The Viking Portable Library

Each Portable Library volume is made up of representative works of a favorite modern or classic author, or is a comprehensive anthology on a special subject. The format is designed for compactness and for pleasurable reading. The books average about 700 pages in length. Each is intended to fill a need not hitherto met by any single book. Each is edited by an authority distinguished in his field, who adds a thoroughgoing introductory essay and other helpful material. Most "Portables" are available both in durable cloth and in stiff paper covers.

This Portable Library
WORLD BIBLE
is adapted from

THE BIBLE OF THE WORLD

Edited by

ROBERT O. BALLOU

In Collaboration with

FRIEDRICH SPIEGELBERG, PH.D., S.T.M.
(COLUMBIA UNIVERSITY)

And with the Assistance and Advice of

HORACE L. FRIESS, PH.D.
(COLUMBIA UNIVERSITY)

The Viking Portable Library

WORLD BIBLE

Edited by Robert O. Ballou

NEW YORK

The Viking Press

The Decorations on the Halftitles in
This Volume Are by
BORIS ARTZYBASHEFF

THE VIKING PORTABLE LIBRARY WORLD BIBLE
Copyright 1944 by Robert O. Ballou

Condensed from THE BIBLE OF THE WORLD,
Copyright 1939 by Robert O. Ballou
Copyright © renewed 1967 by Robert O. Ballou

Printed and bound in U.S.A. by The Colonial Press Inc.
Published in May 1944

Twenty-seventh printing September 1971

SBN 670-78366-8 (hardbound)
SBN 670-01005-7 (paperbound)

Library of Congress catalog card number: 44-4542

Published simultaneously in Canada
by The Macmillan Company of Canada Limited

Contents

The Buddhist

The Parsi

The Jew and the Christian

The Moslem

SELECTIONS FROM MOHAMMEDAN
SCRIPTURES:

The Confucianist

483

Master Kung

SELECTIONS FROM CONFUCIANIST SCRIPTURES:

The Taoist

SELECTIONS FROM TAOIST SCRIPTURES:

Acknowledgements

Grateful acknowledgement is made to the following authors, translators, and publishers for permissions to reprint the scriptural selections used in this volume:

Selections from *The Rig-Veda.* From *The Hymns of the Rig-Veda.* (Two volumes.) Translated by Ralph T. H. Griffith. Benares: E. J. Lazarus, 1896.

Selections from *The Atharva-Veda.* From *Hymns of the Atharva-Veda.* (Two volumes.) Translated by Ralph T. H. Griffith. Benares: E. J. Lazarus, 1895.

Selection from *The Satapatha Brahmana.* From *The Sacred Books of the East.* Translated by Julius Eggeling. Edited by F. Max Müller. Oxford: Clarendon Press, 1900.

Selections from *The Upanishads.* Translated by F. Max Müller. From *The Sacred Books of the East.*

Selections from *The Bhagavad Gita.* From *The Bhagavad Gita, or the Lord's Song.* Translated by Annie Besant. Wheaton, Ill.: The Theosophical Press, 1929.

Selection from *The Vishnu Purana.* From *The Vishnu-puranam.* Translated by H. H. Wilson. Calcutta: H. C. Dass, 1894.

Selections from *The Garuda Purana.* From *The Garuda Purana.* Edited by Manmatha Nath Dutt. Calcutta: Society for the Resuscitation of Indian Literature, 1908.

Selections from *The Markandeya Purana.* From *The Markandeya Puranam.* Edited by Manmatha Nath Dutt. Calcutta: H. C. Dass, 1896.

Selections from *The Atma Bodha.* From *Sankaracharya, His Life and Teachings.* By Sita Nath Dutta. Calcutta: H. C. Dass, 1899.

Selections from *The Hitopadesa.* From *The Hitopadesa.* Translated by Francis Johnson. London: Chapman and Hall, 1928.

Selections from *The Works of Sri Ramakrishna.* From *The Sayings of Sri Ramakrishna.* Compiled by Swami Abhedananda. New York: The Vedanta Society, 1903.

The Foundation of the Kingdom of Righteousness (from the *Mahavagga*). Reprinted from *The Life of Gotama the Buddha*. By E. H. Brewster. London: Kegan Paul, Trench Trubner, and Co., Ltd.; New York: E. P. Dutton, 1926.

The Nine Incapabilities (from *The Pasadika Suttanta*), *The Aryan Eightfold Path* (from the *Maha Satipatthana Suttanta*), *On Theology* (from *The Tevigga Sutta*), and *The Fall and Rise of Social Behaviour* (from *The Chakkavatti Sihanada Suttanta*). Reprinted from *Dialogues of the Buddha*. Translated by T. W. and C. A. F. Rhys-Davids. London: Henry Frowde, Oxford University Press, 1938.

Questions Which Tend Not to Edification (from the *Majjhima-Nikaya*) and *Discussion of Dependent Origination* from the *Maha-Nidana-Sutta of the Digha-Nikaya*). Reprinted from *Buddhism in Translations*. By Henry Clarke Warren. Cambridge: Harvard University Press, 1915.

A Sermon to the Monks (from *The Itivuttaka*). Reprinted from *Minor Anthologies of the Pali Canon*. Translated by F. L. Woodward. London: Humphrey Milford, Oxford University Press, 1935.

Selections from *The Dhammapada*. Reprinted from *Lectures on the Science of Religion with a Paper on Buddhist Nihilism and a Translation of the Dhammapada or Path of Virtue*. By F. Max Müller. New York: Scribner, Armstrong and Co., 1872.

Selections from *Buddaghosha's Parables*. Reprinted from *Buddhaghosha's Parables*. Translated by Captain T. E. Rogers. London: Trubner and Co., 1870.

Selections from *The Lotus of the True Law*. Translated by H. Kern. Reprinted from *The Sacred Books of the East*.

Selections from *The Diamond Sutra*. Reprinted from *The Diamond Sutra, or Prajna-Paramita*. Translated from the Chinese by William Gemmell. London: Kegan Paul, Trench Trubner, and Co., 1912.

Asvaghosha's Doctrine of Suchness. Reprinted from *Acvaghosha's Discourse on the Awakening of Faith in the Mahayana*. Translated from the Chinese by Teitaro Suzuki. Chicago: Open Court Publishing Co., 1900.

"Elegant Sayings" of the Lamas. Reprinted from *Tibetan Yoga and Secret Doctrines, or Seven Books of Wisdom of*

the Great Path. Arranged and edited by W. Y. Evans-Wentz. London: Humphrey Milford, 1935.

All selections from the *Zendavesta* (including selections specifically noted as from the *Vendidad*) and all selections from the *Pahlavi Texts* (including those specifically noted as from the *Bundahis*) are reprinted from *The Sacred Books of the East*.

Selections from *The Gathas*. Reprinted from *The Hymns of Zoroaster*. Translated by Kenneth Sylvan Guthrie. London: George Bell; Brooklyn: Comparative Literature Press, 1914.

Selections from the Judeo-Christian Scriptures. Reprinted from the Authorized Version of the King James Translation.

Selections from *The Koran*. Reprinted from *El Kor'an, or The Koran*. Translated from the Arabic by J. M. Rodwell. London: Bernard Quaritch, 1876.

Selections from *The Masnavi*. Reprinted from *The Masnavi*. Translated by C. E. Wilson. London: Probsthain and Co., 1910.

Selections from *The Forty-Two Traditions of An-Nawawi*. Reprinted from *The Forty-Two Traditions of An-Nawawi*. Translated by Eric F. F. Bishop. In *The Moslem World*. Hartford: The Hartford Seminary Foundation, April 1939.

Selections from the *Li Ki*. Reprinted from *The Sacred Books of the East*.

The Song of How Tsieh. Reprinted from *The Chinese Classics*. Translated by James Legge. London: Trubner and Co., 1871.

Plea to an Ancestor and *How Vast Is God*. Reprinted from *The Sacred Books of the East*.

In Praise of Ancestors, On Letting Alone, and *Admonition*. Reprinted from *The Chinese Classics*.

Selections from *The Analects of Confucius, The Great Learning, The Doctrine of the Steadfast Mean*, and *The Works of Mencius*. Reprinted from a translation by Charles A. Wong, published in China without the imprint of a publisher or date.

Selections from *The Book of Filial Piety*. Reprinted from *The Book of Filial Duty*. Translated from the Chinese by Ivan Chen. London: John Murray; New York: E. P. Dutton, 1920.

Selections from the *Tao-Te King*. Reprinted from *The Tao Te Ching*. Translated by Ch'u Ta-Kao. London: The Buddhist Lodge, 1937.

Selections from *The Works of Chuang-Tze*. Reprinted from *Chuang Tzu, Mystic, Moralist and Social Reformer*. Translated from the Chinese by Herbert A. Giles. London: Bernard Quaritch, 1889.

The true religion of the future will be the fulfilment of all the religions of the past—the true religion of humanity, that which, in the struggle of history, remains as the indestructible portion of all the so-called false religions of mankind. There never was a false god, nor was there ever really a false religion, unless you call a child a false man. All religions, so far as I know them, had the same purpose; all were links in a chain which connects heaven and earth, and which is held, and always was held, by one and the same hand.

—F. MAX MÜLLER, in a letter to the Rev. M. K. Schermerhorn, 1883.

The idea of God constitutes the general foundation of a people. Whatever is the form of a religion, the same is the form of a state and its constitution; it springs from religion.

—GEORGE WILHELM HEGEL, *Philosophy of History*

General Introduction

Man's basic problem is his need to find a way to live in constructive peace in the face of forces which tend to thrust him into destructive conflict. There is nothing new in this. Centuries ago some of the wisest of men faced the problem and set forth a method for its solution: a way of life based upon a social idealism which must begin with the most intimate relations between individuals and extend to the most enlightened co-operation between nations, in order to make war, the fear of war, and the worst of man's miseries only bitter memories of the past.

The kind of idealism required for this tremendous accomplishment, the idealism which so often colours statements made by religious theorists of the West, has often been called "Christian." To be sure, it is, yet this is only a small part of the truth, for these ideals of world brotherhood and international human morality were uttered in many places long before the birth of Jesus of Nazareth.

During the greatest of all religious eras (roughly from 800 to 500 B.C.), India, China, Persia, and Israel were all injecting into human thought what was then a new force. Without question, this force has been one of the most powerful influences in human life, for, persisting without material change to the present day, it has determined every statement of idealistic social purpose to which we now pay homage.

Religion, as we conceive the meaning of the term

3

today, may be said to consist of three conceptions and the actions which spring from them: man's conception of the source of his being, of his self, and of other human beings and his own proper relation to them. In primitive, polytheistic religions there was little if any connexion between the first conception and the last two. Religion, born of fear and questioning, consisted chiefly in the propitiation of gods and spirits through sacrifices and ceremonies performed in the hope that supernatural protection and favour would be bestowed upon the worshipper. Gods were thought of as beings possessed of great though limited might, who often exerted their power in malignant ways unless properly wooed by offerings or circumvented by witchcraft. Their relationship to men was more like that of autocratic rulers exacting tribute than that of loving heavenly fathers whose concern was for the welfare of their earthly children.

But with the appearance in India of the *Upanishads* (800 to 600 B.C.), Gautama, the Buddha (560 to 480 B.C.), and Mahavira (599 to 527 B.C.), of Confucius (551 to 479 B.C.) and Lao Tze (604 to 517? B.C.) in China, Zarathushtra (660 to 583 B.C.) in Persia, and the Pre-Exilic prophets (750 to 586 B.C.) in Israel, sacrifices, ceremonies, propitiations, ceased to be enough to make up the religious life of man. The whole god-concept was changing. In Mahavira's Jainism the existence of all gods was denied and man's religious duty consisted entirely of thought and behaviour unconnected with any form of worship. In the Hindu *Upanishads* and in Taoism the ruling principle of the universe was conceived as a single intangible, indescribable force (*Brahma, Brahman,* or *Atman* in the *Upanishads, Tao* in Taoism). In each case it was a benevolent force, working for the welfare of mankind. In the original

Indian Buddhism "the gods" were recognized, but as creatures who needed salvation as badly as did man himself, while, by implication, the Upanishadic conception of Brahman was denied. Here, as in Jainism, meditation and social behaviour were substituted for worship. Questions about divinity and immortality were "questions which tended not to edification." Confucius "preferred not speaking" about God, but spoke of "the ordinances of heaven" and human conduct instead. And in Zoroastrianism and the Judaism of this period God was worshipped as a single personal, universal benevolent force, a loving Father-God whose care was for the well-being of his children, the human race.

Accompanying these changed god-concepts were changes in the religious rules which determined human conduct. In India the highest desideratum of the religious was the cessation of rebirths. In Upanishadic Hinduism this was achieved through a mystical union with Brahma; in Buddhism and Jainism through the attainment of Nirvana. In Confucianism, Taoism, and the Judaism of this period, the reward sought was the good life on earth, distinguished by peace, prosperity, and happiness; in Zoroastrianism the goal was Paradise after death. But regardless of differences in the states sought as the result of the religious life, all agreed that they could be achieved only through individual purity of heart and mind, good work, and righteous loving-kindness to one's fellow-men in recognition of the essential unity of men, each with all others, and each and all with the divine principle. It was in these days, rather than in those which made Bethlehem of Judea famous, that the principle of "peace on earth, goodwill to men" first began to sweep across the world like a cleansing wind.

Denied and flaunted century after century by conquests, wars, racial and sectarian persecution, commercial greed, social and political ambition, and fanatical disagreements, this ideal yet remains the prayer of the truly devout and the hope of all of the peoples of the world whose lives have been swayed by these religions and Christianity.

It may be argued that Hinduism and Zoroastrianism do not belong in any category which groups the religions of goodwill. It is quite true that greater emphases were placed in the *Upanishads* upon philosophy, "union with Brahma," and ceremonial sacrifice than upon social ethics, and that the degrading caste system and the subordination of women were perpetuated by them. Yet there are many ethical and humanitarian principles of the highest order enunciated in the *Upanishads*, and set forth by them, for the first time in India, as prerequisites to the religious life. The very concept of union with and through Brahma intimates the unity of the human race. And it is significant that the religious philosophy of Gautama, the Buddha, growing as it did directly out of the period of Upanishadic influence, included one of the highest codes of individual purity and social ethics which has ever been formulated. In Zoroastrianism, though ethical precepts are more difficult to find than in Confucianism, Buddhism, Taoism, and later Judaism, those which occur are of the highest order, and a whole philosophy of social behaviour is innate in the Zoroastrian emphasis upon the righteousness of work.

The similarity of the fundamental principles of all these creeds (which, with Christianity, one might well call "the good-will religions," for this phrase designates their greatest distinguishing quality) may be seen by examining a few statements from several of them.

In the *Upanishads* we read:

As all spokes are contained in the axle and felly of a wheel, all beings are contained in the Atman.

Who knows that one whose dwelling is love, he indeed is a teacher.

As he acts, so will he be. He becomes pure by good deeds and bad by bad deeds. Whatever deed he does, that will he reap.

Be subdued, give, be merciful.

Sacrifice, study, charity, are the first branch of the law.

The good is one thing, the pleasant another. It is well with him who clings to the good; he who chooses the pleasant, misses his end.

The Atman cannot be gained by the Veda, nor by much learning. He who has not first turned away from wickedness, or whose mind is not at rest, he can never obtain the Atman.

From Buddhist texts:

Hatred does not cease by hatred at any time. Hatred ceases by love. This is an old rule.

Do not kill nor cause slaughter.

One's own self conquered is better than all other people.

Let a man overcome anger by love, let him overcome evil by good; let him overcome the greedy by liberality, the liar by truth.

A man does not become a Brahmana by his plaited hair, by his family, or by birth; in whom there is truth and righteousness, he is blessed, he is a Brahmana.

To one in whom love dwells, all in the world are brothers.

From the Zoroastrian Scriptures:

He who relieves the poor makes Ahura king.

Whether one is lord of little or much, let him show love to the righteous.

From Confucianist Scriptures:

What you do not want done to yourself, do not do to others.

Return justice for injury, and kindness for kindness.

The tendency of man's nature is good.

Wisdom, benevolence, and fortitude, these are the universal virtues.

To give one's self earnestly to the duties due to men may be called wisdom. . . . The man of perfect virtue, wishing to be established himself, seeks also to establish others; wishing to be enlarged himself, he seeks also to enlarge others. To be able to judge of others what is nigh in ourselves;—this may be called the art of virtue.

Love all men. Know all men.

From the Scriptures of Taoism:

Keep on good terms with men.

He who loves the world as he does his own body can be entrusted with the world.

So far as arms are concerned, they are implements of ill omen. He who takes delight in the slaughter of men cannot have his will done in the world.

The sage makes the self of the people his self.

To the good I act with goodness. To the bad I also act with goodness. To the faithful I act with faith. To the faithless I also act with faith.

I have three treasures. The first is called love; the second is called moderation; the third is called not venturing to go ahead of the world.

Return love for great hatred.

The virtuous resort to agreement.

The universe and I came into being together, and I, and everything therein, are one.

Everything has Tao within it and continues to produce it without end. The endless love of the sage for his fellow-man is based on the same principle.

From the words of Pre-Exilic Hebrew prophets:

Take away from me the noise of thy songs, for I will not bear the melody of thy voice. But let justice roll down as waters, and righteousness as a mighty stream.

Can two walk together, except they be agreed?

Forasmuch as your treading is upon the poor, and ye take from him burdens of wheat, ye have built houses of hewn stone, but ye shall not dwell in them, ye have planted vineyards but ye shall not drink wine from them.

I hate, I despise, your feast days.

Let no man strive, or reprove another.

I desire mercy, not sacrifice, and the knowledge of God more than burnt offerings.

Keep mercy and judgment, and wait on thy God continually.

Do justly, love kindness, and walk humbly with thy God.

Behold, saith Jehovah, I will make a new covenant. . . . I will put my law in their inward parts, and in their heart will I write it.

Woe to him that increaseth that which is not his. Because thou hast spoiled many nations, all the remnant of the people shall spoil thee; because of men's blood, and for the violence of the land, of the city, and of all that dwell therein.

Oppress not the stranger, the fatherless, and the widow, and shed not innocent blood.

Thus saith the Lord, Let not the wise man glory in wisdom, neither let the mighty glory in his might. Let not the rich man glory in his riches. But let him that glorieth, glory in this, that he understandeth and knoweth me, that I am the Lord which exercise lovingkindness, judgment, and righteousness in the earth: for in these things I delight.

Christianity, growing directly out of later Judaism, perhaps gave a greater emphasis to the basic conception of brotherly love as a motivating force in intercourse between all peoples. Yet the fundamental conception of benevolent good-will, of peaceful agreement, of *laissez faire* and loving kindness from all to all, was well established several centuries before the birth of Jesus. And it is of the deepest significance that, in the final alignment of forces in twentieth-century global warfare, the powerful nations in which the ideals of the "good-will religions" had taken firmest hold were fighting together against two mighty nations in one of which the ideal had never been firmly established and in the other of which years of organized destruction of the ideal had preceded entry into war. Regardless of differences in theology which exist among members of the United Nations, they found themselves in almost automatic common agreement to stamp out those forces which completely abrogated the principles of international morality in their determination to make many human beings subject to the will of a few. The people of each of the United Nations understood, without explanations, the statements of social idealism which issued from the others, for as joint heirs of the "good-will religions" they stood on common, ancient, holy ground.

With even that much union achieved by means of the awful flux of war, will it be lost when the grim immediacy has passed? Shall we ever return to the blind inadequacy of attempted isolation from our fellows in a world in which the spatial distances of even a quarter of a century ago have, through the radio and the airplane, become so ineffective that the myth of the separate interests of nations and races has lost every verisimilitude?

Are we capable of making some sort of permanent world union successful? Can we find the key to understanding between the peoples of the world which will make it unnecessary for us to engage in world-wide warfare every quarter of a century? Where shall we start on our search for understanding the peoples of the East, for instance, who, to most of us, have seemed as far removed from our lives and interests as the characters in a fairy tale?

Carlyle had an answer to that question. In *Heroes and Hero Worship* he wrote:

It is well said, in every sense, that a man's religion is the chief fact with regard to him. A man's or a nation of men's. By religion I do not mean the church creed which he professes, the articles of faith which he will sign and, in words or otherwise, assert; not this wholly, in many cases not this at all. We see men of all kinds of professed creeds attain to almost all degrees of worth or worthlessness under each or any of them. This is not what I call religion, this profession and assertion, which is often a profession and assertion from the outworks of the man, from the mere argumentative region of him, if even so deep as that. But the thing a man does practically believe (and this is often enough without asserting it even to himself, much less to others), the thing a man does practically lay to heart, and know for certain, concerning his vital relations to this mysterious universe, and his duty and destiny there, that is in all cases the primary thing for him, and creatively determines all the rest. That is his religion, or, it may be, his mere scepticism and no-religion: the manner in which he feels himself to be spiritually related to the unseen world or no-world, and I say, if you tell me what that is, you tell me to a very great extent what the man is, what the kind of things he will do is. Of a man or of a nation we inquire, therefore, first of all, what religion they had.

Unfortunately, there is frequently a wide gulf existing between the statements of the scriptures and the religious and secular practices of those whose canons they are. All scriptures have had their interpreters and commentators, those who would add to them and those who would detract from them, and those who would fit them to their own uses. Organized Hinduism, Oriental Buddhism, Taoism, and Confucianism to-day bear little relation to the ideals of the *Upanishads*, of Gautama, Lao Tze, or Confucius. Nor do the lives or even the protestations of the average Jew and Christian adequately reflect the words of the Hebrew prophets and Jesus.

The scriptures do not tell us what religion men have to-day. Yet their ancient idealism and their pure impassioned search for God and a way of life capable of establishing human happiness were never more pertinent. Though we and the Buddhists, the Hindus, the Parsis, the Confucianists, the Taoists, and all the others who have sadly divided human ranks by doctrinaire labels, may have largely missed the way, the scriptural signposts pointing to the path of return are still unblemished. They are still waiting to be read, still showing the ancient unity of social idealism among all true followers of "the good-will religions."

Behind the making of the *Viking Portable Library World Bible* there has been a triple stimulus—the beauty and goodness of the scriptures here represented, their universal applicability to the problems of modern living, and the belief that knowledge of these scriptures and the basic unity of their social principles can become a contribution to a much-needed understanding among the peoples of the world.

All of the selections printed here are taken from *The Bible of the World*, and have been chosen only if they seemed to the editor to contribute to an understanding of the basic faiths which they represent. Mere stories, history, and the descriptions of ceremonial rites, which do not in themselves contribute to knowledge of religious faith, have been omitted. The book is not intended as a substitute for the *Bible of the World* which serves a more comprehensive purpose for the serious student or reader who wishes to go farther in his examination of individual religions than is possible in this much smaller volume. Rather, the attempt here is to present the gist of each of the world's eight most influential religious faiths, as revealed by their basic scriptures, in one compact volume for the reader who has little leisure.

The order in which the scriptural selections are presented is not chronological, nor is any evaluation of relative importance intimated by their arrangement. The world's great religions fall into three groups, those which originated with the descendants of the Indo-European races (Hinduism, Buddhism, and Zoroastrianism), those which originated with the Semitic races (Judeo-Christianity and Mohammedanism), and those which originated with the Turanian races (Confucianism and Taoism). These groupings, and the order noted above, have been followed in the *World Bible*.

At a famous meeting of the Free Religious Association of America held in Boston during the last half of the nineteenth century, a somewhat overzealous minister quoted certain passages from the Christian Gospels, adding that these could not be matched in the sacred books of any other religion. At this point Ralph Waldo Emerson, who was in the audience, rose and said quietly, "The gentleman's remark proves only how narrowly he has read."

One aim of the *Viking Portable Library World Bible* is to make it possible for those whose time for reading and research is limited to disprove "the gentle-man's remark" for themselves, and in so doing, to add their quota to a better understanding between the peoples of the world.

THE HINDU

The Worshippers of Brahma

Herdsmen, shepherds, tillers of the soil, warriors, and wanderers—a race of white men dwelt once upon the plains of Central Asia. Whence they came and when, how long they lived there, what the details of their daily lives were, when and why they separated to wander far from their ancient home and in different directions from it, no one knows, for they left behind them no record—at least none which has yet been plainly read. Bits of correlated evidence indicate that they were both agricultural and nomadic, making long stops to raise crops for their herds and flocks, then pushing on to new locations.

At some time, or times, in their migrations, some went far to the west, some to the east. They were apparently a people of astounding vigour and ingenuity, these Indo-Europeans who called themselves *Arya*, a people who conquered the inhabitants of whatever country they entered, forcing upon them their forms of religion and government, and their customs. One of the western offshoots founded the Persian kingdom. Another established Athens and Lacedaemon, beginnings of the Greek nation. A third went to an inland point on a long peninsula shaped like a boot where, on seven hills, they built the city which became Rome. Another group went to the land which is now Spain, and still another crossed the sea to what is now Cornwall, England.

Over the passes of the Hindu Kush mountains went one of the most powerful of the wandering groups, down

17

into the Valley of the Indus, and settled there, where the earth was watered by the melting of everlasting snows on the heights above. They brought with them the elements of an as yet unrecorded religion. Little is known about it, but its vestiges may be found in the faiths later developed among their descendants. They worshipped a "sky father" who, in the language of those who went into India, was *Dyaush pitar*, who became *Zeus pater* in Greek, *Diespiter* or Jupiter in Latin, and, in conception if not etymologically, *Ahura Mazda* in Zoroastrianism. ("Our Heavenly Father" in later Judaism and in Christianity?) They paid homage also to his daughter *Ushas*, the Dawn, who became *Eos* or *Heos* in Greek and *Aurora* in Latin, to his consort Mother Earth, *Privithi* (Greek *Gaia Meter*) and the sun god *Surya* (Greek Helios). *Yama* became, with *Yami*, the Adam and Eve of Hinduism (and later the ruler of the regions of the dead). *Yima*, "the good shepherd," became the first man of the Persian religion. In their religious rites these people who went into India drank the fermented juice of the mountain plant *Soma*, and worshipped *Soma* as a god. The Persians sanctified the same plant, calling it *Haoma*, and developed a tradition that Zarathushtra talked with an angel of that name.

In India this race of white men became joined with aboriginal tribes already there, eliminating those among them who were troublesome. They began to establish and record a religion that has fathered more conceptions and gone through more mutations than any other under the sun. So that, if one asks concerning an inhabitant of India, "What religion had he?" it is necessary, before answering, to ask in return, "In what part of India did he live, and when, and under the influence of what leader or leaders?"

L. D. Barnett says:

Hinduism is not one homogeneous growth of religious thought. . . . It is, on the contrary, an aggregation of minor growths, some of cognate origin, some of foreign provenance, all grouped under the shadow of one mighty tree. . . . Its churches are as well the stately cathedral where scholars and princes worship, as the humblest shrine where villagers offer flowers to some god born of their own hearts, or the wayside spot haunted by some godling who may have dwelt there long before Hindus came into India, or may have arrived there last week.

Within this mighty force of varied expression that sways the religious impulses of nearly 250,000,000 human souls there is, and has been of old, room for the widest range of theological variance, from the most complicated worship of a multiplicity of gods to the most exalted recognition of, and homage to, the one God, the mighty unexplained force which created and rules the universe. These conceptions have changed from time to time, from scripture to scripture, from group to group, and from individual to individual within a group. As the almost unbelievably large volume of Indian sacred literature has grown, and the followers of Indian religious concepts have split into innumerable sects, it has become impossible to state succinctly and comprehensively the details of Hinduist theology. Yet there are central threads which run through all phases of it—relics of the early, unrecorded Indo-European religion, and other concepts which have grown out of later conditions of life and changing trends of thought.

In the Valley of the Indus the newcomers composed, and at some later date recorded, the most ancient of all the world's scriptures, the *Vedas*, of which the *Rig-*

Veda is the oldest. No one knows when it was written. Estimates date it as far back as 4000 B.C., but conservative scholarship says merely that the 10,000 stanzas which compose it (more than the bulk of the *Iliad* and the *Odyssey* together) were written "earlier than 1000 B.C." The title of the work means "Stanzas of praise," though some of the later hymns are blessings and curses.

The *Yajur-Veda* repeats many of the hymns of the *Rig-Veda*, with additional stanzas, and contains short prayers and long, solemn litanies. The *Sama-Veda*, devoted chiefly to worship of *Indra*, is the *Veda* of music, and also contains a number of verses borrowed from the *Rig*. The *Atharva-Veda* contains 730 hymns, a number of which are charms of witchcraft, blessings, and curses. Its chief value lies in its revelations of popular practices, superstitions, and folklore.

By far the most important and interesting of these four ancient books is the *Rig-Veda* with its questioning, its wonder, and its frequent deep humility. Many of the hymns, written before the frequent repetition of theological concepts by priests had bred authoritarian certainty, are filled with an awed, wondering search for answers that might have come from a child. "What covered in, and where? And what gave shelter? Was water there?" asks the singer of the "Creation" hymn. "What was above it then, and what below it? Who verily knows whence it was born, and whence comes, this creation? He, the first origin, he verily knows it, or perhaps he knows not." Even God, the almighty creator, perhaps even his knowledge was not absolute!

In this earliest of all the Hindu religious books there is only one brief mention of caste, which later became so important a part of all Hindu religious belief. The society of earliest Vedic times was of simple organization, patriarchal, with rajas ruling as chieftains and often by hereditary succession. The father ruled the household and offered the religious sacrifices. The wife was mistress of the house, assisted at the sacrifice (hence Yasodhara's complaint at Gautama's abandonment of her—see the introduction to the Buddhist scriptures), and shared in the control of the children, of slaves, and of unmarried brothers and sisters of the husband.

The *Rig-Veda* says that there are 33 gods, though these do not include some of the minor deities, and even some of the 33 seem to have been of little importance. Several of these, notably *Indra* (the god who protected his people in battle), *Agni* (the god of fire), *Mitra* (the sun god, deity of the Mithraists), and *Varuna*, were brought with them from their earlier Asiatic home, along with *Dyaush pitar, Ushas*, and the others mentioned earlier. Traces of all of these are found also in the Persia of Zarathushtra's time.

The characteristics of *Indra* are of particular interest in thinking of the god-concepts of the world's religions. Most peoples have attributed to a god an especial interest in their welfare in battle. In the early days of Judaism the God of Israel was not a peaceful deity but "a mighty man of war." It was Jehovah who sent the plagues to torture the Egyptians in retaliation for their persecution of the Jews, who caused the waters of the Red Sea to part so that the Children of Israel could cross over on dry land, and then to come together again to overwhelm the Egyptians. It was Jehovah who brought calamities to the enemies of Israel who had stolen the Ark of the Covenant, Jehovah who always fought beside his people and made one of them equal to many from among those who followed other gods. Even Jesus, whose followers think of him as symbolizing the ideal of "peace on earth, goodwill toward men," is reported to have said, "I bring you not peace but a sword."

And there is a strange and persistent reminder of this ancient concept in modern times. Since the beginning of World War II story after story of miraculous escapes from death have filtered into the news. Flyers forced down at sea, drifting for days on a raft, made shore or were rescued after daily prayers and the singing of hymns were begun. A boy in a submerged submarine, which could not surface because its mechanism had jammed, prayed then fainted, and in his fall jarred loose the fouled mechanism and the ship rose to the surface. Bullets were deflected from the vital parts of religious soldiers by the sacred talismen they wore. The English Channel, during the five terrible days when the British Army was being evacuated from Dunkirk, was miraculously calm in answer to the prayers of the British people.

It is not to question the faith out of which these stories have come that they are mentioned here, but merely to point out that here again is the conception of a God of war protecting his people in battle, as did Jehovah in the early days of the Old Testament, as Indra did in the pre-historic days of the great Indo-European migrations.

Apparently the earlier inhabitants of India, whom the newcomers found there, believed that the powers of nature were manifestations of gods. Frequently the same god had more than one name. Of these, several were added to the pantheon of the invaders, making a confusing catalogue of many names.

But the deities thus designated had not all existed from the beginning of time. They too were created, along with the sky, the earth, the creatures of earth, and man. ("The gods are later than this world's production," says the *Rig* "Creation" hymn.) In the earlier hymns of the *Rig*, creation is believed to have taken place through some phenomenon of natural generation without any personal god acting in the process. In later hymns there is introduced the idea of a personal creator, *Prajapati*, a physical being whose body was divided, his head becoming the sky, his feet the earth, his navel the air, his eye the sun, and his breath the wind.

In the *Rig-Veda* the conception of life after death is vague. *Yama* is the ruler of the region to which persons go after death, whether they have led good or bad lives, but the character of that region or the manner of existence there seems clouded in mystery. The nearest approach to any idea of salvation consists in a state of happy and prosperous being on this earth before death. In the later *Atharva-Veda* there is described a dark pit below earth into which the evil are hurled after death, and there is a vague intimation that the good go to a happier place. It is only in the still later *Upanishads* and the *Mahabharata* that there emerges a clear belief in a hell for the wicked and a heaven for the righteous, inhabited during the intervals between rebirths.

By the time of the *Brahmanas* (probably about 800 B.C. and later) many of the peoples who had originally settled in the Valley of the Indus had pushed on to the Valley of the Ganges, where there was rain only at the time of the monsoons. In addition to hardships imposed by frequent droughts, there was the depressing effect of a more difficult climate. The daily tasks necessary to maintaining life became more onerous, and apparently the dark-skinned aborigines, set off from the white invaders by the sad and ancient barrier of colour, were compelled to perform many of these

tasks under duress. It is at this time that the system
of castes (so integral a part of orthodox Hindu religious
belief) became important. The human race, the *Brahmanas* say, was divided at the time of its creation into
the *Brahman*, or priestly class, who now became the
real rulers of the people; the *Rajanya* or *Kshatriya*, the
warriors; the *Vaisya*, composed of farmers, artisans,
and tradesmen; and the *Sudra*, or serfs. (For a later
explanation of the creation of the castes by Brahma,
see "The Creation of Castes" from the *Markandeya
Purana*, p. 76.)

As the caste system, emphasized in the *Brahmanas*,
grew in importance, the position of the lowest class
was demeaned to the point where neither gods nor
men would speak to the *Sudra*. As time added new
complexities to Hinduism and its reflections in Hindu
society, castes themselves were divided. Robert Hume,
in *The World's Living Religions*, says that in modern
times "there are over 2,000 mutually exclusive sub-
castes in the Hindu system."

In the *Brahmanas* there is developed the creation
story of the golden egg, which floated about for a year
in a universe which was entirely water (even as in
the first chapter of Genesis). At the end of this time
the egg broke into two parts and "a man, this *Prajapati*"
was produced from it. In the later *Upanishads* one half
of the golden egg is said to have become the sky, the
other half the earth. In the *Satapatha Brahmana, Prajapati*, having emerged from the golden egg, from his
breath creates the *Devas* as gods who, entering the sky,
produce light, and the *Asuras* from his "downward
breathing" (or flatulence) who, entering the earth as
evil spirits, become demons and produce darkness.

Here is evidence on which to base an interesting
speculation (it can be no more than that) as to whether

religious differences may have been at least one of the causes which divided the Indo-Europeans who went to Persia from those who went to India, for in the Persian religion the *Daevas* are the demons, while from the godlike *Ahuras* there emerges the mighty Ahura Mazda, the universal God of Zoroastrianism. One cannot but think here also of the regions of upper light (goodness) and nether darkness (evil) of Zoroastrianism, and of the heaven and hell so clearly conceived in Christianity some 800 years after the writing of the *Brahmanas*.

The joyousness which so often pervaded the *Vedas* now disappears in a pessimistic conviction that life is a burden and rebirth a misfortune. This became a most important basis for the creed of Gautama Buddha, approximately 300 years later.

Something else of great significance was happening to Indian religious belief at the time of the *Brahmanas*. Even then the religious observances were becoming cluttered with complicated ceremonials conducted by the priests. The gods were being constantly propitiated by material sacrifices. But the fertile minds of Indian thinkers were beginning to question the materialistic complexity of these practices and the multiplicity of the gods to whom homage was given. An intangible spirituality was invading Hindu thought.

With the *Upanishads* (800-600 B.C.) Hinduism entered a new phase centering upon the conception of Brahma as the supreme God. The names of the other gods are simply names of the various powers of the absolute, impersonal, indescribable being which created and rules the universe. (See "How Many Gods?" p. 50.) In the earlier writings the word *Brahma* or *Brahman* had meant "sacred knowledge" or "sacred utterance." Now, closely connected, in some uses synonymous, with Brahma is the concept of *Atman*, the universal soul or Self which is within us all, which is, indeed, our being. (See "The Universal Self," p. 39 and "The Education of Svetaketu," p. 54.) Through recognition of and devotion to this Self, and through following certain rules of social ethics, one may achieve union with Brahma, thus partaking of divinity and thus perhaps avoiding the repeated misery of rebirths.

The end of the *Upanishads* period was the beginning of the most exciting and productive era in the religious history of the world. At about this time Zarathushtra was proclaiming the exalted rule of the one god Ahura Mazda in Persia, and in connexion with this pure and vigorous monotheism was urging upon his followers one of the most virile ethical codes based upon works which the world has ever known. In China at about this time Confucius was bringing order and new meaning to the ancient Chinese formalism through emphasis upon social and political principles which still cry for adoption in the relations of man to man and nation to nation, and Lao Tze was decrying all kinds of ceremony and urging a mystical return, through Tao, to the state of goodness which is every man's heritage from the nature which creates him. In Israel the Pre-Exilic prophets, Amos, Hosea, the first Isaiah, Micah, Zephaniah, Jeremiah, Nahum, and Habakkuk, were preparing the way for a strict monotheism by preaching a righteous, forgiving, loving Jehovah, supreme among the nations, with whom one may find union through purity of heart and righteous social conduct. (Micah summarized man's religious duty thus: "To do justly, and to love kindness, and to walk humbly with thy God.") And in India itself, less than 100 years later, the great Gautama Buddha, thoroughly familiar with and strongly influenced by the *Upanishads,* though he was to reject the concept of union with Brahma, was to preach some of the most exalted principles of purity and social righteousness which have ever issued from the mouth of man. No other age in history, not even that which marks the birth of Christianity 600 years later, can be compared with this for its religious consciousness.

Between the time of the *Upanishads* and the beginning of the Christian era there were compiled the *Ordinances of Manu* (about 250 B.C.), a long and complicated book of laws, cosmology, and legends, which exalts the *Vedas*, re-emphasizes the religious obligation to recognize the rigid separation of castes, and lays down many elevated moral principles.

At about the time that Mary and Joseph made their historic trip to Bethlehem and the Magi (probably Zoroastrian priests) came to the manger to adore the infant Jesus, there was written one of the greatest of all the Hindu scriptures, the *Bhagavad Gita* or "Lord's Song." Hinduism, now thoroughly established in India, here enters what is perhaps its most exalted phase and becomes a spiritual religion of devotion to God and to righteous social conduct. The *Gita*, because of the beauty of its composition and the fact that it contains more concepts compatible with Christianity than any of the other early Hindu scriptures, has for long been a favourite with Western scholars, by whom it has been translated into English more than 40 times.

The work consists of a long dramatic poem in which a new name, that of *Krishna*, first appears in Hindu theology as "the Blessed Lord." Some Indian scholars believe that he was an actual human being, an early Messiah of Hinduism. Quoting frequently from the *Upanishads* (as Christ so often quoted from the earlier Hebrew writers), Krishna explains the universality of God, the single identity of all messiahs and saviours, the immortality of the soul, and the possibility of avoiding rebirth through devotion to God and righteousness. He says:

I am the source of the forthgoing of the whole universe and the place of its dissolving. . . . All this is threaded on me, as rows of pearls on a string. I am the sapidity in waters, I the radiance in moon and sun; the word of power in all the Vedas, sound in ether, and virility in men; the pure fragrance of earths and the brilliance of fire am I; the life in all beings am I. . . . Know me as the eternal seed of all things. I am the reason of the reason-endowed, the splendour of all splendid things am I. And I the strength of the strong, devoid of desire and passion. In beings I am desire not contrary to duty. . . . I the oblation; I the sacrifice, I the ancestral offering; I the fire-giving herb; . . . I the Father of this universe; the Mother, the Supporter, the Grandsire, the Holy One to be known, . . . the Path, Husband, Lord, Witness, Abode, Shelter, Lover, Origin, Dissolution, Foundation, Treasure-house, Seed imperishable. I give heat; I hold back and send forth rain; immortality and also death, being and non-being am I. The same am I to all beings; there is none hateful to me or dear. He who offereth to me with devotion a leaf, a flower, a fruit, water, that I accept from the striving self. They verily who worship me with devotion, they are in me, and I also in them.

Whenever there is decay of righteousness and exaltation of unrighteousness, then I myself come forth; for the protection of the good, for the destruction of evil-doers, for the sake of firmly established righteousness, I am born from age to age. He who thus knoweth my divine birth and action, in its essence, having abandoned the body, cometh not to birth again, but cometh unto me. Freed from passion, fear and anger, filled with me, taking refuge in me, purified in the fire of wisdom, many have entered into my being. However men approach me, even so do I welcome them, for the path men take from every side is mine.

Of the immortality of the soul he says this, speaking to Arjuna who is disconsolate before the horror of slaying other human beings in battle:

Thou grievest for those that should not be grieved for, yet speakest words of wisdom. The wise grieve neither for the living nor for the dead. Nor at any time verily was I not, nor thou, nor these princes of men, nor verily shall we ever cease to be, hereafter. . . . Know that to be indestructible by whom all this is pervaded. . . . He who regardeth this as a slayer, and he who thinketh he is slain, both of them are ignorant. He slayeth not, nor is he slain. He is not born, nor doth he die; nor having been, ceaseth he any more to be; unborn, perpetual, eternal and ancient, he is not slain when the body is slaughtered.

Thus in India, immediately preceding the time when Christ was to proclaim eternal life for all who, through faith, achieved union with him. And while Christ was preaching "Know the truth, and the truth will make you free," Krishna, in the *Bhagavad Gita*, was saying, "Even if thou art the most sinful of all sinners, yet shalt thou cross over all sin by the raft of wisdom."

Following the great *Bhagavad Gita*, there was a decline in the exaltation of Hindu religious thought. The epics and *Puranas*, written during the first 250 years of the Christian era, consist of tales, traditions, social rules, and proverbs.

If one were to attempt to state the fundamental beliefs which permeate all the various mutations of

Hinduism (with the exception of the earliest Vedic religion) they would include the worship of the supreme Brahma; the doctrine of *Karma*, that continuing force of one's deeds which determines one's state of being in all existences; the transmigration of the soul, which brings one back to the earth time after time through rebirths; and the caste system, which rigidly divides the human race into classes.

Throughout the centuries Hinduism has been the field for constant reform movements. Roughly five centuries before Christ, Mahavira and Gautama Buddha made their great contributions in Jainism and Buddhism, both of which were reform movements rather than attempts to establish new religions. Later Tiruvalluvar, Manikka-Vasagar, Ramanuja, Madhava, and Ramananda all preached theologies which varied markedly from the concepts of the earlier sacred books and included some beliefs completely consistent with those of the personal God and conscious immortality of Christianity. Nanak, who lived from A.D. 1469 to 1538, in establishing Sikhism, tried to codify a religion which would be acceptable to both Hindus and Moslems. Chaitanya tried to abolish the caste system during the first quarter of the sixteenth century by preaching the equality of all men in the eyes of God. Sri Ramakrishna, the great modern teacher, has blended much that is best in the most advanced Western religious thought with the most profound of ancient Eastern wisdom. And there have been many others.

Today the great rival of the ancient Brahmanical faith in the land of its birth is Mohammedanism, yet Robert Hume estimates the number of Hindu worshippers in India as over 239,000,000. The faith includes a wide variety of beliefs and a humble respect for the creeds of others.

There is much to appeal to the Western mind in present-day Hindu thought and religion. But perhaps the greatest appeal is still made by the vaguely recorded theological concepts of the ancient Indo-Europeans from which the Hindus sprang, those men who, in awe and humility, worshipped *Dyaush pitar*, the "Sky-Father," for through that concept we, who are their descendants, find ourselves irrevocably bound to them in a unity of religious yearning which has persisted in the face of all mutations.

In one of his lectures on "The Science of Religion," delivered in 1870, F. Max Müller said:

> Thousands of years have passed since the Aryan nations separated to travel to the North and the South, the West and the East; they have each formed languages, they have each founded empires and philosophies, they have each built temples and razed them to the ground; they have all grown older, and it may be wiser and better; but when they search for a name for what is most exalted and yet most dear to every one of us, when they wish to express both awe and love, the infinite and the finite, they can but do what their old fathers did when gazing up to the eternal sky, and feeling the presence of a Being as far as far, and as near as near can be, they can but combine the selfsame words, and utter once more the primeval Aryan prayer, Heaven-Father, in that form which will endure forever, "Our Father which art in heaven."

HINDU SCRIPTURES

From the Rig-Veda

Creation

Then was not non-existent nor existent: there was no
    realm of air, no sky beyond it.
What covered in, and where? and what gave shelter?
    Was water there, unfathomed depth of water?

Death was not then, nor was there aught immortal: no
    sign was there, the day's and night's divider.
That One Thing, breathless, breathed by its own
    nature: apart from it was nothing whatsoever.

Darkness there was: at first concealed in darkness this
    All was undiscriminated chaos.
All that existed then was void and formless: by the
    great power of warmth was born that unit.

Who verily knows and who can here declare it, whence
    it was born and whence comes this creation?
The gods are later than this world's production. Who
    knows then whence it first came into being?

He, the first origin of this creation, whether he formed
    it all or did not form it,
Whose eye controls this world in highest heaven, he
    verily knows it, or perhaps he knows not.

Dialogue Between Yama and Yami

Fain would I win my friend to kindly friendship. So
    may the sage, come through the air's wide ocean,
Remembering the earth and days to follow, obtain a
    son, the issue of his father.

Yea, this the immortals seek of thee with longing,
    progeny of the sole existing mortal.
Then let thy soul and mine be knit together, and as a
    loving husband take thy consort.

I, Yami, am possessed by love of Yama, that I may
    rest on the same couch beside him.
I as a wife would yield me to my husband. Like car-
    wheels let us speed to meet each other.

They stand not still, they never close their eyelids, those
    sentinels of gods who wander round us.
Not me—go quickly, wanton, with another, and hasten
    like a chariot wheel to meet him.

I will not fold mine arms about thy body; they call it
    sin when one comes near his sister.
Not me,—prepare thy pleasures with another: thy
    brother seeks not this from thee, O fair one.

Embrace another, Yami; let another, even as the wood-
    bine rings the tree, enfold thee.
Win thou his heart and let him win thy fancy, and he
    shall form with thee a blest alliance.

To Varuna

Sing forth a hymn sublime and solemn, grateful to
glorious Varuna, imperial ruler,
Who hath struck out, like one who slays the victim,
earth as a skin to spread in front of Surya.

In the tree-tops the air he hath extended, put milk in
kine and vigorous speed in horses,
Set intellect in hearts, fire in the waters, Surya in
heaven and Soma on the mountain.

Varuna lets the big cask, opening downward, flow
through the heaven and earth and air's mid-region.
Therewith the universe's sovran waters earth as the
shower of rain bedews the barley.

If we have sinned against the man who loves us, have
ever wronged a brother, friend, or comrade,
The neighbour ever with us, or a stranger, O Varuna,
remove from us the trespass.

If we, as gamesters cheat at play, have cheated, done
wrong unwittingly or sinned of purpose,
Cast all these sins away like loosened fetters, and,
Varuna, let us be thine own beloved.

To Agni, in Praise of Night and Day

One-half of day is dark, and bright the other: both
atmospheres move on by sage devices.
Agni Vaisvanara, when born as sovran, hath with his
lustre overcome the darkness.

I know not either warp or woof, I know not the web
they weave when moving to the contest.

Whose son shall here speak words that must be spoken
   without assistance from the Father near him?

For both the warp and woof he understandeth, and in
   due time shall speak what should be spoken,
Who knoweth as the immortal world's protector, descending, seeing with no aid from other.

He is the priest, the first of all: behold him. Mid mortal
   men he is the light immortal.
Here was he born, firm-seated in his station, immortal,
   ever waxing in his body.

A firm light hath been set for men to look on: among
   all things that fly the mind is swiftest.
All gods of one accord, with one intention, move unob-
   structed to a single purpose.

All the gods bowed them down in fear before thee,
   Agni, when thou wast dwelling in the darkness.
O Universal One, be gracious to assist us, may the
   Immortal favour us and help us

To Liberality

The gods have not ordained hunger to be our death:
   even to the well-fed man comes death in varied
   shape.
The riches of the liberal never waste away, while he
   who will not give finds none to comfort him.

The man with food in store who, when the needy comes
   in miserable case begging for bread to eat,
Hardens his heart against him—even when of old he
   did him service—finds not one to comfort him.

Let the rich satisfy the poor implorer, and bend his
    eye upon a longer pathway.
Riches come now to one, now to another, and like the
    wheels of cars are ever rolling.

From the Atharva-Veda

A Charm Against Fear

As heaven and earth are not afraid, and never suffer
    loss or harm,
Even so, my spirit, fear not thou.

As day and night are not afraid, nor ever suffer loss
    or harm,
Even so, my spirit, fear not thou.
As sun and moon are not afraid, nor ever suffer loss
    or harm,
Even so, my spirit, fear not thou.

As Brahmanhood and princely power fear not, nor
    suffer loss or harm,
Even so, my spirit, fear not thou.
As truth and falsehood have no fear, nor ever suffer
    loss or harm,
Even so, my spirit, fear not thou.

As what hath been and what shall be fear not, nor
    suffer loss or harm,
Even so, my spirit, fear not thou.

One Common Spirit

Prajapati engenders earthly creatures: may the benevolent ordainer form them,
Having one common womb, and mind, and spirit. He
who is lord of plenty give me plenty!

To Heaven and Earth

All hail to heaven!
All hail to earth!
All hail to air!
All hail to air!
All hail to heaven!
All hail to earth!

Mine eye is sun and my breath is wind, air is my soul
and earth my body.
I verily who never have been conquered give up my
life to heaven and earth for keeping.

Exalt my life, my strength, my deed and action; increase
my understanding and my vigour.
Be ye my powerful keepers, watch and guard me, ye
mistresses of life and life's creators! Dwell ye within
me, and forbear to harm me.

From the Satapatha Brahmana

The Creation of Prajapati and the Gods

Verily, in the beginning this universe was water,
nothing but a sea of water. The waters desired, "How
can we be reproduced?" They toiled and performed

fervid devotions; when they were becoming heated, a golden egg was produced. The year, indeed, was not then in existence: this golden egg floated about for as long as the space of a year.

In a year's time a man, this Prajapati, was produced therefrom; and hence a woman, a cow, or a mare brings forth within the space of a year; for Prajapati was born in a year.

Desirous of offspring, he went on singing praises and toiling. He laid the power of reproduction into his own self. By the breath of his mouth he created the gods: the gods were created on entering the sky; and this is the godhead of the gods (deva) that they were created on entering the sky (div). Having created them, there was, as it were, daylight for him; and this also is the godhead of the gods that, after creating them, there was, as it were, daylight (diva) for him.

And by the downward breathing (flatulence) he created the Asuras: they were created on entering this earth. Having created them there was, as it were, darkness for him.

He knew, "Verily, I have created evil for myself since, after creating, there has come to be, as it were, darkness for me."

Now what daylight, as it were, there was for him, on creating the gods, of that he made the day; and what darkness, as it were, there was for him on creating the Asuras, of that he made the night: they are these two, day and night.

Now, these are the deities who were created out of Prajapati,—Agni, Indra, Soma, and Parameshth in Prajapatya.

From the Upanishads

The Universal Self[1]

I

In the beginning this was Self alone, in the shape of a person. He looking round saw nothing but his Self. He feared, and therefore any one who is lonely fears. He thought, "As there is nothing but myself, why should I fear?" Thence his fear passed away. For what should he have feared? Verily fear arises from a second only.

But he felt no delight. He wished for a second. He was so large as man and wife together. He then made this his Self to fall in two, and thence arose husband and wife.

He knew, "I indeed am this creation, for I created all this."

And when they say, "Sacrifice to this or sacrifice to that god," each god is but his manifestation, for he is all gods.

He (Brahman or the Self) cannot be seen, for, in part only, when breathing, he is breath by name; when speaking, speech by name; when seeing, eye by name; when hearing, ear by name; when thinking,

---

[1] The word "Self" here must not be interpreted to mean the individual personal self, as we use the word in English. Nor is "soul," as it is sometimes translated, an adequate rendering. What is meant here is the universal soul, or universal self which is in each of us, that "Self" which existed before all else, which is the source of all life and being. Perhaps the conception in Western thought most nearly akin to it is "God within us." Instead of being the egotistic conception which on casual inspection it may seem to be, it is, on the contrary, the most extreme humility before that essence of divinity which pervades the human soul and mind.

mind by name. All these are but the names of his acts. And he who worships (regards) him as the one or the other, does not know him, for he is apart from this when qualified by the one or the other. Let men worship him as Self, for in the Self all these are one. This Self is the footstep of everything, for through it one knows everything. And as one can find again by footsteps what was lost, thus he who knows this finds glory and praise.

This, which is nearer to us than anything, this Self, is dearer than a son, dearer than wealth, dearer than all else.

And if one were to say to one who declares another than the Self dear, that he will lose what is dear to him, very likely it would be so. Let him worship the Self alone as dear. He who worships the Self alone as dear, the object of his love will never perish.

Now if a man worships another deity, thinking the deity is one and he another, he does not know.

II

Now when Yajnavalkya was going to enter upon another state, he said: "Maitreyi, verily I am going away from this my house into the forest. Forsooth, let me make a settlement between thee and that Katyayani, my other wife."

Maitreyi said: "My lord, if this whole earth, full of wealth belonged to me, tell me, should I be immortal by it?"

"No," replied Yajnavalkya; "like the life of rich people will be thy life. But there is no hope of immortality by wealth."

And Maitreyi said: "What should I do with that by which I do not become immortal? What my lord knoweth of immortality, tell that to me."

Yajnavalkya replied: "Thou who are truly dear to me, thou speakest dear words. Come, sit down, I will explain it to thee, and mark well what I say."

And he said: "Verily, a husband is not dear, that you may love the husband; but that you may love the Self through the husband, therefore a husband is dear.

"Verily, a wife is not dear, that you may love the wife; but that you may love the Self through the wife, therefore a wife is dear.

"Verily, sons are not dear, that you may love the sons; but that you may love the Self through the sons, therefore sons are dear.

"Verily, wealth is not dear, that you may love wealth; but that you may love the Self through the wealth, therefore wealth is dear.

"Verily, the Brahman-class is not dear, that you may love the Brahman-class; but that you may love the Self through the Brahman-class, therefore the Brahman-class is dear.

"Verily, the Kshatriya-class is not dear, that you may love the Kshatriya-class; but that you may love the Self through the Kshatriya-class, therefore the Kshatriya-class is dear.

"Verily, the worlds are not dear, that you may love the worlds; but that you may love the Self through the worlds, therefore the worlds are dear.

"Verily, the Devas are not dear, that you may love the Devas; but that you may love the Self through the Devas, therefore the Devas are dear.

"Verily, creatures are not dear, that you may love the creatures; but that you may love the Self through the creatures, therefore are creatures dear.

"Verily, everything is not dear, that you may love everything; but that you may love the Self through everything, therefore everything is dear.

"Verily, the Self is to be seen, to be heard, to be perceived, to be marked, O Maitreyi! When we see, hear, perceive, and know the Self, then all this is known.

"As all waters find their centre in the sea, all touches in the skin, all tastes in the tongue, all smells in the nose, all colours in the eye, all sounds in the ear, all precepts in the mind, all knowledge in the heart, all actions in the hands, all movements in the feet, and all the Vedas in speech;

"As a lump of salt, when thrown into water, becomes dissolved into water, and could not be taken out again, but wherever we taste (the water) it is salt—thus verily, O Maitreyi, does this great Being, endless, unlimited, consisting of nothing but knowledge, rise from out these elements, and vanish again in them. This is enough, O beloved, for wisdom.

"For when there is duality, then one sees the other, one smells the other, one hears the other, one salutes the other, one perceives the other, one knows the other; but when the Self only is all this, how should he smell another, how should he see another, how should he hear another, how should he salute another, how should he perceive another, how should he know another? How should he know him by whom he knows all this? How, O beloved, should he know himself, the knower?"

The House of Death

(*Vajasravasa, desirous of heavenly rewards, surrenders at a sacrifice all that he possesses. He has a son named Nachiketas. When the promised presents are being given to the priests, faith enters into the heart of Nachiketas, who is still a boy.*)

Nachiketas *(thinking)*: Unblessed, surely, are the worlds to which a man goes by giving as his promised present at a sacrifice cows which have drunk water, eaten hay, given their milk, and are barren.

(Knowing that his father has promised to give up all that he possesses, and therefore his son also, he speaks to his father.)

Nachiketas: Dear father, to whom wilt thou give me? *(His father does not answer.)*

Nachiketas *(again)*: Dear father, to whom wilt thou give me? *(Still his father does not answer.)*

Nachiketas *(for the third time)*: Dear father, to whom wilt thou give me?

Vajasravasa *(angrily)*: I shall give thee unto Death!

Nachiketas *(as if to himself)*: I go as the first, at the head of many who have still to die; I go in the midst of many who are now dying. What will be the work of Yama, the ruler of the departed, which to-day he has to do unto me? Look back how it was with those who came before, look forward how it will be with those who come hereafter. A mortal ripens like corn, like corn he springs up again.

(Nachiketas enters into the abode of Yama [Death], and there is no one to receive him. Thereupon one of the attendants of Yama speaks.)

Attendant: Fire enters into the houses, when a Brahmana enters as a guest. That fire is quenched by this peace-offering—bring water, O Vaivasvata! A Brahmana that dwells in the house of a foolish man without receiving food to eat destroys his hopes and expectations, his possessions, his righteousness, his sacred and his good deeds, and all his sons and cattle.

(Yama, returning to his house after an absence of three nights, during which time Nachiketas has

received no hospitality from him, speaks in apology.)

Death: O Brahmana, as thou, a venerable guest, hast dwelt in my house three nights without eating, therefore choose now three boons, Hail to thee! and welfare to me!

Nachiketas: O Death, as the first of the three boons I choose that Gautama, my father, be pacified, kind, and free from anger towards me; and that he may know me and greet me, when I shall have been dismissed by thee.

Death: Through my favour thy father will know thee, and be again towards thee as he was before. He shall sleep peacefully through the night, and free from anger, after having seen thee freed from the mouth of death.

Nachiketas: In the heaven-world there is no fear; thou art not there, O Death, and no one is afraid on account of old age. Leaving behind both hunger and thirst, and out of the reach of sorrow, all rejoice in the world of heaven. Thou knowest, O Death, the fire-sacrifice which leads us to heaven; tell it to me, for I am full of faith. Those who live in the heaven-world reach immortality—this I ask as my second boon.

Death: I tell it thee, learn it from me, and when thou understandest that fire-sacrifice which leads to heaven, know, O Nachiketas, that it is the attainment of the endless worlds, and their firm support, hidden in darkness.

(*Death then tells him of that fire-sacrifice, the beginning of all the worlds, and what bricks are required for the altar, and how many, and how they are to be placed. And Nachiketas repeats all as it has been told to him.*)

Death: I give thee now another boon: that fire-sacrifice

shall be named after thee. Choose now, O Nachiketas, thy third boon.

Nachiketas: There is that doubt, when a man is dead—some saying, he is; others, he is not. This I should like to know, taught by thee; this is the third of my boons.

Death: On this point even the gods have doubted formerly; it is not easy to understand. That subject is subtle. Choose another boon, O Nachiketas, do not press me, and let me off that boon.

Nachiketas: On this point even the gods have doubted indeed, and thou, Death, hast declared it to be not easy to understand, and another teacher like thee is not to be found—surely no other boon is like unto this.

Death: Choose sons and grandsons who shall live a hundred years, herds of cattle, elephants, gold, and horses. Choose the wide abode of earth, and live thyself as many harvests as thou desirest. If thou canst think of any boon equal to that, choose wealth, and long life. Be king, Nachiketas, on the wide earth. I make thee the enjoyer of all desires. Whatever desires are difficult to attain among mortals, ask for them according to thy wish; these fair maidens with their chariots and musical instruments—such are indeed not to be obtained by men—be waited on by them whom I give to thee, but do not ask me about dying.

Nachiketas: These things last till to-morrow, O Death, for they wear out this vigour of all the senses. Even the whole of life is short. Keep thou thy horses, keep dance and song for thyself. No man can be made happy by wealth. Shall we possess wealth, when we see thee? Shall we live, as long as thou rulest? Only that boon which I have chosen is to be chosen by me. What mortal, slowly decaying here below, and knowing, after having approached them, the freedom from decay enjoyed by the immortals, would delight in a long life, after he has pondered on the pleasures which arise from beauty and love? No, that on which there is this doubt, O Death, tell us what there is in that great hereafter. Nachiketas does not choose another boon but that which enters into the hidden world.

Death: The good is one thing, the pleasant another; these two, having different objects, chain a man. It is well with him who clings to the good; he who chooses the pleasant, misses his end. The good and pleasant approach man: the wise goes round about them and distinguishes them. Yea, the wise prefers the good to the pleasant, but the fool chooses the pleasant through greed and avarice.

Thou, O Nachiketas, after pondering all pleasures that are or seem delightful, hast dismissed them all. Thou hast not gone into the road that leadeth to wealth, in which many men perish.

Wide apart and leading to different points are these two, ignorance, and what is known as wisdom. I believe Nachiketas to be one who desires knowledge, for even many pleasures did not tear thee away. Fools dwelling in darkness, wise in their own conceit, and puffed up with vain knowledge, go round and round, staggering to and fro, like blind men led by the blind. The hereafter never rises before the eyes of the careless child, deluded by the delusion of wealth. "This is the world," he thinks, "there is no other"—thus he falls again and again under my sway.

The knowing Self is not born, it dies not; it sprang from nothing, nothing sprang from it. The Ancient is unborn, eternal, everlasting; he is not killed, though the body is killed. If the killer thinks that he kills, if the killed think that he is killed, they do not understand; for this one does not kill, nor is that one killed.

The Self, smaller than small, greater than great, is hidden in the heart of that creature. A man who is free from desires and free from grief sees the majesty of the Self by the grace of the Creator.

(Death continues)

Know the Self to be sitting in the chariot, the body to be the chariot, the intellect the charioteer, and the mind the reins. The senses they call the horses, the objects of the senses their roads. When he (the highest Self) is in union with the body, the senses, and the mind, then wise people call him the Enjoyer.

He who has no understanding and whose mind (the reins) is never firmly held, his senses (horses) are unmanageable, like vicious horses of a charioteer. But he who has understanding and whose mind is always firmly held, his senses are under control, like good horses of a charioteer.

He who has no understanding, who is unmindful and always impure, never reaches that place, but enters into the round of births. But he who has understanding, who is mindful and always pure, reaches indeed that place, whence he is not born again. But he who has understanding for his charioteer, and who holds the reins of the mind, he reaches the end of his journey, and that is the highest place of Vishnu.

When that incorporated (Brahman) who dwells in the body is torn away and freed from the body, what remains then? No mortal lives by the breath that goes up and by the breath that goes down. We live by another, in whom these two repose.

Well then, O Gautama, I shall tell thee this mystery, the old Brahman, and what happens to the Self, after reaching death. Some enter the womb in order to have a body, as organic beings, others go into inorganic matter, according to their work and according to their knowledge.

As the one fire, after it has entered the world, though one, becomes different according to whatever it burns, thus the one Self within all things becomes different, according to whatever it enters, and exists also without. As the one air, after it has entered the world, though one, becomes different according to whatever it enters, thus the one Self within all things becomes different, according to whatever it enters, and exists also without. As the sun, the eye of the whole world, is not contaminated by the external impurities seen by the eyes, thus the one Self within all things is never contaminated by the misery of the world, being himself without.

There is one ruler, the Self within all things, who makes the one form manifold. The wise who perceive him within their Self, to them belongs eternal happiness, not to others. There is one eternal thinker, thinking non-eternal thoughts, who, though one, fulfils the desires of many. The wise who perceive him within their Self, to them belongs eternal peace, not to others.

The sun does not shine there, nor the moon and the stars, nor these lightnings, and much less this fire. When he shines, everything shines after him; by his light all this is lighted.

Whatever there is, the whole world, when gone forth from the Brahman, trembles in its breath. That Brahman is a great terror, like a drawn sword. Those who know it become immortal. From terror of Brahman fire burns, from terror the sun burns, from terror Indra and Vayu, and Death, as the fifth, run away.

If a man cannot understand this before the falling asunder of his body, then he has to take body again in the worlds of creation.

Beyond the senses is the mind, beyond the mind is the highest created Being, higher than that Being is the Great Self, higher than the Great, the highest Undeveloped. Beyond the Undeveloped is the Person, the all-pervading and entirely imperceptible. Every creature that knows him is liberated, and obtains immortality. His form is not to be seen, no one beholds him with the eye. He is imagined by the heart, by wisdom, by the mind. Those who know this, are immortal.

He, the Self, cannot be reached by speech, by mind, or by the eye. How can it be apprehended except by him who says: "He is"? By the words "He is," is he to be apprehended, and by admitting the reality of both the invisible Brahman and the visible world, as coming from Brahman. When he has been apprehended by the words "He is," then his reality reveals itself.

When all desires that dwell in his heart cease, then the mortal becomes immortal, and obtains Brahman. When all the ties of the heart are severed here on earth, then the mortal becomes immortal—here ends the teaching.

The Person not larger than a thumb, the inner Self, is always settled in the heart of men. Let a man draw that Self forth from his body with steadiness, as one draws the pith from a reed. Let him know that Self as the Bright, as the Immortal; yes, as the Bright, as the Immortal.

(*Having received this knowledge taught by Death and the whole rule of Yoga [meditation], Nachiketas became free from passion and death, and obtained Brahman. Thus it will be with another also who knows thus what relates to the Self. May he protect us both!*

*May he enjoy us both! May we acquire strength to-
gether! May our knowledge become bright! May we
never quarrel! Om! Peace! peace! peace! Hari, Om!)*

How Many Gods?

Then Vidagdha Sakalya asked him: "How many gods
are there, O Yajnavalkya?" He replied with this formula: "As many as are mentioned in the formula of the
hymn of praise addressed to the Visvedevas, viz. three
and three hundred, three and three thousand."

"Yes," he said, and asked again: "How many gods
are there really, O Yajnavalkya?"

"Thirty-three," he said.

"Yes," he said, and asked again: "How many gods
are there really, O Yajnavalkya?"

"Six," he said.

"Yes," he said, and asked again: "How many gods
are there really, O Yajnavalkya?"

"Three," he said.

"Yes," he said, and asked again: "How many gods
are there really, O Yajnavalkya?"

"Two," he said.

"Yes," he said, and asked again: "How many gods
are there really, O Yajnavalkya?"

"One and a half (adhyardha)," he said.

"Yes," he said, and asked again: "How many gods
are there really, O Yajnavalkya?"

"One," he said.

"Yes," he said, and asked: "Who are these three and
three hundred, three and three thousand?"

Yajnavalkya replied: "They are only the various
powers."

The Light of Man

Yajnavalkya came to Janaka Vaideha, and he did not mean to speak with him. But when formerly Janaka Vaideha and Yajnavalkya had a disputation on the Agnihotra, Yajnavalkya had granted him a boon, and he chose that he might be free to ask him any question he liked. Yajnavalkya granted it, and thus the king was the first to ask him a question.

"Yajnavalkya," he said, "what is the light of man?"

Yajnavalkya replied: "The sun, O king; for, having the sun alone for his light, man sits, moves about, does his work, and returns."

Janaka Vaideha said: "So indeed it is, O Yajnavalkya. When the sun has set, O Yajnavalkya, what is then the light of man?"

Yajnavalkya replied: "The moon indeed is his light; for, having the moon alone for his light, man sits, moves about, does his work, and returns."

Janaka Vaideha said: "So indeed it is, O Yajnavalkya. When the sun has set, O Yajnavalkya, and the moon has set, what is the light of man?"

Yajnavalkya replied: "Fire indeed is his light; for, having fire alone for his light, man sits, moves about, does his work, and returns."

Janaka Vaideha said: "When the sun has set, O Yajnavalkya, and the moon has set, and the fire is gone out, what is then the light of man?"

Yajnavalkya replied: "Sound indeed is his light; for, having sound alone for his light, man sits, moves about, does his work, and returns. Therefore, O king, when one cannot see even one's own hand, yet when a sound is raised, one goes towards it."

Janaka Vaideha said: "So indeed it is, O Yajnavalkya. When the sun has set, O Yajnavalkya, and the moon has set, and the fire is gone out, and the sound hushed, what is then the light of man?"

Yajnavalkya said: "The Self indeed is his light; for, having the Self alone as his light, man sits, moves about, does his work, and returns."

Janaka Vaideha said: "Who is that Self?"

Yajnavalkya replied: "He who is within the heart, surrounded by the pranas (senses), the person of light, consisting of knowledge. And there are two states for that person, the one here in this world, the other in the other world, and as a third an intermediate state, the state of sleep. When in that intermediate state, he sees both those states together, the one here in this world, and the other in the other world.

"If a man clearly beholds this Self as Brahman, and as the lord of all that is and will be, then he is no more afraid. This eternal being that can never be proved, is to be perceived in one way only; it is spotless, beyond the ether, the unborn Self, great and eternal. Let a wise Brahmana, after he has discovered him, practise wisdom. Let him not seek after many words, for that is mere weariness of the tongue."

My Self Within the Heart

All this is Brahman. Let a man meditate on that visible world as beginning, ending, and breathing in it, the Brahman.

Now man is a creature of will, According to what his will is in this world, so will he be when he has departed this life. Let him therefore have this will and belief:

The intelligent, whose body is spirit, whose form is light, whose thoughts are true, whose nature is like ether, omnipresent and invisible, from whom all works,

all desires, all sweet odours and tastes proceed; he who
embraces all this, who never speaks, and is never surprised, he is my self within the heart, smaller than a
corn of rice, smaller than a corn of barley, smaller
than a mustard seed, smaller than a canary seed or
the kernel of a canary seed. He also is my self within
the heart, greater than the earth, greater than the
sky, greater than heaven, greater than all these worlds.

He from whom all works, all desires, all sweet odours
and tastes proceed, who embraces all this, who never
speaks and who is never surprised, he, my self within
the heart, is that Brahman. When I shall have departed
hence, I shall obtain him (that Self). He who has this
faith has no doubt; thus said Sandilya, yea, thus he
said.

The Sun Is Brahman

Aditya (the sun) is Brahman, this is the doctrine,
and this is the fuller account of it:

In the beginning this was non-existent. It became
existent, it grew. It turned into an egg. The egg lay
for the time of a year. The egg broke open. The two
halves were one of silver, the other of gold.

The silver one became this earth, the golden one the
sky, the thick membrane of the white the mountains,
the thin membrane of the yolk the mist with the clouds,
the small veins the rivers, the fluid the sea.

And what was born from it that was Aditya, the
sun.

The Education of Svetaketu

Hari, Om. There lived once Svetaketu Aruneya, the grandson of Aruna. To him his father, Uddalaka, the son of Aruna, said: "Svetaketu, go to school; for there is none belonging to our race, darling, who, not having studied the Veda, is, as it were, a Brahmana by birth only."

Having begun his apprenticeship with a teacher when he was twelve years of age, Svetaketu returned to his father when he was twenty-four, having then studied all the Vedas—conceited, considering himself well-read, and stern.

His father said to him: "Svetaketu, as you are so conceited, considering yourself so well-read, and so stern, my dear, have you ever asked for that instruction by which we hear what cannot be heard, by which we perceive what cannot be perceived, by which we know what cannot be known?"

"What is that instruction, Sir?" he asked.

The father replied: "My dear, as by one clod of clay all that is made of clay is known, the difference being only a name, arising from speech, but the truth being that all is clay; and as, my dear, by one nugget of gold all that is made of gold is known, the difference being only a name, arising from speech, but the truth being that all is gold; and as, my dear, by one pair of nail-scissors all that is made of iron is known, the difference being only a name, arising from speech, but the truth being that all is iron—thus, my dear, is that instruction."

The son said: "Surely those venerable men, my teachers, did not know that. For if they had known it, why should they not have told it me? Do you, Sir, therefore tell me that." "Be it so," said the father.

"In the beginning, my dear, there was that only which is, one only, without a second. It thought, May I be many, may I grow forth. It sent forth fire. That fire thought, may I be many, may I grow forth. It sent forth water. And therefore whenever anybody anywhere is hot and perspires, water is produced on him from fire alone.

"Water thought, may I be many, may I grow forth. It sent forth earth (food). Therefore whenever it rains anywhere, most food is then produced. From water alone is eatable food produced.

"As the bees, my son, make honey by collecting the juices of distant trees, and reduce the juice into one form, and as these juices have no discrimination, so that they might say, I am the juice of this tree or that, in the same manner, my son, all these creatures, when they have become merged in the True (either in deep sleep or in death), know not that they are merged in the True. Whatever these creatures are here, whether a lion, or a wolf, or a boar, or a worm, or a midge, or a gnat, or a mosquito, that they become again and again. Now that which is that subtle essence, in it all that exists has its self. It is the True. It is the Self, and thou, O Svetaketu, art it."

"Please, Sir, inform me still more," said the son.

"Be it so, my child," the father replied.

"These rivers, my son, run, the eastern like the Ganga, towards the east, the western like the Sindhu, towards the west. They go from sea to sea (i.e. the clouds lift up the water from the sea to the sky, and send it back as rain to the sea). They become indeed sea. And as those rivers, when they are in the sea, do not know, I am this or that river, in the same manner, my son, all these creatures, when they have come back from the True, know not that they have come back from the True. Whatever these creatures are here, whether a lion, or a wolf, or a boar, or a worm, or a midge, or a gnat, or a mosquito, that they become again and again.

"That which is that subtile essence, in it all that exists has its self. It is the True. It is the Self, and thou, O Svetaketu, art it."

"Please, Sir, inform me still more," said the son.

"Be it so, my child," the father replied.

"If someone were to strike at the root of this large tree here, it would bleed, but live. If he were to strike at its stem, it would bleed, but live. If he were to strike at its top, it would bleed, but live. Pervaded by the living Self that tree stands firm, drinking in its nourishment and rejoicing; but if the life (the living Self) leaves one of its branches, that branch withers; if it leaves a second, that branch withers; if it leaves a third, that branch withers. If it leaves the whole tree, the whole tree withers.

"In exactly the same manner, my son, know this. This body indeed withers and dies when the living Self has left it; the living Self dies not.

"That which is that subtile essence, in it all that exists has its self. It is the True. It is the Self, and thou, O Svetaketu, art it."

The Power of God

Those who know the High Brahman, the vast, hidden in the bodies of all creatures, and alone enveloping everything, as the Lord, they become immortal.

Some wise men, deluded, speak of nature, and others

of time as the cause of everything; but it is the greatness of God by which this Brahma-wheel is made to
turn. It is at the command of him who always covers
this world, the knower, the time of time, who assumes
qualities and all knowledge, it is at his command that
this work, creation, unfolds itself, which is called earth,
water, fire, air, and ether; he who, after he has done
that work and rested again, and after he has brought
together one essence (the self) with the other (matter),
with one, two, three, or eight, with time also and with
the subtile qualities of the mind, who, after starting the
works endowed with the three qualities, can order all
things, yet when, in the absence of all these, he has
caused the destruction of the work, goes on, being in
truth different from all that he has produced; he is the
beginning, producing the causes which unite the soul
with the body, and, being above the three kinds of time,
past, present, future, he is seen as without parts, after
we have first worshipped that adorable god, who has
many forms, and who is the true source of all things, as
dwelling in our own mind.

He is the one God, hidden in all beings, all-pervading, the self within all beings, watching over all works,
dwelling in all beings, the witness, the perceiver, the
only one, free from qualities. He is the one ruler of
many who seem to act, but really do not act; he makes
the one seed manifold. The wise who perceive him
within their self, to them belongs eternal happiness, not
to others. He is the eternal among eternals, the thinker
among thinkers, who, though one, fulfils the desires of
many. He who has known that cause which is to be
apprehended by Samkhya (philosophy) and Yoga
(religious discipline), he is freed from all fetters.

The sun does not shine there, nor the moon and the

stars, nor these lightnings, and much less this fire. When he shines, everything shines after him; by his light all this is lightened.

He makes all, he knows all, the self-caused, the knower, the time of time, who assumes qualities and knows everything, the master of nature and of man, the lord of the three qualities, the cause of the bondage, the existence, and the liberation of the world.

Seeking for freedom I go for refuge to that God who is the light of his own thoughts, he who first creates Brahman and delivers the Vedas to him; who is without parts, without actions, tranquil, without fault, without taint, the highest bridge to immortality—like a fire that has consumed its fuel.

Only when men shall roll up the sky like a hide, will there be an end of misery, unless God has first been known.

From the Bhagavad Gita

Revolt Against War

Having seen arrayed the army of the Pandavas, the Prince Duryodhana approached his teacher, and spake these words:

"Behold this mighty host of the sons of Pandu, O teacher, arrayed by the son of Drupada, thy wise disciple. Insufficient seems this army of ours, though marshalled by Bhishma, while that army of theirs seems sufficient, though marshalled by Bhima; therefore in the rank and file let all, standing firmly in their respective divisions, guard Bhishma, even all ye generals."

Then, beholding the sons of Dhritarashtra standing arrayed, and the flight of missiles about to begin, he whose crest is an ape, the son of Pandu, took up his bow, and spake this word to Hrishikesa:

"In the midst, between the two armies, stay my chariot, O Achyuta, that I may behold these standing, longing for battle, with whom I must strive in this out-breaking war. And gaze on those here gathered together, ready to fight, desirous of pleasing in battle the evil-minded son of Dhritarashtra."

Thus addressed by Arjuna, Hrishikesa, having stayed that best of chariots in the midst, between the two armies, over against Bhishma, Drona and all the rulers of the world, said:

"O Partha, behold these Kurus gathered together."

Then saw Partha standing there, uncles and grand-fathers, teachers, mother's brothers, cousins, sons and grandsons, comrades, fathers-in-law, and benefactors also in both armies; seeing all these kinsmen thus standing arrayed, Arjuna, deeply moved to pity, this uttered in sadness:

"Seeing these my kinsmen, O Krishna, arrayed, eager to fight, my limbs fail and my mouth is parched, my body quivers, and my hair stands on end, Gandiva slips from my hand, and my skin burns all over, I am not able to stand, my mind is whirling, and I see adverse omens, O Kesava. Nor do I foresee any advantage from slaying kinsmen in battle.

"For I desire not victory, O Krishna, nor kingdom, nor pleasures; what is kingdom to us, O Govinda, what enjoyment, or even life? Those for whose sake we desire kingdom, enjoyments and pleasures, they stand here in battle, abandoning life and riches—teachers, fathers, sons, as well as grandfathers, mother's brothers, fathers-in-law, grandsons, brothers-in-law, and other relatives. These I do not wish to kill, though myself slain, O

Madhusudana, even for the sake of the kingship of the three worlds; how then for earth?"

Having thus spoken on the battlefield, Arjuna sank down on the seat of the chariot, casting away his bow and arrow, his mind overborne by grief.

The Blessed Lord said: "Thou grievest for those that should not be grieved for, yet speakest words of wisdom. The wise grieve neither for the living nor for the dead. Nor at any time verily was I not, nor thou, nor these princes of men, nor verily shall we ever cease to be, hereafter. As the dweller in the body experienceth in the body childhood, youth, old age, so passeth he on to another body; the steadfast one grieveth not thereat. The contacts of matter, O son of Kunti, giving cold and heat, pleasure and pain, they come and go, impermanent; endure them bravely.

"The man whom these torment not, balanced in pain and pleasure, steadfast, he is fitted for immortality. The unreal hath no being; the real never ceaseth to be; the truth about both hath been perceived by the seers of the essence of things. Know that to be indestructible by whom all this is pervaded. Nor can any work the destruction of that imperishable One. These bodies of the embodied One, who is eternal, indestructible and immeasurable, are known as finite. Therefore fight, O Bharata. He who regardeth this as a slayer, and he who thinketh he is slain, both of them are ignorant. He slayeth not, nor is he slain. He is not born, nor doth he die; nor having been, ceaseth he any more to be; unborn, perpetual, eternal and ancient, he is not slain when the body is slaughtered. Who knoweth him indestructible, perpetual, unborn, undiminishing, how can that man slay, O Partha, or cause to be slain?

"As a man, casting off worn-out garments, taketh new ones, so the dweller in the body, casting off worn-out bodies, entereth into others that are new. Weapons cleave him not, nor fire burneth him, nor waters wet him, nor wind drieth him away. Uncleavable he, incombustible he, and indeed neither to be wetted nor dried away; perpetual, all-pervasive, stable, immovable, ancient. Unmanifest, unthinkable, immutable, he is called; therefore knowing him as such, thou shouldst not grieve. Or if thou thinkest of him as being constantly born and constantly dying, even then, O mighty-armed, thou shouldst not grieve. For certain is death for the born, and certain is birth for the dead; therefore over the inevitable thou shouldst not grieve."

The Rule of Action

Arjuna said: "With these perplexing words thou only confusest my understanding; therefore tell me with certainty the one way by which I may reach bliss."

The Blessed Lord said: "In this world there is a two-fold path, as I before said, O sinless one: that of yoga by knowledge, of the Sankhyas; and that of yoga by action, of the Yogis.

"Man winneth not freedom from action by abstaining from activity, nor by mere renunciation doth he rise to perfection. Nor can any one, even for an instant, remain really actionless; for helplessly is every one driven to action by the qualities born of nature. Who sitteth, controlling the organs of action, but dwelling in his mind on the objects of the senses, that bewildered man is called a hypocrite. But who, controlling the senses by the mind, O Arjuna, with the organs of action without attachment, performeth yoga by action, he is worthy. Perform thou right action, for action is superior to inaction, and, inactive, even the maintenance of thy body would not be possible.

"The world is bound by action, unless performed for the sake of sacrifice; for that sake, free from attachment, O son of Kunti, perform thou action. Having in ancient times emanated mankind together with sacrifice, the lord of emanation said: 'By this shall ye propagate; be this to you the giver of desires; with this nourish ye the shining ones, and may the shining ones nourish you; thus nourishing one another, ye shall reap the supremest good. For nourished by sacrifice, the shining ones shall bestow on you the enjoyments you desire.'

"He who on earth doth not follow the wheel thus revolving, sinful of life and rejoicing in the senses, he liveth in vain. But the man who rejoiceth in the Self with the Self is satisfied, and is content in the Self, for him verily there is nothing to do; for him there is no interest in things done in this world, nor any in things not done, nor doth any object of his depend on any being. Therefore, without attachment, constantly perform action which is duty, for, by performing action without attachment, man verily reacheth the Supreme.

"Whatsoever a great man doeth, that other men also do; the standard he setteth up, by that the people go. Let no wise man unsettle the mind of ignorant people attached to action; but acting in harmony with me let him render all action attractive.

"All actions are wrought by the qualities of nature only. Even the man of knowledge behaves in conformity with his own nature; beings follow nature; what shall restraint avail? Affection and aversion for the objects of sense abide in the senses; let none come under the dominion of these two; they are obstructors of the path. Better one's own duty though destitute of merit, than the duty of another, well-discharged. Better death in the discharge of one's own duty; the duty of another is full of danger."

The Rule of Wisdom

The Blessed Lord said: "Many births have been left behind by me and by thee, O Arjuna. I know them all, but thou knowest not thine, O Parantapa. Though unborn, the imperishable Self, and also the lord of all beings, brooding over nature, which is mine own, yet I am born through my own power.

"Whenever there is decay of righteousness, O Bharata, and there is exaltation of unrighteousness, then I myself come forth; for the protection of the good, for the destruction of evil-doers, for the sake of firmly establishing righteousness, I am born from age to age.

"He who thus knoweth my divine birth and action, in its essence, having abandoned the body, cometh not to birth again, but cometh unto me, O Arjuna. Freed from passion, fear and anger, filled with me, taking refuge in me, purified in the fire of wisdom, many have entered into my being. However men approach me, even so do I welcome them, for the path men take from every side is mine, O Partha.

"They who long after success in action on earth worship the shining ones; for in brief space verily, in this world of men, success is born of action.

"'What is action, what inaction?' Even the wise are herein perplexed. It is needful to discriminate action, to discriminate unlawful action, and to discriminate inaction; mysterious is the path of action. He who seeth inaction in action, and action in inaction, he is wise among men, he is harmonious, even while performing all action.

"Whose works are all free from the moulding of desire, whose actions are burned up by the fire of wisdom, him the wise have called a sage. Having abandoned attachment to the fruit of action, always content, nowhere seeking refuge, he is not doing anything, although doing actions.

"Even if thou art the most sinful of all sinners, yet shalt thou cross over all sin by the raft of wisdom. As the burning fire reduces fuel to ashes, O Arjuna, so doth the fire of wisdom reduce all actions to ashes. Verily, there is no purifier in this world like wisdom; he that is perfected in yoga finds it in the Self in due season.

"The man who is full of faith obtaineth wisdom, and he also who hath mastery over his senses; and, having obtained wisdom, he goeth swiftly to the supreme peace. But the ignorant, faithless, doubting self goeth to destruction; nor this world, nor that beyond, nor happiness, is there for the doubting self."

The Nature of God

The Blessed Lord said: "Among thousands of men scarce one striveth for perfection; of the successful strivers scarce one knoweth me in essence. Earth, water, fire, air, ether, mind, and reason also and egoism— these are the eightfold division of my nature.

"Know this to be the womb of all beings. I am the source of the forthgoing of the whole universe and likewise the place of its dissolving. There is naught whatsoever higher than I. All this is threaded on me, as rows of pearls on a string.

"I am the sapidity in waters, I the radiance in moon and sun; the word of power in all the Vedas, sound in ether, and virility in men; the pure fragrance of earths and the brilliance in fire am I; the life in all beings am I, and the austerity in ascetics. Know me as the eternal seed of all beings. I am the reason of the reason-endowed, the splendour of splendid things am I. And I the strength of the strong, devoid of desire and passion. In beings I am desire not contrary to duty. The natures that are harmonious, active, slothful, these know as from me; not I in them, but they in me.

"All this world, deluded by these natures made by the three qualities, knoweth not me, above these, imperishable. This divine illusion of mine, caused by the qualities, is hard to pierce; they who come to me, they cross over this illusion."

The Lord of All

The Blessed Lord said: "By me all this world is pervaded in my unmanifested aspect; all beings have root in me, I am not rooted in them. As the mighty air everywhere moving is rooted in the ether, so all beings rest rooted in me—thus know thou.

"Hidden in nature, which is mine own, I emanate again and again all this multitude of beings, helpless, by the force of nature. Under me as supervisor nature sends forth the moving and unmoving; because of this, the universe revolves.

"The foolish disregard me, when clad in human semblance, ignorant of my supreme nature, the great Lord of beings; empty of hope, empty of deeds, empty of wisdom, senseless, partaking of the deceitful, brutal and demoniacal nature.

"Others also, sacrificing with the sacrifice of wisdom, worship me as the One and the Manifold everywhere present.

"I the oblation; I the sacrifice; I the ancestral offering; I the fire-giving herb; the mantram I; I also the butter; I the fire; the burnt offering I; I the Father of this universe, the Mother, the Supporter, the Grandsire, the Holy One to be known, the Word of Power, and also the Ric, Sama, and Yajur, the Path, Husband, Lord, Witness, Abode, Shelter, Lover, Origin, Dissolution, Foundation, Treasure-house, Seed imperishable. I give heat; I hold back and send forth the rain; immortality and also death, being and non-being am I.

"To those men who worship me alone, thinking of no other, to those ever harmonious, I bring full security. They who worship the shining ones go to the shining ones; to the ancestors go the ancestor-worshippers; to the elementals go those who sacrifice to elementals; but my worshippers come unto me. He who offereth to me with devotion a leaf, a flower, a fruit, water, that I accept from the striving self, offered as it is with devotion.

"The same am I to all beings; there is none hateful to me nor dear. They verily who worship me with devotion, they are in me, and I also in them. Even if the most sinful worship me, with undivided heart, he too must be accounted righteous, for he hath rightly resolved; speedily he becometh dutiful and goeth to eternal peace.

"On me fix thy mind; be devoted to me; sacrifice to me; prostrate thyself before me; harmonized thus in the Self, thou shalt come unto me, having me as thy supreme goal."

The Rule of Devotion

The Blessed Lord said: "Those verily who, renouncing all actions in me and intent on me, worship meditating on me, with wholehearted yoga, these I speedily lift up from the ocean of death and existence, O Partha, their minds being fixed on me.

"If also thou art not equal to constant practice, be intent on my service; performing actions for my sake, thou shalt attain perfection. If even to do this thou hast not strength, then, taking refuge in union with me, renounce all fruit of action with the self controlled.

"Better indeed is wisdom than constant practice; than wisdom, meditation is better; than meditation, renunciation of the fruit of action; on renunciation follows peace.

"He who beareth no ill-will to any being, friendly and compassionate, without attachment and egoism, balanced in pleasure and pain, and forgiving, ever content, harmonious with the self controlled, resolute, with mind and reason dedicated to me, he, my devotee, is dear to me.

"He from whom the world doth not shrink away, who doth not shrink away from the world, freed from the anxieties of joy, anger, and fear, he is dear to me.

"He who wants nothing, is pure, expert, passionless, untroubled, renouncing every undertaking, he, my devotee, is dear to me. He who neither loveth nor hateth, nor grieveth, nor desireth, renouncing good and evil, full of devotion, he is dear to me.

"Alike to foe and friend, and also in fame and ignominy, alike in cold and heat, pleasures and pain, destitute of attachment, taking equally praise and reproach, silent, wholly content with what cometh, homeless, firm in mind, full of devotion, that man is dear to me.

"They verily who partake of this life-giving wisdom as taught herein, endued with faith, I their supreme object, devotees, they are surpassingly dear to me."

The Good Man and the Evil

"Fearlessness, cleanness of life, steadfastness in the Yoga of wisdom, alms-giving, self-restraint and sacrifice and study of the scriptures, austerity and straightforwardness, harmlessness, truth, absence of wrath, renunciation, peacefulness, absence of crookedness, compassion to living beings, uncovetousness, mildness, modesty, absence of fickleness, vigour, forgiveness, fortitude, purity, absence of envy and pride—these are his who is born with the divine properties.

"Hypocrisy, arrogance and conceit, wrath and also harshness and unwisdom are his who is born with demoniacal properties.

"Holding this view, these ruined selves of small understanding, of fierce deeds, come forth as enemies for the destruction of the world. Surrendering themselves to insatiable desires, possessed with vanity, conceit and arrogance, holding evil ideas through delusion, they engage in action with impure resolves. Giving themselves over to unmeasured thought whose end is death, regarding the gratification of desires as the highest, feeling sure that this is all, held in bondage by a hundred ties of expectation, given over to lust and anger, they strive to obtain by unlawful means hoards of wealth for sensual enjoyments.

"Self-glorifying, stubborn, filled with the pride and intoxication of wealth, they perform lip-sacrifices for ostentation, contrary to scriptural ordinance. Given over to egoism, power, insolence, lust and wrath, these malicious ones hate me in the bodies of others and in their own.

"Therefore let the scriptures be thy authority, in determining what ought to be done, or what ought not to be done. Knowing what hath been declared by the ordinances of the scriptures, thou oughtest to work in this world."

From the Vishnu Purana

The General Duties of Man

Vishnu being worshipped, a man obtains the consummation of all earthly desires and attains to the regions of the celestials and of Brahma and even final liberation. He is the true worshipper of Vishnu who observes duly the duties of the four castes and rules of four Asramas. There is no other means of satisfying Vishnu. He who offers sacrifices, sacrifices to him; he who recites prayers, prays to him; he who injures living beings, injures him; for Hari is identical with all living beings. Therefore, he who observes duly the duties of his caste is said to worship the glorious Janardana. O lord of earth, the Brahmana, the Kshatriya, the Vaisya, the Sudra, by attending to the duties prescribed by his caste, best worships Vishnu. He who does not vilify another either in his presence, or in his absence, who does not speak untruth, does not injure others, pleases Kesava the best. Kesava is best pleased with him, O king, who does not covet another's wife, wealth, and who does not bear ill feeling towards any. O lord of men, Kesava is pleased with him who neither beats nor slays any animate thing. O lord of men, Govinda is pleased with that man who is ever intent upon serving the gods, the Brahmanas and his spiritual preceptor. Hari is always satisfied with him who is ever anxious for the welfare of all creatures, his children and his own soul. Vishnu is always pleased with that pure-minded man whose mind is not sullied with anger and other passions. He best worships Vishnu, O king, who observes the duties laid down by scripture for every caste and condition of life; there is no other mode.

From the Garuda Purana

Of Associates

Double-tongued are the snakes and the malicious; their cruel mouths are the source of many an evil to man. Avoid the company of an erudite miscreant: is not the serpent that bears a gem on its hood doubly dangerous for the stone? Who is he that dreadeth not the malicious who work mischief without any provocation and who are but the serpents in human form? Words of spite drop down from the mouths of the malicious; the fangs of serpents secrete deadly venom.

Sit in the assembly of the honest; combine with those that are good and virtuous; nay, seek out a noble enemy where enmity cannot be helped and have nothing to do with the wicked and the unrighteous. Even in bondage thou shalt live with the virtuous, the erudite and the truthful; but not for a kingdom shalt thou stay with the wicked and the malicious.

The vile are ever prone to detect the faults of others, though they be as small as mustard seeds, and persistently shut their eyes against their own, though they be as large as Vilva fruits. I come to the conclusion, after much deliberation, that pleasure exists not where desire or affection has room to be. True happiness lies in the extinction of all emotions. Apprehension is where affec-

tion is. Where there is affection there is misery. Pain
has its root in love or affection. Renounce affection and
you shall be happy. This human body is a theatre of
pleasure and pain, and they come into being with the
self of a man. Dependence or bondage is misery. Liberty or emancipation is the only happiness vouchsafed
to man.

Never stay in a lonely place with your own daughters, sisters or stepmothers. The fiend of lust takes advantage of solitude and pleads evil counsel to the heart
to which the learned have been known to yield. How
absurd is the love god in his frolics!

A courtesan is a dependant even in respect of her
sleep, the sole aim of her life being to regale the hearts
of her visitors as long as they can decently bear their
wine. She is a sort of perpetual smiling machine, being
obliged to hammer out a horse-laugh, even with the
weight of a life-long grief, misery and futility lying
heavy on her heart. Her person is sold to others for
money, while she often meets a violent death. Fire,
water, a king, a woman, a fool, or a serpent used or
provoked by another, should be regarded as fatal.
What wonder is it that a man well-versed in letters will
pass as an erudite one? What is surprising in the fact
that a king who is learned in the science of politics will
rule justly as a virtuous prince? What is there to wonder, if a young and beautiful woman, proud and conscious of her charms, leads a gay and fast life? What
is there to surprise, if an indigent person commits a
crime?

How can I believe a rich man to be an anchorite,
and a drunken woman chaste? Trust not the untrust-
worthy nor confide any secret in your friend, lest he
might betray you in a fit of anger. A vast, deep and
child-like faith in all, a universal clemency, and a close

and watchful veiling of his own god-like inherent
virtues, are the traits which mark a noble soul.

Karma

A man is the creator of his own fate, and even in his
fœtal life he is affected by the dynamics of the works
of his prior existence. Whether confined in a mountain
fastness or lulling on the bosom of a sea, whether
secure in his mother's lap or held high above her head,
a man cannot fly from the effects of his own prior
deeds.

This human body entombs a self which is nothing if
not emphatically a worker. It is the works of this self
in a prior existence which determine the nature of its
organism in the next, as well as the character of the diseases, whether physical or mental, which it is to fall a
prey to.

A man reaps that at that age, whether infancy, youth
or old age, at which he had sowed it in his previous
birth. The Karma of a man draws him away from a
foreign country and makes him feel its consequence
even in spite of his will. A man gets in life what he is
fated to get, and even a god cannot make it otherwise.

A Duty to Children

The parents of a child are but his enemies when
they fail to educate him properly in his boyhood. An
illiterate boy, like a heron amidst swans, cannot shine
in the assembly of the learned. Learning imparts a
heightened charm to a homely face. Knowledge is the
best treasure that a man can secretly hoard up in life.
Learning is the revered of the revered. Knowledge
makes a man honest, virtuous and endearing to the

society. It is learning alone that enables a man to better the condition of his friends and relations. Knowledge is the holiest of the holies, the god of the gods, and commands the respect of crowned heads; shorn of it a man is but an animal. The fixtures and furniture of one's house may be stolen by thieves; but knowledge, the highest treasure, is above all stealing.

From the Markandeya Purana

Sumati Instructs His Father

A certain high-minded Brahmana, born in the race of Bhrigu, said to his gentle son Sumati, resembling one void of sense at the time of his investiture with the sacred thread:

Study the Vedas, O Sumati, in due order being intent upon serving your preceptor and depending upon alms. Then entering the life of a householder do you celebrate excellent sacrifices and beget desirable offspring and then enter into woods. When you shall live in the forest, O child, and, leaving the company of your wife, lead the life of a mendicant, you will attain to that Brahman, approaching whom no one grieves. Being thus urged on by his father out of parental affection with nectarine words, he, smiling, said:

O father, all that you advise me to study has been exhaustively read by me together with various other branches of learning and diverse mechanical arts. Ten thousand births more come to my recollection.

I was born as a Brahmana, a Kshatriya, a Vaisya and a Sudra, and again as a beast, a worm, a deer and a bird. I was born in the houses of the royal entertainers and war-like kings, as I have been born in your house. I became servants and slaves of many men and I came by mastery, lordship, and poverty.

Thus revolving on the perilous wheel of the world, I have attained to this knowledge, O father, which is instrumental to the attainment of liberation.

Hear, O father, a true account of what I have experienced again and again. This wheel of a world is undecaying, still it has no existence.

He who has never uttered a falsehood, he who has not made a distinction of love, he who believes in God and who is reverential, meets with happy death. Those who are intent upon adoring the deities and Brahmanas, who are free from spite, who are pure in spirit, are liberal and bashful, meet with easy death. He who does not forsake virtue through lust, anger or spite, he who keeps his promise and is gentle, meets with easy death. But he who does not give water to one who is thirsty, food to one who is hungry, is assailed by them when death presents itself. Those who give fuel conquer cold, those who give sandal conquer heat; but those who afflict people come by a dreadful pain destroying the very life.

Those worst of men, who cause ignorance and stupefaction, attain great fear and are crushed by fierce pangs. Those that give false evidence, or speak falsely, or satisfy the orders of a wicked man, or disregard the Vedas, die in ignorance. The dreadful and vicious-souled followers of Yama, breathing hellish smell around, with nooses and maces in hands, approach them. And when they come within the range of their vision they all tremble and continually wail for their brothers, mothers and sons. Then their speech becomes indistinct, O father, and is composed of one letter; their eyes roll and their faces are dried up with fear and sighs. Then with breath running high, sight dimmed and assailed by pain, such a one renounces his body. Then going before the body, for undergoing affliction consequent upon his acts, he assumes another body not sprung from a father or a mother but which has the same age, condition and habitation as assigned to the other body.

Then the emissaries of Yama quickly bind him with dreadful nooses and drag him to the south, trembling with the stroke of the rod. Then he is dragged by the emissaries of Yama, sending out dreadful, inauspicious yells through grounds rough with Kusa, thorns, ant-hills, pins and stones, glowing with flames at places, covered with pits, blazing with the heat of the sun and burning with its rays. Dragged by the dreadful emissaries and eaten by hundreds of jackals, the sinful person goes to Yama's house through a fearful passage.

But those who have distributed umbrellas and shoes, those who have given away cloth, as well as those who have given away food, go easily by that way.

Going through such sufferings, losing all control over self and assailed by sin, a man is taken, on the twelfth day, to the city of Dharma. When his body is burnt he experiences a great burning sensation; and when his body is beaten or cut he feels a great pain.

His body being thus destroyed, a creature, although walking into another body, suffers eternal misery on account of his own adverse actions.

A man repeatedly goes through a cycle of births and deaths. In this way, he rolls like a clock on the wheel of the world. Sometimes a man attains heaven, some-times he goes to hell and sometimes a dead man reaps both heaven and hell. And sometimes born again in this earth he reaps the fruits of his own acts. And some-times enjoying the fruits of his own acts within a short

time he breathes his last. Sometimes, O best of Brahmanas, living in heaven or hell for a short time on account of his limited merit or demerit he is born in this
earth.

O father, the dwellers of heaven are seen by them
to enjoy happiness—and then those, brought down to
perdition, think that there is a great misery in hell.
Even in heaven there is incomparable misery, for from
the time of ascension every one conceives in his mind,
"I shall fall." Beholding the people of hell, they attain
to mighty misery thinking day and night, "I shall be
brought to this condition."

Mighty is the pain of living in the womb, of being
born from a female, of the infancy of one when born,
and that of decrepitude as well. There is also great
misery in youth influenced by lust, malice and anger;
old age is also full of miseries and the culmination of
this is death. Mighty is the pain of those who are
carried away by force by the emissaries of Yama and
thrown into hell; then again is birth in the womb and
death and hell.

The Creation of Castes

From the mouth of Brahma, meditating on truth
and entering upon the functions of creation, were produced a thousand pairs. They, thus born, were all
moved by the quality of Satwa, and were joined to the
right understanding. Another thousand pairs he created
from his breast. They all were moved by the quality
of Rajas, and were full of strength and invincible. Another thousand pairs he created again from his thigh.
They were moved by the two qualities of Rajas and
Tamas, and were full of energy and enterprise. From
his two feet he created another thousand pairs. They

were all moved by the quality of Tamas, and were without beauty, and of little understanding.

In this way, after the establishment of the means of subsistence for them, the Lord himself established honour and precedence among them according to their respective rights and qualifications.

From Sankaracharya's Atma Bodha

Knowledge of Spirit

The spirit is smothered, as it were, by ignorance, but so soon as ignorance is destroyed, spirit shines forth, like the sun when released from clouds. After the soul, afflicted by ignorance, has been purified by knowledge, knowledge disappears, as the seed or berry of the Kataka after it has purified water.

Like an image in a dream the world is troubled by love, hatred, and other poisons. So long as the dream lasts, the image appears to be real; but on awaking it vanishes.

The world appears real, as an osyter-shell appears to be silver; but only so long as the Brahman remains unknown, he who is above all, and indivisible. That Being, true, intelligent, comprehends within itself every variety of being, penetrating and permeating all as a thread which strings together beads.

In consequence of possessing diverse attributes, the supreme existence appears manifold, but when the attributes are annihilated, unity is restored. In consequence of those diverse attributes, a variety of names and conditions are supposed proper to the spirit, just as a variety of tastes and colours are attributed to water.

All that belongs to the body (must be considered) as the product of ignorance. It is visible; it is perishable as bubbles of air (on the surface of water); but that which has not these signs must be recognized as pure spirit which says of itself, "I am Brahman. Because I am distinct from body, I experience neither birth, old age, decrepitude, nor extinction, and detached from organs of sense, I have no longer any connexion with their objects, such as sound."

This conception, "I am Brahman itself," incessantly entertained, disperses the hallucinations born of ignorance, as medicine disperses sickness.

Seated in a desert place, exempt from passion, master of his senses, let man represent to himself this spirit, one and infinite, without allowing his thoughts to stray elsewhere.

Considering the visible universe as annihilated in spirit, let a man, pure through intelligence, constantly contemplate the One Spirit, as he might contemplate luminous ether.

From the Hitopadesa

Proverbs

Amongst all things, knowledge is truly the best thing; from its not being liable ever to be stolen, from its not being purchasable, and from its being imperishable.

Of a son unborn, dead, or a fool,—better the two first than the last. The two first cause unhappiness once; but the last, perpetually.

The mind is lowered, O son, through association

with inferiors. With equals it attains equality; and with superiors, superiority.

No labour bestowed upon a worthless thing can be productive of fruit; even by a hundred efforts a crane cannot be made to talk like a parrot.

As one's life is dear to himself, so also are those of all beings. The good show compassion towards all living beings because of their resemblance to themselves.

He who looks on another's wife as a mother, on another's goods as a clod of earth, and on all creatures as himself, is a wise man.

From covetousness anger proceeds; from covetousness lust is born; from covetousness come delusion and perdition. Covetousness is the cause of sin.

Six faults ought to be avoided by a man seeking prosperity in this world: sleep, sloth, fear, anger, laziness, prolixity.

In this life there is none more happy than he who has a friend to converse with, a friend to live with, and a friend to chat with.

As long as danger is at a distance, it should be dreaded: but when a man perceives danger to be present, he should act in a becoming manner.

Fitting hospitality must be shown even towards an enemy arrived at the house. The tree does not withdraw from the wood-cutter the shade at its side.

The good show pity even to worthless beings. The moon withholds not its light from the hovel of the outcast.

"Is this one of our tribe or a stranger?" is the calculation of the narrow-minded; but to those of a noble disposition the world itself is but one family.

From the Works of Sri Ramakrishna

Many Paths to the One God

You see many stars at night in the sky but find them not when the sun rises; can you say that there are no stars in the heaven of day? So, O man! because you behold not God in the days of your ignorance, say not that there is no god.

As one and the same material, water, is called by different names by different peoples, one calling it water, another eau, a third aqua, and another pani, so the one Sat-chit-ananda, the everlasting-intelligent-bliss, is invoked by some as God, by some as Allah, by some as Jehovah, by some as Hari, and by others as Brahman.

As one can ascend to the top of a house by means of a ladder or a bamboo or a staircase or a rope, so diverse are the ways and means to approach God, and every religion in the world shows one of these ways.

Different creeds are but different paths to reach the Almighty. Various and different are the ways that lead to the temple of Mother Kali at Kalighat (Calcutta). Similarly, various are the ways that lead to the house of the Lord. Every religion is nothing but one of such paths that lead to God.

As the young wife in a family shows her love and respect to her father-in-law, mother-in-law, and every other member of the family, and at the same time loves her husband more than these; similarly, being firm in thy devotion to the deity of thy own choice (Ishta-Devata), do not despise other deities, but honour them all.

Bow down and worship where others kneel, for where so many have been paying the tribute of adoration the kind Lord must manifest himself, for he is all mercy.

The Sat-chit-ananda has many forms. The devotee who has seen God in one aspect only, knows him in that aspect alone. But he who has seen him in manifold aspects is alone in a position to say, "All these forms are of one god and God is multiform." He is formless and with form, and many are his forms which no one knows.

The Vedas, Tantras, and the Puranas and all the sacred scriptures of the world have become as if defiled (as food thrown out of the mouth becomes polluted), because they have been constantly repeated by and have come out of human mouths. But the Brahman or the Absolute has never been defiled, for no one as yet has been able to express it by human speech.

The magnetic needle always points towards the north, and hence it is that the sailing vessel does not lose her course. So long as the heart of man is directed towards God, he cannot be lost in the ocean of wordliness.

Verily, verily, I say unto thee, he who longs for him, finds him. Go and verify this in thine own life; try for three consecutive days with genuine earnestness and thou art sure to succeed.

God cannot be seen so long as there is the slightest taint of desire; therefore have thy small desires satisfied, and renounce the big desires by right reasoning and discrimination.

Knowledge and love of God are ultimately one and the same. There is no difference between pure knowledge and pure love.

The master said, "Everything that exists is God." The pupil understood it literally, but not in the right spirit.

While he was passing through the street he met an elephant. The driver shouted aloud from his high place, "Move away! Move away!" The pupil argued in his mind, "Why should I move away? I am God, so is the elephant God; what fear has God of himself?" Thinking thus, he did not move. At last the elephant took him up in his trunk and dashed him aside. He was hurt severely, and going back to his master, he related the whole adventure. The master said: "All right. You are God, the elephant is God also, but God in the shape of the elephant-driver was warning you from above. Why did you not pay heed to his warnings?"

The Avatara or Saviour is the messenger of God. He is like the viceroy of a mighty monarch. As when there is some disturbance in a far-off province, the king sends his viceroy to quell it, so whenever there is a decline of religion in any part of the world, God sends his Avatara there. It is one and the same Avatara that, having plunged into the ocean of life, rises up in one place and is known as Krishna, and diving down again rises in another place and is known as Christ.

On the tree of absolute existence-knowledge-bliss (Sat-chit-ananda) there hang innumerable Ramas, Krishnas, Buddhas, Christs, etc., out of which one or two come down to this world now and then and produce mighty changes and revolutions.

Ornaments cannot be made of pure gold. Some alloy must be mixed with it. A man totally devoid of Maya will not survive more than twenty-one days. So long as the man has a body, he must have some Maya, however small it may be, to carry on the functions of the body.

Hast thou got, O preacher, the badge of authority? As the humblest servant of the king authorized by him is heard with respect and awe, and can quell the riot by showing his badge; so must thou, O preacher, obtain first the order and inspiration from God. So long as thou hast not this badge of divine inspiration thou mayest preach all thy life, but only in vain.

What is true preaching like? Instead of preaching to others, if one worships God all that time, that is enough preaching. He who strives to make himself free is the real preacher. Hundreds come from all sides, no one knows whence, to him who is free, and are taught by him. When a rosebud blooms, the bees come from all sides uninvited and unasked.

Throw an unbaked cake of flour into hot butter, it will make a sort of boiling noise. But the more it is fried, the less becomes the noise; and when it is fully fried, the bubbling ceases altogether. So long as a man has little knowledge, he goes about lecturing and preaching, but when the perfection of knowledge is obtained, man ceases to make vain displays.

The seeds of Vajrabantul do not fall to the bottom of the tree. They are carried by the wind far off and take root there. So the spirit of a prophet manifests itself at a distance and he is appreciated there.

The sunlight is one and the same wherever it falls, but only bright surfaces like water, mirrors and polished metals can reflect it fully. So is the divine light. It falls equally and impartially on all hearts, but only the pure and clean hearts of the good and holy can fully reflect it.

Every man should follow his own religion. A Christian should follow Christianity, a Mohammedan should follow Mohammedanism, and so on. For the Hindus the ancient path, the path of the Aryan Rishis, is the best.

People partition off their lands by means of boundaries, but no one can partition off the all-embracing sky overhead. The indivisible sky surrounds all and includes all. So common man in ignorance says, "My religion is the only one, my religion is the best." But when his heart is illumined by true knowledge, he knows that above all these wars of sects and sectarians presides the one indivisible, eternal, all-knowing bliss.

As a mother, in nursing her sick children, gives rice and curry to one, and sago arrowroot to another and bread and butter to a third, so the Lord has laid out different paths for different men suitable to their natures.

Dispute not. As you rest firmly on your own faith and opinion, allow others also the equal liberty to stand by their own faiths and opinions. By mere disputation you will never succeed in convincing another of his error. When the grace of God descends on him, each one will understand his own mistakes.

So long as the bee is outside the petals of the lily, and has not tasted the sweetness of its honey, it hovers round the flower emitting its buzzing sound; but when it is inside the flower, it noiselessly drinks its nectar. So long as a man quarrels and disputes about doctrines and dogmas, he has not tasted the nectar of true faith; when he has tasted it, he becomes quiet and full of peace.

People of this age care for the essence of everything. They will accept the essential of religion and not its non-essentials (that is, the rituals, ceremonials, dogmas and creeds).

Honour spirit and form, both sentiment within and symbol without.

Common men talk bagfuls of religion but act not a grain of it, while the wise man speaks little, but his whole life is a religion acted out.

What you wish others to do, do yourself.

The tender bamboo can be easily bent, but the full-grown bamboo breaks when attempt is made to bend it.

It is easy to bend young hearts towards God, but the heart of the old escapes the hold when so drawn.

Those who live in the world and try to find salvation are like soldiers that fight protected by the breastwork of a fort, while the ascetics who renounce the world in search of God are like soldiers fighting in the open field. To fight from within the fort is more convenient and safer than to fight in the open field.

The spiritual gain of a person depends upon his sentiments and ideas, proceeds from his heart and not from his visible actions. Two friends, while strolling about, happened to pass by a place where Bhagavat (the word of God) was being preached. One of them said: "Brother, let us go there for a while and hear the good words spoken." The other replied, "No friend, what is the use of hearing the Bhagavatam? Let us spend the time in yonder public-house in amusement and pleasure." The first one did not consent to this. He went to the place where the Bhagavatam was being read and began to hear it. The other went to the public-house, but did not find the pleasure that he had anticipated there and was thinking all the while, "Alas, me! Why have I come here? How happy is my friend hearing all the while the sacred life and deeds of Hari (Lord)." Thus he meditated on Hari even though in a public-house. The other man who was hearing the Bhagavatam also did not find pleasure in it. Sitting there, he began to blame himself, saying, "Alas! Why did I not accompany my friend to the public-house? What a great pleasure he must be enjoying at this time there!" The result was that he who was sitting where the Bhagavatam was preached meditated on the pleasure of the public-house and acquired the fruit of the sin of going to the public-house because of his bad thoughts; while the man who had gone to the public-house acquired the merit of hearing the Bhagavatam because of his good heart.

A wife once spoke to her husband, saying, "My dear, I am very anxious about my brother. For the last few days he has been thinking of renouncing the world and of becoming a Sannyasin, and has begun preparations for it. He has been trying gradually to curb his desires and reduce his wants." The husband replied, "You need not be anxious about your brother. He will never become a Sannyasin. No one has ever renounced the world by making long preparations." The wife asked, "How then does one become a Sannyasin?" The husband answered, "Do you wish to see how one renounces the world? Let me show you." Saying this, instantly he tore his flowing dress into pieces, tied one piece round his loins, told his wife that she and all women were henceforth his mother, and left the house never to return.

If I hold up this cloth before me, you will not see me any more, though I shall be as near you. So also God is nearer to you than anything else, yet because of the screen of egoism you cannot see him.

If you find that you cannot make this "I" go, then let it remain as the "servant I." There is not much to fear of mischief in the "I" which knows itself as "I am the servant of God; I am his devotee." Sweets beget dyspepsia, but the crystallized sugar candy is not among the sweets, for it has not that injurious property.

The "servant I," the "I" of a devotee, or the "I" of a child is like the line drawn with a stick on a sheet of water. It does not last long.

If you feel proud, feel so in the thought that you are the servant of God, the son of God. Great men have the nature of children. They are always children before God, so they have no egoism. All their strength is of God, belonging to and coming from him, nothing of themselves.

There are two egos—one ripe and the other unripe. "Nothing is mine; whatever I see, feel or hear, nay, even this body, is not mine. I am always eternal, free, and all-knowing"—the ego that has this idea is the ripe one, while the unripe ego is that which thinks, "This is my house, my child, my wife, my body, etc."

When shall I be free? When the "I" has vanished. "I and mine" is ignorance; "Thou and thine" is true knowledge. The true devotee always says, "O Lord, thou art the doer, thou doest everything. I am only a machine. I do whatever thou makest me to do. And all this is thy glory. This home and this family are thine, not mine; I have only the right to serve as thou ordainest."

When the knowledge of Self is gained, all fetters fall off of themselves. Then there is no distinction between a Brahmana and a Sudra, a high caste or a low caste. In that state the sacred-thread-sign of caste falls away of itself. But so long as a man has the consciousness of distinction and difference, he should not forcibly throw it off.

The spiritual-minded belong to a caste of their own irrespective of all social conventions.

When a man is on the plains he sees the lowly grass and the mighty pine tree and says, "How big is the tree and how small is the grass!" But when he ascends the mountain and looks from its high peak on the plain below, the mighty pine tree and the lowly grass blend into one indistinguishable mass of green verdure. So in the sight of the worldly there are differences of rank and position—one is a king, another is a cobbler, one a father, another a son, and so on—but when the divine sight is opened, all appear as equal and one, and there remains no distinction of good and bad, high and low.

When I look upon chaste women of respectable families, I see in them the divine Mother arrayed in the garb of a chaste lady; and again, when I look upon the public women of the city, sitting in their verandas, arrayed in the garb of immorality and shamelessness, I see in them also the divine Mother sporting in a different way.

Man is like a pillow-case. The colour of the one may be red, that of another blue, that of a third black, but all contain the same cotton. So it is with man,—one is beautiful, another is black, a third holy, a fourth wicked, but the divine One dwells within them all.

If you fill an earthen vessel with water and set it apart upon a shelf, the water in it will dry up in a few days; but if you place the same vessel immersed in water, it will remain filled as long as it is kept there. Even so is the case of your love for the Lord God. Fill and enrich your bosom with the love of God for a time and then employ yourself in other affairs, forgetting him all the while, and then you are sure to find within a short time that your heart has become poor and vacant and devoid of that precious love. But if you keep your heart immersed always in the ocean of divine love, your heart is sure to remain ever full to overflowing with the water of the divine love.

A man after fourteen years' penance in a solitary forest obtained at last the power of walking on water. Overjoyed at this, he went to his Guru and said, "Master, master, I have acquired the power of walking on water." The master rebukingly replied, "Fie, O child! is this the result of thy fourteen years' labours?

Verily thou hast obtained only that which is worth a penny; for what thou hast accomplished after fourteen years' arduous labour ordinary men do by paying a penny to the boatman."

So long as one does not become simple like a child, one does not get divine illumination. Forget all the worldly knowledge that thou hast acquired and become as ignorant as a child, and then wilt thou get the divine wisdom.

The Saints and the Saviours

A place was enclosed by means of a high wall. The men outside did not know what sort of place it was. Once four persons determined to find out what was inside by scaling the wall with a ladder. As soon as the first man ascended to the top of the wall, he laughed out, "Ha, ha, ha!" and jumped in. The second also, as soon as he ascended, similarly laughed aloud and jumped in, and so did the third. When the fourth and last man got up to the top of the wall, he found stretched beneath him a large and beautiful garden containing pleasant groves and delicious fruits. Though strongly tempted to jump down and enjoy the scene, he resisted the temptation, and coming down the ladder, preached the glad tidings about the beautiful garden to all outsiders. The Brahman is like the walled garden. He who sees it forgets his own existence and with ecstatic joy rushes headlong unto it to attain to Moksha or absolute freedom. Such are the holy men and liberated saints of the world. But the saviours of humanity are those who see God and, being at the same time anxious to share their happiness of divine vision with others, refuse the final liberation (Moksha), and willingly undergo the troubles of rebirth in the world in order to teach and lead struggling humanity to its ultimate goal.

The Protection of God

A Jnani (knower of God) and a Premika (lover of God) were once passing through a forest. On the way they saw a tiger at a distance. The Jnani said, "There is no reason why we should flee; the Almighty God will certainly protect us." At this the Premika said, "No, brother, come, let us run away. Why should we trouble the Lord for what can be accomplished by our own exertions?"

The Converted Snake

A snake dwelt in a certain place. No one dared to pass by that way; for whoever did so was instantaneously bitten to death. Once a Mahatman (high-souled one) passed by that road, and the serpent ran after the sage in order to bite him. But when the snake approached the holy man he lost all his ferocity and was overpowered by the gentleness of the Yogin. Seeing the snake, the sage said: "Well, friend, thinkest thou to bite me?" The snake was abashed and made no reply. At this the sage said: "Hearken, friend; do not injure anybody in the future." The snake bowed and nodded assent. The sage went his own way, and the snake entered his hole, and thenceforward began to live a life of innocence and purity without even attempting to harm any one. In a few days all the neighbourhood began to think that the snake had lost all his venom and was no more dangerous, and so every one began to tease him. Some pelted him; others dragged him mercilessly by the tail, and in this way there was no end to his troubles. Fortunately the sage again passed by that way and, seeing the bruised and battered condition of the good snake, was very much moved, and inquired the cause of his distress. At this the snake replied: "Holy Sir, this is because I do not injure any one after your advice. But alas! they are so merciless!" The sage smilingly said: "My dear friend, I simply advised you not to bite any one, but I did not tell you not to frighten others. Although you should not bite any creature, still you should keep every one at a considerable distance by hissing at him."

Similarly, if thou livest in the world, make thyself feared and respected. Do not injure any one, but be not at the same time injured by others.

The Aspects of God

Be not like Ghanta Karna in thy bigotry. There was a man who worshipped Shiva but hated all other deities. One day Shiva appeared to him and said, "I shall never be pleased with thee so long as thou hatest the other gods." But the man was inexorable. After a few days Shiva again appeared to him and said, "I shall never be pleased with thee so long as thou hatest." The man kept silent. After a few days Shiva again appeared to him. This time he appeared as Hari-har, namely, one side of his body was that of Shiva, and the other side that of Vishnu. The man was half pleased and half displeased. He laid his offerings on the side representing Shiva, and did not offer anything to the side representing Vishnu. Then Shiva said, "Thy bigotry is unconquerable. I, by assuming this dual aspect, tried to convince thee that all gods and goddesses are but various aspects of the one Absolute Brahman."

THE BUDDHIST

The Buddha and the World
He Sought to Save

Every year in the Valley of the Ganges, 80 miles north of Benares, the floods descended upon the little village of Kapilavastu, sweeping away in a night the work of months of labour on farms and homes. Every year, in the wake of the monsoon, drought and famine took their bitter toll of human life. Cholera, dysentery and diabetes, venomous snakes, tigers and other predatory beasts decimated the human population. The Brahmanas, priests of Brahmanism, ancient of ancients among the world's religions, chanted their *Vedas*, made the ancient fire sacrifices, followed religiously the Nachiketa rite, appeased, with this formalism and that, the many deifications of the powers of Brahma, rigorously held their caste separate from all others, and preached the separations of each of the others from the rest, in their search for union with Brahma. But all their Vedic chanting and formal sacrifices, all their purifications and promises, all of their utterances of names given to an increasing and complex multiplication of the personalized powers of Brahma, did nothing to alleviate the lot of the common man in his struggle against climate, topography, social environment, and economic conditions. His indeed was a life of bitter suffering and hopelessness.

Into this environment, about 560 B.C., was born Gautama, who harmoniously shares with Moses and Isaiah, the later prophets of Israel and Christ, with

95

Lao Tze, Confucius, Chuang Tze, Zoroaster, and St. Paul, the distinction of having given to the world its most exalted precepts of social ethics.

And it is noteworthy that in Western Christian philosophy there are always Christian students who attempt to synthesize Buddhism and Christianity, through drawing analogies between the teachings of the Christ and those of the Buddha, and that in China, where Buddhism is one of the three great ancient religions, a convert to Christianity may still hold to much of his Buddhist faith and find no inconsistency between the old and the new. Indeed, were it not for the accident of time and place and the fact that Christ was a Jew, Christianity might have absorbed into its own complex credo many of the admonitions of Buddhism which deal with social principles as easily as it took over the scriptures of Judaism and made of them the bulk of its Holy Bible.

There is little which is known to be factual in the record of the Buddha's origin and early life, yet in spite (or perhaps because) of this, no other religious leader has had woven about him such a wealth of flowery story and so many legends of supernatural phenomenon. As in the story of Christ, Gautama, according to the elaborate traditional account in one of the Buddhist's sacred books, was conceived immaculately, his birth was accompanied by many miraculous phenomena, he was recognized at once by wise men as the divine leader of a world whose pleasures he was to renounce in order to fulfill his messianic purpose.

In effect there is a strange and somewhat attenuated analogy between the origin of Christ, who was "conceived of the Holy Ghost" and who thus through his identification in the trinity ("Father, Son, and Holy Ghost") may be said literally to have taken part in his own conception, and that of the Buddha, who (again according to the traditional account) "had become a superb white elephant, and was wandering on Gold Hill. Descending thence, he ascended Silver Hill [where his future mother was lying under the watchful eyes of four guardian angels] and approaching from the north, he plucked a white lotus with his silvery trunk, and trumpeting loudly, went into the golden mansion. And three times he walked round his mother's couch, with his right side towards it, and striking her on the right side, he seemed to enter her womb. Thus the conception took place." And thus he became his own earthly father, as Christ, through his identification with the Holy Ghost, became partly his.

When Christ was born there was, according to the Gospels, "a multitude of the heavenly host praising God, and saying, 'Glory to God in the Highest, and on earth, peace, goodwill toward men,'" and a great star left its fixed place in the heavens to travel to a spot directly over the manger in which the Virgin and her son lay, thus leading wise men and shepherds to the spot. When the Buddha was born, according to the Buddhist sacred books, a great sal-tree bent low over the mother so that she could grasp it and ease her labour pains, there "came four pure-minded Maha-Brahma angels bearing a golden net" on which to receive the holy child, and the "delighted hosts of the heaven of the thirty-three held a celebration, waving their cloaks and giving other signs of joy." And at this instant there were also born Yasodhara, who was to become the wife of Gautama, and the mother of his child; Channa, who was later to be Gautama's faithful attendant; and Kanthaka, one of the most beautiful and wise horses in all legend, who finally carried Gautama away to his great retirement and, when he had to leave his master, hung his head, wept, and finally died of a broken heart.

If we were to attempt to list parallels in the social teachings of Christ and the Buddha, the list would be long indeed, as would such a list drawn up to compare the ethical precepts of any two of the great "goodwill" religions. It may justifiably be said that such parallels as these but indicate similar visions of the only path to human happiness in the minds of similarly righteous and wise leaders of men. But there are more striking parallels between early Buddhism and early Christianity than between any of the other two great religions. The stories of the penitent and impenitent robber and the prodigal son, common to both Christian and Buddhist doctrine, are cases in point.

Perhaps a more revealing comparison, however, may be made between the story of Christ and the widow's son, and the story of the Buddha and Kisagotami (see p. 142). In both situations the Messiah was faced with a woman grieving over the death of a dearly beloved son. Each (if we are to believe both the Buddhist and Christian stories) was possessed of the same miraculous powers. Yet they acted differently. Christ restored the son to life which meant, in all realism, that either the mother would again face the sorrow of her son's death, or the son would meet the grief attendant upon the death of his mother. Gautama, on the other hand, performed no miracle of physical restoration. Instead, by placing Kisagotami in a situation in which she learned from the mouths of others that "the living are few, but the dead are many," he forced upon her a realization of the universality of death, and thus acceptance of her own sorrow through a philosophy which could rise above it.

In these two stories is a typical comparison between

the emphasis of Christianity and that of Buddhism. Christianity emphasizes the need to obtain a future salvation through faith, and demonstration of the power of that faith in miracles. Buddhism emphasizes the desirability of achieving salvation in this life, as a path to Nirvana, through enlightenment.

During the rejoicing of the gods upon the birth of Gautama an ascetic named Kaldevala, hearing them, asked the cause of their celebration, and when he learned it, went at once to King Suddhodana in Kapila-vastu (husband of queen Maha-Maya, the Buddha's mother). In paying homage to the divine infant (who had been named Siddharta by the king), Kaldevala announced that the child would, as a young man, see four signs, "a decrepit man, a diseased man, a dead man, and a monk," and that these signs would make him go into retirement to prepare for his ministry as a Buddha.

Apprehensive at the thought of losing his son and heir to the throne, the king (who, according to another more interesting but no more easily documented legend, was not a king at all but the head of a thoroughly democratic government) caused guards to be posted far and wide about the village to prevent the approach of any individual whose condition might be interpreted as one of the four signs. But the gods put his efforts to naught for, on four successive days, while taking divinely inspired drives, Gautama saw all of the signs.

Sitting on his couch meditating on them, he saw the women about him who had been sent by the king to entertain him and keep him from leaving. The women, wearied by his inattention, had gone to sleep, and with his eyes sharpened by the signs he had seen, he saw them "with their bodies wet with trickling phlegm and spittle; some grinding their teeth, and muttering and talking in their sleep; some with their mouths open; and some with their dresses fallen apart so as plainly to disclose their loathesome nakedness. . . . To him that magnificent apartment, as splendid as the palace of Sakka, began to seem like a cemetery filled with dead bodies impaled and left to rot."[1]

Thereupon he rose quickly and ordered Channa, his faithful attendant who had been sleeping at the threshold of his door, to saddle Kanthaka.

Gautama's son had just been born and he had not yet seen it. For one human moment he hesitated at Yasodhara's door, where she slept with the infant Rahula (so named by Gautama—the word meaning "impediment") in the circle of her arm. Then, quietly closing the door, he went quickly out and vaulted onto the back of the waiting Kanthaka. "My dear Kanthaka," he said, "save me now this one night; and then, when thanks to you I have become a Buddha, I will save the world of gods and men."

A marvellous horse was this Kanthaka—18 cubits long according to the story, and of corresponding height, of super-equine strength, and "white all over like a conch shell." His neighing and stamping were so loud that they could be heard all over the village, and so, in order to prevent his betrayal of the Buddha's departure, the gods muffled the sound of his voice, "and at every step he took they placed the palms of their hands under his feet."

When the three, Gautama, Kanthaka, and Channa (holding onto Kanthaka's tail while Gautama rode) came at midnight to the gate of the city, they found it locked by order of the King, who had made this one last effort to prevent his son's departure. In a flowery

[1] Henry Clarke Warren, *Buddhism* in *Translations* (Cambridge: Harvard University Press, 1915).

declaration of the miraculous power which dwelt in the Buddha, the tale now says that if the gate had not opened Gautama, who "had a vigour and a strength that was equal to the strength of ten thousand million elephants, or a hundred thousand million men," would have leaped over it, carrying Kanthaka and Channa with him, or Channa or Kanthaka would have done the same, but, faced by this threefold ability, "the divinity that inhabited the gate opened it for them."

When he finally had reached the place chosen for his retirement, Gautama discharged Channa and Kanthaka, and these two, grieving, went slowly home, where the mournful sounds uttered by Kanthaka, and the tears which flowed from the eyes of both horse and man, announced to the entire village that their beloved prince had left them.

Chief among the mourners were Gautami, "the king's principal queen," and Yasodhara, wife of Gautama and mother of Rahula. Gautami mourned, weeping:

Beautiful, soft, black, and all in great waves, growing each from its own special root, those hairs of his are tossed on the ground, worthy to be encircled by a royal diadem. With his long arms and lion-gate, his bull-like eye, and his beauty bright like gold, his broad chest, and his voice deep as a drum or a cloud,—should such a hero as this dwell in a hermitage?

Those two feet of his, tender, with their beautiful web spread between the toes [one of the thirty-two physical manifestations of Buddhaship], with their ankles concealed, and soft like a blue lotus,— how can they, bearing a wheel marked in the middle [another of the physical manifestations] walk on the hard ground of the skirts of the forest?[2]

2 *Ibid.*

But the plaint of Yasodhara was a more human and realistic one.

> If he wishes to practise a religious life after abandoning me his lawful wife widowed,—where is his religion, who wishes to follow practices without his lawful wife to share them with him? . . . He does not see that husband and wife are both consecrated in sacrifices, and both purified by the rites of the Veda, and both destined to enjoy the same results afterwards,—he therefore grudges me a share in his merit. . . .
>
> Even if I am unworthy to look on my husband's face with its long eyes and bright smile, still is this poor Rahula never to roll about in his father's lap? Alas! the mind of that wise hero is terribly stern,—gentle as his beauty seems it is pitilessly cruel,—who can desert of his own accord such an infant son with his inarticulate talk, one who would charm even an enemy![3]

This poignant cry marks one of the most human and understandable passages in all of the fantastic, naïvely beautiful, legendary account of the early life of Gautama. (For much more extended selections from the same source, see *The Bible of the World*, pp. 181 ff.)

For seven years Gautama remained in retirement, at first following the rules of fasting, self-mortification, and meditation, which marked the retreats of the ascetics of Brahmanism. "At the hours for eating, he, longing to cross the world whose farther shore is so difficult to reach, interrupted his fast with single jujube fruits, sesame seeds, and rice. Having only skin and bone remaining, with his fat, flesh and blood entirely wasted, yet, though diminished, he still shone with undiminished grandeur like the ocean."

[3] *Ibid.*

But strangely he found no virtue in this. It was "like trying to tie the air in knots." "This is not the way," he reflected, "to passionlessness, nor to perfect knowledge, nor to liberation. . . . True calm is properly obtained by the constant satisfaction of the senses. . . . True meditation is produced in him whose mind is self-possessed and at rest. . . . This means is based upon eating food."[4]

Then, having eaten, he sat down under a tree, resolved not to move until he had attained complete enlightenment. Because of this the tree is known in Buddhist dogma as the *boddhi* (enlightenment) or bo-tree.

And now occurs another strange parallel in the stories of Christ and Gautama. As Jesus, fasting in the wilderness, was approached by Satan (and as Zoroaster was approached by the fiend in the form of a beautiful woman) so Gautama was tempted by Mara, the spirit of evil and "enemy of liberation," with "his three sons, Confusion, Gaiety, and Pride, and his three daughters, Lust, Delight, and Thirst," who tried to persuade the Buddha to return to his lawful place as a member of the Kshatriya caste, and assume his royal status in the Sakya clan. Failing in this, Mara urged Gautama to enter Nirvana at once, thus avoiding the burden of life. But the Buddha, firm in his resolve, did not move from his position until his enlightenment was complete and he was ready to gather his disciples about him and instruct them, by word of mouth, in the doctrine which has since become known as Buddhism.

For the rest of his life he wandered as a mendicant with his disciples through his native Maghada in Northern India, much as Christ did with his in Judea, preaching "and delivering from their ills the blind, the

[4] *Ibid.*

humpbacked, the lame, the insane, the maimed, and the destitute." As Christ and his disciples ate with publicans and sinners, so the Buddha and his disciples graciously accepted the hospitality of the courtesan, Ambapali. At the age of eighty he died after having first given his disciples final instructions at a gathering which, in many respects, resembles the Last Supper in the Christian story.

As Christ was born, lived, and died a Jew, grounded in and wholly committed to the religion of his fathers, so was Gautama born, so did he live, and so did he die, a Hindu devoted to the underlying spiritual and ethical truths of Hinduism. The purpose of neither was to found a new religion; each spent his life trying to cleanse an old. For just as the Jewish congregation at the time of the birth of Jesus was fouled with hypocrisies and cluttered with a formalism that obscured the underlying spiritual truths uttered by the great Hebrew prophets, so had the Brahmanas in the India of 560 B.C. allowed their complicated and obscure formalisms to become an empty shell in which there existed little of the true spirit of the ancient *Vedas*. From the beautiful and simple statement in the *Upanishads* of an intangible supreme force whose powers had been given various names (see "How Many Gods?" p. 50), they had descended to the conception of a complicated polytheism in which every object, animate and inanimate, might contain not only one but many gods, each with different powers. And as the Jewish Pharisees of Christ's time had adopted a hypocritical attitude of superiority to all other peoples in the world, excluding all others from any hope of salvation, so had the Brahmanical caste system excluded any but the high priests from any thought of religious worthiness.

To understand the influences behind the doctrine

which Gautama preached in an effort to overcome these evils, one must think back to the low estate of the common man who was his contemporary—the man who was the creature of floods, famine, pestilence, and lack of social or economic opportunity, the man who represented by far the great majority of those who lived in and near Kapilavastu, the place of the Buddha's birth, and the conception of the lack of dignity in earthly human life and the constantly recurring birth on earth, belief in which had been firmly established by Hinduism.

Gautama, while emphasizing even more deeply the burden of life, offered release from it through living so that Nirvana (in which no further births were necessary) might be achieved by the fully enlightened. But his way was different from that of those who advocated "union with Brahma." The fundamental statement of his doctrine was made by him in the "Four Noble Truths," which may be summarized as follows:

All existence involves suffering.

All suffering is caused by indulging desires.

All suffering will cease with the suppression of desires.

To achieve this suppression, and to gain Nirvana after a suitable number of preparatory existences, one must follow the "Noble Eightfold Path" of right belief, right aspiration, right speech, right action, right livelihood, right endeavour, right thought, and right meditation.

Although the pattern of his enlightenment shows how similar it was in the perception of basic spiritual truths to that of the ancient Rishis who bequeathed the *Vedas* to Hinduism, he denied many of the tenets of Brahmanism. The way to enlightenment was not through mortification and fasting, as Brahmanism proclaimed, but this extreme should be avoided along with the other extreme of a life devoted to pleasures and lusts. He refused to recognize the divisions of caste: "A man does not become a Brahmana by his family or by birth," he said. "In whom there is truth and righteousness, he is blessed, he is a Brahmana." Nor were the blessings of religious salvation to be denied to any one, regardless of his station or caste. "My doctrine makes no distinction between high and low, rich and poor; it is like the sky; it has room for all, like water it washes all alike."

One of the beautiful Buddhist stories, illustrative of this, tells how Ananda, the Buddha's beloved disciple, coming to a well, asked a girl of low and despised caste (as Christ asked the woman of Samaria) for a drink of water. But she, fearing a gift from her hands would make him unclean (as the woman of Samaria feared that Christ did not know that she was one with whom the Jews were forbidden to have intercourse) declined, telling him her caste. Ananda said: "My sister, I did not ask thee concerning thy caste or thy family. I beg water of thee, if thou canst give it me. To him in whom love dwells, the whole world is but one family."

Gautama also denied, by indirection, the existence of Brahma, and thus the possibility of that union with Brahma sought by the Brahmanas. "Is there a single one of the Brahmanas, or a single teacher of the Brahmanas, or even a single one of those ancient Rishis of the Brahmanas versed in the three *Vedas*, who has ever seen Brahma face to face?" he asks. And upon his companion answering "no," he asks again, "Does it not follow, then, that it is foolish talk to point the way to a state of union with that which we have not seen?"

Yet strangely, while denying the intangible all-pervading Brahma, he did not deny the existence of many gods. But they were not, in his conception, beings to be worshipped, but rather creatures with very human attributes, subject to human burdens, and needing to be saved as well as men.

He claimed for himself no exclusiveness nor peculiarity. He was the enlightened one, the perfect one, but there had been many other Buddhas, similarly enlightened, similarly perfect, and there would be many more. Whoever had followed or would follow, one of these was equal in merit to one of his own disciples. And whoever followed the law as he expounded it did honour not only to himself but to all Buddhas.

The ruling law in Buddhism to which both men and gods were subject was Karma, that powerful accumulation of the effect of one's deeds, which carried over from rebirth to rebirth until, through long and assiduous following of the "Noble Eightfold Path," an advantageous Karma outweighed a disadvantageous one. "Not in the sky, nor in the midst of the sea," says the *Dhammapada*, "not if we enter into the clefts of the mountains, is there known a spot where a man might be freed from an evil deed." (One is reminded here of the Negro spiritual, "O the foxes have holes in the ground, and the birds have nests in the air, and everything has a hiding place, but we poor sinners ain't got nowhere." Indeed many Negro spirituals, with their accent on the burden of life, are reminiscent of Buddhism.)

But there is, within his philosophy, as in Hinduism, a conception of heaven and of hells in which one may dwell between earthly incarnations, depending upon one's Karma. In order to avoid the worst of these hells between earthly existences, to achieve a pleasant estate upon rebirth, and to gain a cessation of rebirths at last,

one must live according to some of the most exalted
precepts of purity and social righteousness ever uttered,
yet one must regard the world and earthly existence as
transitory and of worth only as a path to Nirvana. But
when asked to define this blessed state Gautama
evaded the task, just as Confucius always avoided dis-
cussing either God or life after death. Questions such
as this, questions as to future existence or non-existence,
Gautama said, were all "questions which tend not to
edification." Let a man follow the Noble Eightfold
Path. That was enough.

There are many beliefs in Buddhist theology which
seem strange to Western Christian or Jewish minds.
Yet if we seek the truths of Buddhism on the more
easily perceived plane of ethical concepts, an ear at-
tuned to the teachings of the prophets of Israel and
Christ will hear much that is familiar in the words of
the Buddha. In Buddhism one who has achieved enlightenment is incapable of deliberately depriving a
living creature of life, of stealing, of sexual impurity, of
"laying up treasure for indulgence in worldly pleasure,"
of taking a wrong course through partiality, hate,
stupidity, or fear. He will renounce slander, abuse, and
idle talk. He makes an effort to insure "that evil and bad
states which have not arisen within him may not arise;
. . . That he may put away evil and bad states which
have arisen within him, . . . That good states which
have not arisen may arise, and that good states which
have arisen may persist, may not grow blurred, may
multiply." He gives up lust, ill-will, delusion, wrath,
pride, and spite. He knows "the ripening of sharing
gifts, . . . the value of goodwill which is the heart's
release." He is not "covetous in his desires, not fierce in
his longing, not malevolent of heart, not of mind corrupt." He recognizes that "there are these two gifts,

the carnal and the spiritual. Of these two, the spiritual is pre-eminent." He heeds these precepts of the *Dhammapada*; "Hatred does not cease by hatred at any time: hatred ceases by love—this is an old rule." "All men love life; remember that thou art like unto them, and do not kill, nor cause slaughter." "Do not speak harshly to any one; those who are spoken to will answer thee in the same way. Angry speech is painful: blows for blows will touch thee." "Let a man leave anger, let him forsake pride, let him overcome all bondage!" "Speak the truth, do not yield to anger; give, if thou art asked." "Let a man overcome anger by love, let him overcome evil by good; let him overcome the greedy by liberality, the liar by truth!"

Surely here is a description which applies as well to the way of life of a good Christian as to that of a good follower of the Buddha.

The Scriptures of Buddhism are the *Tripitaka*, or "Three Baskets" of wisdom, the *Vinaya Pitaka* (Discipline Basket) containing rules for members of the order, the *Sutta Pitaka* (Teaching Basket) containing the words of the Buddha, and the *Abhidhamma Pitaka* (Metaphysical Basket) in which are elucidations of abstruse points of doctrine. The whole of the *Tripitaka* is in 29 subdivisions of which much is still untranslated and some not even printed in its original Pali, the common dialect of North Central India. When finally translated the whole text will, according to Robert E. Hume, probably occupy 10,000 pages. Like the *Vedas*, the texts of the *Pitakas* were not at first written down but transmitted orally from generation to generation of students until, about 250 B.C., the Buddhist convert, King Asoka, ordered them to be committed to writing. During his reign Buddhism spread rapidly in the land of its origin.

By the time of the birth of Jesus, the religion of the Buddha had crossed the frontiers of India and penetrated as far east as China. During the life of Mohammed it declined in India, but was gaining ground in Japan. It has spread through Burma, Ceylon, and Siam. To-day it is almost extinct in the land of its birth but, in modified forms which it has acquired in the lands of its adoption, it flourishes side by side with Confucianism, Taoism, Shinto, and other religions.

Like its mighty parent, Hinduism, Buddhism has gone through many transformations and appeared in many forms since its founder's death. The legend of the Buddha's miraculous conception, which has been included in this introduction, was not preached by Gautama himself (just as Christ did not report the story of his miraculous conception), but grew up long after his death along with a number of other birth stories. These accompanied his deification in the evolving Buddhist system known as *Mahayana* or the "Great Vehicle," in which prayer has become an important part of the ritual. Thus the Enlightened One (as he called himself), who scouted the idea of a God to be prayed to, is himself evoked as deity. This practice may be attributed, at least in part, to a doctrine which the Buddha is said to have taught, namely that 24 Buddhas had appeared before him, and that 5,000 years after his death, when the world has become deeply sunk in unrighteousness, a new Buddha, Maitreya, who is all kindliness, will come to save the world. As a result of this teaching, Buddhists look forward to the coming of Maitreya much as fundamentalist Christians look for the second coming of Christ.

The "Little Vehicle" or *Hinayana* Buddhism, accepted widely in Ceylon, Siam, and Burma, regards Gautama as a human being and a great teacher of fundamental truths. In Tibet and Nepal another modification has taken place. Here it is believed that there were three Buddhas whose lives on earth preceded that of Gautama, that he was the fourth, and that Maitreya will be the fifth. Each of these five has a spiritual counterpart called a *Dyani* Buddha who dwells in the heavenly world and, since he never takes human form, is never subjected to earthly corruption. And attached to each of the Dyani is a *Bodhisattva*, who may be either a man, an animal, or an angel, and who is capable of producing other beings in an ascending scale of goodness. Each of the fifteen is revered by name. Mixed in with this modification of the Buddhist doctrine is much of the older Vedic religion, including a god of the thunder who is clearly the Indra of the Indo-Europeans and the early Vedists.

In Tibet there has developed a hierarchy of Buddhist priests headed by the Dalai Lama, the supposedly perfect and infallible head of the church. Incense is burned to statues of the Buddha and prayers said, chanted, and read. So great is the efficacy of these prayers supposed to be that even the mechanical manipulation of them is thought to have great virtue. Prayers are printed and enclosed in wheels which, when turned by men, wind, or water, are thought to ascend to the Buddha and bring virtue to the maker or manipulator.

In the sixth century A.D. Mahayana Buddhism reached Japan by way of China and Korea. Resisted at first and its symbols destroyed, it gained prestige when an epidemic of small pox increased after destruction of some images of the Buddha. In the eighth century it was encouraged by governmental sanction, and eventually achieved great power in the Land of the Rising Sun.

But Mahayana Buddhism was already far afield from the doctrines of Gautama, with its deifications and its prayers, and in the ninth century the Japanese carried it still farther by splitting it into various sects. The *Tendai*, followers of Saicho, find manifestations of the Buddha in Vedic gods, Hindu idols, and Shinto symbols. The *Shingon*, or "True Word" sect, seek Buddhahood for each individual. The *Jodo*, or "Pure Land" sect, influenced by Christianity's conception of Heaven, seek Paradise through the Buddha who preached that gods were not to be worshipped, and that not Paradise but Nirvana was the highest goal!

One of the most interesting of the later sects is *Zen* Buddhism, founded about A.D. 1187 by Eisai, a monk who had studied in China. In essence it is a strange combination of Buddhism, Taoism, and an obscure mysticism. It includes the Buddhist concept of Nirvana and the mystic "way" of Taoism, and lays great stress both on overstatement of the obvious and on paradox in its teaching. (For a number of selections from Zen books see *The Bible of the World*, pp. 351 ff.)

But we are less concerned in this book with the various mutations of religious thought which parade under the name of Buddhism than we are with the teachings of its founder. T. W. Rhys Davids has estimated the number of Buddhists in the world as 500,-000,000. Surely the Western peoples could hope for no greater expression of belief in the ethical precepts of Jesus Christ in the Eastern world than that half a billion human beings should accept and live by those precepts which were enunciated by Gautama, the Buddha.

BUDDHIST SCRIPTURES

From Early Buddhist Books

The Foundation of the Kingdom of Righteousness

(THE FIRST SERMON ASCRIBED TO GAUTAMA BUDDHA)

And the Blessed One thus addressed the five monks: "There are two extremes, monks, which he who has given up the world ought to avoid.

"What are these two extremes? A life given to pleasures, devoted to pleasures and lusts; this is degrading, sensual, vulgar, ignoble, and profitless.

"And a life given to mortifications; this is painful, ignoble, and profitless.

"By avoiding these two extremes, monks, the Tathagata has gained the knowledge of the middle path which leads to insight, which leads to wisdom, which conduces to calm, to knowledge, to Sambodhi (supreme enlightenment), to Nirvana.

"Which, monks, is this middle path the knowledge of which the Tathagata has gained, which leads to insight, which leads to wisdom, which conduces to calm, to knowledge, to Sambodhi, to Nirvana?

"It is the noble eightfold path, namely: right views, right intent, right speech, right conduct, right means of livelihood, right endeavour, right mindfulness, right meditation.

"This, monks, is the middle path the knowledge of which the Tathagata has gained, which leads to insight, which leads to wisdom, which conduces to calm, to knowledge, to perfect enlightenment, to Nirvana.

"This, monks, is the noble truth of suffering: birth is suffering; decay is suffering; death is suffering; presence of objects we hate is suffering; separation from objects we love is suffering; not to obtain what we desire is suffering.

"In brief, the five aggregates which spring from grasping, they are painful.

"This, monks, is the noble truth concerning the origin of suffering: verily it originates in that craving which causes the renewal of becomings, is accompanied by sensual delight, and seeks satisfaction now here, now there; that is to say, craving for pleasures, craving for becoming, craving for not becoming.

"This, monks, is the noble truth concerning the cessation of suffering. Verily, it is passionlessness, cessation without remainder of this very craving; the laying aside of, the giving up, the being free from, the harbouring no longer of, this craving.

"This, monks, is the noble truth concerning the path which leads to the cessation of suffering. Verily, it is this noble eightfold path, that is to say, right views, right intent, right speech, right conduct, right means of livelihood, right endeavour, right mindfulness and right meditation."

The Nine Incapabilities

(WORDS ASCRIBED TO GAUTAMA BUDDHA)

The brother who is arahant, in whom the intoxicants are destroyed, who has lived the life, who has done his task, who has laid low his burden, who has attained salvation, who has utterly destroyed the fetter of rebirth, who is emancipated by the true gnosis, he is incapable of perpetrating nine things:

1. He is incapable of deliberately depriving a living creature of life.

2. He is incapable of taking what is not given so that it constitutes theft.

3. He is incapable of sexual impurity.

4. He is incapable of deliberately telling lies.

5. He is incapable of laying up treasure for indulgence in worldly pleasure as he used to do in the life of the house.

6. He is incapable of taking a wrong course through partiality.

7. He is incapable of taking a wrong course through hate.

8. He is incapable of taking a wrong course through stupidity.

9. He is incapable of taking a wrong course through fear.

These nine things the arahant in whom the mental intoxicants are destroyed, who has lived the life, whose task is done, whose burden is laid low, who has attained salvation, who has utterly destroyed the fetter of becoming, who is emancipated by the true gnosis, is incapable of perpetrating.

The Aryan Eightfold Path

The Exalted One said:

"And what, bhikkhus, is the Aryan truth concerning the way that leads to the cessation of ill?

"This is that Aryan eightfold path, to wit, right view, right aspiration, right speech, right doing, right livelihood, right effort, right mindfulness, right rapture.

"And what, bhikkhus, is right view?

"Knowledge, bhikkhus, about ill, knowledge about the coming to be of ill, knowledge about the cessation of ill, knowledge about the way that leads to the cessation of ill. This is what is called right view.

"And what, bhikkhus, is right aspiration?

"The aspiration towards renunciation, the aspiration towards benevolence, the aspiration towards kindness. This is what is called right aspiration.

"And what, bhikkhus, is right speech?

"Abstaining from lying, slander, abuse and idle talk. This is what is called right speech.

"And what, bhikkhus, is right doing?

"Abstaining from taking life, from taking what is not given, from carnal indulgence. This is what is called right doing.

"And what, bhikkhus, is right livelihood?

"Herein, O bhikkhus, the Aryan disciple, having put away wrong livelihood, supports himself by right livelihood.

"And what, bhikkhus, is right effort?

"Herein, O bhikkhus, a brother makes effort in bringing forth will that evil and bad states that have not arisen within him may not arise; to that end he stirs up energy, he grips and forces his mind. That he may put away evil and bad states that have arisen within him he puts forth will, he makes effort, he stirs up energy, he grips and forces his mind. That good states which have not arisen may arise he puts forth will, he makes effort, he stirs up energy, he grips and forces his mind. That good states which have arisen may persist, may not grow blurred, may multiply, grow abundant, develop and come to perfection, he puts forth will, he makes effort, he stirs up energy, he grips and forces his mind. This is what is called right effort.

"And what, bhikkhus, is right mindfulness?

"Herein, O bhikkhus, a brother, as to the body, continues so to look upon the body, that he remains ardent, self-possessed and mindful, having overcome both the hankering and the dejection common in the world. And in the same way as to feelings, thoughts and ideas, he so looks upon each, that he remains ardent, self-possessed and mindful, having overcome the hankering and the dejection that is common in the world. This is what is called right mindfulness.

"And what, bhikkhus, is right rapture?

"Herein, O bhikkhus, a brother, aloof from sensuous appetites, aloof from evil ideas, enters into and abides in the first Jhana, wherein there is cogitation and deliberation, which is born of solitude and is full of joy and ease. Suppressing cogitation and deliberation, he enters into and abides in the second Jhana, which is self-evoked, born of concentration, full of joy and ease, in that, set free from cogitation and deliberation, the mind grows calm and sure, dwelling on high. And further, disenchanted with joy, he abides calmly contemplative while, mindful and self-possessed, he feels in his body that ease whereof Aryans declare: 'He that is calmly contemplative and aware, he dwelleth at ease.' So does he enter into and abide in the third Jhana. And further, by putting aside ease and by putting aside malaise, by the passing away of the happiness and of the melancholy he used to feel, he enters into and abides in the fourth Jhana, rapture of utter purity of mindfulness and equanimity, wherein neither ease is felt nor any ill. This is what is called right rapture.

"This, bhikkhus, is the Aryan truth concerning the way leading to the cessation of ill."

Questions Which Tend Not to Edification

Thus have I heard.

On a certain occasion the Blessed One was dwelling at Savatthi in Jetavana monastery in Anathapindika's Park. Now it happened to the venerable Malunkyaputta, being in seclusion and plunged in meditation, that a consideration presented itself to his mind.

Then the venerable Malunkyaputta arose at eventide from his seclusion, and drew near to where the Blessed One, was; and having drawn near and greeted the Blessed One, he sat down respectfully at one side. And seated respectfully at one side, the venerable Malunkyaputta spoke to the Blessed One as follows:

"Reverend Sir, it happened to me, as I was just now in seclusion and plunged in meditation, that a consideration presented itself to my mind, as follows: 'These theories which the Blessed One has left unelucidated, has set aside and rejected,—that the world is eternal, that the world is not eternal, . . . that the saint neither exists nor does not exist after death,—these the Blessed One does not elucidate to me. I will draw near to the Blessed One and inquire of him concerning this matter. If the Blessed One will elucidate them to me, in that case will I lead the religious life under the Blessed One. If the Blessed One will not elucidate them, I will abandon religious training and return to the lower life of a layman.'"

"The religious life, Malunkyaputta, does not depend on the dogma that the world is eternal, nor on the dogma that the world is not eternal. Whether the dogma obtain, Malunkyaputta, that the world is eternal, or that the world is not eternal, there still remain birth, old age, death, sorrow, lamentation, misery, grief, and

despair, for the extinction of which in the present life
I am prescribing.

"Accordingly, Malunkyaputta, bear always in mind
what it is that I have not elucidated, and what it is
that I have elucidated. And what, Malunkyaputta,
have I not elucidated? I have not elucidated, Malunkyaputta, that the world is eternal; I have not elucidated
that the world is not eternal. . . . I have not elucidated
that the saint neither exists nor does not exist after
death. And why, Malunkyaputta, have I not elucidated
this? Because, Malunkyaputta, this profits not, nor has
to do with the fundamentals of religion, nor tends to
aversion, absence of passion, cessation, quiescence, the
supernatural faculties, supreme wisdom, and Nirvana;
therefore have I not elucidated it.

"And what, Malunkyaputta, have I elucidated?
Misery, Malunkyaputta, have I elucidated; the origin
of misery have I elucidated; the cessation of misery
have I elucidated; and the path leading to the cessation
of misery have I elucidated. And why, Malunkyaputta,
have I elucidated this? Because, Malunkyaputta, this
does profit, has to do with the fundamentals of religion,
and tends to aversion, absence of passion, cessation,
quiescence, knowledge, supreme wisdom, and Nirvana;
therefore have I elucidated it. Accordingly, Malunkyaputta, bear always in mind what it is that I have not
elucidated, and what it is that I have elucidated."

Thus spake the Blessed One; and, delighted, the
venerable Malunkyaputta applauded the speech of the
Blessed One.

Discussion of Dependent Origination

Thus have I heard.
On a certain occasion the Blessed One was dwelling

among the Kurus where was the Kuru-town named Kammasadhamma.

Then drew near the venerable Ananda to where the Blessed One was; and having drawn near and greeted the Blessed One, he sat down respectfully at one side. And seated respectfully at one side, the venerable Ananda spoke to the Blessed One as follows:

"O wonderful is it, Reverend Sir! O marvellous is it, Reverend Sir! How profound, Reverend Sir, is dependent origination, and of how profound an appearance! To me, nevertheless, it is as clear as clear can be."

"O Ananda, say not so! O Ananda, say not so! Profound, Ananda, is dependent origination, and profound of appearance. It is through not understanding this doctrine, Ananda, through not penetrating it, that thus mankind is like an entangled warp, or to an ensnarled web, or to munja-grass and pabbaja-grass, and fails to extricate itself from punishment, suffering, perdition, rebirth.

"Ananda, if it be asked, 'Do old age and death depend on anything?' the reply should be, 'Old age and death depend on birth.'

"Ananda, if it be asked, 'Does birth depend on anything?' the reply should be, 'Birth depends on existence.'

"Ananda, if it be asked, 'Does existence depend on anything?' the reply should be, 'Existence depends on attachment.'

"Ananda, if it be asked, 'Does attachment depend on anything?' the reply should be, 'Attachment depends on desire.'

"Ananda, if it be asked, 'Does desire depend on anything?' the reply should be, 'Desire depends on sensation.'

"Ananda, if it be asked, 'Does sensation depend on anything?' the reply should be, 'Sensation depends on contact.'

"Ananda, if it be asked, 'Does contact depend on anything?' the reply should be, 'Contact depends on the mental and physical phenomena.'

"Ananda, if it be asked, 'Do the mental and physical phenomena depend on anything?' the reply should be, 'The mental and physical phenomena depend on consciousness.'

"Ananda, if it be asked, 'Does consciousness depend on anything?' the reply should be, 'Consciousness depends on the mental and physical phenomena.'

"Thus, Ananda, on the mental and physical phenomena depends consciousness;

"On consciousness depends the mental and physical phenomena;

"On the mental and physical phenomena depends contact;

"On contact depends sensation;

"On sensation depends desire;

"On desire depends attachment;

"On attachment depends existence;

"On existence depends birth;

"On birth depend old age and death, sorrow, lamentation, misery, grief, and despair. Thus does this entire aggregation of misery arise."

On Theology

Then the young Brahmana Vasettha and the young Brahmana Bharadvaga went on to the place where the Exalted One was.

And when they had come there, they exchanged with the Exalted One the greetings and compliments of politeness and courtesy, and sat down beside him.

And while they were thus seated the young Brahmana Vasettha said to the Exalted One:

"As we, Gautama, were taking exercise and walking up and down, there sprang up a conversation between us on which was the true path and which the false. Regarding this matter, Gautama, there is a strife, a dispute, a difference of opinion between us."

"Wherein, then, O Vasettha, is there a strife, a dispute, a difference of opinion between you?"

"Concerning the true path and the false, Gautama. Various Brahmanas, Gautama, teach various paths. Are all those saving paths? Are they all paths which will lead him, who acts according to them, into a state of union with Brahma?"

"Vasettha, is there a single one of the Brahmanas versed in the three Vedas who has ever seen Brahma face to face?"

"No, indeed, Gautama."

"Well, then, Vasettha, those ancient Rishis of the Brahmanas versed in the three Vedas, the authors of the verses, the utterers of the verses, whose ancient form of words so chanted, uttered, or composed, the Brahmanas of to-day chant over again or repeat; intoning or reciting exactly as has been intoned or recited; did even they speak thus, saying: 'We know it, we have seen it, where Brahma is, whence Brahma is, whither Brahma is'?"

"Not so, Gautama!"

"Then you say, Vasettha, that none of the Brahmanas, or of their teachers, or of their pupils, even up to the seventh generation, has ever seen Brahma face to face. And that even the Rishis of old, the authors and utterers of the verses, of the ancient form of words which the Brahmanas of to-day so carefully intone and recite precisely as they have been handed down—even they did not pretend to know or to have seen where or whence or whither Brahma is. So that the Brahmanas versed in the three Vedas have forsooth said thus: 'What we know not, what we have not seen, to a state of union with that we can show the way, and can say: "This is the straight path, this is the direct way which makes for salvation, and leads him, who acts according to it, into a state of union with Brahma!'"

"Now what think you, Vasettha? Does it not follow, this being so, that the talk of the Brahmanas, versed though they be in the three Vedas, turns out to be foolish talk?"

"In sooth, Gautama, that being so, it follows that the talk of the Brahmanas versed in the three Vedas is foolish talk!"

The Fall and Rise of Social Behaviour

(WORDS ASCRIBED TO GAUTAMA BUDDHA)

When poverty was become rife, a certain man took that which others had not given him, what people call by theft. Him they caught, and brought before the king, saying: This man, O king, has taken that which was not given him, and that is theft.

Thereupon the king spake thus to the man: Is it true, sirrah, that thou hast taken what no man gave thee, hast committed what men call theft?

It is true, O king.

But why?

O king, I have nothing to keep me alive.

Then the king bestowed wealth on that man, saying: With this wealth, sirrah, do thou both keep thyself alive, maintain thy parents, maintain children and wife, carry on thy business, and keep up such alms for holy men as shall be of value in the realms above, heavenly gifts, the result whereof shall be happiness here and rebirth in the heavenly worlds.

Even so, O king, replied the man.

Now another man, brethren, took by theft what was not given him. Him they caught and brought before the king, the anointed Kshatriya, and told him, saying: This man, O king, hath taken by theft what was not given him.

And the king spoke and did even as he had spoken and done to the former man.

Now men heard, brethren, that to them who had taken by theft what was not given them, the king was giving wealth. And hearing they thought: Let us then take by theft what has not been given us.

Now a certain man did so. And him they caught and charged before the king, the anointed Kshatriya, who, as before, asked him why he had stolen.

Because, O king, I cannot maintain myself.

Then the king thought: If I bestow wealth on any one soever who has taken by theft what was not given him, there will be hereby an increase of this stealing. Let me now put a final stop to this, inflict condign punishment on him, have his head cut off!

So he bade his men saying: Now, look ye! bind this man's arms behind him with a strong rope and a tight knot, shave his head bald, lead him around with a harsh sounding drum, from road to road, from crossways to crossways, take him out by the southern gate, and to the south of the town, put a final stop to this, inflict on him the uttermost penalty, cut off his head.

Even so, O king, answered the men, and carried out his commands.

Now men heard, brethren, that they who took by theft what was not given them, were thus put to death. And hearing, they thought: Let us also now have sharp swords made ready for ourselves, and them from whom we take what is not given us—what they call theft—let us put a final stop to them, inflict on them the uttermost penalty, and cut their heads off.

And they gat themselves sharp swords, and came forth to sack village and town and city, and to work highway robbery. And them whom they robbed they made an end of, cutting off their heads.

Thus, brethren, from goods not being bestowed on the destitute poverty grew rife; from poverty growing rife stealing increased, from the spread of stealing violence grew apace, from the growth of violence the destruction of life became common, from the frequency of murder both the span of life in those beings and their comeliness also wasted away, so that, of humans whose span of life was eighty thousand years, the sons lived but forty thousand years.

Now among humans of the latter span of life, brethren, a certain man took by theft what was not given him and, even as those others, was accused before the king and questioned if it was true that he had stolen.

Nay, O king, he replied, thus deliberately telling a lie.

Thus, from goods not being bestowed on the destitute, poverty grew rife . . . stealing . . . violence . . . murder . . . until lying grew common. And from lying growing common both the span of life in those beings and the comeliness of them wasted away, so that of humans whose span of life was forty thousand years, the sons lived but twenty thousand years.

Now among humans of the latter life-span, a certain man took by theft what was not given him. Him a certain man reported to the king, the anointed Kshatriya, saying: Such and such a man, O king, has taken by theft what was not given him—thus speaking evil of him.

And so, brethren, from goods not being bestowed on the destitute, poverty grew rife . . . stealing . . . violence . . . murder . . . lying . . . evil speaking grew abundant. And from evil speaking growing abundant, both the life-span of those beings and also the comeliness of them wasted away, so that, of humans whose life-span was twenty thousand years, the sons lived but ten thousand years.

Now among humans of the latter span of life, brethren, some were comely and some were ugly. And so those who were ugly, coveting them that were comely, committed adultery with their neighbours' wives.

Thus from goods not being bestowed on the destitute, poverty . . . stealing . . . violence . . . murder . . . lying . . . evil speaking . . . immorality grew rife. And from the increase of immorality, both the life-span of those beings and also the comeliness of them wasted away, so that, of humans whose life-span was ten thousand years, the sons lived but five thousand years.

Now among humans of the latter span of life, brethren, two things increased, abusive speech and idle talk. And from these two things increasing, both the life-span of those beings and the comeliness of them wasted away, so that, of humans whose life-span was five thousand years, some sons lived but two and a half, some but two, thousand years.

Among humans of a life-span of two thousand years and a half, covetousness and ill-will waxed great. And thereby . . . the sons lived but a thousand years.

Among humans of the latter span of life, brethren, false opinions grew. And thereby the life-span of those beings and the comeliness of them wasted, so that, of humans whose span of life was a thousand years, the sons lived but five hundred years.

Among humans of the latter span of life, brethren,

three things grew apace: incest, wanton greed, and perverted lust. Thereby the life-span of those beings and their comeliness wasted, so that, of humans whose span of life was five hundred years, some sons lived but two and a half centuries, some only two centuries.

Among humans of a life-span, brethren, of two and a half centuries, these things grew apace—lack of filial piety to mother and father, lack of religious piety to holy men, lack of regard for the head of the clan.

Thus, brethren, from goods not being bestowed on the destitute, poverty grew great . . . stealing . . . violence . . . murder . . . lying . . . evil speaking . . . adultery . . . abusive and idle talk . . . covetousness and ill-will . . . false opinions . . . incest, wanton greed and perverted lust . . . till finally lack of filial and religious piety and lack of regard for the head of the clan grew great. From these things growing, the life-span of those beings and the comeliness of them wasted, so that, of humans whose span of life was two and a half centuries, the sons lived but one century.

There will come a time, brethren, when the descendants of those humans will have a life-span of ten years. Among humans of this life-span, maidens of five years will be of a marriageable age. Among such humans these kinds of tastes (savours) will disappear: ghee, butter, oil of tila, sugar, salt. Among such humans kudrusa grain will be the highest kind of food. Even as to-day, rice and curry is the highest kind of food, so will kudrusa grain be then. Among such humans the ten moral courses of conduct will altogether disappear, the ten immoral courses of action will flourish excessively; there will be no word for moral among such humans— far less any moral agent. Among such humans, brethren, they who lack filial and religious piety, and show no respect for the head of the clan—'tis they to whom homage and praise will be given, just as to-day homage and praise are given to the filial-minded, to the pious and to them who respect the heads of their clans.

Among such humans, brethren, there will be no such thoughts of reverence as are a bar to inter-marriage with mother, or mother's sister, or mother's sister-in-law, or teacher's wife, or father's sister-in-law. The world will fall into promiscuity, like goats and sheep, fowls and swine, dogs and jackals.

Among such humans, brethren, keen mutual enmity will become the rule, keen ill-will, keen animosity, passionate thoughts even of killing, in a mother towards her child, in a child towards its mother, in a father towards his child and a child towards its father, in brother to brother, in brother to sister, in sister to brother. Just as a sportsman feels towards the game that he sees, so will they feel.

Among such humans, brethren, there will arise a sword-period of seven days, during which they will look on each other as wild beasts; sharp swords will appear ready to their hands, and they, thinking, This is a wild beast, this is a wild beast, will with their swords deprive each other of life.

Then to some of those beings it will occur: Let us not slay just any one; nor let just any one slay us! Let us now, therefore, betake ourselves to dens of grass, or dens in the jungle, or holes in trees, or river fastnesses, or mountain clefts, and subsist on roots and fruits of the jungle. And they will do so for those seven days. And at the end of those seven days, coming forth from those dens and fastnesses and mountain clefts, they will embrace each other, and be of one accord comforting one another, and saying: Hail, O mortal, that thou livest still! O happy sight to find thee still alive!

Then this, brethren, will occur to those beings: Now, only because we had gotten into evil ways, have we had this heavy loss of kith and kin. Let us therefore now do good. What can we do that is good? Let us now abstain from taking life. That is a good thing that we may take up and do. And they will abstain from slaughter, and will continue in this good way. Because of their getting into this good way, they will increase again both as to their span of life and as to their comeliness. And to them thus increasing in life and comeliness, to them who lived but one decade, there will be children who will live for twenty years.

Then this, brethren, will occur to those beings: Now we, because we have gotten into good ways, increase in length of life and comeliness. Let us now do still more good. Let us now abstain from taking what is not given, let us abstain from adultery, let us now abstain from lying, let us now abstain from evil speaking, let us now abstain from abuse and from idle talk, let us now abstain from covetousness, from ill-will, from false opinions, let us now abstain from the three things—incest, wanton greed and perverted desires; let us now be filial towards our mothers, and our fathers, let us be pious towards holy men, let us respect the head of clans, yea, let us continue to practise each of these good things.

So they will practise these virtues. And because of the good they do they will increase in length of life, and in comeliness, so that the sons of them who lived but twenty years will come to live forty years. And the sons of these sons will come to live eighty years; their sons to one hundred and sixty years; their sons to three hundred and twenty years; their sons to six hundred and forty years; their sons to two thousand years; their sons to four thousand years; their sons to eight thousand years; their sons to twenty thousand years; their sons to forty thousand years; and the sons of those that lived forty thousand years will come to live eighty thousand years.

Among humans living eighty thousand years, brethren, maidens are marriageable at five hundred years of age. Among such humans there will be only three kinds of disease—appetite, non-assimilation and old age. Among such humans, this India will be mighty and prosperous, the villages, towns and royal cities will be so close that a cock could fly from each one to the next.

A Sermon to the Monks

This was said by the Exalted One, said by the Arahant, so I have heard:

Monks, I am your surety for not returning to birth. Do ye give up lust, ill-will, delusion, wrath, spite, pride. I am your surety for not returning.

Monks, the man who does not understand and comprehend the all, who has not detached his mind therefrom, who has not abandoned the all, can make no growth in extinguishing ill. But, monks, he who does understand and comprehend the all, who has detached his mind therefrom, who has abandoned the all, he makes growth in extinguishing ill.

Monks, for the monk who is a learner not yet come to mastery of mind, but who dwells aspiring for peace from the bond, making it a matter concerning what is outside the self, I see no other single factor so helpful as friendship with the lovely. Monks, one who is a friend of the lovely abandons the unprofitable and makes the profitable to become.

Here, monks, I discern a certain person with mind at peace to be such because I compass his thoughts with my mind; and, if at this moment this person were to make an end, he would be put just so into the heaven-world according to his deserts. What is the reason for that? His mind at peace. Indeed it is because of a mind at peace, monks, that in this way certain beings, when the body breaks up, after death arise again in the happy bourn, in the heaven-world.

Monks, if beings knew, as I know, the ripening of sharing gifts, they would not enjoy their use without sharing them, nor would the taint of stinginess obsess the heart and stay there. Even if it were their last bit, their last morsel of food, they would not enjoy its use without sharing it, if there were any one to receive it. But inasmuch, monks, as beings do not know, as I know, the ripening of sharing gifts, therefore they enjoy their use without sharing them, and the taint of stinginess obsesses their heart and stays there.

Monks, whatsoever grounds there be for good works undertaken with a view to rebirth, all of them are not worth one sixteenth part of that goodwill which is the heart's release; goodwill alone, which is the heart's release, shines and burns and flashes forth in surpassing them. Just as, monks, the radiance of all the starry bodies is not worth one sixteenth part of the moon's radiance, but the moon's radiance shines and burns and flashes forth in surpassing them, even so, monks, goodwill . . . flashes forth in surpassing good works undertaken with a view to rebirth.

Monks, two dhamma-teachings of the wayfarer arahant, a rightly awakened one, take place one after the other. What two? "Look at evil as evil" is the first dhamma-teaching. "Seeing evil as evil, be disgusted therewith, be cleansed of it, be freed of it" is the second dhamma-teaching.

Monks, ignorance leads the way to the attainment of unprofitable things; shamelessness and disregard of blame follow after. But, monks, knowledge leads the way to the attainment of profitable things, shrinking and fear of blame follow after.

Monks, there are these two conditions of Nirvana. What two? The condition of Nirvana with the basis still remaining and that without basis. Of what sort, monks, is the condition of Nirvana which has the basis still remaining? Herein, monks, a monk is arahant, one who has destroyed the cankers, who has lived the life, done what was to be done, laid down the burden, won the goal, worn out the fetter of becoming, one released by perfect knowledge. In him the five sense-faculties still remain, through which, as they have not yet departed, he experiences sensations pleasant and unpleasant, undergoes pleasure and pain. In him the end of lust, malice and delusion, monks, is called "the condition of Nirvana with the basis still remaining."

And of what sort, monks, is the condition of Nirvana that is without basis?

Herein a monk is arahant . . . released by perfect knowledge, but in him in this very life all things that are sensed have no delight for him, they have become cool. This is called "the condition of Nirvana without basis." So, monks, these are the two conditions of Nirvana.

Monks, do ye delight in solitary communing; delighted by solitary communing, given to mental calm in the inner self, not neglecting musing, possessed of insight, do ye foster resort to empty places? One of two fruits is to be looked for in those who do these things, namely, gnosis in this very life or, if there be still a basis, not-return to this world.

Monks, there are these three persons found existing in the world. What three? The one who is like a drought, the one who rains locally and the one who pours down everywhere.

And how, monks, is a person like a drought?

Herein, monks, a certain person is not a giver to all alike, no giver of food and drink, clothing and vehicle, flowers, scents and unguents, bed, lodging and light to recluses and Brahmanas, to wretched and needy beggars. In this way, monks, a person is like a drought.

And how, monks, is a person like a local rainfall?

In this case a person is a giver to some, but to others he gives not; be they recluses and Brahmanas or wretched, needy beggars, he is no giver of food and drink . . . lodging and lights. In this way a person is like a local rainfall.

And how, monks, does a person rain down every-where?

In this case a certain person gives to all, be they recluses and Brahmanas or wretched, needy beggars; he is a giver of food and drink . . . lodging and lights. In this way a person rains down everywhere.

So these are the three sorts of persons found existing in the world.

Monks, even if a monk should seize the hem of my garment and walk behind me step for step, yet if he be covetous in his desires, fierce in his longing, malevolent of heart, of mind corrupt, careless and unrestrained, not quieted but scatter-brained and uncontrolled in sense, that monk is far from me and I am far from him. What is the cause of that? Monks, that monk sees not dhamma. Not seeing dhamma he sees not me. Monks, even though a monk should dwell a hundred yoyanas away, yet if he be not covetous in his desires, not fierce in his longing, not malevolent of heart, not of mind corrupt, but with mindfulness set up and composed,

calmed, one-pointed in mind and restrained in sense,—
then indeed that one is nigh unto me and I am nigh
unto him. What is the cause of that? Monks, that monk
sees dhamma. Seeing dhamma he sees me.

Monks, there are these two gifts, the carnal and the
spiritual. Of these two gifts the spiritual gift is pre-
eminent. Monks, there are these two sharings together,
the sharing of the carnal and the sharing of the spiritual. Of these two sharings together the sharing of the
spiritual is pre-eminent. Monks, there are these two
acts of kindness, the carnal and the spiritual. Of these
two acts of kindness the spiritual is pre-eminent.

Monks, I am a Brahmana, one to ask a favour of, ever
clean-handed, wearing my last body, incomparable
physician and surgeon. Ye are my own true sons, born
of my mouth, born of dhamma, created by dhamma,
my spiritual heirs, not carnal heirs.

Monks, do ye live perfect in virtue, do ye live perfect
in the performance of the obligations, restrained with
the restraint of the obligations, perfect in the practice
of right behaviour; seeing danger in the slightest faults,
undertake and train yourselves in the training of the
precepts. For him who so lives . . . so restrained . . .
who undertakes the training of the precepts, what else
remains to be done?

From the Dhammapada

The Twin Verses

All that we are is the result of what we have thought:
it is founded on our thoughts, it is made up of our
thoughts. If a man speaks or acts with an evil thought,

pain follows him, as the wheel follows the foot of the ox that draws the carriage.

All that we are is the result of what we have thought: it is founded on our thoughts, it is made up of our thoughts. If a man speaks or acts with a pure thought, happiness follows him, like a shadow that never leaves him.

"He abused me, he beat me, he defeated me, he robbed me"—in those who harbour such thoughts hatred will never cease.

"He abused me, he beat me, he defeated me, he robbed me"—in those who do not harbour such thoughts hatred will cease.

For hatred does not cease by hatred at any time: hatred ceases by love—this is an old rule.

The world does not know that we must all come to an end here; but those who know it, their quarrels cease at once.

He who lives looking for pleasures only, his senses uncontrolled, immoderate in his food, idle, and weak, Mara will certainly overthrow him, as the wind throws down a weak tree.

He who lives without looking for pleasures, his senses well controlled, moderate in his food, faithful and strong, him Mara will certainly not overthrow, any more than the wind throws down a rocky mountain.

They who imagine truth in untruth, and see untruth in truth, never arrive at truth, but follow vain desires.

They who know truth in truth, and untruth in untruth, arrive at truth, and follow true desires.

As rain breaks through an ill-thatched house, passion will break through an unreflecting mind.

As rain does not break through a well-thatched house, passion will not break through a well-reflecting mind.

Thought

As a fletcher makes straight his arrow, a wise man makes straight his trembling and unsteady thought, which is difficult to guard, difficult to hold back.

As a fish taken from his watery home and thrown on the dry ground, our thought trembles all over in order to escape the dominion of Mara, the tempter.

It is good to tame the mind, which is often difficult to hold in and flighty, rushing wherever it listeth; a tamed mind brings happiness.

Let the wise man guard his thoughts, for they are difficult to perceive, very artful, and they rush wherever they list: thoughts well guarded bring happiness.

Before long, alas! this body will lie on the earth, despised, without understanding, like a useless log.

Whatever a hater may do to a hater, or an enemy to an enemy, a wrongly directed mind will do him greater mischief.

Not a mother, not a father, will do so much, nor any other relatives; a well-directed mind will do us greater service.

The Fool

Long is the night to him who is awake; long is a mile to him who is tired; long is life to the foolish who do not know the true law.

If a traveller does not meet with one who is his better, or his equal, let him firmly keep to his solitary journey; there is no companionship with a fool.

"These sons belong to me, and this wealth belongs to me"; with such thoughts a fool is tormented. He himself does not belong to himself; how much less sons and wealth?

If a fool be associated with a wise man even all his life, he will perceive the truth as little as a spoon perceives the taste of soup.

If an intelligent man be associated for one minute only with a wise man, he will soon perceive the truth, as the tongue perceives the taste of soup.

"One is the road that leads to wealth, another the road that leads to Nirvana"—if the Bhikkhu, the disciple of Buddha, has learnt this, he will not yearn for honour, he will strive after separation from the world.

Punishment

All men tremble at punishment, all men love life; remember that thou art like unto them, and do not kill, nor cause slaughter.

He who, seeking his own happiness, punishes or kills beings who also long for happiness, will not find happiness after death.

Do not speak harshly to any one; those who are spoken to will answer thee in the same way. Angry speech is painful: blows for blows will touch thee.

Old Age

How is there laughter, how is there joy, as this world is always burning? Do you not seek a light, ye who are surrounded by darkness?

Look at this dressed-up lump, covered with wounds, joined together, sickly, full of many schemes, but which has no strength, no hold!

This body is wasted, full of sickness, and frail; this heap of corruption breaks to pieces, life indeed ends in death.

After one has looked at those grey bones, thrown

away like gourds in the autumn, what pleasure is there left in life?

After a stronghold has been made of the bones, it is covered with flesh and blood, and there dwell in it old age and death, pride and deceit.

The brilliant chariots of kings are ·destroyed, the body also approaches destruction, but the virtue of good people never approaches destruction—thus do the good say to the good.

A man who has learnt little, grows old like an ox; his flesh grows, but his knowledge does not grow.

Looking for the maker of this tabernacle, I have run through a course of many births, not finding him; and painful is birth again and again. But now, maker of the tabernacle, thou hast been seen; thou shalt not make up this tabernacle again. All thy rafters are broken, thy ridge-pole is sundered; the mind, approaching the Eternal, has attained to the extinction of all desires.

Anger

Let a man leave anger, let him forsake pride, let him overcome all bondage! No sufferings befall the man who is not attached to name and form, and who calls nothing his own.

He who holds back rising anger like a rolling chariot, him I call a real driver; other people are but holding the reins.

Let a man overcome anger by love, let him overcome evil by good; let him overcome the greedy by liberality, the liar by truth!

Speak the truth, do not yield to anger; give, if thou art asked for little; by these three steps thou wilt go near the gods.

Proverbs

Earnestness is the path of Nirvana, thoughtlessness the path of death. Those who are earnest do not die, those who are thoughtless are as if dead already.

Earnest among the thoughtless, awake among the sleepers, the wise man advances like a racer, leaving behind the hack.

He who understands that his body is like froth, and has learnt that it is as unsubstantial as a mirage, will break the flower-pointed arrow of Mara, and never see the king of death.

Death carries off a man who is gathering flowers, and whose mind is distracted, as a flood carries off a sleeping village.

As the bee collects nectar and departs without injuring the flower, or its colour or scent, so let a sage dwell in his village.

One's own self conquered is better than all other people.

Even though a speech be a thousand words, but made up of senseless talk, one word of sense is better, which if a man hears, he becomes quiet.

The best of ways is the eightfold path; the best of truths the four words; the best of virtues passionlessness; the best of men he who has eyes to see.

He who does not rouse himself when it is time to rise, who, though young and strong is full of sloth, whose will and thought are weak, that lazy and idle man never finds the way to knowledge.

What ought to be done is neglected, what ought not to be done is done; the desires of unruly, thoughtless people are always increasing.

But they whose whole watchfulness is always directed to their body, who do not follow what ought not to be done, and who steadfastly do what ought to be done, the desires of such watchful and wise people will come to an end.

He who says what is not goes to hell; he also who, having done a thing, says I have not done it. After death both are equal: they are men with evil deeds in the next world.

Better it would be to swallow a heated iron ball, like flaring fire, than that a bad unrestrained fellow should live on the charity of the land.

Four things does a reckless man gain who covets his neighbour's wife—demerit, an uncomfortable bed, thirdly, punishment, and lastly, hell.

As a grass-blade, if badly grasped, cuts the arm, badly practised asceticism leads to hell.

If anything is to be done, let a man do it, let him attack it vigorously! A careless pilgrim only scatters the dust of his passions more widely.

They who are ashamed of what they ought not to be ashamed of, and are not ashamed of what they ought to be ashamed of, such men, embracing false doctrines, enter the evil path.

They who fear when they ought not to fear, and fear not when they ought to fear, such men, embracing false doctrines, enter the evil path.

They who see sin where there is no sin, and see no sin where there is sin, such men, embracing false doctrines, enter the evil path.

They who see sin where there is sin, and no sin where there is no sin, such men, embracing the true doctrine, enter the good path.

A man does not become a Brahmana by his plaited hair, by his family, or by birth; in whom there is truth and righteousness, he is blessed, he is a Brahmana.

I do not call a man a Brahmana because of his origin

or of his mother. He is indeed arrogant, and he is wealthy; but the poor, who is free from all attachments, him I call indeed a Brahmana.

Him I call indeed a Brahmana who is free from anger, dutiful, virtuous, without appetites, who is subdued, and has received his last body.

Him I call indeed a Brahmana who does not cling to sensual pleasures, like water on a lotus leaf, like a mustard seed on the point of a needle.

Him I call indeed a Brahmana who without hurting any creatures, whether feeble or strong, does not kill nor cause slaughter.

Him I call indeed a Brahmana who is tolerant with the intolerant, mild with the violent, and free from greed among the greedy.

Him I call indeed a Brahmana from whom anger and hatred, pride and hypocrisy have dropped like a mustard seed from the point of a needle.

Him I call indeed a Brahmana who utters true speech, instructive and free from harshness, so that he offend no one.

Him I call indeed a Brahmana who takes nothing in the world that is not given him, be it long or short, small or large, good or bad.

Him I call indeed a Brahmana who in this world has risen above both ties, good and evil, who is free from grief, from sin, and from impurity.

From Buddaghosha's Parables

The Story of Kisagotami

Kisagotami became in the family way, and when the ten months were completed, gave birth to a son. When the boy was able to walk by himself, he died. The young girl, in her love for it, carried the dead child clasped to her bosom, and went about from house to house asking if any one would give her some medicine for it. When the neighbours saw this, they said, "Is the young girl mad that she carries about on her breast the dead body of her son!" But a wise man thinking to himself, "Alas! this Kisagotami does not understand the law of death, I must comfort her," said to her, "My good girl, I cannot myself give medicine for it, but I know of a doctor who can attend to it." The young girl said, "If so, tell me who it is." The wise man continued, "Gautama can give medicine, you must go to him."

Kisagotami went to Gautama, and doing homage to him, said, "Lord and master, do you know any medicine that will be good for my boy?" Gautama replied, "I know of some." She asked, "What medicine do you require?" He said, "I want a handful of mustard seed." The girl promised to procure it for him, but Gautama continued, "I require some mustard seed taken from a house where no son, husband, parent, or slave has died." The girl said, "Very good," and went to ask for some at the different houses, carrying the dead body of her son astride on her hip. The people said, "Here is some mustard seed, take it." Then she asked, "In my friend's house has there died a son, a husband, a parent, or a slave?" They replied, "Lady, what is this that you say! The living are few, but the dead are many." Then she went to other houses, but one said, "I have lost a son"; another, "I have lost my parents"; another, "I have lost my slave." At last, not being able to find a single house where no one had died, from which to procure the mustard seed, she began to think, "This is a heavy task that I am engaged in. I am not the only one whose son is dead. In the whole of the Savatthi country, everywhere children are dying, parents are dying." Thinking thus, she acquired the law of fear, and putting away her affection for her child, she summoned up resolution, and left the dead body in a forest; then she went to Gautama and paid him homage. He said to her, "Have you procured the handful of mustard seed?" "I have not," she replied; "the people of the village told me, 'The living are few, but the dead are many.'" Gautama said to her, "You thought that you alone had lost a son; the law of death is that among all living creatures there is no permanence." When Gautama had finished preaching the law, Kisagotami was established in the reward of Sotapatti; and all the assembly who heard the law were also established in the reward of Sotapatti.

Some time afterwards, when Kisagotami was one day engaged in the performance of her religious duties, she observed the lights in the houses now shining, now extinguished, and began to reflect, "My state is like these lamps." Gautama, who was then in the Gandhakuti building, sent his sacred appearance to her, which said to her, just as if he himself were preaching, "All living beings resemble the flame of these lamps, one moment lighted, the next extinguished; those only who have arrived at Nirvana are at rest." Kisagotami, on hearing this, reached the stage of a Rahanda possessed of intuitive knowledge.

From the Lotus of the True Law

The Wheel of the Law

The Lord addressed the venerable Sariputra:

It is not by reasoning, Sariputra, that the law is to be found: it is beyond the pale of reasoning, and must be learnt from the Tathagata. It is for a sole object, a lofty object, that the Buddha, the Tathagata, appears in the world. To show all creatures the sight of Tathagata-knowledge does the Buddha, the Tathagata, appear in the world; to open the eyes of creatures for the sight of Tathagata-knowledge does the Buddha, the Tathagata, appear in the world.

Now the word of my commandment, as contained in nine divisions, has been published according to the varying degree of strength of creatures. Such is the device I have shown in order to introduce creatures to the knowledge of the giver of boons. And to those in the world who have always been pure, wise, good-minded, compassionate sons of Buddha and done their duty under many kotis of Buddhas will I make known amplified Sutras.

There is no envy whatever in me; no jealousy, no desire, nor passion. Therefore I am the Buddha, because the world follows my teaching.

If I spoke to the creatures, "Vivify in your minds the wish for enlightenment," they would in their ignorance all go astray and never catch the meaning of my good words. From lust they run into distress; they are tormented in the six states of existence and people the cemetery again and again; they are overwhelmed with misfortune, as they possess little virtue. They are continually entangled in the thickets of sectarian theories,

such as, "It is and it is not; it is thus and it is not thus."
In trying to get a decided opinion on what is found in
the sixty-two heretical theories they come to embrace
falsehood and continue in it. They are hard to correct,
proud, hypocritical, crooked, malignant, ignorant, dull;
hence they do not hear the good Buddha-call, not once
in kotis of births.

This event to-day will be hard to be understood by
the ignorant who imagine they see here a sign, as they
are proud and dull. But the Bodhisattvas, they will
listen to me.

At certain times, at certain places, somehow do the
leaders appear in the world, and after their appearance
will they whose view is boundless at one time or another preach a similar law. Just as the blossom of the
glomerous fig-tree is rare, albeit sometimes, at some
places, and somehow it is met with, as something
pleasant to see for everybody, as a wonder to the world
including the gods; so wonderful and far more wonderful is the law I proclaim. Any one who, on hearing a
good exposition of it, shall cheerfully accept it and
recite but one word of it, will have done honour to all
Buddhas.

Ye are my children, I am your father, who has removed you from pain, from the triple world, from fear
and danger, when you had been burning for many
kotis of aeons. And I am teaching blessed rest (Nirvana) in so far as, though you have not yet reached
final rest, you are delivered from the trouble of the
mundane whirl, provided you seek the vehicle of the
Buddhas.

When the creatures in this world delight in low and
contemptible pleasures, then the Chief of the world,
who always speaks the truth, indicates pain as the first
great truth. And to those who are ignorant and too

simple-minded to discover the root of that pain I lay open the way: "Awaking of full consciousness, strong desire is the origin of pain."

Always try, unattached, to suppress desire. This is my third truth, that of suppression. It is an infallible means of deliverance; for by practising this method one shall become emancipated. And from what are they emancipated, Sariputra? They are emancipated from chimeras. Yet they are not wholly freed; the Chief declares that they have not yet reached final and complete rest in this world.

Why is it that I do not pronounce one to be delivered before one's having reached the highest, supreme enlightenment? Because such is my will; I am the ruler of the law, who is born in this world to lead to beatitude.

This, Sariputra, is the closing word of my law which now at the last time I pronounce for the weal of the world including the gods. Preach it in all quarters. And if someone speaks to you these words, "I joyfully accept," and with signs of utmost reverence receives this Sutra, thou mayst consider that man to be unable to slide back.

But do not speak of this matter to haughty persons, nor to conceited ones, nor to Yogins who are not self-restrained; for the fools, always revelling in sensual pleasures, might in their blindness scorn the law manifested.

Now hear the dire results when one scorns my skilfulness and the Buddha-rules for ever fixed in the world. After having disappeared from amongst men, they shall dwell in the lowest hell during a whole kalpa, and thereafter they shall fall lower and lower, the fools, passing through repeated births for many intermediate kalpas. And when they have vanished from amongst the inhabitants of hell, they shall further descend to the condition of brutes, be even as dogs and jackals, and become a sport to others.

And whenever they assume a human shape, they are born crippled, maimed, crooked, one-eyed, blind, dull, and low, they having no faith in my Sutra.

And since I am fully aware of it, I command thee, Sariputra, that thou shalt not expound a Sutra like this before foolish people.

But those who are sensible, instructed, thoughtful, clever, and learned, who strive after the highest supreme enlightenment, to them expound its real meaning. Those who, full of energy and ever kind-hearted, have a long time been developing the feeling of kindness, have given up body and life, in their presence thou mayst preach this Sutra. Those who show mutual love and respect, keep no intercourse with ignorant people, and are content to live in mountain caverns, to them expound this hallowed Sutra. Those who are not irascible, ever sincere, full of compassion for all living beings, and respectful towards the Sugata, before those thou mayst propound this Sutra.

I preach with ever the same voice, constantly taking enlightenment as my text. For this is equal for all; no partiality is in it, neither hatred nor affection. I am inexorable, bear no love nor hatred towards any one, and proclaim the law to all creatures without distinction, to the one as well as the other.

I re-create the whole world like a cloud shedding its water without distinction; I have the same feelings for respectable people as for the low; for moral persons as for the immoral; for the depraved as for those who observe the rules of good conduct; for those who hold sectarian views and unsound tenets as for those whose views are sound and correct. I preach the law to the inferior in mental culture as well as to persons of superior understanding and extraordinary faculties; inaccessible to weariness, I spread in season the rain of the law.

The Lord having thus spoken, the venerable Maha-Kasyapa said: Lord, if the beings are of different disposition, will there be for those who have left the triple world one Nirvana, or two, or three? The Lord replied: Nirvana, Kasyapa, is a consequence of understanding that all laws (things) are equal. Hence there is but one Nirvana, not two, not three.

As the rays of the sun and moon descend alike on all men, good and bad, without deficiency in one case or surplus in the other; so the wisdom of the Tathagata shines like the sun and moon, leading all beings without partiality.

The strength of charity or kindness is my abode; the apparel of forbearance is my robe; and voidness or complete abstraction is my seat; let the preacher take his stand on this and preach.

From the Diamond Sutra

The Transcendent Wisdom

Thus have I heard concerning our Lord Buddha:

Upon a memorable occasion, the venerable Subhuti, pressing together the palms of his hands, respectfully raised them towards Lord Buddha, saying: "Honoured of the worlds! if a good disciple, whether man or woman, seeks to obtain supreme spiritual wisdom, what immutable law shall sustain the mind of that disciple, and bring into subjection every inordinate desire?"

The Lord Buddha replied to Subhuti, saying: "By

this wisdom shall enlightened disciples be enabled to bring into subjection every inordinate desire! Every species of life, whether hatched in the egg, formed in the womb, evolved from spawn, produced by metamorphosis, with or without form or intelligence, possessing or devoid of natural instinct—from these changeful conditions of being, I command you to seek deliverance, in the transcendental concept of Nirvana. Thus, you shall be delivered from an immeasurable, innumerable, and illimitable world of sentient life; but, in reality, there is no world of sentient life from which to seek deliverance. And why? Because, in the minds of enlightened disciples, there have ceased to exist such arbitrary concepts of phenomena as an entity, a being, a living being, or a personality.

"Moreover, Subhuti, it is imperative that an enlightened disciple, in the exercise of charity, should act independently of phenomena. Is it possible to estimate the distance comprising the illimitable universe of space? It is equally impossible to estimate the merit of an enlightened disciple, who discharges the exercise of charity, unperturbed by the seductive influences of phenomena. Subhuti, the mind of an enlightened disciple ought thus to be indoctrinated.

"Is it possible that by means of his physical body, the Lord Buddha may be clearly perceived? Every form or quality of phenomena is transient and illusive. When the mind realizes that the phenomena of life are not real phenomena, the Lord Buddha may then be clearly perceived.

"Even at the remote period of five centuries subsequent to the Nirvana of the Lord Buddha, there will be many disciples observing the monastic vows, and assiduously devoted to good works. These, hearing this scripture proclaimed, will believe in its immutability, and similarly conceive within their minds a pure, un-mingled faith. Besides, it is important to realize that faith thus conceived is not exclusively in virtue of the insular thought of any particular Buddha, but because of its affiliation with the concrete thoughts of myriad Buddhas, throughout infinite ages. Therefore, amongst the beings destined to hear this scripture proclaimed, many, by momentary reflection, will intuitively conceive a pure and holy faith."

The Lord Buddha addressed Subhuti, saying: "What think you? Has the Lord Buddha really attained to supreme spiritual wisdom? Or has he a system of doctrine which can be specifically formulated?"

Subhuti replied, saying: "As I understand the meaning of the Lord Buddha's discourse, he has no system of doctrine which can be specifically formulated; nor can the Lord Buddha express, in explicit terms, a form of knowledge which can be described as supreme spiritual wisdom. And why? Because what the Lord Buddha adumbrated in terms of the law is transcendental and inexpressible. Being a purely spiritual concept, it is neither consonant with law, nor synonymous with anything apart from the law. Thus is exemplified the manner by which wise disciples and holy Buddhas, regarding intuition as the law of their minds, severally attained to different planes of spiritual wisdom."

The Lord Buddha addressed Subhuti, saying: "What think you? If a benevolent person bestowed as alms an abundance of the seven treasures sufficient to fill the universe, would there accrue to that person a considerable merit?"

Subhuti replied, saying: "A very considerable merit, honoured of the worlds!"

The Lord Buddha rejoined, saying: "If a disciple adhered with implicit faith to a stanza of this scripture, and diligently explained it to others, the intrinsic merit of that disciple would be relatively greater. And why? Because, Subhuti, the holy Buddhas, and the law by which they attained to supreme spiritual wisdom, severally owe their inception to the truth of this sacred scripture. Subhuti, what is ordinarily termed the Buddhic law is not really a law attributive to Buddha.

"What think you? You disciples, do not affirm that the Lord Buddha reflects thus within himself, 'I bring salvation to every living being.' Subhuti, entertain no such delusive thought! Because in reality there are no living beings to whom the Lord Buddha can bring salvation. If there were, the Lord Buddha would necessarily assume the reality of such arbitrary concepts as an entity, a being, a living being, and a personality. Subhuti, what the Lord Buddha adverted to as an entity is not in reality an entity; it is only understood to be an entity, and believed in as such, by the common, uneducated people.

"In what attitude of mind should it be diligently explained to others? Not assuming the permanency or the reality of earthly phenomena, but in the conscious blessedness of a mind at perfect rest. And why? Because, the phenomena of life may be likened unto a dream, a phantasm, a bubble, a shadow, the glistening dew, or lightning flash, and thus they ought to be contemplated."

From Asvaghosha's Awakening of Faith

Asvaghosha's Doctrine of Suchness

In the one soul we may distinguish two aspects. The one is the soul as suchness, the other is the soul as birth-and-death. Each in itself constitutes all things, and both are so closely interrelated that one cannot be separated from the other.

What is meant by the soul as suchness is the oneness of the totality of things, the great all-including whole, the quintessence of the doctrine. For the essential nature of the soul is uncreate and eternal.

Therefore all things in their fundamental nature are not nameable or explicable. They cannot be adequately expressed in any form of language. They are without the range of apperception. They are universals. They have no signs of distinction. They possess absolute sameness. They are subject neither to transformation, nor to destruction. They are nothing but the one soul, for which suchness is another designation. Therefore they cannot be fully explained by words or exhausted by reasoning.

In the essence of suchness, there is neither anything which has to be excluded, nor anything which has to be added.

The soul as birth-and-death comes forth (as the law of causation) from the Tathagata's womb. But the immortal (i.e., suchness) and the mortal (i.e., birth-and-death) coincide with each other. Though they are not identical, they are not a duality. Thus when the absolute soul assumes a relative aspect by its self-affirmation it is called the all-conserving mind.

The same mind has a twofold significance as the organizer and the producer of all things.

Again it embraces two principles: (1) enlightenment; (2) non-enlightenment.

Enlightenment is the highest quality of the mind. As it is free from all limiting attributes of subjectivity, it is like unto space, penetrating everywhere, as the unity of all. That is to say, it is the universal Dharmakaya of all Tathagatas.

The multitude of people are said to be lacking in enlightenment, because ignorance prevails there from all eternity, because there is a constant succession of confused subjective states from which they have never been emancipated.

But when they transcend their subjectivity, they can then recognize that all states of mentation, viz., their appearance, presence, change, and disappearance (in the field of consciousness) have no genuine reality. They are neither in a temporal nor in a spatial relation with the one soul, for they are not self-existent.

When you understand this, you also understand that enlightenment in appearance cannot be manufactured, for it is no other thing than enlightenment in its suchness, which is uncreate and must be discovered.

To illustrate: a man who is lost goes astray because he is bent on pursuing a certain direction; and his confusion has no valid foundation other than that he is bent on a certain direction.

It is even the same with all beings. They become unenlightened, foster their subjectivity and go astray, because they are bent on enlightenment.

While the essence of the mind is eternally clean and pure, the influence of ignorance makes possible the existence of a defiled mind. But in spite of the defiled mind, the mind itself is eternal, clear, pure, and not subject to transformation.

When the oneness of the totality of things is not recognized, then ignorance as well as particularization arises, and all phases of the defiled mind are thus developed. But the significance of this doctrine is so extremely deep and unfathomable that it can be fully comprehended by Buddhas and by no others.

When the mind is disturbed, it fails to be a true and adequate knowledge; it fails to be a pure, clean essence; it fails to be eternal, blissful, self-regulating, and pure; it fails to be tranquil. On the contrary, it will become transient, changeable, unfree, and therefore the source of falsity and defilement, while its modifications outnumber the sands of the Ganges. But when there is no disturbance in the essence of the mind, we speak of suchness as being the true, adequate knowledge, and as possessing pure and clean merits that outnumber the sands of the Ganges.

When the mind is disturbed it will strive to become conscious of the existence of an external world and will thus betray the imperfection of its inner condition. But as all infinite merits in fact constitute the one mind which, perfect in itself, has no need of seeking after any external things other than itself, so suchness never fails to actualize all those Buddha-dharmas, that, outnumbering the sands of the Ganges, can be said to be neither identical nor non-identical with the essence of the mind, and that therefore are utterly out of the range of our comprehension. On that account suchness is designated the Tathagata's womb or the Tathagata's Dharmakaya.

The body has infinite forms. The form has infinite attributes. The attribute has infinite excellencies. And the accompanying rewards of Bodhisattvas, that is, the region where they are predestined to be born by their previous karma, also has infinite merits and ornamentations. Manifesting itself everywhere, the body of Bliss is infinite, boundless, limitless, unintermittent in its action, directly coming forth from the mind.

From the Tibetan Doctrine

"Elegant Sayings" of the Lamas

A hen, when at rest, produceth much fruit;
A peacock, when it remaineth still, hath a handsome tail;
A gentle horse hath a swift pace;
The quiescence of a holy man is the sign of his being a sage.

Not to be cheered by praise,
Not to be grieved by blame,
But to know thoroughly one's own virtues or powers
Are the characteristics of an excellent man.

In the same place where the great Lord Buddha is present
Who would acknowledge any other man?
When the sun hath arisen, though there be many bright stars in the sky,
Not one of them is visible.

A foolish man proclaimeth his qualifications;
A wise man keepeth them secret within himself;
A straw floateth on the surface of water,
But a precious gem placed upon it sinketh.

It is only narrow-minded men that make such distinc-
    tions
As "This is our friend, this our enemy";
A liberal-minded man showeth affection for all,
For it is uncertain who may yet be of aid to one.

An excellent man, like precious metal,
Is in every way invariable;
A villain, like the beams of a balance,
Is always varying, upwards and downwards.

The greatest wealth consisteth in being charitable,
And the greatest happiness in having tranquillity of
    mind.
Experience is the most beautiful adornment;
And the best comrade is one that hath no desires.

Men of little ability, too,
By depending upon the great, may prosper;
A drop of water is a little thing,
But when will it dry away if united to a lake?

Hurtful expressions should never be used,
Not even against an enemy;
For inevitably they will return to one,
Like an echo from a rock.

When about to perform any great work,
Endeavour to have a trustworthy associate;
If one would burn down a forest,
The aid of a wind is, of course, needed.

To him who knoweth the true nature of things,
What need is there of a teacher?
To him who hath recovered from illness,

What need is there of a physician?
To him who hath crossed the river,
What need is there of a boat?

An astronomer maketh calculations and divinations
concerning the motions of the moon and the stars,
But he doth not divine that in his own household his
own womenfolk, being at variance, are misbe-
having.

In eating, sleeping, fearing, and copulating, men and
beasts are alike;
Man excelleth the beast by engaging in religious practices.
So why should a man, if he be without religion, not
be equal to the beast?

Although many stars shine, and that ornament of the
earth, the moon, also shineth,
Yet when the sun setteth, it becometh night.

The science which teacheth arts and handicrafts
Is merely science for the gaining of a living;
But the science which teacheth deliverance from
worldly existence,
Is not that the true science?

That which one desireth not for oneself,
Do not do unto others.

The foolish are like ripples on water,
For whatsoever they do is quickly effaced;
But the righteous are like carvings upon stone,
For their smallest act is durable.

The supreme path of altruism is a short-cut,
Leading to the realm of the conquerors,—
A track more speedy than that of a racing horse;
The selfish, however, know naught of it.

Charity produceth the harvest in the next birth.
Chastity is the parent of human happiness.
Patience is an adornment becoming to all.
Industry is the conductor of every personal accomplishment.
Meditation is the clarifier of a beclouded mind.
Intellect is the weapon which overcometh every enemy.

Gloat not, even though death and misfortune overwhelm thine enemies;
Boast not, even though thou equal Indra in greatness.
Some there are who turn inside out their whole interior
By means of over-talkativeness.

Be humble and meek if thou would be exalted;
Praise every one's good qualities if thou would have friends.

Relinquish an evil custom even though it be of thy fathers and ancestors;
Adopt a good custom even though it be established among thine enemies:
Poison is not to be taken even though offered by one's mother;
But gold is acceptable even from one who is inimical.

Be not too quick to express the desire of thy heart.
Be not short-tempered when engaged in a great work.
Be not jealous of a devotee who is truly religious and pious.

Consult not him who is habituated and hardened to
evil-doing.
Rogues there are even in religious orders;
Poisonous plants grow even on hills of medicinal herbs.

Some there are who marvel not at others removing
mountains,
But who consider it a heavy task when obliged to carry
a bit of fleece.

He who is ever ready to take the credit for any action
when it hath proved successful
And is equally ready to throw the blame on others
when it goeth wrong in the least,
And who is ever looking for faults in those who are
learned and righteous,
Possesseth the nature of a crow.

Preaching religious truth to an unbeliever is like feed-
ing a venomous serpent with milk.

Although a cloth be washed a hundred times,
How can it be rendered clean and pure
If it be washed in water which is dirty?

He who knoweth the precepts by heart, but faileth to
practise them,
Is like unto one who lighteth a lamp and then shutteth
his eyes.

Who can say with certainty that one will live to see the
morrow?

How can it be just to kill helpless and inoffensive
creatures?

THE PARSI

The Religion Which Might Have Been Ours

On a marble throne high above the narrow strait which stretched between the island of Salamis and the southern coast of Attica, in 480 B.C., the great Xerxes sat waiting to watch his navy defeat the Greek fleet. At his back burned the city of Athens, fired by the torches of his soldiers. At the pass of Thermopylae lay the bodies of 300 Spartans with that of their leader, Leonidas, slain by the Asiatic hosts of the Persian Empire. There remained only the task of destroying the Greek fleet, to wipe out the bitter shame of the Persian failure at Marathon ten years before, and to establish the Persian Empire in Greece, from whence it could sweep throughout Europe.

The Persian ships outnumbered the Greek fleet three to one, and were of heavier construction. But the Greeks, using the same superior strategy at sea that Miltiades had used on land at Marathon, sank 200 of the Persian vessels, captured others, and drove the rest from the strait.

The flight of the terror-stricken Xerxes signalized not only the end of his dream of conquest in Europe, but also a vastly changed religious prospect for the Western World. For, according to no less an authority than the late Max Müller, had it not been for the Persian defeats at the decisive battles of Marathon and Salamis, if, in other words, the western march of the Persian Empire had not been stopped there, Zoroastrianism rather than Judeo-Christianity would undoubtedly have been the prevailing religion of Europe and the Americas. Yet in spite of these crushing military and naval defeats, the resulting decline of the Persian Empire, and the eventual near-extinction of Zoroastrianism, so great was this religion's vitality and so appealing to the human heart were many of its conceptions and precepts that much of Zarathushtra's creed lives on in the religions of Israel and Christ.

The date when a branch of the Indo-European family moved into Persia, like the date of their brothers' entrance into India, is unknown. It is probable that the migration took place between the time when Abraham was said to have made his compact with Yaweh (about 2000 B.C.) and when Moses led the Children of Israel out of their captivity in Egypt (about 1200 B.C.). Evidences of Indo-European names and of worship of the old Indo-European gods are found among the Mitanni of the upper Euphrates valley during the century 1400-1300 B.C.

The region upon which the newcomers settled was an elevated tableland, parts of which were well watered, but which included areas that needed irrigation to make its fruitful soil productive. Irrigation and tillage meant food and social solidity; sloth and neglect brought social ruin.

Evidences of their early religion are scant, but show many traces of similarity to the Vedic religion of India. They paid homage to the sun god *Mitra*, whom they called *Mithra*, the sky god *Varuna* (who is sometimes called *Ahura*, equivalent of the Indian *Asura* and forerunner of the one God Ahura Mazda), the fire god *Agni*, and the old thunderer, *Indra*. There is evidence that Ahura Mazda existed in their conceptions before the birth of Zoroaster, but apparently as only one of a list of gods, just as, in the earlier conception of the

Jews, Yaweh was one of many gods, the tribal god of Abraham, and only later became Jehovah, the one God, maker of heaven and earth. The early Persians believed that all good things came to them from a region of light above and all evil from a region of darkness below.

Unto this people who depended upon rigorous tillage of the soil for their livelihood, was born Zarathushtra or Zoroaster about 660 B.C. Thus his influence was felt in that great age of religious consciousness and reformation, a little more than half a millennium before the birth of Christ, during which, in India, the *Upanishads* were furthering a conception of Brahma as the supreme God, and Gautama Buddha, the great enlightener, was born, when in China, Confucius and Lao Tze were quickening the moral and religious perceptions of men, and in Israel the Pre-Exilic prophets were paving the way for the pure monotheism of later Judaism.

There is no certainty as to the exact locality of Zarathushtra's birth or of the details of his early life. The traditional accounts are interesting chiefly because of the fundamental similarity which exists between the stories of his birth and those of other great leaders. Here, too, the sense of shame that accompanies the thought of sex in many early religions is evidenced by a tradition of sexless conception. How-tsieh, one of the "first ancestors" of China, was conceived when his mother "stepped upon a footprint of God." The conception of the Buddha came about when the Buddha himself, in the form of a white elephant, struck his future mother on the side with his trunk while she was dreaming. Jesus was immaculately conceived of a virgin by the Holy Ghost. And the conception of Zarathushtra took place when his mother, also a virgin (who "dazzled by the radiance of her body"), took the milk that had miraculously appeared in two white virgin cows, after they had eaten from a branch of the sacred Haoma plant on which the archangels had carried Zarathushtra's spirit to earth.

During his childhood, according to the same accounts in the *Pahlavi Texts*, he showed many evidences of wisdom and enlightenment, as did Christ preaching in the temple, and Gautama when he saw "the four signs." He early enunciated the principle of duality in the universe. "When I looked upwards," he said, "I saw that our souls that go up to the sky will go up to the best existence. When I looked downwards I saw the demon and the fiend, the wizard and the witch, become buried below in the earth and fall paralysed back to hell." When he was thirty he announced his righteous purpose, after having talked at great length with the archangels. And as Satan tempted Christ and Mara attempted to turn the Buddha from his mission, "forth rushed *Angra Mainyu*, the deadly, the Daeva of the Daevas," and attempted to slay Zarathushtra before he could preach his gospel of righteousness.

During the early years of his ministry he is reported to have had several visions in which he spoke with archangels and Ahura Mazda. For ten years, using these visions as evidence of his authority, he sought converts in vain. Then, after long pleading, he succeeded in converting the monarch Vishtaspa, and, under royal patronage, the success of the new religion became assured in the country of its birth. In his forty-seventh year, according to the *Pahlavi Texts* (in his seventy-eighth according to the more generally accepted theory of the scholar A. V. W. Jackson), Zarathushtra died, leaving behind him a lusty religion built on love of earth and its fruits, whole-souled worship of the one God Ahura Mazda, an enlightened ethical code, and the healing goodness of work. Such a creed towered high above the ceremonial polytheism which had existed in Iran before his birth.

The inclusive name for the sacred scriptures of Zoroastrianism is *Avesta*. The books include the *Yasna*, of which the seventeen *Gathas* or psalms are a part, the *Visperad*, the *Vendidad*, and the *Yashts*.

In Zarathushtra's doctrine there was no place for a sterile asceticism or profitless ceremonials. His was a worship of life in its full burgeoning; the highest religious exercise possible was complete co-operation with the beneficent forces of nature.

His theology was fundamental and simple. Ahura Mazda is the omniscient and potentially omnipotent creator of the universe, who made the good earth and instructed man to till it. Delaying full realization of his omnipotence and undoing as many of his good works as possible was Angra Mainyu "who is all death" and "who counter-created" evil. But the heavenly helpers, "Good Thought, Perfect Righteousness," and others will eventually make it possible for Ahura Mazda to destroy Angra Mainyu and achieve his righteous all-powerfulness.

Ahura Mazda makes rigid demands of righteousness upon mankind. This righteousness consists of truthfulness, kindness, benevolence, justice, devotion to God, and good works, especially in the field of agriculture where weedless stands of grain are more efficacious in the matter of salvation than are prayers. Here is no place for a hypocrisy which may build a reputation for sanctity on pious words, prayers, and religious ceremonies. A man's field may be seen! All matters connected with agriculture are given an accented religious importance. Earth itself is surrounded by special sanctity and is almost personified in the *Zenda-*

vesta in which Ahura Mazda recounts the five places in which "the earth feels most happy," the five where it "feels sorest grief," and the five kinds of persons who "rejoice the earth with greatest joy." The five places of the earth's happiness, in the order of their importance, are as follows: The first is where "one of the faithful steps forward." The second is "where one of the faithful erects a house with a priest within, with cattle, with a wife, with children, and good herds within" and "wherein afterwards the cattle continue to thrive, virtue to thrive, fodder to thrive, the dog to thrive, the wife to thrive, the child to thrive, the fire to thrive, and every blessing of life to thrive." The third place of the earth's greatest happiness is "where one of the faithful sows most corn, grass, and fruit, where he waters ground that is dry, or drains ground that is too wet." The fourth is the place "where there is most increase of flocks and herds," the fifth "where flocks and herds yield most dung."

So sacred is the holy earth that it must not be contaminated by the touch of dead bodies, which putrefy quickly in the Persian climate. Instead of being buried, these are disposed of by being deposited in "towers of silence" on grills where the birds may pick the bones clean of flesh before they at last drop to the ground. Indeed the earth "feels the sorest grief . . . where most corpses of dogs and men lie buried," according to the *Zendavesta*, and "the first who rejoices the earth with greatest joy" is he who "digs out of it most corpses of dogs and men."

The emphasis upon the goodness and usefulness of the dog is one of the most beautiful details in this religion of shepherds and cattlemen which, but for two defeats in battle, might have been the religion of the Western World. "The dog, with the prickly back, with the long and thin muzzle . . . is the good creature among the creatures of the Good Spirit. . . . Whosoever shall smite either a shepherd's dog or a house-dog, his soul, when passing to the other world, shall fly howling louder and more sorely grieved than the sheep does in the lofty forest where the wolf ranges."

Various strict rules protect this "good creature among the creatures." If a bitch whelps while at large, she and her puppies are the strict responsibility of the man nearest whose house she is. He must care for her and for her puppies until they are old enough to care for themselves, and if one of them dies through his neglect he is to suffer the same penalty as if he had killed it, which is to say the same penalty as he would if he had killed a man.

There is no animal worship involved in this, no superstitious formalism of sacred beast. The dog is "of the earth, earthly." The Zoroastrian attitude towards him is simply one of the evidences of the lustiness and at the same time the gentleness of Zarathushtra's creed. By Zoroastrian rules dog life was protected as human life was, first perhaps because of his usefulness to a people dependent upon herds and flocks, but also because of a recognition of the character of the dog which has marked true and realistic dog lovers of all times.

In Ahura Mazda we find for the first time in the history of any religion a clear and vigorous conception of the universal loving Father-God as the only imaginable God—a conception which eventually came to us through later Judaism and Christianity. Ahura Mazda is "the father of the Toiling Good Mind within us." His daughter is Piety. He is the one "with the bounteous spirit." He is "the creator of all." He is "Lord of the Good Spirit." "The souls of the righteous . . . will dwell in eternal immortality . . . in his kingdom." He is "the

Lord of saving power, a friend, a brother, a father to us, Mazda Lord!" He has many names, among which are "the One of whom questions are asked, the Herd-giver, the Strong One, Perfect Holiness, Understanding, Knowledge, Weal, Most Beneficent, He in whom there is no harm, Unconquerable One, All-seeing One, and Healing One." His is "the glory that cannot be forcibly seized."

Intended especially for Zoroastrian priests there are "five dispositions" and ten admonitions with which all instruction as to religion is connected. The five dispositions are innocence, discrimination between thoughts, words, and deeds ("to distinguish destruction from indestructiveness, and production from unproductiveness"), authoritativeness, steadfastness in religion, and to struggle prayerfully day and night with your own fiend.

The ten admonitions are: (1) Proceed with good repute. (2) Avoid evil repute. (3) Do not beat your teacher with a stick. (4) Whatever is taught to you deliver back to the worthy. (5) Rewards for the doers of good works and punishment for the workers of evil must be established by law, in other words, they are not to be administered by the clergy. (6) Keep the way of the good open to your house. (7) Do not remain in impenitence of sin. (8) Force malice away from your thoughts. (9) Keep ever progressing with the progress of this religion, do not go backwards. (10) Obey the ruler and the priestly authority.

The simplicity and broadness of these rules for the priesthood are in marked contrast to the elaboration of parallel rules in the Indian religions, and the radical character of the ninth admonition marks Zoroaster as a man with vision and a forward-looking intellect almost unparalleled among religious law makers.

For consideration of the nature of the Zorastrian heaven and hell, the veneration paid the souls of the faithful, and the reverence for the "undying, shining, swift-horsed sun," we leave you to the texts themselves.

What if this religion, instead of Judeo-Christianity, had become our faith? Would we have a vastly different theology and code of ethical conduct?

We would believe in a loving Father-God who is omniscient and concerned with the welfare of his children. We would have, instead of Jesus, Zarathushtra who, while not peculiarly the son of God, was sent to earth by God to spread his doctrine and do his work. We would look forward to "the Kingdom of God." We would have the ancient statement of a region of darkness and a region of light, of heaven and hell, of the good power in conflict with the evil. We would have Angra Mainyu, instead of Satan—a mere difference in name. We would have angels and archangels. We would have a statement of the final resurrection of the dead very similar to that in the Judeo-Christian Bible.

These things we have now. Did they come to us from the pious and vigorous mind of Zarathushtra by way of the later prophets of Israel and Christ, or were they original conceptions of Judeo-Christianity?

How well acquainted the chroniclers of the Jewish Old Testament were with the Persian branch of the Indo-European wanderers is evidenced by their frequent references to the Medes, the Persians, and the Hittites. But there is also definite evidence of borrowings from Zoroastrianism in the religious creeds which Christianity absorbed from later Judaism. Up to the time of the exile, the source of both good and evil in the religion of the Israelites was thought to be the God Jehovah. But after the exile, which is to say after the influence of Zarathushtra's monotheistic doctrine began to be felt, the Old Testament writers recorded the doctrine that Jehovah was the one God of the universe and a God of pure righteousness, while Satan was charged with all evil creations. It is probable that Satan—or the devil of later Judaism and Christianity—is none other than Angra Mainyu, the arch daeva of Zoroastrianism. The elaborate angelology and demonology of later Judaism, the idea of a divine judgment and a final resurrection, and a future life in a region which may be definitely described—all seem to have come from the doctrines of Zarathushtra though there is no definite proof of this. Indeed there are Christian and Hebrew commentators who believe that Zoroastrianism borrowed these conceptions from later Judaism, but they speak with less conviction than do those who hold the opposite view. Almost certainly the Magi who are said to have visited Jesus in the manger were Zoroastrian priests, and Christ's word "paradise" was taken from the Persian *pairidaeza*.

In the field of human ethics and social behaviour we would have in Zoroastrianism a code which, if followed, would produce a state of human welfare that would be difficult to surpass. Perhaps the chief differences would be in matters of emphasis. While Zoroastrianism and Christianity both state the necessity of faith and works, the emphasis in Christianity is on faith, in Zoroastrianism on works.

When Alexander the Great conquered Persia, and Greek cities were established there, the decline of Zoroastrianism began. Under the Mohammedans the decline continued until to-day there are scarcely ten thousand followers of Zarathushtra in the land of his birth—they call themselves *Parsis*, from Pars or Persia—and about one hundred thousand in India.

ZOROASTRIAN SCRIPTURES

From the Bundahis

The Order of Creation

The first of Ahura Mazda's creatures of the world was the sky, and his good thought, by good procedure, produced the light of the world, along with which was the good religion of the Mazdayasnians.

Of Ahura Mazda's creatures of the world, the first was the sky; the second, water; the third, earth; the fourth, plants; the fifth, animals; the sixth, mankind.

Ahura Mazda produced illumination between the sky and the earth, the constellation stars and those also not of the constellations, then the moon, and afterwards the sun.

The Ancestry of the World

On the nature of men it says in revelation, that Gayomard, in passing away, gave forth seed; that seed was thoroughly purified by the motion of the light of the sun, and Neryosang kept charge of two portions, and Spendarmad received one portion. And in forty years, with the shape of a one-stemmed Rivas-plant, and the fifteen years of its fifteen leaves, Matro and Matroyao grew up from the earth in such a manner that their arms rested behind on their shoulders, and one joined to the other they were connected together and both alike. And the waists of both of them were brought close and so connected together that it was not clear which was the male and which the female, and which was the one whose living soul of Ahura Mazda was not away. As it is said thus: "Which is created before, the soul or the body?" And Ahura Mazda said that the soul is created before, and the body after, for him who was created; it is given into the body that it may produce activity, and the body is created only for activity; hence the conclusion is this, that the soul is created before and the body after.

And both of them changed from the shape of a plant into the shape of a man, and the breath went spiritually into them, which is the soul; and now, moreover, in that similitude a tree had grown up whose fruit was the ten varieties of man.

Ahura Mazda spoke to Mashya and Mashyoi thus: "You are man, you are the ancestry of the world, and you are created perfect in devotion by me; perform devotedly the duty of the law, think good thoughts, speak good words, do good deeds, and worship no demons!"

Both of them first thought this, that one of them should please the other, as he is a man for him; and the first deed done by them was this, when they went out they washed themselves thoroughly; and the first words spoken by them were these, that Ahura Mazda created the water and earth, plants and animals, the stars, moon, and sun, and all prosperity whose origin and effect are from the manifestation of righteousness.

And, afterwards, antagonism rushed into their minds, and their minds were thoroughly corrupted, and they exclaimed that the evil spirit created the water and earth, plants and animals, and other things as aforesaid. That false speech was spoken through the will of the demons, and the evil spirit possessed himself of this first enjoyment from them; through that false speech they both became wicked, and their souls are in hell until the future existence.

And they had gone thirty days without food, covered with clothing of herbage; and after the thirty days they went forth into the wilderness, came to a white-haired goat, and milked the milk from the udder with their mouths. When they had devoured the milk Mashya said to Mashyoi thus: "My delight was owing to it when I had not devoured the milk, and my delight is more delightful now when it is devoured by my vile body."

That second false speech enhanced the power of the demons, and the taste of the food was taken away by them, so that out of a hundred parts one part remained.

Afterwards, in another thirty days and nights, they came to a sheep, fat and white-jawed, and they slaughtered it; and fire was extracted by them out of the wood of the lote-plum and box-tree, through the guidance of the heavenly angels, since both woods were most productive of fire for them; and the fire was stimulated by their mouths; and the first fuel kindled by them was dry grass, kendar, lotos, date palm leaves, and myrtle; and they made a roast of the sheep.

And they dropped three handfuls of the meat into the fire, and said: "This is the share of the fire." One piece of the rest they tossed to the sky, and said: "This is the share of the angels." A bird, the vulture, advanced and carried some of it away from before them, as a dog ate the first meat.

And first a clothing of skins covered them; afterwards, it is said, woven garments were prepared from a cloth woven in the wilderness.

And they dug out a pit in the earth, and iron was obtained by them and beaten out with a stone, and without a forge they beat out a cutting edge from it; and they cut wood with it, and prepared a wooden shelter from the sun.

Owing to the gracelessness which they practised, the demons became more oppressive, and they themselves carried on unnatural malice between themselves; they advanced one against the other, and smote and tore their hair and cheeks.

Then the demons shouted out of the darkness thus: "You are man; worship the demon! so that your demon of malice may repose."

Mashya went forth and milked a cow's milk, and poured it out towards the northern quarter; through that the demons became more powerful, and owing to them they both became so dry-backed that in fifty winters they had no desire for intercourse, and though they had had intercourse they would have had no children.

And on the completion of fifty years the source of desire arose, first in Mashya and then in Mashyoi, for Mashya said to Mashyoi thus: "When I see thy shame my desires arise." Then Mashyoi spoke thus: "Brother Mashya! when I see thy great desire I am also agitated." Afterwards, it became their mutual wish that the satisfaction of their desires should be accomplished, as they reflected thus: "Our duty even for those fifty years was this."

From them was born in nine months a pair, male and female; and owing to tenderness for offspring the mother devoured one, and the father one. And afterwards Ahura Mazda took tenderness for offspring away from them, so that one may nourish a child, and the child may remain.

The Flood

On the conflict of the creations of the world with the antagonism of the evil spirit it is said in revelation, that the evil spirit, even as he rushed in and looked upon the pure bravery of the angels and his own violence, wished to rush back. The spirit of the sky is himself like one of the warriors who has put on armour; he arrayed the sky against the evil spirit, and led on in the contest, until Ahura Mazda had completed a rampart around, stronger than the sky and in front of the sky. And his guardian spirits of warriors and the righteous, on war horses and spear in hand, were around the sky; such-like as the hair on the head is the similitude of those who held the watch of the rampart. And no passage was found by the evil spirit, who rushed back; and he beheld the annihilation of the demons and his own impotence, as Ahura Mazda did his own final triumph, producing the renovation of the universe for ever and everlasting.

The second conflict was waged with the water, because, as the star Tistar was in Cancer, the water which is in the subdivision they call Avrak was pouring, on the same day when the destroyer rushed in, and came again into notice for mischief in the direction of the west. For every single month is the owner of one constellation; the month Tir is the fourth month of the year, and Cancer the fourth constellation from Aries, so it is the owner of Cancer, into which Tistar sprang, and displayed the characteristics of a producer of rain; and he brought on the water aloft by the strength of the wind.

Tistar was converted into three forms, the form of a man and the form of a horse and the form of a bull; thirty days and nights he was distinguished in brilliance, and in each form he produced rain ten days and nights. Every single drop of that rain became as big as a bowl, and the water stood the height of a man over the whole of this earth; and the noxious creatures on the earth being all killed by the rain, went into the holes of the earth.

And afterwards the wind spirit, so that it might not be contaminated, stirred up the wind and atmosphere as the life stirs in the body; and the water was all swept away by it, and was brought out to the borders of the earth, and the wide-formed ocean arose therefrom. The noxious creatures remained dead within the earth, and their venom and stench were mingled with the earth, and in order to carry that poison away from the earth Tistar went down into the ocean in the form of a white horse with long hoofs.

And Apaosh, the demon, came meeting him in the likeness of a black horse with clumsy hoofs; a mile away from him fled Tistar, through the fright which drove him away. And Tistar begged for success from Ahura Mazda, and Ahura Mazda gave him strength and power, as it is said, that unto Tistar was brought at once the strength of ten vigorous horses, ten vigorous camels, ten vigorous bulls, ten mountains, and ten rivers. A mile away from him fled Apaosh, the demon, through fright at his strength; on account of this they speak of an arrow-shot with Tistar's strength in the sense of a mile.

Afterwards, with a cloud for a jar—thus they call the measure which was a means of the work—he seized upon the water and made it rain most prodigiously, in drops like bulls' heads and men's heads, pouring in handfuls and pouring in armfuls, both great and small. On the production of that rain the demons Aspengargak and Apaosh contended with it, and the fire Vazist turned its club over; and owing to the blow of the club Aspengargak made a very grievous noise, as even now, in a conflict with the producer of rain, a groaning and raging are manifest. And ten nights and days rain was produced by him in that manner, and the poison and venom of the noxious creatures which were in the earth were all mixed up in the water, and the water became quite salt, because there remained in the earth some of those germs which noxious creatures ever collect.

Afterwards, the wind, in the same manner as before, restrained the water, at the end of three days, on various sides of the earth; and the three great seas and twenty-three small seas arose therefrom.

From the Vendidad

The First Man

Zarathushtra asked Ahura Mazda:

O Ahura Mazda, most beneficent Spirit, Maker of the material world, thou Holy One!

Who was the first mortal, before myself, Zarathushtra, with whom thou, Ahura Mazda, didst converse, whom thou didst teach the religion of Ahura, the religion of Zarathushtra?

Ahura Mazda answered:

The fair Yima, the good shepherd, O holy Zarathushtra! he was the first mortal, before thee, Zarathushtra.

Unto him, O Zarathushtra, I, Ahura Mazda, spake, saying: "Well, fair Yima, son of Vivanghat, be thou the preacher and the bearer of my religion!"

And the fair Yima, O Zarathushtra, replied unto me, saying:

"I was not born, I was not taught to be the preacher and the bearer of thy religion."

Then I, Ahura Mazda, said thus unto him, O Zarathushtra:

"Since thou dost not consent to be the preacher and the bearer of my religion, then make thou my world increase, make my world grow: consent thou to nourish, to rule, and to watch over my world."

And the fair Yima replied unto me, O Zarathushtra, saying:

"Yes! I will make thy world increase, I will make thy world grow. Yes! I will nourish, and rule, and watch over thy world. There shall be, while I am king, neither cold wind nor hot wind, neither disease nor death."

Then I, Ahura Mazda, brought two implements unto him: a golden seal and a poniard inlaid with gold. Behold, here Yima bears the royal sway!

Thus, under the sway of Yima, three hundred winters passed away, and the earth was replenished with flocks and herds, with men and dogs and birds and with red blazing fires, and there was room no more for flocks, herds, and men.

Then Yima stepped forward, in light, southwards, on the way of the sun, and afterwards he pressed the earth with the golden seal, and bored it with the poniard, speaking thus:

"O Spenta Armaiti, kindly open asunder and stretch thyself afar, to bear flocks and herds and men."

And Yima made the earth grow larger by one-third than it was before, and there came flocks and herds and men, at their will and wish, as many as he wished.

Thus, under the sway of Yima, six hundred winters passed away, and the earth was replenished with flocks and herds, with men and dogs and birds and with red blazing fires, and there was room no more for flocks, herds, and men.

Then Yima stepped forward, in light, southwards, on the way of the sun, and afterwards he pressed the earth with the golden seal, and bored it with the poniard, speaking thus:

"O Spenta Armaiti, kindly open asunder and stretch thyself afar, to bear flocks and herds and men."

And Yima made the earth grow larger by two-thirds than it was before, and there came flocks and herds and men, at their will and wish, as many as he wished.

Thus, under the sway of Yima, nine hundred winters passed away, and the earth was replenished with flocks and herds, with men and dogs and birds and with red blazing fires, and there was room no more for flocks, herds, and men.

Then Yima stepped forward, in light, southwards, on the way of the sun, and afterwards he pressed the earth with the golden seal, and bored it with the poniard, speaking thus:

"O Spenta Armaiti, kindly open asunder and stretch thyself afar, to bear flocks and herds and men."

And Yima made the earth grow larger by three-thirds than it was before, and there came flocks and herds and men, at their will and wish, as many as he wished.

The Evil Winters

The Maker, Ahura Mazda, called together a meeting of the celestial Yazatas in the Airyana Vaego of high renown, by the Vanguhi Daitya.

The fair Yima, the good shepherd, called together a meeting of the best of the mortals, in the Airyana Vaego of high renown, by the Vanguhi Daitya.

To that meeting came Ahura Mazda, in the Airyana Vaego of high renown, by the Vanguhi Daitya; he came together with the celestial Yazatas.

To that meeting came the fair Yima, the good shepherd, in the Airyana Vaego of high renown, by the Vanguhi Daitya; he came together with the best of the mortals.

And Ahura Mazda spake unto Yima, saying:

"O fair Yima, son of Vivanghat! Upon the material world the evil winters are about to fall, that shall bring the fierce, deadly frost; upon the material world the evil winters are about to fall, that shall make snow-flakes fall thick, even on the highest tops of mountains.

"And the beasts that live in the wilderness, and those that live on the tops of the mountains, and those that live in the bosom of the dale shall take shelter in underground abodes.

"Before that winter, the country will bear plenty of grass for cattle, before the waters have flooded it. Now after the melting of the snow, O Yima, a place wherein the footprint of a sheep may be seen will be a wonder in the world.

"Therefore make thee a Vara, long as a riding-ground on every side of the square, and thither bring the seeds of sheep and oxen, of men, of dogs, of birds, and of red blazing fires.

"Therefore make thee a Vara, long as a riding-ground on every side of the square, to be an abode for men; a Vara, long as a riding-ground on every side of the square, for oxen and sheep.

"There thou shalt make waters flow in a bed a hathra long; there thou shalt settle birds, on the green that never fades, with food that never fails. There thou shalt establish dwelling-places, consisting of a house with a balcony, a courtyard, and a gallery.

"Thither thou shalt bring the seeds of men and women, of the greatest, best, and finest on this earth; thither thou shalt bring the seeds of every kind of cattle, of the greatest, best, and finest on this earth.

"Thither thou shalt bring the seeds of every kind of tree, of the highest of size and sweetest of odour on this earth; thither thou shalt bring the seeds of every kind of fruit, the best of savour and sweetest of odour. All those seeds shalt thou bring, two of every kind, to be kept inexhaustible there, so long as those men shall stay in the Vara.

"There shall be no humpbacked, none bulged forward there; no impotent, no lunatic; no one malicious, no liar; no one spiteful, none jealous; no one with decayed tooth, no leprous to be pent up, nor any of the brands wherewith Angra Mainyu stamps the bodies of mortals.

"In the largest part of the place thou shalt make nine streets, six in the middle part, three in the smallest. To the streets of the largest part thou shalt bring a thousand seeds of men and women; to the streets of the middle part, six hundred; to the streets of the smallest part, three hundred. That Vara thou shalt seal up with thy golden seal, and thou shalt make a door, and a window self-shining within."

And Yima did as Ahura Mazda wished.

From the Zendavesta

The One of Whom Questions Are Asked

Zarathushtra asked Ahura Mazda: "O Ahura Mazda, most beneficent Spirit, Maker of the material world, thou Holy One! What of the Holy World is the strongest?"

Ahura Mazda answered: "Our name, O Spitama Zarathushtra! who are the Amesha-Spentas, that is the strongest part of the Holy Word."

Then Zarathushtra said: "Reveal unto me that name of thine, O Ahura Mazda!"

Ahura Mazda replied unto him: "My name is the One of whom questions are asked, O holy Zarathushtra!

"My second name is the Herd-giver.

"My third name is the Strong One.

"My fourth name is Perfect Holiness.

"My fifth name is All good things created by Mazda, the offspring of the holy principle.

"My sixth name is Understanding;

"My seventh name is the One with understanding.

"My eighth name is Knowledge;

"My ninth name is the One with knowledge.

"My tenth name is Weal;

"My eleventh name is He who produces weal.

"My twelfth name is AHURA (the Lord).

"My thirteenth name is the Most Beneficent.

"My fourteenth name is He in whom there is no harm.

"My fifteenth name is the Unconquerable One.

"My sixteenth name is He who makes the true account.

"My seventeenth name is the All-seeing One.

"My eighteenth name is the Healing One.

"My nineteenth name is the Creator.

"My twentieth name is MAZDA (the All-knowing One).

"Worship me, O Zarathushtra, by day and by night, with offerings of libations well accepted. I will come unto thee for help and joy, I, Ahura Mazda; the good, holy Sraosha will come unto thee for help and joy; the waters, the plants, and the Fravashis of the holy ones will come unto thee for help and joy."

The Fatherhood of God

Yea, I will speak forth; hear ye; now listen, ye who from near, and ye who from afar have come seeking the knowledge. Now ponder ye clearly all that concerns him. Not for a second time shall the false teacher slay our life of the mind, or the body. The wicked is hemmed in with his faith and his tongue!

Yea, I will declare him whose blessings the offerers will seek for, those who are living now, as well as those who have lived aforetime, as will they also who are coming hereafter. Yea, even the souls of the righteous will desire them in the eternal immortality. Those things they will desire which are blessings to the righteous but woes to the wicked. And these hath Ahura Mazda established through his kingdom, he, the creator of all.

Him in our hymns of homage and of praise would I faithfully serve, for now with mine eye, I see him clearly, Lord of the good spirit, of word, and action, I knowing through my righteousness him who is Ahura Mazda. And to him not here alone, but in his home of song, his praise we shall bear.

Yea, him with our better mind we seek to honour, who desiring good, shall come to us to bless in weal and sorrow. May he, Ahura Mazda, make us vigorous through Khshathra's royal power, our flocks and men in thrift to further, from the good support and bearing of his Good Mind, itself born in us by his righteousness.

Him would we magnify and praise who hath despised the Daeva-gods and alien men, them who before held him in their derision. Far different are these from him who gave him honour. This latter one is through the Saoshyant's bounteous faith, who likewise is the Lord of saving power, a friend, brother, or father to us, Mazda Lord!

The Mazdayasnian Confession

I drive the Daevas hence; I confess as a Mazda-worshipper of the order of Zarathushtra, estranged from the Daevas, devoted to the lore of the Lord, a praiser of the bountiful Immortals; and to Ahura Mazda, the good and endowed with good possessions, I attribute all things good, to the Holy One, the resplendent, to the glorious, whose are all things what-soever which are good; whose is the kine, whose is Asha (the righteous order pervading all things pure), whose are the stars, in whose lights the glorious beings and objects are clothed.

And I choose Piety, the bounteous and the good, mine may she be. And therefore I loudly deprecate all rob-bery and violence against the sacred kine, and all drought to the wasting of the Mazdayasnian villages.

To that religious sanctity to which the waters apper-tain, do I belong, to that sanctity to which the plants, to that sanctity to which the kine of blessed gift, to that religious sanctity to which Ahura Mazda, who made both kine and holy men, belongs, to that sanctity do I. Of that creed which Zarathushtra held, which

Kavi Vistaspa, and those two, Frashaostra and Gam-
aspa; yea, of that religious faith which every Saoshyant
who shall yet come to save us, the holy ones who do
the deeds of real significance, of that creed, and of that
lore, am I.

A Mazda-worshipper I am, of Zarathushtra's order;
so do I confess, as a praiser and confessor, and I therefore praise aloud the well-thought thought, the word
well spoken, and the deed well done.

The Earth

O Maker of the material world, thou Holy One!
Which is the first place where the earth feels most
happy? Ahura Mazda answered: It is the place whereon one of the faithful steps forward, O Spitama Zarathushtra! lifting up his voice in good accord with
religion, and beseeching Mithra, the lord of the rolling
country-side, and Rama Hvastra.

O Maker of the material world, thou Holy One!
Which is the second place where the earth feels most
happy? Ahura Mazda answered: It is the place whereon
one of the faithful erects a house with a priest within,
with cattle, with a wife, with children, and good herds
within; and wherein afterwards the cattle continue to
thrive, virtue to thrive, fodder to thrive, the dog to
thrive, the wife to thrive, the child to thrive, the fire to
thrive, and every blessing of life to thrive.

O Maker of the material world, thou Holy One!
Which is the third place where the earth feels most
happy? Ahura Mazda answered: It is the place where
one of the faithful sows most corn, grass, and fruit,
O Spitama Zarathushtra! where he waters ground that
is dry, or drains ground that is too wet.

O Maker of the material world, thou Holy One!

Which is the fourth place where the earth feels most happy? Ahura Mazda answered: It is the place where there is most increase of flocks and herds.

O Maker of the material world, thou Holy One! Which is the fifth place where the earth feels most happy? Ahura Mazda answered: It is the place where flocks and herds yield most dung.

O Maker of the material world, thou Holy One! Which is the first place where the earth feels sorest grief? Ahura Mazda answered: It is the neck of Arezura, whereon the hosts of fiends rush forth from the burrow of the Drug.

O Maker of the material world, thou Holy One! Which is the second place where the earth feels sorest grief? Ahura Mazda answered: It is the place wherein most corpses of dogs and of men lie buried.

O Maker of the material world, thou Holy One! Which is the third place where the earth feels sorest grief? Ahura Mazda answered: It is the place whereon stand most of those Dakhmas on which the corpses of men are deposited.

O Maker of the material world, thou Holy One! Which is the fourth place where the earth feels sorest grief? Ahura Mazda answered: It is the place wherein are most burrows of the creatures of Angra Mainyu.

O Maker of the material world, thou Holy One! Which is the fifth place where the earth feels sorest grief? Ahura Mazda answered: It is the place whereon the wife and children of one of the faithful, O Spitama Zarathushtra! are driven along the way of captivity, the dry, the dusty way, and lift up a voice of wailing.

O Maker of the material world, thou Holy One! Who is the first that rejoices the earth with greatest joy? Ahura Mazda answered: It is he who digs out of it most corpses of dogs and men.

O Maker of the material world, thou Holy One! Who is the second that rejoices the earth with greatest joy? Ahura Mazda answered: It is he who pulls down most of those Dakhmas on which the corpses of men are deposited. Let no man alone by himself carry a corpse. If a man alone by himself carry a corpse, the Nasu rushes upon him. This Drug Nasu falls upon and stains him, even to the end of the nails, and he is unclean, thenceforth, for ever and ever.

O Maker of the material world, thou Holy One! What shall be the place of that man who has carried a corpse alone? Ahura Mazda answered: It shall be the place on this earth wherein is least water and fewest plants, whereof the ground is the cleanest and the driest and the least passed through by flocks and herds, by the fire of Ahura Mazda, by the consecrated bundles of Baresma, and by the faithful.

O Maker of the material world, thou Holy One! Who is the third that rejoices the earth with greatest joy? Ahura Mazda answered: It is he who fills up most burrows of the creatures of Angra Mainyu.

O Maker of the material world, thou Holy One! Who is the fourth that rejoices the earth with greatest joy? Ahura Mazda answered: It is he who sows most corn, grass, and fruit, O Spitama Zarathushtra! who waters ground that is dry, or drains ground that is too wet. Unhappy is the land that has long lain unsown with the seed of the sower and wants a good husbandman, like a well-shapen maiden who has long gone childless and wants a good husband. He who would till the earth, O Spitama Zarathushtra! with the left arm and the right, with the right arm and the left, unto him will she bring forth plenty of fruit: even as it were a lover sleeping with his bride on her bed; the bride will bring forth children, the earth will bring forth plenty of fruit. He who would till the earth, O Spitama Zarathushtra! with the left arm and the right, with the right arm and the left, unto him thus says the earth: "O thou man! who dost till me with the left arm and the right, with the right arm and the left, here shall I ever go on bearing, bringing forth all manner of food, bringing corn first to thee." He who does not till the earth, O Spitama Zarathushtra! with the left arm and the right, with the right arm and the left, unto him thus says the earth: "O thou man! who dost not till me with the left arm and the right, with the right arm and the left, ever shalt thou stand at the door of the stranger, among those who beg for bread; the refuse and the crumbs of the bread are brought unto thee, brought by those who have profusion of wealth."

O Maker of the material world, thou Holy One! What is the food that fills the religion of Mazda? Ahura Mazda answered: It is sowing corn again and again, O Spitama Zarathushtra! He who sows corn, sows righteousness: he makes the religion of Mazda walk, he suckles the religion of Mazda; as well as he could do with a hundred man's feet, with a thousand woman's breasts, with ten thousand sacrificial formulas.

O Maker of the material world, thou Holy One! Who is the fifth that rejoices the earth with greatest joy? Ahura Mazda answered: It is he who kindly and piously gives to one of the faithful who tills the earth.

Reward of the Faithful

"O Maker of the material world, thou Holy One! Where are the rewards given? Where does the rewarding take place? Where is the rewarding fulfilled? Whereto do men come to take the reward that, during their life in the material world, they have won for their souls?"

Ahura Mazda answered: "When the man is dead, when his time is over, then the wicked, evil-doing Daevas cut off his eyesight. On the third night, when the dawn appears and brightens up, when Mithra, the god with beautiful weapons, reaches the all-happy mountains, and the sun is rising:

"Then the fiend, named Vizaresha, O Spitama Zarathushtra, carries off in bonds the souls of the wicked Daeva-worshippers who live in sin. The soul enters the way made by Time, and open both to the wicked and to the righteous. At the head of the Chinvad bridge, the holy bridge made by Mazda, they ask for their spirits and souls the reward for the worldly goods which they gave away here below.

"Then comes the beautiful, well-shapen, strong and well-formed maid, with the dogs at her sides, one who can distinguish, who has many children, happy, and of high understanding.

"She makes the soul of the righteous one go up above the Haraberezaiti; above the Chinvad bridge she places it in the presence of the heavenly gods themselves.

"Up rises Vohumano from his golden seat; Vohumano exclaims: 'How hast thou come to us, thou holy one, from that decaying world into this undecaying one?'

"Gladly pass the souls of the righteous to the golden seat of Ahura Mazda, to the golden seat of the Amesha-Spentas, to the Garo-nmanem, the abode of Ahura Mazda, the abode of the Amesha-Spentas, the abode of all the other holy beings."

Hymn to the Sun

We sacrifice unto the undying, shining, swift-horsed Sun.

When the light of the sun waxes warmer, when the

brightness of the sun waxes warmer, then up stand the heavenly Yazatas, by hundreds and thousands: they gather together its glory, they make its glory pass down, they pour its glory upon the earth made by Ahura, for the increase of the world of holiness, for the increase of the creatures of holiness, for the increase of the undying, shining, swift-horsed Sun.

And when the sun rises up, then the earth, made by Ahura, becomes clean; the running waters become clean, the waters of the wells become clean, the waters of the sea become clean, the standing waters become clean; all the holy creatures, the creatures of the Good Spirit, become clean.

Should not the sun rise up, then the Daevas would destroy all the things that are in the seven Karshvares, nor would the heavenly Yazatas find any way of withstanding or repelling them in the material world.

He who offers up a sacrifice unto the undying, shining, swift-horsed Sun—to withstand darkness, to withstand the Daevas born of darkness, to withstand the robbers and bandits, to withstand the Yatus and Pairikas, to withstand death that creeps in unseen—offers it up to Ahura Mazda, offers it up to the Amesha-Spentas, offers it up to his own soul. He rejoices all the heavenly and worldly Yazatas, who offers up a sacrifice unto the undying, shining, swift-horsed Sun.

The Fravashis of the Faithful

We worship the good, strong, beneficent Fravashis of the faithful, who show beautiful paths to the waters, who show a beautiful growth to the fertile plants, who showed their paths to the stars, the moon, the sun, and the endless lights, that had stood before for a long time in the same place, without moving forward, through the oppression of the Daevas and the assaults of the Daevas. And now they move around in their far-revolving circle for ever, till they come to the time of the good restoration of the world.

We worship Zarathushtra, the lord and master of all the material world, the man of the primitive law; the wisest of all beings, the best-ruling of all beings, the brightest of all beings, the most glorious of all beings, the most worthy of sacrifice amongst all beings, the most worthy of prayer amongst all beings, the most worthy of propitiation amongst all beings, the most worthy of glorification amongst all beings, whom we call well-desired and worthy of sacrifice and prayer as much as any being can be, in the perfection of his holiness.

We worship this earth; we worship those heavens; we worship those good things that stand between the earth and the heavens and that are worthy of sacrifice and prayer and are to be worshipped by the faithful man.

We worship the souls of the wild beasts and of the tame.

We worship the souls of the holy men and women, born at any time, whose consciences struggle, or will struggle, or have struggled, for the good.

We worship the spirit, conscience, perception, soul, and Fravashi of the holy men and holy women who struggle, will struggle, or have struggled, and teach the law, and who have struggled for holiness.

The Fravashis of the faithful, awful and overpowering, awful and victorious; the Fravashis of the men of the primitive law; the Fravashis of the next-of-kin; may these Fravashis come satisfied into this house; may they walk satisfied through this house!

The Abodes of the Soul

At the end of the third night, when the dawn appears, it seems to the soul of the faithful one as if it were brought amidst plants and scents. it seems as if a wind were blowing from the region of the south, from the regions of the south, a sweet-scented wind, sweeter-scented than any other wind in the world.

And it seems to him as if his own conscience were advancing to him in that wind, in the shape of a maiden fair, bright, white-armed, strong, tall-formed, high-standing, thick-breasted, beautiful of body, noble, of a glorious seed, of the size of a maid in her fifteenth year, as fair as the fairest things in the world.

And the soul of the faithful one addresses her, asking: "What maid art thou, who art the fairest maid I have ever seen?"

And she, being his own conscience, answers him: "O thou youth of good thoughts, good words, and good deeds, of good religion, I am thy own conscience!

"Everybody did love thee for that greatness, goodness, fairness, sweet-scentedness, victorious strength and freedom from sorrow, in which thou dost appear to me;

"And so thou, O youth of good thoughts, good words, and good deeds, of good religion! didst love me for that greatness, goodness, fairness, sweet-scentedness, victorious strength, and freedom from sorrow, in which I appear to thee.

"When thou wouldst see a man making derision and deeds of idolatry, or rejecting the poor and shutting his door, then thou wouldst sit singing the Gathas and worshipping the good waters and Atar, the son of Ahura Mazda, and rejoicing the faithful that would come from near or from afar.

"I was lovely and thou madest me still lovelier; I was fair and thou madest me still fairer; I was desirable and thou madest me still more desirable; I was sitting in a forward place and thou madest me sit in the foremost place, through this good thought, through this good speech, through this good deed of thine; and so henceforth men worship me for my having long sacrificed unto and conversed with Ahura Mazda."

The first step that the soul of the faithful man made, placed him in the good-thought paradise; the second step that the soul of the faithful man made, placed him in the good-word paradise; the third step that the soul of the faithful man made, placed him in the good-deed paradise; the fourth step that the soul of the faithful man made, placed him in the endless lights.

At the end of the third night, when the dawn appears, it seems to the soul of the wicked one as if it were brought amidst snow and stench, and as if a wind were blowing from the region of the north, from the regions of the north, a foul-scented wind, the foulest-scented of all the winds in the world.

The first step that the soul of the wicked man made laid him in the evil-thought hell; the second step that the soul of the wicked man made laid him in the evil-word hell; the third step that the soul of the wicked man made laid him in the evil-deed hell; the fourth step that the soul of the wicked man made laid him in the endless darkness.

Of the Dog

"Which is the good creature among the creatures of the Good Spirit that from midnight till the sun is up goes and kills thousands of the creatures of the Evil Spirit?"

Ahura Mazda answered: "The dog with the prickly back, with the long and thin muzzle, the dog Vanghapara, which evil-speaking people call the Duzaka; this is the good creature among the creatures of the Good Spirit that from midnight till the sun is up goes and kills thousands of the creatures of the Evil Spirit.

"And whosoever, O Zarathushtra! shall kill the dog kills his own soul for nine generations, nor shall he find a way over the Chinvad bridge, unless he has, while alive, atoned for his sin."

"O Maker of the material world, thou Holy One! If a man kill the dog, what is the penalty that he shall pay?"

Ahura Mazda answered: "A thousand stripes with the Aspahe-astra, a thousand stripes with the Sraosho-karana.

"Whosoever shall smite either a shepherd's dog, or a house-dog, or a Vohunazga dog, or a trained dog, his soul when passing to the other world, shall fly howling louder and more sorely grieved than the sheep does in the lofty forest where the wolf ranges.

"No soul will come and meet his departing soul and help it, howling and grieved in the other world; nor will the dogs that keep the Chinvad bridge help his departing soul howling and grieved in the other world.

"A dog has the characters of eight sorts of people:

"He has the character of a priest, of a warrior, of a husbandman, of a strolling singer, of a thief, of a disu, of a courtesan, and of a child.

"He eats the refuse, like a priest; he is easily satisfied, like a priest; he is patient, like a priest; he wants only a small piece of bread, like a priest; in these things he is like unto a priest.

"He marches in front, like a warrior; he fights for the beneficent cow, like a warrior; he goes first out of the house, like a warrior; in these things he is like unto a warrior.

"He is watchful and sleeps lightly, like a husbandman; he goes first out of the house, like a husbandman; he returns last into the house, like a husbandman; in these things he is like unto a husbandman.

"He is fond of singing, like a strolling singer; he wounds him who gets too near, like a strolling singer; he is ill-trained, like a strolling singer; he is changeful, like a strolling singer; in these things he is like unto a strolling singer.

"He is fond of darkness, like a thief; he prowls about in darkness, like a thief; he is a shameless eater, like a thief; he is therefore an unfaithful keeper, like a thief; in these things he is like unto a thief.

"He is fond of darkness like a disu; he prowls about in darkness, like a disu; he is a shameless eater, like a disu; he is therefore an unfaithful keeper, like a disu; in these things he is like unto a disu.

"He is fond of singing, like a courtesan; he wounds him who gets too near, like a courtesan; he roams along the roads, like a courtesan; he is ill-trained, like a courtesan; he is changeful, like a courtesan; in these things he is like unto a courtesan.

"He is fond of sleep, like a child; he is tender like snow, like a child; he is full of tongue, like a child; he digs the earth with his paws, like a child; in these things he is like unto a child!

"If those two dogs of mine, the shepherd's dog and the house-dog, pass by any one of my houses, let them never be kept away from it.

"For no house could subsist on the earth made by Ahura, but for those two dogs of mine, the shepherd's dog and the house-dog."

"O Maker of the material world, thou Holy One!

When a dog dies, with marrow and seed dried up, whereto does his ghost go?"

Ahura Mazda answered: "It passes to the spring of the waters, O Spitama Zarathushtra! and there out of them two water-dogs are formed: out of every thousand dogs and every thousand she-dogs, a couple is formed, a water-dog and a water she-dog."

"O Maker of the material world, thou Holy One! If a bitch be near her time, which is the worshipper of Mazda that shall support her?"

Ahura Mazda answered: "He whose house stands nearest, the care of supporting her is his; so long shall he support her, until the whelps be born.

"If he shall not support her, so that the whelps come to grief, for want of proper support, he shall pay for it the penalty for wilful murder.

"He shall take her to rest upon a litter of nemovanta or of any foliage fit for a litter; so long shall he support her, until the young dogs are capable of self-defence and self-subsistence.

"It lies with the faithful to look in the same way after every pregnant female, either two-footed or four-footed, two-footed woman or four-footed bitch."

From the Pahlavi Texts

Instructions to Priests

About the five dispositions of priests, and the ten admonitions with which all instruction as to religion is connected:

Of those five dispositions the first is innocence.

The second is discrimination among thoughts, words,

and deeds; to fully distinguish the particulars of destruction from indestructiveness, such as noxious creatures from cattle; and of production from unproductiveness, such as the righteous and worthy from the wicked and unworthy.

The third is authoritativeness, because that priestly master is always wiser and speaking more correctly who is taught wisely and teaches with more correct words.

The fourth is to understand and consider the ceremonial as the ceremonial of Ahura Mazda, and the essentials with all goodness, beneficence, and authority; to be steadfast in his religion, and to consider the indications of protection which are established for his religion. To maintain the reverence of the luminaries prayerfully, also the reverence of the emanations from the six archangels, be they fire, be they earth, or be they of bodily form, and of the creatures which are formed by them; also the pure cleansing from dead matter, menstruation, bodily refuse, and other hurtfulness; this is in order that they may be characterized, and thereby constituted, as better-principled, more sensible, and purer, and they may become less faulty. The reverence of mankind is to consider authoritatively about knowledge and property; the reverence of cattle is about fodder, little hardship, and moderate maintenance; the reverence of plants is about sowing and ripening for the food of the worthy. The ceremonial which is glorifying all the sacred beings, praises the luminaries and worldly creations improperly, and is antagonistic to them, because complete glorification is proper through complete recitation of the ritual; and the ceremonial of any one whatever is his own proper duty professionally, so long as it is possible to keep proceeding with very little sinfulness.

The fifth is to struggle prayerfully, day and night, with your own fiend, and all life long not to depart from steadfastness, nor allow your proper duty to go out of your hands.

And the first of those ten admonitions is to proceed with good repute, for the sake of occasioning approving remarks as to the good repute of your own guardian and teacher, high-priest and master.

The second is to become awfully refraining from evil repute, for the sake of evil repute not occurring to relations and guardians.

The third is not to beat your own teacher with a snatched-up stick, and not to bring scandal upon his name, for the sake of annoying him, by uttering that which was not heard from your own teacher.

The fourth is that whatever is taught liberally by your own teacher, you have to deliver back to the worthy, for the sake of not extorting a declaration of renown from the righteous.

The fifth is that the reward of doers of good works and the punishment of criminals have to be established by law, for the sake of progress.

The sixth is to keep the way of the good open to your house, for the sake of making righteousness welcome in your own abode.

The seventh is that, for the sake of not developing the fiend insensibly in your reason, you are not to keep it with the religion of the good, nor to remain in impenitence of sin.

The eighth is that, for the sake of severing the fiend from the reason, you have to force malice away from your thoughts, and to become quickly repentant of sin.

The ninth is to fully understand the forward movement of the religion, also to keep the advancing of the religion further forwards, and to seek your share of duty therein; and on a backward movement, when adversity happens to the religion, to have the religion back again, and to keep your body in the continence of religion.

The tenth is that there is to be a period of obedience towards the ruler and priestly authority, the high-priesthood of the religious.

The Righteous Man

For what purpose is a righteous man created for the world, and in what manner is it necessary for him to exist in the world?

When the persistent one accomplished that most perfect and wholly miraculous creation of the lord, and his unwavering look—he made a spirit of observant temperament, which was the necessary soul, the virtuous lord of the body moving into the world. And the animating life, the preserving guardian spirit, the acquiring intellect, the protecting understanding, the deciding wisdom, the demeanour which is itself a physician, the impelling strength, the eye for what is seen, the ear for what is heard, the nose for what is smelt, the mouth for recognizing flavour, the body for approaching the assembly of the righteous, the heart for thinking, the tongue for speaking, the hand for working, the foot for walking, these which make life comfortable, these which are developments in creating, these which are to join the body, these which are to be considered perfected, are urged on by him continuously, and the means of industry of the original body are arranged advisedly. And by proper regulation, and the recompense of good thoughts, good words, and good deeds, he announced and adorned conspicuous, patient, and virtuous conduct; and that procurer of the indispensable did not forget to keep men in his own true service and proper bounds, the supreme sovereignty of the creator.

And man became a pure glorifier and pure praiser of that all-good friend, through the progress which is his wish. Because pure friendship arises from sure meditation on every virtue, and from its existence no harm whatever arose; pure glorifying arises from glorifying every goodness, and from its existence no vileness whatever arose; and pure praising arises from all prosperity, and from its existence no distress whatever arose.

A righteous man is the creature by whom is accepted that occupation which is provided for him, and is fully watchful in the world so that he will not be deceived by the rapacious fiend.

The Chinvad Bridge

How are the Chinvad bridge, the Daitih peak, and the path of the righteous and wicked; how are they when one is righteous, and how when one is wicked?

The reply is this, that thus the high-priests have said, that the Daitih peak is in Airyana-Vaego, in the middle of the world; reaching unto the vicinity of that peak is that beam-shaped spirit, the Chinvad bridge, which is thrown across from the Alburz enclosure back to the Daitih peak. As it were that bridge is like a beam of many sides, of whose edges there are some which are broad, and there are some which are thin and sharp; its broad sides are so large that its width is twenty-seven reeds, and its sharp sides are so contracted that in thinness it is like the edge of a razor. And when the souls of the righteous and wicked arrive it turns to that side which is suitable to their necessities, through the great glory of the creator and the command of him who takes the just account.

Moreover, the bridge becomes a broad bridge for the righteous, as much as the height of nine spears—and the length of those which they carry is each separately three reeds—; and it becomes a narrow bridge for the wicked, even unto a resemblance to the edge of a razor. And he who is of the righteous passes over the bridge, and a worldly similitude of the pleasantness of his path upon it is when thou shalt eagerly and unweariedly walk in the golden-coloured spring, and with the gallant body and sweet-scented blossom in the pleasant skin of that maiden spirit, the price of goodness. He who is of the wicked, as he places a footstep on to the bridge, on account of affliction and its sharpness, falls from the middle of the bridge, and rolls over head-foremost. And the unpleasantness of his path to hell is in similitude such as the worldly one in the midst of that stinking and dying existence, there where numbers of the sharp-pointed darts are planted out inverted and point upwards.

The Nature of Heaven

How are the nature of heaven and the comfort and pleasure which are in heaven?

The reply is this, that it is lofty, exalted, and supreme, most brilliant, most fragrant, and most pure, most supplied with beautiful existences, most desirable, and most good, and the place and abode of the sacred beings. And in it are all comfort, pleasure, joy, happiness, and welfare, more and better even than the greatest and supremest welfare and pleasure in the world; and there is no want, pain, distress, or discomfort whatever in it; and its pleasantness and the welfare of the angels are from that constantly beneficial place, the full and undiminishable space, the good and boundless world.

And the freedom of the heavenly from danger from evil in heaven is like unto their freedom from disturbance, and the coming of the good angels is like unto the heavenly ones' own good works provided. This prosperity and welfare of the spiritual existence is more than that of the world, as much as that which is unlimited and everlasting is more than that which is limited and demoniacal.

The Nature of Hell

How are the nature of hell, and the pain, discomfort, punishment, and stench of hell?

The reply is this, that it is sunken, deep, and descending, most dark, most stinking, and most terrible, most supplied with wretched existences, and most bad, the place and cave of the demons and fiends. And in it is no comfort, pleasantness, or joy whatever; but in it are all stench, filth, pain, punishment, distress, profound evil, and discomfort; and there is no resemblance of it whatever to worldly stench, filthiness, pain, and evil. And since there is no resemblance of the mixed evil of the world to that which is its sole-indicating good, there is also a deviation of it from the origin and abode of evil.

And so much more grievous is the evil in hell than even the most grievous evil on earth, as the greatness of the spiritual existence is more than that of the world; and more grievous is the terror of the punishment on the soul than that of the vileness of the demons on the body. And the punishment on the soul is from those whose abode it has become, from the demons and darkness—a likeness of that evil to hell—the head of whom is Aharman the deadly.

And the words of the expressive utterance of the high-priests are these, that where there is a fear of every other thing it is more than the thing itself, but hell is a thing worse than the fear of it.

The Two Regions

It is in scripture thus declared, that light was above and darkness below, and between those two was open space. Ahura Mazda was in the light, and Aharman in the darkness; Ahura Mazda was aware of the existence of Aharman and of his coming for strife; Aharman was not aware of the existence of light and of Ahura Mazda. It happened to Aharman, in the gloom and darkness, that he was walking humbly on the borders, and meditating other things he came up to the top, and a ray of light was seen by him; and because of its antagonistic nature to him he strove that he might reach it, so that it might also be within his absolute power. And as he came forth to the boundary, accompanied by certain others, Ahura Mazda came forth to the struggle for keeping Aharman away from his territory; and he did it through pure words, confounding witchcraft, and cast him back to the gloom.

The Resurrection

Zarathushtra asked of Ahura Mazda thus: "Whence does a body form again, which the wind has carried and the water conveyed? and how does the resurrection occur?" Ahura Mazda answered thus: "When through me the sky arose from the substance of the ruby, without columns, on the spiritual support of far-compassed light; when through me the earth arose, which bore the material life, and there is no maintainer of the worldly creation but it; when by me the sun and moon and stars were conducted in the firmament of luminous bodies; when by me corn was created so that, scattered about in the earth, it grew again and returned with increase; when by me colour of various kinds was created in plants; when by me fire was created in plants and other things without combustion; when by me a son was created and fashioned in the womb of a mother, and the structure severally of the skin, nails, blood, feet, eyes, ears, and other things was produced; when by me legs were created for the water, so that it flows away, and the cloud was created which carries the water of the world and rains there where it has a purpose; when by me the air was created which conveys in one's eyesight, through the strength of the wind, the lowermost upward according to its will, and one is not able to grasp it with the hand outstretched; each one of them, when created by me, was herein more difficult than causing the resurrection, for it is an assistance to me in the resurrection that they exist, but when they were formed it was not forming the future out of the past.

"Observe that when that which was not was then produced, why is it not possible to produce again that which was? for at that time one will demand the bone from the spirit of earth, the blood from the water, the hair from the plants, and the life from fire, since they were delivered to them in the original creation."

First, the bones of Gayomard are roused up, then those of Mashya and Mashyoi, then those of the rest of mankind; in the fifty-seven years of Soshyans they prepare all the dead, and all men stand up; whoever is righteous and whoever is wicked, every human creature, they rouse up from the spot where its life departs.

Afterwards, when all material living beings assume again their bodies and forms, then they assign them a single class.

Of the light accompanying the sun, one-half will be for Gayomard, and one-half will give enlightenment among the rest of men, so that the soul and body will know that this is my father, and this is my mother, and this is my brother, and this is my wife, and these are some other of my nearest relations.

Then is the assembly of the Sadvastaran, where all mankind will stand at this time; in that assembly every one sees his own good deeds and his own evil deeds; and then, in that assembly, a wicked man becomes as conspicuous as a white sheep among those which are black.

Afterwards, they set the righteous man apart from the wicked; and then the righteous is for heaven, and they cast the wicked back to hell. Three days and nights they inflict punishment bodily in hell, and then he beholds bodily those three days' happiness in heaven. As it says that, on the day when the righteous man is parted from the wicked, the tears of every one, thereupon, run down unto his legs.

Afterwards, the fire and halo melt the metal of Shatvairo, in the hills and mountains, and it remains on this earth like a river. Then all men will pass into that melted metal and will become pure; when one is righteous, then it seems to him just as though he walks continually in warm milk; but when wicked, then it seems to him in such manner as though, in the world, he walks continually in melted metal.

Afterwards, with the greatest affection, all men come together, father and son and brother and friend ask one another thus: "Where hast thou been these many years, and what was the judgment upon thy soul? hast thou been righteous or wicked?" All men become of one voice and administer loud praise to Ahura Mazda and the archangels.

Ahura Mazda completes his work at that time, and the creatures become so that it is not necessary to make any effort about them.

From the Gathas

Exhortation to the Faithful

Now will I speak out: Listen and hear,
You who, from far and near, have come to seek my
    word;
Now I exhort you clearly to impress on your memory
    the evil teacher and his faults; for
No longer shall the evil teacher—druj that he is!—
    destroy the second life,
In the speech of his tongue misleading to the evil life.

Now will I speak out: At the beginning of life
The holier Mentality said to the opposing Mentality
    who was more hostile,
"Neither our thoughts, doctrines, plans,
Beliefs, utterances, deeds,
Individualities, nor souls agree."

Now will I speak out! Of that which at the beginning
    of life
The knowing Ahura Mazda said:
"Those who do not practise the Word,
As I consider and declare it,
They shall have woe at the end of life."

Now will I speak out what is the best of life:

Through Justice, O Mazda, have I discovered thee, who
     hast created him;

That Mazda is the father of the working Good Dis-
     position;

And that Love, who produces good deeds, is his daugh-
     ter;

And that the all-detecting Ahura is not to be deceived.

Now will I, who am the utterer of this Word which
     is the best for mortal men to hear,

Speak out what the most bounteous Ahura Mazda said
     to me:

"Those who, for the attainment of this mystic manthric
     Word grant me their obedience,

They shall come up with Health, and Immortality,

With the deeds of the good Mentality."

Let the preparers for the conversion of the world, both
     those who were, and those who are yet becoming

Wish for the profits of the compensations;

The successful soul of the Ashaist abiding in Im-
     mortality

With enduringness; while the Drujists shall endure
     griefs,

And all this Ahura Mazda creates through the coming
     of the Kingdom.

Thou shalt seek to win Mazda with such praises of
     reverence as for instance this psalm:

"With my own eyes shall I now behold the heaven

Of the good Mentality of word and deed;

Having, through Justice, known Ahura Mazda,

To whom let us, in heaven, set down adorations for
     the filling of the paradise Garodman."

Him, Mazda, along with Good Disposition, shalt thou
    seek to satisfy for us,
Because it is he who, by his will, makes our fortune or
    misfortune.
May Ahura Mazda through his realm
Grant, for the group of herdsmen, prospering of our
    cattle and men
By the proficiency of Good Disposition, through Justice.

How shalt thou, O individual believer, with hymns of
    Love, magnify
Him who is reputed to be Ahura Mazda for eternity;
Since through Justice and Good Disposition he has
    promised us
That in his realm we shall obtain Health and Immor-
    tality;
But we shall obtain that his heavenly dwelling through
    vitality and enduringness.

Whoever, therefore, in the future scorns the Daevas
And the men who scorn Zarathushtra,
And all others—lukewarm neutrals—except whoever
    is devoted to Zarathushtra,
Shall be considered, by the bounteous individuality of
    Zarathushtra, who is Saviour and Master-of-the-
    house
As his friend, brother, or father,—O Ahura Mazda!

A Prayer for Guidance

O Ahura Mazda, this I ask of thee: speak to me truly!
How should I pray, when I wish to pray to one like
    you?
May one like you, O Mazda, who is friendly, teach one
    like me?

And may you give us supporting aids through the
    friendly Justice,
And tell us how you may come to us with Good Dis-
    position?

O Ahura Mazda, this I ask of thee: speak to me truly!
Whether at the beginning of the best life
The retributions will be of profit to their recipients?
And whether he, who is bounteous to all through
    Justice, and who watches the end
Through his Mentality,—whether he is the life-healing
    friend of the people?

O Ahura Mazda, this I ask of thee: speak to me truly!
Who was the first father of Justice by giving birth to
    him?
Who established the sunlit days and the star glister-
    ing sphere and the Milky Way?
Who, apart from thee, established the law by which
    the moon waxes and wanes?
These and other things would I like to know!

O Ahura Mazda, this I ask of thee: speak to me truly!
Who was from beneath sustaining the earth and the
    clouds
So that they would not fall down? Who made the
    waters and the plants?

Who yoked the two swift ones, thunder and lightning,
    to the wind and to the clouds?
Who is the creator of Good Disposition?

O Ahura Mazda, this I ask of thee: speak to me truly!
Who produced well-made lights and darkness?

Who produced sleep, well-induced through laborious
    waking?

Who produced the dawns and the noon through the
    contrast with the night

Whose daily changes act for the enlightened believers
    as monitors of their interests?

O Ahura Mazda, this I ask of thee: speak to me truly!

Is the message I am about to proclaim genuine?

Does Love support Justice through deeds?

Dost thou with Good Disposition destine the realm for
    these believers?

For whom but these believers didst thou shape the
    fortune-bringing cattle?

O Ahura Mazda, this I ask of thee: speak to me truly!

Who shaped prized Love with Power?

Who, by guidance, rendered sons reverent to their
    fathers?

It is I who strive to learn to recognize thee

Through the bounteous Mentality, as giver of all good
    things!

O Ahura Mazda, this I ask of thee: speak to me truly!

I would like to know what sort of a purpose is thine,
    that I may be mindful of it;

What are thy utterances, about which I asked through
    the aid of Good Disposition;

The proper knowledge of life through Justice—

How shall my soul, encouraged by bliss, arrive at that
    good reward?

O Ahura Mazda, this I ask of thee: speak to me truly!

How may I accomplish the sanctification of those spirits

To whom thou, the well-disposed Master of the coming
 Kingdom,
Hast pronounced promises about its genuine blessings,
Promising that those spirits shall dwell in the same
 dwelling with Justice and Good Disposition?

O Ahura Mazda, this I ask of thee: speak to me truly!
How will Love actually, in deeds, extend over those
 persons
To whom thy spirit was announced as a doctrine?
On account of whom I first was elected, and whom I
 love;
All others I look upon with hostility of mentality!

O Ahura Mazda, this I ask of thee: speak to me truly!
How shall I carry out the object inspired by you,
Namely, my attachment to you, in order that my speech
 may grow mighty, and
That by that word of mine the adherent of Justice
May in the future commune with Health, and Im-
 mortality?

The Choice Between Right and Wrong

But thus, O souls desirous of hearing, I will utter those
 things worthy to be remembered by the expert-
 knower,
The praises for Ahura, and hymns worthy of Good
 Disposition,
And things well remembered with the aid of Justice,
 and the propitious omens beheld through the lights
 of the stars, or of the altar-flames.

Listen with your ears to the best information; behold
 with your sight, and with your mind;

Man by man, each for his own person, distinguishing
    between both confessions,
Before this great crisis. Consider again!

At the beginning both these Mentalities became con-
    scious of each other,
The one being a Mentality better in thought, and word,
    and deed, than the other Mentality who is bad.
Now let the just man discriminate between these two,
    and choose the benevolent one, not the bad one.

But when the twin-Mentalities came together, they
    produced
The first life, and lifelessness, and settled on the state
    of the last condition of existence,
The worst for the Drujists, but for the Ashaists the best
    mind.

The Drujist chose between these twin-Mentalities, the
    one who perpetrated the worst deeds,
But he who was inspired by the most bountiful Men-
    tality that is clothed upon by the most adamantine
    stone-quarried heavens as a garment,
And he who cheerfully satisfied Ahura Mazda with
    sincere deeds, chose Justice.

The Daevaists did not discriminate accurately between
    these two, because
Just as they were deliberating, there came upon them
    a delusion so that they should choose the worst
    Mind,
So that, all together, they rushed over to Fury, through
    which they afflict the life of man with disease.

And to this man now sick came Mazda Ahura with the
    Power realm, with Good Disposition, and with
    Justice,
And Love endowed the sick body of man with firmness
    and endurance
So that he may become the first of those surviving the
    tests of passing through the metallic trials and
    through the retributions.

And thereupon, when the punishments of those male-
    factors shall occur,
Then the saved man shall obtain for thee, O Mazda,
    with the help of Good Disposition, the Power
    realm,
Which will be the fulfilment of the world's destiny, and
    this will be obtained by those who shall deliver the
    Druj into the two hands of Justice.

And may we be those who shall make life progressive
    or purposeful!
Assemble together, along with Justice, O Ahura Mazda,
    and come hither
So that here where our thoughts formerly developed
    separately, they may now mature together, fuse,
    and become wisdom.

THE JEW
AND THE CHRISTIAN

The Jew and the Christian

Out of the land of Egypt, out of a swamp of bulrushes, out of the loins of a slave woman 1200 years before the birth of Christ, came the child who was to become the supreme lawmaker of all time. The religion of Judaism, for which he laid the foundation, and that of Christianity, which was its child, are to-day the strong bases of Western religious culture.

There is no story of the miraculous conception or birth of Moses such as those which record the origins of Jesus, of Gautama Buddha, and of Zarathushtra. There were no voices of angels singing to herald the coming of the great Hebrew leader, no moving star or other phenomena of nature to lead shepherds and wise men to the bed of the child, no bending down of trees over the mother, as in the story of the birth of the Buddha, no luminosity about the place of *accouchement*, such as that which we are told shone about Zarathushtra's birthplace three days before his birth. There were no prophets either at his birth or during his childhood to proclaim his divinity. Nor did Moses ever claim for himself any divine qualities which set him apart from other mortals.

The greatest of all the leaders of the Jews was a child of his people, hidden at birth in the bulrushes on the bank of an Egyptian river by his mother in order that he might escape the edict of Pharaoh that every child of the Hebrews should be killed. And though we are told that he later saw God, talked with him, and received directly from the omnipotent hand the stone tablets containing the Ten Commandments, he remained a man of his people to the day of his death and beyond.

From time immemorial the Jews had prophesied the coming of a Messiah. Christians believe that the prophecy was fulfilled in the birth of Jesus. The orthodox Jews' dissension from this belief does not arise from protestation that Moses was this long-heralded Messiah. They still await a divine leader in human form, and are content to regard one of the world's most dramatic stories—that of the life of Moses—as the narrative of a natural phenomenon and Moses as a thoroughly human being. They are satisfied to say, in the words of Deuteronomy, "There arose not a prophet since in Israel like unto Moses, whom the Lord knew face to face."

Yet if a religion which is swayed by so many cross currents and has so many leaders in it as has Judaism may be said to have a personal founder, surely that man is Moses. With Aaron as his lieutenant, he led the Children of Israel out of their bondage in Egypt and during forty years of wandering held them together, strengthened them in their heart-breaking discouragements, instructed them, laid down laws for them which he enforced with an iron hand, and gave them the Ten Commandments in the form recognized to-day by both Jew and Christian. By pleading, demonstration, threats, denunciations, and even ruthless slaughter of the recalcitrant, he induced them to worship only Jehovah, thus paving the way for the monotheism which is the basis of Western theology.

To understand the complex pattern of the Jewish religion, it is necessary to look back to times long prior to the birth of Moses, to a time probably before the Iranian branch of Indo-Europeans migrated to Persia.

The Jews were then a group of Semitic tribes wandering on the Arabian desert and slowly drifting towards Palestine, constantly seeking better pastures for their herds of sheep and goats.

There is evidence that even at this early date they recognized a code of laws enunciated in ten sentences which they called "the Ten Commands." Some of these are identical in meaning with edicts of the Ten Commandments. Some are not. But they are undoubtedly the parent of the later code. (See *The Bible of the World*, p. 1368.) The stories of the origins of the earth and of man may already have been established much as we have them today in Genesis. The story of Adam and Eve in its essentials may, or may not, have had some relation to a basic legend believed by that other great race of religious men, the Indo-Europeans, who told the story of Mashya and Mashyoi in Persia and that of Yama and Yami in India. The story of the flood and the ark which Noah built appears in its essential details in the earlier Babylonian *Epic of Gilgamish.* (See *The Bible of the World*, pp. 1366, 1367.) Some of the laws later enunciated in the Old Testament (notably those of exact retaliation) are from the Code of Hammurabai, a Babylonian king who ruled about 2250 B.C. who is probably identical with the King Amraphel of Genesis 14, 1. According to the Babylonian story this code, inscribed on tablets, was given to Hammurabai by the sun god himself, an almost exact parallel to the story of Jehovah giving Moses the Ten Commandments.

Obviously, then, Judaism owes much to earlier religions. But it has contributed to the present much more than it has borrowed from the past.

That contribution began even before the birth of Moses when, about 2000 B.C., the Jews wandered from

"Ur of the Chaldees" westward to found a nation. Because in their migration they crossed the Euphrates River, they were called "Hebrews" from a word which means "to cross over." Genesis tells us that they were led by the patriarch Abraham.

Some scholars now question the existence of the individual man Abraham, believing rather that this was the designation of a tribe, but the name stands in Jewish belief for one of the greatest of all the early patriarchs, the first of the strong Jewish leaders whose names have been preserved, the "father of the faithful," and the "friend of God."

At the time of Abraham his people believed in many gods. These gods had been given names after first having been worshipped merely as natural phenomena or objects. The Hebrews accorded their worship to individual deities as their fancies—or their beliefs in relative godly strengths—dictated. But the God of Abraham was *Yaweh*, Yaweh the strong, Yaweh whose power, so Abraham said, was far greater than the combined strength of all the other gods. Abraham and Yaweh had made a compact whereby the great god had agreed to accept the Hebrews as his chosen people, to take a special interest in them, and to further their well-being so long as they acknowledged him alone as their god, gave no homage to other gods, and did his will.

Now the doing of his will was a complex matter. Sacrifices, burnt offerings heaped upon an altar, prayers and incantations—these he wanted, but they were not in themselves enough. The will of Yaweh was that the people of Abraham should, in their daily lives, follow a course of conduct which had in view the well-being and happiness of their fellow tribesmen. Thus an ethical pattern was woven into the religion along with its rites and ceremonies. It did not yet include the concept of world brotherhood. Ethical conduct towards members of the tribe of Abraham was one thing—that to others, another. But even here was the beginning of an ethical code which later was to dominate the Western World.

Abraham's compact with Yaweh did not constitute the monotheism, the belief that there is one God only, which Judaism and its child Christianity accept to-day, but was rather "henotheism," the worship of one god, while recognizing others. Until long after the death of Moses the existence of other gods was believed in by the Jews. The first commandment did not say "Thou shalt believe that there are no other gods but me," but rather "Thou shalt have no other gods before me." This tacit recognition of the existence of other gods was reinforced by such admonitions as "Revile not the gods." When God appeared to Moses in the burning bush he did not say, "I am the only God," nor did he apparently feel that the simple words "I am God" were enough to make him known. He identified himself among the gods by saying "I am the God of thy father, the God of Abraham, the God of Isaac, and the God of Jacob." Even years later, when Moses' leadership had ended with his death and Joshua, having led his people through a long lifetime, was about to die, he urged them to "put away the strange gods which are among you, and incline your hearts unto the Lord God of Israel."

Directly descended from Abraham, through his son Isaac, was Jacob, twin brother of Esau. Jacob, whose name later became Israel, was the father of twelve sons who became heads of the twelve tribes of Israel. Esau meanwhile headed another tribe near Canaan who became known as the Edomites.

The story of the twelve sons of Jacob—how one of

them, Joseph, was sold by his brothers and carried into
Egypt, how Joseph rose to leadership under the powerful Pharaoh, of how he brought his people to live
there in a land of plenty, how he and his master died,
and how another Pharaoh enslaved the Hebrews—is
told in the later part of Genesis and the first part of
Exodus.

Then rose the mighty figure of Moses, grandson of a
Hebrew slave named Levi, who was adopted by the
daughter of Pharaoh when she found him hidden in the
bulrushes. As a son of the royal household he might
have cast his lot in with the Egyptian overlords. But
the Pharaoh's daughter had engaged Moses' own mother
(who had thrust herself forward through subterfuge)
to nurse him, and from her he must have been well
schooled in the manner of his birth and the history of
his people. When as a young man he saw the burdens
laid upon the Hebrews, he was overcome with sadness.
This rapidly grew into anger and drove Moses to kill
an Egyptian who was beating a Jew. Escaping from the
wrath of the Pharaoh, he went into the land of Midian
where he married and had the first of several en-
counters with Yaweh who, speaking from the midst of
a burning bush, said that his name was "I Am" (just
as, in the later Hinduist *Upanishads*, Yama tells Nachiketas that God can be named only by the words "He
Is"). Reaffirming the ancient covenant with Abraham,
Yaweh said that he had come to strengthen his people.
With Moses acting as his spokesman and executive,
he would lead them out of their captivity.

How Moses courageously faced the Pharaoh, de-
manding and finally accomplishing the release of the
Hebrews (with the help of "I Am" and the plagues he
sent upon the Egyptians), how he led them across the
Red Sea and to the very edge of the Promised Land

with the fire by night and the cloud by day which Yaweh sent to guide them, is told in the magnificent story of Exodus. This story is of primary importance in the belief of devout Jews to this day, for they have not forgotten Yaweh's ancient covenant with Abraham, and God's help in their deliverance from Egypt is one of the basic evidences that he fulfilled his part of that compact.

After the death of Moses the Hebrew people passed through centuries of viscissitudes as a nation. These are important from a religious point of view only in so far as the changing circumstances influenced their religious, and therefore, their ethical concepts—those two forces which, as early as Abraham, were becoming so strongly enmeshed with tribal feeling that the three were to become one. Their attitude towards God, their attitude towards themselves as a united and exclusive people, and their standards of ethical conduct merged in the one mighty phenomenon of Judaism.

For nearly a century in the time of the kings they enjoyed prosperity and peace. Then, during the reign of Rehoboam, when the nation was in the throes of political dissension and revolt against high taxation, once more the people were divided. Now the two groups became a northern and a southern kingdom, "Israel" and "Judah." In both kingdoms prosperity brought luxury and with it a falling away from the ancient worship of Yaweh. Many adopted the licentious practices of the Canaanitish religion and worshipped the Canaanitish gods. Their covenant with Yaweh forgotten, an increase in the commercial spirit brought with it exploitation, extortion, the selling of the poor into slavery for debts, immorality, and wars.

Rising to the need of the times came a succession of great leaders. They have been called prophets, but perhaps it would be more accurate to call them sociologists and religious truth-tellers. For their teachings were based upon a deep understanding of the human heart and mind, a keen knowledge of the ills and needs of their people, and an exalted vision of righteous justice.

One can only speculate on how much or how little they were influenced by other similar religious phenomena which were occurring throughout the world. This great age of religious awakening took place a little more than half a millennium before the birth of Christ and gave the *Upanishads* with their conception of the supreme Brahma, Gautama Buddha, and Mahavira to India, Confucius and Lao Tze to China, and the great monotheistic and work-revering Zarathushtra to Persia. In Greece men sought elevation of the human soul through beauty in one of the world's greatest periods of art. Rome was spreading its civilization through conquest and leaving its mark indelibly upon world society through the Roman genius in law making.

In Israel these seers and moral leaders saw the threatened disintegration of national unity and morality, and reminded their people over and over of their covenant with Yaweh and their debt to him for their deliverance from slavery. They warned them that greed, dishonesty, cruelty, intolerance, lasciviousness, materialism, and sloth were the instruments of national suicide. Perhaps they were strongly influenced by contemporary Zoroastrianism, for whereas Jehovah had previously been represented as the source of all things, both good and evil, he was now credited only with good while Satan (parallel of the Zoroastrian Angra Mainyu) was thought to create evil. Other evidences point to possible extensive borrowing of concepts from the fertile and vital religion of the great Persian.

But regardless of how much Judaism may have taken

from Zoroastrianism or other religions, its own utterances at this time were vastly more important. It was combining, with such force, conviction, and practicality as had never before been achieved, a theology and a social code. It was building an ethical religion in which man was to achieve salvation through co-operation with the one God, omnipotent Lord of the universe and loving, merciful father of us all, in whose godhead we could participate through righteousness and love in the service of our fellow-men.

Considering the later prophets and the earlier leaders as one group, no other religious history has within it such an assembly of giants—Abraham and Moses, Elijah (who is reported to have raised a man from the dead and miraculously filled a widow's pitcher with milk centuries before Christ was said to have performed similar miracles), Elisha, Amos, Hosea, Joel, Micah, the dour and sorrowful Jeremiah (first to suggest that others besides Jews might share in the blessings of Jehovah-worship), Nahum, Habbakuk, Zephaniah, Ezekiel, Job of the many trials and great faith, Isaiah to whose loving Father-God all men were equal regardless of race, colour, or time or place of their births, and the deep-throated Daniel, saved by faith from the jaws of lions, who could dream and sing while he told of the holiness of Jehovah, and the glory which slept in the souls of men, waiting only for a reign of human righteousness to awaken it and vivify the human world.

But no nation has ever realized the visions of greatness seen by its spiritual leaders. Century by century the moral and religious practices of the Jews declined until, like coins which become so worn that their original values cannot be deciphered, they had little in common with the teachings of the great prophets. It was time for a new vision and a new leader.

Twelve hundred years after the death of Moses, about the time when Krishna in the *Bhagavad Gita* was calling India to righteous living and devotion to God, when Buddhism was flooding eastward into China and Japan, and Zoroastrianism was falling away from the greatness which its founder had brought to it, there was born in Bethlehem of Judea a Jew who was to descend upon the Hebrew congregation like a storm from heaven. Crying for repentance and rededication to God, he offered salvation in holy loving kindness to all who would follow him.

Jesus of Nazareth was well versed in the religion of his fathers and dedicated, as were those great religious leaders whose concepts he carried on, to worship of "the God of Abraham, the God of Isaac, and the God of Jacob," Jehovah, who was now seen as the one God, omnipotent ruler of the universe and loving father of mankind. As he grew to manhood Jesus saw a Hebrew nation whose religious life consisted largely in external observances, in rituals and sacrifices, in petty dietary laws and other domestic rules, rather than in that spiritual co-operation with God through humility, social righteousness, and faith of which the later prophets spoke. He saw a priestly class who hypocritically held themselves above others—as the priests of Hinduism did at the time of Gautama's birth—and a people who believed that they were the chosen of God and thus the superiors of all other peoples. Intolerance, bigotry, hypocrisy, and materialism were like acid poisons eating away the soul of Israel.

There were other great Jewish leaders who saw these things, others who were carrying on and advancing the religious thought of the prophets. One of the most notable of these, the incomparable Rabbi Hillel, was still living when Jesus was born. He preached the

Golden Rule of Reciprocity (which Confucius had taught in China and Gautama Buddha in India more than half a millennium before) and other principles of humility, worship of the one God, and universal brotherhood, which became such essential parts of Christ's doctrine. But the Hebrew nation as a whole heeded these exhortations as little as they had those of Isaiah—as little as the Christian nations of the twentieth century heed the doctrines of Jesus Christ.

The mission which Jesus set for himself was essentially no different from that to which Isaiah, Amos, Jeremiah, Ezekiel, Hillel, and the other great Jewish leaders had devoted their lives. Each of these and Jesus tried to bring understanding and a reawakened consciousness of the need of righteousness to his people, just as Confucius and Lao Tze in China, Gautama Buddha in India, and Zarathushtra in Persia had done. It was no part of the intention or effort of any one of these to overthrow the religion of his fathers and set up a new religion in its place. Many of Christ's most forceful admonitions, including his great commandments—"The Lord thy God is one God. Thou shalt love the Lord thy God with all thy heart, and thy neighbour as thyself"—were direct quotations from the Old Testament. The Golden Rule he quoted (with a slight change to make it positive instead of negative) from Hillel. He announced his purpose (Luke 4: 18-19) in the words of an Old Testament prophet: "The Lord annointed me to preach good tidings to the poor. He hath sent me to proclaim release to the captives and recovering of sight to the blind, to set at liberty them that are bruised, to proclaim the acceptable year of the Lord." (Isaiah 61: 1-2.) He said that he had come not to destroy, but to fulfil, the Jewish laws. He at all times observed the Jewish religious ceremonies rigorously.

Even his cry of despair on the cross, "My God, my God, why hast thou forsaken me?" evidenced his preoccupation with Hebrew religious texts, for it is a direct quotation from an Old Testament Psalm.

Racially and religiously Christ was born, lived, and died a loyal Jew, He sought merely to strengthen observance of the Jewish law and widen his people's understanding of the merciful, loving, Father-God whose Lordship was attested by the Jewish spiritual leaders who preceded him. He wanted to impress upon his people the doctrine that devotion to God was meaningless unless it was expressed first of all in devotion to one's fellow-men.

The life of Jesus is shrouded in mystery and mysticism. As in the earlier stories of Gautama Buddha and Zarathushtra, the scriptural story tells of the miraculous conception of Jesus, of homage paid to him at birth by wise men (probably Zoroastrian priests) who recognized his divinity, of his temptation by Satan (as Buddha was tempted by Mara and Zarathushtra assaulted by a personification of evil), of many miracles which he performed during his ministry, and, as a last proof of his divinity, of his resurrection after death.

Jesus' reception during his life was a stormy one. The multitudes, drawn by his tremendous personal magnetism and his never failing understanding and kindness, flocked to him, proclaimed his goodness and greatness, and many of them acknowledged him as the Son of God and the long-awaited Messiah. But powerful forces in the Jewish congregation, jealous of his popularity, incensed by his denunciation of some of them, and bitterly critical of his disregard for formalism, his willingness to violate some of the minor laws of the Jews, and his heretical claim that he was the Son of God, repudiated him, conspired to kill him, saw him crucified, and, after his death, persecuted his followers.

It is probably to that persecution that we owe the spread of Judeo-Christianity to the West and its influence upon modern life, for reaction from it produced the ministry of Paul. In the beginning those who followed the doctrines of Jesus, the Jew from Nazareth, were thought of merely as the representatives of a new Jewish sect, just as the first Buddhists were merely representatives of a new sect in Hinduism. There was nothing startling or revolutionary in the appearance of one more sect. Judaism had survived many divisions and the infusions of many interpretations. But the doctrine of Jesus, after his death, was singularly unsuccessful among the Jews. It was only when the convert, Paul, turned from the persecuting Jews and began his almost fanatic proselytizing among the Gentiles that the doctrine spread into Greece and Rome and thence to the rest of the Western World.

During Paul's ministry, in the first century after the death of Jesus, the followers of Christ's doctrine (or more properly the followers of Christ's doctrine as interpreted by Paul and his colleagues) definitely left the Jewish congregation, called themselves Christians, and established the Christian Church at Antioch. Thus occurred the greatest and most tragic schism in the religious history of the Western World, and one which Christ himself never intended and never foresaw.

None of the story of Jesus in any form which is now extant was recorded during his lifetime. The earliest writings of the New Testament are in the Acts of the Apostles and the Pauline Epistles, written A.D. 50-65. The four Gospels, which tell the story of Christ's life, were written A.D. 65-150. The three called "the Synoptics" because they "see together" or present substantially

the same point of view (Matthew, Mark, and Luke)
were written first. The last, the Gospel of John, was
written much later and presents a somewhat different
theological concept which has much that relates it to
the religions of India and China. "In the beginning
was the Word," John writes, "and the Word was with
God, and the Word was God." Thus he was presenting
a concept which was very like that of the Tao in Taoism
and the Brahman of the *Upanishads*. Indeed, Chinese
translations of the Gospel of John begin, "In the beginning was the *Tao*, and the *Tao* was with God, and the
Tao was God," repeating the concept of one of the
verses of the *Tao-Te King*, basic scripture of Taoism.

There are logical questions to be asked, pertinent to
contemporary social problems, in view of the history
of New Testament writing. Would the Gospels, and
thus the story of the life of Christ, ever have been
written at all and preserved for us had it not been for
the passionate ministry of Paul and his colleagues?
How much of the point of view in the Gospels, the Acts
of the Apostles, and the Epistles, how much of the
point of view of the Christian Church to-day, and how
much of the separation between Jew and Gentile to-
day, rise directly from Paul's point of view rather than
from the doctrines of Christ himself? These questions
have been asked many times and no attempt to answer
them will be made here. They are raised simply because they are healthy questions for the mind of any
one approaching the subject of Christ's place in the
religious history of the Western World or the subject
of a world emerging from the most destructive war in
history and hoping for a society based upon the brotherhood of man. They are raised because they emphasize
once more the indisputable fact that Jesus (regardless
of the question of his special divinity, which Christians

assert and Jews deny) was one in a long line of great Jewish spiritual leaders who together gave the world the religious and ethical foundations of Western civilization which are threatened to-day by a vast complex of international antagonisms.

The Christian cannot, if he wishes to understand his own beliefs, separate Christ from his predecessors, nor can the Jew, if he wishes to understand the full flowering of the religious thought of his Old Testament prophets, ignore its logical development in the doctrine of Jesus Christ. That there should ever have been any separation between the doctrines of Israel and those of Christianity is a sad commentary on the Jew's lack of understanding of Isaiah, Ezekiel, Hillel, and his other great leaders, and the Christian's lack of understanding of the Jew whom he calls Saviour.

The sacred books of the Jew and the Christian are contained in what the Western World calls the Holy Bible, of which the Old Testament only is acknowledged by the orthodox Jew, while the Christian Church has added to it the New Testament containing the Gospels, the Pauline writings, and certain other books. During the early years of the Christian Church there was a movement by the Christians to abolish the Old Testament entirely and to accept only the New as the Christian Bible. Fortunately it failed, else Christianity would have been robbed of far the greater part of its scriptures, including the scriptural bases on which Christ built his doctrine.

The Old Testament of Judaism contains 39 books arranged in three groups known as the Law (the first five books, called the *Torah* by Jews and the *Pentateuch* by Christians), the Prophets, and the Writings. These books are still read in the original (Hebrew, with the exception of about half the book of Daniel, parts of Ezra, and one verse of Jeremiah, which are in Aramaic) in all orthodox Jewish synagogues. In the Christian Bible they have been rearranged into 39 books. The New Testament consists of 27 books which were originally written in Greek during the first century of the Christian era.

There are also other books, which are considered apocryphal by many. But those of the Old Testament Apocrypha are still included in the Bibles of the Greek and Roman Catholic Churches, which also take some of their traditions from the New Testament Apocrypha, though they do not include the books of this group in their Bible.

None of these apocryphal books are included in this volume. (For extensive selections from both New and Old Testament Apocrypha, see *The Bible of the World.*) Here selections from the Old Testament and the New are given in one group, as by far the largest part of the Western World knows them.

JUDEO-CHRISTIAN
SCRIPTURES

THE OLD TESTAMENT

From the Book of Genesis

Creation

In the beginning God created the heaven and the earth. And the earth was without form and void; and darkness was upon the face of the deep; and the Spirit of God moved upon the face of the waters.

And God said, Let there be light: and there was light. And God saw the light that it was good: and God divided the light from the darkness. And God called the light Day, and the darkness he called Night: and the evening and the morning were the first day.

And God said, Let there be a firmament in the midst of the waters; and let it divide the waters from the waters. And God made the firmament, and divided the waters which were under the firmament from the waters which were above the firmament: and it was so. And God called the firmament Heaven: and the evening and the morning were the second day.

And God said, Let the waters under the heaven be gathered together unto one place, and let the dry land appear: and it was so. And God called the dry land Earth; and the gathering together of the waters called the Seas: and God saw that it was good.

And God said, Let the earth bring forth grass, the herb yielding seed, and fruit yielding fruit after his kind, whose seed is in itself, upon the earth: and it was so. And the earth brought forth grass, and herb yielding seed after his kind, and the tree yielding fruit, whose seed was in itself, after his kind: and God saw that it was good.

And the evening and the morning were the third day.

And God said, Let there be lights in the firmament of the heaven, to divide the day from the night; and let them be for signs, and for seasons, and for days, and years. And let them be for lights in the firmament of the heaven to give light upon the earth: and it was so. And God made two great lights; the greater light to rule the day, and the lesser light to rule the night: he made the stars also. And God set them in the firmament of the heaven to give light upon the earth, and to rule over the day, and over the night, and to divide the light from the darkness: and God saw that it was good.

And the evening and the morning were the fourth day.

And God said, Let the waters bring forth abundantly the moving creature that hath life, and fowl that may fly above the earth in the open firmament of heaven. And God created great whales, and every living creature that moveth, which the waters brought forth abundantly after their kind, and every winged fowl after his kind: and God saw that it was good. And God blessed them, saying, Be fruitful and multiply, and fill the waters in the seas, and let fowl multiply in the earth.

And the evening and the morning were the fifth day.

And God said, Let the earth bring forth the living creature after his kind, cattle, and creeping thing, and beast of the earth after his kind: and it was so. And God made the beast of the earth after his kind, and cattle after their kind, and everything that creepeth upon the earth after his kind: and God saw that it was good.

And God said, Let us make man in our image, after our likeness: and let them have dominion over the fish of the sea, and over the fowl of the air, and over the cattle, and over all the earth, and over every creeping thing that creepeth upon the earth. So God created man in his own image, in the image of God created he him; male and female created he them. And God blessed them, and God said unto them, Be fruitful, and multiply, and replenish the earth, and subdue it: and have dominion over the fish of the sea, and over the fowl of the air, and over every living thing that moveth upon the earth.

And God said, Behold, I have given you every herb bearing seed, which is upon the face of all the earth, and every tree, in the which is the fruit of a tree yielding seed; to you it shall be for meat. And to every beast of the earth, and to every fowl of the air, and to every thing that creepeth upon the earth, wherein there is life, I have given every green herb for meat: and it was so.

And God saw every thing that he had made: and behold, it was very good. And the evening and the morning were the sixth day.

The Garden of Eden

Thus the heavens and the earth were finished, and all the host of them. And on the seventh day God ended his work which he had made; and he rested on the seventh day from all his work which he had made. And God blessed the seventh day, and sanctified it: because that in it he had rested from all his work which God created and made.

These are the generations of the heavens and of the earth when they were created, in the day that the Lord God made the earth and the heavens, and every plant of the field before it was in the earth, and every herb of the field before it grew: for the Lord God had not caused it to rain upon the earth, and there was not a man to till the ground. But there went up a mist from the earth, and watered the whole face of the ground. And the Lord God formed man of the dust of the ground, and breathed into his nostrils the breath of life; and man became a living soul.

And the Lord God planted a garden eastward in Eden; and there he put the man whom he had formed. And out of the ground made the Lord God to grow every tree that is pleasant to the sight, and good for food; the tree of life also in the midst of the garden; and the tree of knowledge of good and evil.

And the Lord God took the man, and put him into the garden of Eden, to dress it, and to keep it.

And the Lord God commanded the man, saying, Of every tree of the garden thou mayest freely eat: but of the tree of the knowledge of good and evil, thou shalt not eat of it: for in the day that thou eatest thereof thou shalt surely die.

And the Lord God said, It is not good that the man should be alone: I will make him an help meet for him.

And out of the ground the Lord God formed every beast of the field, and every fowl of the air, and brought them unto Adam to see what he would call them; and whatsoever Adam called every living creature, that was the name thereof. And Adam gave names to all cattle, and to the fowl of the air, and to every beast of the field: but for Adam there was not found an help meet for him.

And the Lord God caused a deep sleep to fall upon Adam, and he slept; and he took one of his ribs, and closed up the flesh instead thereof: and the rib, which the Lord God had taken from man, made he a woman, and brought her unto the man.

And Adam said, This is now bone of my bones, and flesh of my flesh: she shall be called Woman, because she was taken out of man. Therefore shall a man leave his father and his mother, and shall cleave unto his wife: and they shall be one flesh. And they were both naked, the man and his wife, and were not ashamed.

The Fall of Man

Now the serpent was more subtle than any beast of the field which the Lord God had made: and he said unto the woman, Yea, hath God said, Ye shall not eat of every tree of the garden?

And the woman said unto the serpent, We may eat of the fruit of the trees of the garden: but of the fruit of the tree which is in the midst of the garden, God hath said, Ye shall not eat of it, neither shall ye touch it, lest ye die.

And the serpent said unto the woman, Ye shall not surely die: for God doth know, that in the day ye eat thereof, then your eyes shall be opened; and ye shall be as gods, knowing good and evil.

And when the woman saw that the tree was good for food, and that it was pleasant to the eyes, and a tree to be desired to make one wise; she took of the fruit thereof, and did eat; and gave also unto her husband with her, and he did eat. And the eyes of them both were opened, and they knew that they were naked: and they sewed fig-leaves together, and made themselves aprons.

And they heard the voice of the Lord God walking in the garden in the cool of the day: and Adam and his wife hid themselves from the presence of the Lord God amongst the trees of the garden.

And the Lord God called unto Adam, and said unto him, Where art thou?

And he said, I heard thy voice in the garden: and I was afraid, because I was naked; and I hid myself.

And he said, Who told thee that thou wast naked? Hast thou eaten of the tree whereof I commanded thee, that thou shouldest not eat?

And the man said, The woman whom thou gavest to be with me, she gave me of the tree, and I did eat.

And the Lord God said unto the woman, What is this that thou hast done? And the woman said, The serpent beguiled me, and I did eat.

And the Lord God said unto the serpent, Because thou hast done this, thou art cursed above all cattle, and above every beast of the field: upon thy belly shalt thou go, and dust shalt thou eat all the days of thy life: and I will put enmity between thee and the woman, and between thy seed and her seed: it shall bruise thy head, and thou shalt bruise his heel.

Unto the woman he said, I will greatly multiply thy sorrow and thy conception; in sorrow thou shalt bring forth children: and thy desire shall be to thy husband, and he shall rule over thee.

And unto Adam he said, Because thou hast hearkened unto the voice of thy wife, and hast eaten of the tree of which I commanded thee, saying, Thou shalt not eat of it: cursed is the ground for thy sake; in sorrow shalt thou eat of it all the days of thy life; thorns also and thistles shall it bring forth to thee; and thou shalt eat the herb of the field: in the sweat of thy face shalt thou eat bread, till thou return unto the ground;

for out of it wast thou taken: for dust thou art, and unto dust shalt thou return.

And Adam called his wife's name Eve, because she was the mother of all living.

Unto Adam also and to his wife did the Lord God make coats of skins, and clothed them.

And the Lord God said, Behold, the man is become as one of us, to know good and evil: and now, lest he put forth his hand, and take also of the tree of life, and eat, and live for ever: therefore the Lord God sent him forth from the garden of Eden, to till the ground from whence he was taken.

So he drove out the man: and he placed at the east of the garden of Eden cherubims, and a flaming sword which turned every way, to keep the way of the tree of life.

The Murder of Abel

And Adam knew Eve his wife; and she conceived, and bare Cain, and said, I have gotten a man from the Lord. And she again bare his brother Abel: and Abel was a keeper of sheep, but Cain was a tiller of the ground.

And in process of time it came to pass, that Cain brought of the fruit of the ground an offering unto the Lord. And Abel, he also brought of the firstlings of his flock, and of the fat thereof. And the Lord had respect unto Abel, and to his offering: but unto Cain, and to his offering, he had not respect: and Cain was very wroth, and his countenance fell.

And the Lord said unto Cain, Why art thou wroth? And why is thy countenance fallen? If thou doest well, shalt thou not be accepted? and if thou doest not well, sin lieth at the door.

And Cain talked with Abel his brother: and it came

to pass when they were in the field, that Cain rose up against Abel his brother, and slew him.

And the Lord said unto Cain, Where is Abel thy brother? And he said, I know not: Am I my brother's keeper?

And he said, What hast thou done? the voice of thy brother's blood crieth unto me from the ground. And now art thou cursed from the earth, which hath opened her mouth to receive thy brother's blood from thy hand. When thou tillest the ground, it shall not henceforth yield unto thee her strength: A fugitive and a vagabond shalt thou be in the earth.

And Cain said unto the Lord, My punishment is greater than I can bear. Behold, thou hast driven me out this day from the face of the earth; and from thy face shall I be hid; and I shall be a fugitive and a vagabond in the earth; and it shall come to pass, that everyone that findeth me shall slay me.

And the Lord said unto him, Therefore, whosoever slayeth Cain, vengeance shall be taken on him sevenfold. And the Lord set a mark upon Cain, lest any finding him should kill him.

And Cain went out from the presence of the Lord, and dwelt in the land of Nod, on the east of Eden.

The Making of the Ark

And it came to pass, when men began to multiply on the face of the earth, and daughters were born unto them, that the sons of God saw the daughters of men that they were fair; and they took them wives of all which they chose.

And the Lord said, My Spirit shall not always strive with man, for that he also is flesh: yet his days shall be an hundred and twenty years.

There were giants in the earth in those days, and also after that, when the sons of God came in unto the daughters of men, and they bare children to them: the same became mighty men, which were of old, men of renown.

And God saw that the wickedness of man was great in the earth, and that every imagination of the thoughts of his heart was only evil continually. And it repented the Lord that he had made man on the earth, and it grieved him at his heart.

And the Lord said, I will destroy man whom I have created from the face of the earth; both man and beast, and the creeping thing, and the fowls of the air; for it repenteth me that I have made them.

But Noah found grace in the eyes of the Lord. And Noah begat three sons, Shem, Ham, and Japheth.

And God said unto Noah, The end of all flesh is come before me; for the earth is filled with violence through them: and behold, I will destroy them with the earth. Make thee an ark of gopher-wood: rooms shalt thou make in the ark, and shalt pitch it within and without with pitch.

A window shalt thou make to the ark, and in a cubit shalt thou finish it above; and the door of the ark shalt thou set in the side thereof: with lower, second, and third stories shalt thou make it.

And behold, I, even I, do bring a flood of waters upon the earth, to destroy all flesh, wherein is the breath of life, from under heaven: and everything that is in the earth shall die.

But with thee will I establish my covenant: and thou shalt come into the ark, thou, and thy sons, and thy wife, and thy sons' wives with thee. And of every living thing of all flesh, two of every sort shalt thou bring into the ark, to keep them alive with thee: they shall be male and female. Of fowls after their kind, and of cattle after their kind, of every creeping thing of the earth after his kind; two of every sort shall come unto thee, to keep them alive.

And take thou unto thee of all food that is eaten, and thou shalt gather it to thee; and it shall be for food for thee, and for them.

Thus did Noah; according to all that God commanded him, so did he.

The Flood

And the Lord said unto Noah, Come thou and all thy house into the ark: for thee have I seen righteous before me in this generation.

And Noah did according unto all that the Lord commanded him. And Noah was six hundred years old when the flood of waters was upon the earth.

And Noah went in, and his sons, and his wife, and his sons' wives with him, into the ark, because of the waters of the flood. Of clean beasts, and of beasts that are not clean, and of fowls, and of everything that creepeth upon the earth, there went in two and two unto Noah into the ark, the male and the female, as God had commanded Noah.

And it came to pass, after seven days, that the waters of the flood were upon the earth. And the rain was upon the earth forty days and forty nights. And the waters prevailed, and were increased greatly upon the earth: and the ark went upon the face of the waters.

And the waters prevailed exceedingly upon the earth: and all the high hills that were under the whole heaven were covered. Fifteen cubits upward did the waters prevail: and the mountains were covered. And all flesh died that moved upon the earth, both of fowl, and of cattle, and of beast, and of every creeping thing that creepeth upon the earth, and every man: all in whose nostrils was the breath of life, of all that was in the dry land, died. Noah only remained alive, and they that were with him in the ark.

And the waters prevailed upon the earth an hundred and fifty days.

And God remembered Noah, and every living thing, and all the cattle that was with him in the ark: and God made a wind to pass over the earth, and the waters assuaged. The fountains also of the deep, and the windows of heaven were stopped, and the rain from heaven was restrained. And the waters returned from off the earth continually: and after the end of the hundred and fifty days the waters were abated.

And it came to pass in the six hundredth and first year, in the first month, the first day of the month, the waters were dried up from off the earth: and Noah removed the covering of the ark, and looked, and behold, the face of the ground was dry. And in the second month, on the seven and twentieth day of the month, was the earth dried.

And Noah went forth, and his sons, and his wife, and his sons' wives with him: every beast, every creeping thing, and every fowl, and whatsoever creepeth upon the earth, after their kinds, went forth out of the ark.

And Noah builded an altar unto the Lord, and took of every clean beast, and of every clean fowl, and offered burnt-offerings on the altar.

And the Lord smelled a sweet savour; and the Lord said in his heart, I will not again curse the ground any more for man's sake; for the imagination of man's heart is evil from his youth: neither will I again smite any more every thing living, as I have done. While the earth remaineth, seed-time and harvest, and cold and heat, and summer and winter, and day and night, shall not cease.

God's Covenant with Noah

And God blessed Noah and his sons, and said unto them, Be fruitful, and multiply, and replenish the earth. And the fear of you, and the dread of you, shall be upon every beast of the earth, and upon every fowl of the air, upon all that moveth upon the earth, and upon all the fishes of the sea; into your hand are they delivered. Every moving thing that liveth shall be meat for you; even as the green herb have I given you all things. But flesh with the life thereof, which is the blood thereof, shall ye not eat.

And surely your blood of your lives will I require: at the hand of every beast will I require it, and at the hand of man; at the hand of every man's brother will I require the life of man. Whoso sheddeth man's blood, by man shall his blood be shed: for in the image of God made he man.

And God spake unto Noah, and to his sons with him, saying: And I, behold, I establish my covenant with you, and with your seed after you; and with every living creature that is with you, of the fowl, of the cattle, and of every beast of the earth with you, from all that go out of the ark, to every beast of the earth. And I will establish my covenant with you; neither shall all flesh be cut off any more by the waters of a flood; neither shall there any more be a flood to destroy the earth.

And God said: This is the token of the covenant which I make between me and you, and every living creature that is with you, for perpetual generations. I do set my bow in the cloud, and it shall be for a token of a covenant between me and the earth. And it shall come to pass, when I bring a cloud over the earth, that the bow shall be seen in the cloud: and I will remember my covenant, which is between me and you, and every living creature of all flesh; and the waters shall no more become a flood to destroy all flesh.

And the sons of Noah that went forth of the ark, were Shem, and Ham, and Japheth: and Ham is the father of Canaan. These are the three sons of Noah: and of them was the whole earth overspread.

The Tower of Babel

And the whole earth was of one language, and of one speech. And it came to pass, as they journeyed from the east, that they found a plain in the land of Shinar; and they dwelt there.

And they said one to another, Go to, let us make brick, and burn them thoroughly. And they had brick for stone, and slime had they for mortar.

And they said, Go to, let us build us a city, and a tower, whose top may reach unto heaven; and let us make us a name, lest we be scattered abroad upon the face of the whole earth.

And the Lord came down to see the city and the tower, which the children of men builded.

And the Lord said, Behold, the people is one, and they have all one language; and this they began to do: and now nothing will be restrained from them, which they have imagined to do. Go to, let us go down, and there confound their language, that they may not understand one another's speech.

So the Lord scattered them abroad from thence upon

the face of all the earth: and they left off to build the city. Therefore is the name of it called Babel, because the Lord did there confound the language of all the earth: and from thence did the Lord scatter them abroad upon the face of all the earth.

God's Covenant with Abraham

Now the Lord had said unto Abram, Get thee out of thy country, and from thy kindred, and from thy father's house, unto a land that I will shew thee: and I will make of thee a great nation, and I will bless thee, and make thy name great; and thou shalt be a blessing: and I will bless them that bless thee, and curse him that curseth thee: and in thee shall all families of the earth be blessed.

So Abram departed, as the Lord had spoken unto him, and passed through the land unto the place of Sichem, unto the plain of Moreh. And the Canaanite was then in the land.

And the Lord appeared unto Abram, and said, Unto thy seed will I give this land: and there builded he an altar unto the Lord, who appeared unto him.

And he removed from thence unto a mountain on the east of Beth-el, and pitched his tent, having Beth-el on the west, and Hai on the east: and there he builded an altar unto the Lord, and called upon the name of the Lord.

And Abram journeyed, going on still toward the south.

And there was a famine in the land: and Abram went down into Egypt to sojourn there; for the famine was grievous in the land.

And when Abram was ninety years old and nine, the Lord appeared to Abram, and said unto him, I am the

Almighty God; walk before me, and be thou perfect.
And I will make my covenant between me and thee,
and will multiply thee exceedingly.

And Abram fell on his face: and God talked with
him, saying, As for me, behold, my covenant is with
thee, and thou shalt be a father of many nations. Neither
shall thy name any more be called Abram; but thy
name shall be Abraham: for a father of many nations
have I made thee. And I will make thee exceedingly
fruitful, and I will make nations of thee; and kings
shall come out of thee.

And I will establish my covenant between me and
thee, and thy seed after thee, in their generations, for
an everlasting covenant; to be a God unto thee, and to
thy seed after thee. And I will give unto thee, and to
thy seed after thee, the land wherein thou art a stranger,
all the land of Canaan, for an everlasting possession;
and I will be their God.

This is my covenant, which ye shall keep, between me
and you, and thy seed after thee; Every man-child
among you shall be circumcised. And ye shall circum-
cise the flesh of your foreskin; and it shall be a token
of the covenant betwixt me and you. And he that is
eight days old shall be circumcised among you, every
man-child in your generations, he that is born in the
house, or bought with money of any stranger, which is
not of thy seed. He that is born in thy house, and he
that is bought with thy money, must needs be circumcised: and my covenant shall be in your flesh for an
everlasting covenant. And the uncircumcised man-child,
whose flesh of his foreskin is not circumcised, that soul
shall be cut off from his people; he hath broken my
covenant.

And God said unto Abraham, As for Sarai thy wife,
thou shalt not call her name Sarai, but Sarah shall her

name be. And I will bless her, and give thee a son also of her: yea, I will bless her, and she shall be a mother of nations; kings of people shall be of her.

Then Abraham fell upon his face, and laughed, and said in his heart, Shall a child be born unto him that is an hundred years old? and shall Sarah, that is ninety years old, bear?

And Abraham said unto God, O that Ishmael might live before thee!

And God said, Sarah thy wife shall bear thee a son indeed; and thou shall call his name Isaac; and I will establish my covenant with him for an everlasting covenant, and with his seed after him. And as for Ishmael, I have heard thee: Behold, I have blessed him, and will make him fruitful, and will multiply him exceedingly: twelve princes shall he beget, and I will make him a great nation.

But my covenant will I establish with Isaac, which Sarah shall bear unto thee at this set time in the next year. And he left off talking with him, and God went up from Abraham.

And Abraham took Ishmael his son, and all that were born in his house, and all that were bought with his money, every male among the men of Abraham's house; and circumcised the flesh of their foreskin, in the self-same day, as God had said unto him. And Abraham was ninety years old and nine, when he was circumcised in the flesh of his foreskin.

The Birth of Isaac

And Abraham journeyed from thence toward the south country, and dwelled between Kadesh and Shur, and sojourned in Gerar.

And the Lord visited Sarah as he had said, and the Lord did unto Sarah as he had spoken. For Sarah conceived, and bare Abraham a son in his old age, at the set time of which God had spoken to him. And Abraham called the name of his son that was born unto him, whom Sarah bare to him, Isaac. And Abraham circumcised his son Isaac, being eight days old, as God had commanded him. And Abraham was an hundred years old, when his son Isaac was born unto him.

And Sarah said, God hath made me to laugh, so that all that hear will laugh with me. Who would have said unto Abraham, that Sarah should have given children suck? for I have borne him a son in his old age.

Esau and Jacob

And Abraham gave all that he had unto Isaac.

And these are the days of the years of Abraham's life which he lived, an hundred threescore and fifteen years.

Then Abraham gave up the ghost, and died in a good old age, an old man, and full of years; and was gathered to his people. And his sons Isaac and Ishmael buried him in the cave of Machpelah, in the field of Ephron the son of Zohar the Hittite, which is before Mamre; the field which Abraham purchased of the sons of Heth: there was Abraham buried, and Sarah his wife.

And it came to pass after the death of Abraham, that God blessed his son Isaac; and Isaac dwelt by the well Lahai-roi.

And these are the generations of Isaac, Abraham's son: Abraham begat Isaac: and Isaac was forty years

old when he took Rebekah to wife, the daughter of
Bethuel the Syrian of Padan-aram, the sister to Laban
the Syrian.

And Isaac entreated the Lord for his wife, because
she was barren: and the Lord was entreated of him,
and Rebekah his wife conceived. And the children
struggled together within her; and she said, If it be
so, why am I thus? And she went to inquire of the
Lord.

And the Lord said unto her, Two nations are in thy
womb, and two manner of people shall be separated
from thy bowels; and the one people shall be stronger
than the other people; and the elder shall serve the
younger.

And when her days to be delivered were fulfilled,
behold, there were twins in her womb. And the first
came out red, all over like an hairy garment: and they
called his name Esau. And after that came his brother
out, and his hand took hold on Esau's heel; and his
name was called Jacob: and Isaac was three-score years
old when she bare them.

The Family of Jacob

And God said unto Jacob, Arise, go up to Beth-el,
and dwell there: and make there an altar unto God.

Then Jacob said unto his household, and to all that
were with him, Put away the strange gods that are
among you, and be clean and change your garments:
and let us arise, and go up to Beth-el; and I will make
there an altar unto God.

And they gave unto Jacob all the strange gods which
were in their hand, and all their ear-rings which were
in their ears; and Jacob hid them under the oak which
was by Shechem.

And they journeyed: and the terror of God was upon the cities that were round about them, and they did not pursue after the sons of Jacob. So Jacob came to Luz, which is in the land of Canaan, that is Beth-el, he and all the people that were with him.

And God appeared unto Jacob again when he came out of Padan-aram; and blessed him. And God said unto him, Thy name is Jacob: thy name shall not be called any more Jacob, but Israel shall be thy name; and he called his name Israel. And God said unto him, I am God Almighty: be fruitful and multiply; a nation and a company of nations shall be of thee, and kings shall come out of thy loins.

And they journeyed from Beth-el; and there was but a little way to come to Ephrath; and Rachel travailed, and she had hard labour. And it came to pass, when she was in hard labour, that the midwife said unto her, Fear not; thou shalt have this son also. And it came to pass, as her soul was departing (for she died), that she called his name Benoni: but his father called him Benjamin.

And Rachel died, and was buried in the way to Ephrath.

Now the sons of Jacob were twelve: the sons of Leah: Reuben, Jacob's first-born, and Simeon, and Levi, and Judah, and Issachar, and Zebulun; the sons of Rachel: Joseph, and Benjamin; and the sons of Bilhah, Rachel's handmaid: Dan, and Naphtali; and the sons of Zilpah, Leah's handmaid: Gad, and Asher. These are the sons of Jacob, which were born to him in Padan-aram.

Joseph Is Sold by His Brothers

Now Israel loved Joseph more than all his children, because he was the son of his old age: and he made him a coat of many colours. And when his brethren saw that their father loved him more than all his brethren, they hated him, and could not speak peaceably unto him.

And Joseph dreamed a dream. And he said unto them, Hear, I pray you, this dream which I have dreamed: for, behold, we were binding sheaves in the field, and, lo, my sheaf arose, and also stood upright; and, behold, your sheaves stood round about, and made obeisance to my sheaf.

And his brethren said to him, Shalt thou indeed reign over us? Or shalt thou indeed have dominion over us? And they hated him yet the more for his dreams, and for his words.

And he dreamed yet another dream, and told it his brethren, and said, Behold, I have dreamed a dream more: and, behold, the son and the moon and the eleven stars made obeisance to me. And he told it to his father, and to his brethren: and his father rebuked him, and said unto him, What is this dream that thou has dreamed? Shall I and thy mother and thy brethren indeed come to bow down ourselves to thee to the earth? And his brethren envied him; but his father observed the saying.

And his brethren went to feed their father's flock in Shechem.

And Israel said unto Joseph, Do not thy brethren feed the flock in Shechem? Come, and I will send thee unto them. And he said to him, Here am I.

And he said to him, Go, I pray thee, see whether it be well with thy brethren, and well with the flocks; and bring me word again. So he sent him out of the vale of Hebron, and he came to Shechem.

And Joseph went after his brethren, and found them. And when they saw him afar off, even before he came near unto them, they conspired against him to slay him.

And they said one to another, Behold, this dreamer cometh. Come now therefore, and let us slay him, and cast him into some pit; and we will say, Some evil beast hath devoured him: and we shall see what will become of his dreams.

And Reuben heard it, and he delivered him out of their hands; and said, Let us not kill him. Shed no blood, but cast him into this pit that is in the wilderness, and lay no hand upon him; that he might rid him out of their hands, to deliver him to his father again.

And it came to pass, when Joseph was come unto his brethren, that they stript Joseph out of his coat, his coat of many colours that was on him. And they took him, and cast him into a pit: and the pit was empty, there was no water in it. And they sat down to eat bread: and they lifted up their eyes and looked, and behold, a company of Ishmaelites came from Gilead, with their camels bearing spicery, and balm, and myrrh, going to carry it down to Egypt.

And Judah said unto his brethren, What profit is it if we slay our brother, and conceal his blood? Come, and let us sell him to the Ishmaelites, and let not our hand be upon him; for he is our brother, and our flesh: and his brethren were content.

Then there passed by Midianites, merchant-men: and they drew and lifted up Joseph out of the pit, and sold Joseph to the Ishmaelites for twenty pieces of silver: and they brought Joseph into Egypt.

And Reuben returned unto the pit; and, behold, Joseph was not in the pit; and he rent his clothes. And he returned unto his brethren, and said, The child is not: and I, whither shall I go?

And they took Joseph's coat, and killed a kid of the goats, and dipped the coat in the blood; and they sent the coat of many colours, and they brought it to their father; and said, This have we found: know now whether it be thy son's coat or no.

And he knew it, and said, It is my son's coat; an evil beast hath devoured him: Joseph is without doubt rent in pieces.

And Jacob rent his clothes, and put sackcloth upon his loins, and mourned for his son many days. And all his sons and all his daughters rose up to comfort him; but he refused to be comforted; and he said, For I will go down into the grave unto my son mourning. Thus his father wept for him.

Joseph in Egypt

And Joseph was brought down to Egypt: and Potiphar, an officer of Pharoah, captain of the guard, an Egyptian, bought him of the hands of the Ishmaelites, which had brought him down thither.

And Joseph found grace in his sight, and he served him: and he made him overseer over his house, and all that he had he put into his hand. And it came to pass from the time that he had made him overseer in his house, and over all that he had, that the Lord blessed the Egyptian's house for Joseph's sake; and the blessing of the Lord was upon all that he had in the house, and in the field. And he left all that he had in Joseph's hand; and he knew not aught he had, save the bread which he did eat. And Joseph was a goodly person, and well-favoured.

And in seven plenteous years the earth brought forth by handfuls. And Joseph gathered up all the food of the seven years, which were in the land of Egypt, and laid up the food in the cities: the food of the field, which was round about every city, laid he up in the same.

And the seven years of plenteousness, that was in the land of Egypt, were ended. And seven years of dearth began to come, and the dearth was in all lands; but in all the land of Egypt there was bread. And all countries came into Egypt to Joseph for to buy corn; because that the famine was so sore in all lands.

Joseph's Brothers Go into Egypt

Now when Jacob saw that there was corn in Egypt, Jacob said unto his sons, Why do ye look one upon another? Behold, I have heard that there is corn in Egypt: get you down thither, and buy for us from thence; that we may live, and not die.

And Joseph's ten brethren went down to buy corn in Egypt. But Benjamin, Joseph's brother, Jacob sent not with his brethren: for he said, Lest peradventure mischief befall him.

And Joseph saw his brethren, and he knew them, but made himself strange unto them, and spake roughly unto them; and he said unto them, Whence come ye? And they said, From the land of Canaan to buy food.

And Joseph knew his brethren, but they knew not him.

And Joseph remembered the dreams which he dreamed of them, and said unto them, Ye are spies; to see the nakedness of the land ye are come.

And they said unto him, Nay, my lord, but to buy food are thy servants come.

And Joseph said unto them, Hereby ye shall be proved: by the life of Pharaoh ye shall not go forth hence, except your youngest brother come hither. Send one of you, and let him fetch your brother, and ye shall be kept in prison, that your words may be proved, whether there be any truth in you: or else, by the life of Pharaoh, surely ye are spies.

And he put them all together into ward three days, and said unto them the third day, This do, and live; for I fear God: if ye be true men, let one of your brethren be bound in the house of your prison: go ye, carry corn for the famine of your houses: but bring your youngest brother unto me; so shall your words be verified, and ye shall not die.

And Joseph turned himself about from them, and wept; and returned to them again, and communed with them, and took from them Simeon, and bound him before their eyes.

Then Joseph commanded to fill their sacks with corn, and to restore every man's money into his sack, and to give them provision for the way: and thus did he unto them. And they laded their asses with the corn, and departed thence. And as one of them opened his sack to give his ass provender in the inn, he espied his money: for, behold, it was in his sack's mouth.

And he said unto his brethren, My money is restored; and lo, it is even in my sack: and their heart failed them, and they were afraid, saying one to another, What is this that God hath done unto us?

And they came unto Jacob their father unto the land of Canaan, and told him all that befell unto them.

And the famine was sore in the land. And it came to pass, when they had eaten up the corn which they had brought out of Egypt, their father said unto them, Go again, buy us a little food.

And Judah spake unto him, saying, The man did solemnly protest unto us, saying, Ye shall not see my face, except your brother be with you.

And Judah said unto Israel his father, Send the lad

with me, and we will arise and go; that we may live, and not die, both we, and thou, and also our little ones. I will be surety for him; of my hand shalt thou require him: if I bring him not unto thee, and set him before thee, then let me bear the blame for ever: for except we had lingered, surely now we had returned this second time.

And their father Israel said unto them, If it must be so now, do this; take of the best fruits in the land in your vessels, and carry down the man a present, a little balm, and a little honey, spices, and myrrh, nuts, and almonds: and take double money in your hand; and the money that was brought again in the mouth of your sacks, carry it again in your hand; peradventure it was an oversight: take also your brother, and arise, go again unto the man: and God Almighty give you mercy before the man, that he may send away your other brother, and Benjamin. If I be bereaved of my children, I am bereaved.

And the men took that present, and they took double money in their hand, and Benjamin; and rose up, and went down to Egypt, and stood before Joseph. And when Joseph saw Benjamin with them, he said to the ruler of his house, Bring these men home, and slay, and make ready; for these men shall dine with me at noon.

And the man did as Joseph bade; and the man brought the men into Joseph's house. And the men were afraid, because they were brought into Joseph's house; and they said, Because of the money that was returned in our sacks at the first time, are we brought in; that he may seek occasion against us, and fall upon us and take us for bondmen, and our asses.

And they came near to the steward of Joseph's house, and they communed with him at the door of the house. And the man brought the men into Joseph's house, and gave them water, and they washed their feet; and he gave their asses provender. And they made ready the present against Joseph came at noon: for they heard that they should eat bread there.

And when Joseph came home, they brought him the present which was in their hand into the house, and bowed themselves to him to the earth.

And he asked them of their welfare, and said, Is your father well, the old man of whom ye spake? Is he yet alive?

And they answered, Thy servant our father is in good health, he is yet alive. And they bowed down their heads, and made obeisance.

And he lifted up his eyes, and saw his brother Benjamin, his mother's son, and said, Is this your younger brother, of whom ye spake unto me? And he said, God be gracious unto thee, my son.

And Joseph made haste; for his bowels did yearn upon his brother: and he sought where to weep; and he entered into his chamber, and wept there. And he washed his face, and went out, and refrained himself, and said, Set on bread.

And they set on for him by himself, and for them by themselves, and for the Egyptians, which did eat with him, by themselves: because the Egyptians might not eat bread with the Hebrews; for that is an abomination unto the Egyptians. And they sat before him, the first-born according to his birth-right, and the youngest according to his youth: and the men marvelled one at another. And he took and sent messes unto them from before him: but Benjamin's mess was five times so much as any of theirs. And they drank, and were merry with him.

Joseph and His Brothers Are Reconciled

And he commanded the steward of his house, saying, Fill the men's sacks with food, as much as they can carry, and put every man's money in his sack's mouth. And put my cup, the silver cup, in the sack's mouth of the youngest, and his corn-money. And he did according to the word that Joseph had spoken.

As soon as the morning was light, the men were sent away, they, and their asses. And when they were gone out of the city, and not yet far off, Joseph said unto his steward. Up, follow after the men; and when thou dost overtake them, say unto them, Wherefore have ye rewarded evil for good? Is not this it in which my lord drinketh, and whereby indeed he divineth? ye have done evil in so doing.

And he overtook them, and he spake unto them these same words. And they said unto him, Wherefore saith my lord these words? God forbid that thy servants should do according to this thing: behold, the money which we found in our sacks' mouths, we brought again unto thee out of the land of Canaan: how then should we steal out of thy lord's house silver or gold? With whomsoever of thy servants it be found, both let him die, and we also will be my lord's bondmen.

And he said, Now also let it be according unto your words: he with whom it is found shall be my servant; and ye shall be blameless.

Then they speedily took down every man his sack to the ground, and opened every man his sack. And he searched, and began at the eldest, and left at the youngest: and the cup was found in Benjamin's sack. Then they rent their clothes, and laded every man his ass, and returned to the city.

262 THE JEW AND THE CHRISTIAN

And Judah and his brethren came to Joseph's house; for he was yet there: and they fell before him on the ground.

And Joseph said unto them, What deed is this that ye have done? wot ye not that such a man as I can certainly divine?

And Judah said, What shall we say unto my lord? what shall we speak? or how shall we clear ourselves? God hath found out the iniquity of thy servants: behold we are my lord's servants, both we, and he also with whom the cup is found.

And he said, God forbid that I should do so: but the man in whose hand the cup is found, he shall be my servant; and as for you, get you up in peace unto your father.

Then Judah came near unto him, and said, O my lord, let thy servant, I pray thee, speak a word in my lord's ears, and let not thine anger burn against thy servant: for thou art even as Pharaoh. When I come to thy servant my father, and the lad be not with us; (seeing that his life is bound up in the lad's life;) he will die: and thy servants shall bring down the grey hairs of thy servant our father with sorrow to the grave. For thy servant became surety for the lad unto my father, saying, If I bring him not unto thee, then I shall bear the blame to my father for ever. Now therefore, I pray thee, let thy servant abide instead of the lad a bondman to my lord; and let the lad go up with his brethren. For how shall I go up to my father, and the lad be not with me? lest peradventure I see the evil that shall come to my father.

Then Joseph could not refrain himself before all them that stood by him; and he cried, Cause every man to go out from me: and there stood no man with him while Joseph made himself known unto his brethren. And he wept aloud; and the Egyptians and the house of Pharaoh heard.

And Joseph said unto his brethren, I am Joseph; doth my father yet live? And his brethren could not answer him; for they were troubled at his presence.

And Joseph said unto his brethren, Come near to me, I pray you: and they came near: and he said, I am Joseph your brother, whom ye sold into Egypt. Now therefore be not grieved, nor angry with yourselves, that ye sold me hither: for God did send me before you to preserve life. For these two years hath the famine been in the land: and yet there are five years, in the which there shall neither be earing nor harvest. And God sent me before you, to preserve you a posterity in the earth, and to save your lives by a great deliverance. So now it was not you that sent me hither, but God: and he hath made me a father to Pharaoh, and lord of all his house, and a ruler throughout all the land of Egypt. Haste ye, and go up to my father, and say unto him, Thus saith thy son Joseph, God hath made me lord of all Egypt; come down unto me, tarry not: and thou shalt dwell in the land of Goshen, and thou shalt be near unto me, thou, and thy children, and thy children's children, and thy flocks, and thy herds, and all that thou hast: and there will I nourish thee, (for yet there are five years of famine;) lest thou, and thy household, and all that thou hast, come to poverty. And, behold, your eyes see, and the eyes of my brother Benjamin, that it is my mouth that speaketh unto you. And ye shall tell my father of all my glory in Egypt, and of all that ye have seen: and ye shall haste, and bring down my father hither.

And he fell upon his brother Benjamin's neck, and

wept; and Benjamin wept upon his neck. Moreover, he kissed all his brethren, and wept upon them: and after that his brethren talked with him.

And they went up out of Egypt, and came into the land of Canaan unto Jacob their father, and told him, saying, Joseph is yet alive, and he is governor over all the land of Egypt. And Jacob's heart fainted, for he believed them not.

And they told him all the words of Joseph, which he had said unto them: and when he saw the wagons which Joseph had sent to carry him, the spirit of Jacob their father revived: and Israel said, It is enough; Joseph my son is yet alive: I will go and see him before I die.

And they took their cattle, and their goods, which they had gotten in the land of Canaan, and came into Egypt, Jacob, and all his seed with him; his sons, and his sons' sons with him, his daughters, and his sons' daughters, and all his seed brought he with him into Egypt.

The Death of Joseph

And Joseph dwelt in Egypt, he, and his father's house; and Joseph lived an hundred and ten years. And Joseph saw Ephraim's children of the third generation: the children also of Machir, the son of Manasseh, were brought up upon Joseph's knees.

And Joseph said unto his brethren, I die; and God will surely visit you, and bring you out of this land, unto the land which he sware to Abraham, to Isaac, and to Jacob. And Joseph took an oath of the children of Israel, saying, God will surely visit you, and ye shall carry up my bones from hence.

So Joseph died, being an hundred and ten years old: and they embalmed him, and he was put in a coffin in Egypt.

From the Book of Exodus

The Beginning of Persecution

And the children of Israel were fruitful, and increased abundantly, and multiplied, and waxed exceeding mighty; and the land was filled with them.

Now there arose up a new king over Egypt, which knew not Joseph. And he said unto his people, Behold, the people of the children of Israel are more and mightier than we. Come on, let us deal wisely with them; lest they multiply, and it come to pass, that, when there falleth out any war, they join also unto our enemies, and fight against us, and so get them up out of the land.

Therefore they did set over them task-masters, to afflict them with their burdens. And they built for Pharaoh treasure-cities, Pithom, and Raamses. But the more they afflicted them, the more they multiplied and grew. And they were grieved because of the children of Israel. And they made their lives bitter with hard bondage, in mortar, and in brick, and in all manner of service in the field: all their service wherein they made them serve was with rigour.

And the king of Egypt spake to the Hebrew midwives (of which the name of the one was Shiphrah, and the name of the other Puah;) and he said, When ye do the office of a midwife to the Hebrew women, and see them upon the stools; if it be a son, then ye shall kill him; but if it be a daughter, then she shall live.

But the midwives feared God, and did not as the king of Egypt commanded them, but saved the men-children alive.

The Birth of Moses

And there went a man of the house of Levi, and took to wife a daughter of Levi. And the woman conceived and bare a son: and when she saw him that he was a goodly child, she hid him three months. And when she could not longer hide him, she took for him an ark of bulrushes, and daubed it with slime and with pitch, and put the child therein; and she laid it on the flags by the river's brink. And his sister stood afar off, to wit what would be done to him.

And the daughter of Pharaoh came down to wash herself at the river; and her maidens walked along by the river's side: and when she saw the ark among the flags, she sent her maid to fetch it. And when she had opened it, she saw the child: and, behold, the babe wept. And she had compassion on him, and said, This is one of the Hebrews' children.

Then said his sister to Pharaoh's daughter, Shall I go, and call to thee a nurse of the Hebrew women, that she may nurse the child for thee?

And Pharaoh's daughter said to her, Go. And the maid went and called the child's mother.

And Pharaoh's daughter said unto her, Take this child away and nurse it for me, and I will give thee thy wages. And the woman took the child and nursed it.

And the child grew, and she brought him unto Pharaoh's daughter, and he became her son. And she called his name Moses: and she said, Because I drew him out of the water.

The Burning Bush and the Name of God

Now Moses kept the flock of Jethro his father-in-law, the priest of Midian: and he led the flock to the back side of the desert, and came to the mountain of God, even to Horeb.

And the Angel of the Lord appeared unto him in a flame of fire out of the midst of a bush; and he looked, and, behold, the bush burned with fire, and the bush was not consumed. And Moses said, I will now turn aside, and see this great sight, why the bush is not burnt.

And when the Lord saw that he turned aside to see, God called unto him out of the midst of the bush, and said, Moses, Moses! And he said, Here am I.

And he said, Draw not nigh hither: put off thy shoes from off thy feet; for the place whereon thou standest is holy ground. I am the God of thy father, the God of Abraham, the God of Isaac, and the God of Jacob.

And Moses hid his face; for he was afraid to look upon God.

And the Lord said, I have surely seen the affliction of my people which are in Egypt, and have heard their cry by reason of their taskmasters; for I know their sorrows: and I am come down to deliver them out of the hand of the Egyptians, and to bring them up out of that land, unto a good land, and a large, unto a land flowing with milk and honey; unto the place of the Canaanites, and the Hittites, and the Amorites, and the Perizzites, and the Hivites, and the Jebusites. Come now therefore, and I will send thee unto Pharaoh, that thou mayest bring forth my people, the children of Israel, out of Egypt.

And Moses said unto God, Who am I, that I should

go unto Pharaoh, and that I should bring forth the children of Israel out of Egypt?

And he said, Certainly I will be with thee; and this shall be a token unto thee, that I have sent thee: When thou hast brought forth the people out of Egypt, ye shall serve God upon this mountain.

And Moses said unto God, Behold, when I come unto the children of Israel, and shall say unto them, The God of your fathers hath sent me unto you; and they shall say to me, What is his name? what shall I say unto them?

And God said unto Moses, I AM THAT I AM: And he said, Thus shalt thou say unto the children of Israel, I AM hath sent me unto you.

The Passover Is Instituted

And the Lord spake unto Moses and Aaron in the land of Egypt, saying, This month shall be unto you the beginning of months: it shall be the first month of the year to you.

Speak ye unto all the congregation of Israel, saying, In the tenth day of this month they shall take to them every man a lamb according to the house of their fathers, a lamb for an house: and the whole assembly of the congregation of Israel shall kill it in the evening. And they shall take of the blood, and strike it on the two sideposts, and on the upper doorpost of the houses, wherein they shall eat it. And they shall eat the flesh in that night, roast with fire, and unleavened bread; and with bitter herbs they shall eat it.

And thus shall ye eat it; with your loins girded, your shoes on your feet, and your staff in your hand: and ye shall eat it in haste; it is the Lord's passover.

For I will pass through the land of Egypt this night, and will smite all the first-born in the land of Egypt,

both man and beast: and against all the gods of Egypt
I will execute judgment: I am the Lord. And the blood
shall be to you for a token upon the houses where ye
are: and when I see the blood, I will pass over you, and
the plague shall not be upon you to destroy you, when
I smite the land of Egypt.

And this day shall be unto you for a memorial; and
ye shall keep it a feast to the Lord throughout your
generations: ye shall keep it a feast by an ordinance
for ever. Seven days shall ye eat unleavened bread; even
the first day ye shall put away leaven out of your
houses: for whosoever eateth leavened bread, from the
first day until the seventh day, that soul shall be cut
off from Israel. And in the first day there shall be an
holy convocation, and in the seventh day there shall be
an holy convocation to you: no manner of work shall be
done in them, save that which every man must eat, that
only may be done of you.

And ye shall observe the feast of unleavened bread;
for in this selfsame day have I brought your armies out
of the land of Egypt; therefore shall ye observe this day
in your generations by an ordinance for ever. In the first
month, on the fourteenth day of the month at even, ye
shall eat unleavened bread, until the one and twentieth
day of the month at even.

Seven days shall there be no leaven found in your
houses: for whosoever eateth that which is leavened,
even that soul shall be cut off from the congregation of
Israel, whether he be a stranger, or born in the land. Ye
shall eat nothing leavened: in all your habitations shall
ye eat unleavened bread.

And the children of Israel went away, and did as the
Lord had commanded Moses and Aaron, so did they.

And it came to pass, that at midnight the Lord smote
all the first-born in the land of Egypt, from the first-

born of Pharaoh that sat on his throne, unto the first-born of the captive that was in the dungeon; and all the first-born of cattle.

And Pharaoh rose up in the night, he, and all his servar:s, and all the Egyptians; and there was a great cry in Egypt: for there was not a house where there was not one dead.

And he called for Moses and Aaron by night, and said, Rise up, and get you forth from among my people, both ye and the children of Israe!: and go, serve the Lord, as ye have said. Also take your flocks and your herds, as ye have said, and be gone: and bless me also. And the Egyptians were urgent upon the people, that they might send them out of the land in haste; for they said, We be all dead men.

And the people took their dough before it was leavened, their kneading troughs being bound up in their clothes upon their shoulders. And the children of Israel did according to the word of Moses: and they borrowed of the Egyptians jewels of silver, and jewels of gold, and raiment. And the Lord gave the people favour in the sight of the Egyptians, so that they lent unto them such things as they required: and they spoiled the Egyptians.

And the children of Israel journeyed from Rameses to Succoth, about six hundred thousand on foot that were men, beside children. And a mixed multitude went up also with them; and flocks, and herds, even very much cattle. And they baked unleavened cakes of the dough which they brought forth out of Egypt, for it was not leavened: because they were thrust out of Egypt, and could not tarry, neither had they prepared for themselves any victual.

Now the sojourning of the children of Israe! who dwelt in Egypt, was four hundred and thirty years.

They Cross the Red Sea

And it came to pass, when Pharaoh had let the people go, that God led them not through the way of the land of the Philistines, although that was near; for God said, Lest peradventure the people repent when they see war, and they return to Egypt: but God led the people about, through the way of the wilderness of the Red sea: and the children of Israel went up harnessed out of the land of Egypt.

And the Lord went before them by day in a pillar of a cloud, to lead them the way; and by night in a pillar of fire, to give them light: to go by day and night.

And it was told the king of Egypt that the people fled: and the heart of Pharaoh and of his servants was turned against the people, and they said, Why have we done this, that we have let Israel go from serving us?

And he made ready his chariot, and took his people with him: and he took six hundred chosen chariots, and all the chariots of Egypt, and captains over every one of them, and he pursued after the children of Israel.

And when Pharaoh drew nigh, the children of Israel lifted up their eyes, and behold, the Egyptians marched after them; and they were sore afraid: and the children of Israel cried out unto the Lord.

And the Lord said unto Moses, Wherefore criest thou unto me? Speak unto the children of Israel, that they go forward: but lift thou up thy rod, and stretch out thine hand over the sea, and divide it: and the children of Israel shall go on dry ground through the midst of the sea.

And the angel of God which went before the camp of Israel, removed, and went behind them; and the

pillar of the cloud went from before their face, and
stood behind them: and it came between the camp of
the Egyptians and the camp of Israel; and it was a
cloud and darkness to them, but it gave light by night
to these: so that the one came not near the other all
the night.

And the Egyptians pursued, and went in after them,
the Lord caused the sea to go back by a strong east
wind all that night, and made the sea dry land, and
the waters were divided. And the children of Israel
went into the midst of the sea upon the dry ground:
and the waters were a wall unto them on their right
hand, and on their left.

And the Egyptians pursued, and went in after them,
to the midst of the sea, even all Pharaoh's horses, his
chariots, and his horsemen. And it came to pass, that
in the morning-watch the Lord looked unto the host
of the Egyptians through the pillar of fire and of the
cloud, and troubled the host of the Egyptians, and took
off their chariot-wheels, that they drave them heavily:
so that the Egyptians said, Let us flee from the face of
Israel; for the Lord fighteth for them against the
Egyptians.

And the Lord said unto Moses, Stretch out thine hand
over the sea, that the waters may come again upon the
Egyptians, upon their chariots, and upon their horsemen.

And Moses stretched forth his hand over the sea, and
the sea returned to his strength when the morning appeared; and the Egyptians fled against it; and the Lord
overthrew the Egyptians in the midst of the sea. And
the waters returned, and covered the chariots, and the
horsemen, and all the host of Pharaoh that came into
the sea after them: there remained not so much as one
of them.

But the children of Israel walked upon dry land in the midst of the sea; and the waters were a wall unto them on their right hand, and on their left.

Thus the Lord saved Israel that day out of the hand of the Egyptians: and Israel saw the Egyptians dead upon the sea-shore.

God Gives Moses the Ten Commandments

In the third month, when the children of Israel were gone forth out of the land of Egypt, the same day came they into the wilderness of Sinai, and there Israel camped before the mount.

And the Lord came down upon mount Sinai, on the top of the mount: and the Lord called Moses up to the top of the mount; and Moses went up.

And God spake all these words, saying,

I am the Lord thy God, which have brought thee out of the land of Egypt, out of the house of bondage.

Thou shalt have no other gods before me.

Thou shalt not make unto thee any graven image, or any likeness of anything that is in heaven above, or that is in the earth beneath, or that is in the water under the earth: thou shalt not bow down thyself to them, nor serve them: for I the Lord thy God am a jealous God, visiting the iniquity of the fathers upon the children unto the third and fourth generation of them that hate me; and showing mercy unto thousands of them that love me, and keep my commandments.

Thou shalt not take the name of the Lord thy God in vain: for the Lord will not hold him guiltless that taketh his name in vain.

Remember the sabbath-day to keep it holy. Six days shalt thou labour, and do all thy work: but the seventh day is the sabbath of the Lord thy God: in it thou shalt not do any work, thou, nor thy son, nor thy daughter, thy man-servant, nor thy maid-servant, nor thy cattle, nor thy stranger that is within thy gates: for in six days the Lord made heaven and earth, the sea and all that in them is, and rested the seventh day: wherefore the Lord blessed the sabbath-day and hallowed it.

Honour thy father and thy mother; that thy days may be long upon the land which the Lord thy God giveth thee.

Thou shalt not kill.

Thou shalt not commit adultery.

Thou shalt not steal.

Thou shalt not bear false witness against thy neighbour.

Thou shalt not covet thy neighbour's house, thou shalt not covet thy neighbour's wife, nor his man-servant, nor his maid-servant, nor his ox, nor his ass, nor any thing that is thy neighbour's.

Further Laws

He that smiteth a man, so that he die, shall be surely put to death.

If men strive, and hurt a woman with child, so that her fruit depart from her, and yet no mischief follow: he shall be surely punished, according as the woman's husband will lay upon him; and he shall pay as the judges determine. And if any mischief follow, then thou shalt give life for life, eye for eye, tooth for tooth, hand for hand, foot for foot, burning for burning, wound for wound, stripe for stripe.

If a thief be found breaking up, and be smitten that he die, there shall no blood be shed for him.

And if a man entice a maid that is not betrothed,

and lie with her, he shall surely endow her to be his wife. If her father utterly refuse to give her unto him, he shall pay money according to the dowry of virgins.

Thou shalt not suffer a witch to live.

Whosoever lieth with a beast shall surely be put to death.

He that sacrificeth unto any god, save unto the Lord only, he shall be utterly destroyed.

Thou shalt neither vex a stranger, nor oppress him: for ye were strangers in the land of Egypt.

Ye shall not afflict any widow, or fatherless child. If thou afflict them in any wise, and they cry at all unto me, I will surely hear their cry; and my wrath shall wax hot, and I will kill you with the sword; and your wives shall be widows, and your children fatherless.

If thou lend money to any of my people that is poor by thee, thou shalt not be to him as an usurer, neither shalt thou lay upon him usury.

Thou shalt not revile the gods, nor curse the ruler of thy people.

And in all things that I have said unto you, be circumspect: and make no mention of the name of other gods, neither let it be heard out of thy mouth.

Moses Is Given the Tablets of Stone

And he said unto Moses, Come up unto the Lord, thou, and Aaron, Nadab, and Abihu, and seventy of the elders of Israel; and worship ye afar off. And Moses alone shall come near the Lord: but they shall not come nigh; neither shall the people go up with him.

Then went up Moses, and Aaron, Nadab, and Abihu, and seventy of the elders of Israel: and they saw the God of Israel: and there was under his feet as it were a paved work of a sapphire-stone, and as it were the body of heaven in his clearness. And upon the nobles of the children of Israel he laid not his hand: also they saw God, and did eat and drink.

And the Lord said unto Moses, Come up to me into the mount, and be there: and I will give thee tables of stone, and a law, and commandments which I have written; that thou mayest teach them. And Moses rose up, and his minister Joshua: and Moses went up into the mount of God.

And Moses went up into the mount, and a cloud covered the mount. And the glory of the Lord abode upon mount Sinai, and the cloud covered it six days: and the seventh day he called unto Moses out of the midst of the cloud. And the sight of the glory of the Lord was like devouring fire on the top of the mount in the eyes of the children of Israel.

And Moses went into the midst of the cloud, and gat him up into the mount: and Moses was in the mount forty days and forty nights.

From the Book of Leviticus

Various Laws

And the Lord spake unto Aaron, saying,

Do not drink wine nor strong drink, thou, nor thy sons with thee, when ye go into the tabernacle of the congregation, lest ye die: it shall be a statute for ever throughout your generations: and that ye may put difference between holy and unholy, and between unclean and clean.

And the Lord spake unto Moses and to Aaron, saying unto them, Speak unto the children of Israel, saying, These are the beasts which ye shall eat among all the beasts that are on the earth.

Whatsoever parteth the hoof, and is cloven-footed, and cheweth the cud among the beasts, that shall ye eat.

Nevertheless, these shall ye not eat, of them that chew the cud, or of them that divide the hoof: as the camel, because he cheweth the cud, but divideth not the hoof; he is unclean unto you. And the coney, because he cheweth the cud, but divideth not the hoof; he is unclean unto you. And the hare, because he cheweth the cud, but divideth not the hoof; he is unclean unto you. And the swine, though he divide the hoof, and be cloven-footed, yet he cheweth not the cud; he is unclean unto you. Of their flesh shall ye not eat, and their carcass shall ye not touch; they are unclean to you.

And if a stranger sojourn with thee in your land, ye shall not vex him. But the stranger that dwelleth with you shall be unto you as one born among you, and thou shall love him as thyself; for ye were strangers in the land of Egypt: I am the Lord your God.

Whosoever he be of the children of Israel, or of the strangers that sojourn in Israel, that giveth any of his seed unto Molech, he shall surely be put to death: the people of the land shall stone him with stones. And I will set my face against that man, and will cut him off from among his people; because he hath given of his seed unto Molech, to defile my sanctuary, and to profane my holy name.

And when ye reap the harvest of your land, thou shalt not wholly reap the corners of thy field, neither shalt thou gather the gleanings of thy harvest. And thou shalt not glean thy vineyard, neither shalt thou gather every grape of thy vineyard; thou shalt leave them for the poor and stranger: I am the Lord your God.

Thou shalt not curse the deaf, nor put a stumbling-block before the blind, but shalt fear thy God: I am the Lord.

Ye shall do no unrighteousness in judgment; thou shalt not respect the person of the poor, nor honour the person of the mighty: but in righteousness shalt thou judge thy neighbour.

Thou shalt not go up and down as a tale-bearer among thy people; neither shalt thou stand against the blood of thy neighbour; I am the Lord.

Thou shalt not avenge, nor bear any grudge against the children of thy people, but thou shalt love thy neighbour as thyself: I am the Lord.

Ye shall have one manner of law, as well for the stranger, as for one of your own country: for I am the Lord your God.

And if thy brother be waxen poor, and fallen in decay with thee; then thou shalt relieve him: yea, though he be a stranger, or a sojourner; that he may live with thee. Take thou no usury of him, or increase; but fear thy God; that thy brother may live with thee. Thou shalt not give him thy money upon usury, nor lend him thy victuals for increase.

From the Book of Numbers

The Lord's Blessing

And the Lord spake unto Moses, saying, Speak unto Aaron and unto his sons, saying, On this wise ye shall bless the children of Israel, saying unto them,

The Lord bless thee, and keep thee:

The Lord make his face shine upon thee, and be gracious unto thee:

The Lord lift up his countenance upon thee, and give thee peace.

And they shall put my name upon the children of Israel, and I will bless them.

The Cloud and Fire Lead

And on the day that the tabernacle was reared up, the cloud covered the tabernacle, namely, the tent of the testimony: and at even there was upon the tabernacle as it were the appearance of fire, until the morning. So it was always: the cloud covered it by day, and the appearance of fire by night.

And when the cloud was taken up from the tabernacle, then after that the children of Israel journeyed: and in the place where the cloud abode, there the children of Israel pitched their tents. At the commandment of the Lord the children of Israel journeyed; and at the commandment of the Lord they pitched: as long as the cloud abode upon the tabernacle they rested in their tents.

And when the cloud tarried long upon the tabernacle many days, then the children of Israel kept the charge of the Lord, and journeyed not.

At the commandment of the Lord they rested in their tents, and at the commandment of the Lord they journeyed: they kept the charge of the Lord, at the commandment of the Lord by the hand of Moses.

The Water of Meribah

Then came the children of Israel, even the whole congregation, into the desert of Zin the first month: and the people abode in Kadesh; and Miriam died there, and was buried there.

And there was no water for the congregation: and they gathered themselves together against Moses and against Aaron. And the people chode with Moses, and spake, saying, Would God that we had died when our brethren died before the Lord!

And why have ye brought up the congregation of the Lord into this wilderness, that we and our cattle should die there? And wherefore have ye made us to come up out of Egypt, to bring us unto this evil place? It is no place of seed, or of figs, or of vines, or of pomegranates; neither is there any water to drink.

And Moses and Aaron went from the presence of the assembly unto the door of the tabernacle of the congregation, and they fell upon their faces and the glory of the Lord appeared unto them.

And the Lord spake unto Moses, saying: Take the rod, and gather thou the assembly together, thou and Aaron thy brother, and speak ye unto the rock before their eyes; and it shall give forth his water, and thou shalt bring forth to them water out of the rock: so thou shalt give the congregation and their beasts drink.

And Moses took the rod from before the Lord, as he commanded him. And Moses and Aaron gathered the congregation together before the rock, and he said unto them, Hear now, ye rebels; must we fetch you water out of this rock?

And Moses lifted up his hand, and with his rod he smote the rock twice: and the water came out abundantly, and the congregation drank, and their beasts also.

And the Lord spake unto Moses and Aaron, Because ye believed me not, to sanctify me in the eyes of the children of Israel, therefore ye shall not bring this congregation into the land which I have given them. This is the water of Meribah; because the children of

Israel strove with the Lord, and he was sanctified in them.

The Death of Aaron

And the Lord spake unto Moses and Aaron in mount Hor, by the coast of the land of Edom, saying, Aaron shall be gathered unto his people: for he shall not enter into the land which I have given unto the children of Israel, because ye rebelled against my word at the water of Meribah. Take Aaron and Eleazar his son, and bring them up unto mount Hor: and strip Aaron of his garments, and put them upon Eleazar his son: and Aaron shall be gathered unto his people, and shall die there.

And Moses did as the Lord commanded: and they went up into mount Hor in the sight of all the congregation.

And Moses stripped Aaron of his garments, and put them upon Eleazar his son; and Aaron died there in the top of the mount: and Moses and Eleazar came down from the mount.

And when all the congregation saw that Aaron was dead, they mourned for Aaron thirty days, even all the house of Israel.

Joshua Appointed to Succeed Moses

And the Lord said unto Moses, Get thee up into this mount Abarim, and see the land which I have given unto the children of Israel. And when thou hast seen it, thou also shalt be gathered unto thy people, as Aaron thy brother was gathered. For ye rebelled against my commandment in the desert of Zin, in the strife of the congregation, to sanctify me at the water before their eyes: that is the water of Meribah in Kadesh in the wilderness of Zin.

And Moses spake unto the Lord, saying, Let the Lord, the God of the spirits of all flesh, set a man over the congregation, which may go out before them, and which may go in before them, and which may lead them out, and which may bring them in; that the congregation of the Lord be not as sheep which have no shepherd.

And the Lord said unto Moses, Take thee Joshua the son of Nun, a man in whom is the spirit, and lay thine hand upon him; and set him before Eleazar the priest, and before all the congregation: and give him a charge in their sight. And thou shalt put some of thine honour upon him, that all the congregation of the children of Israel may be obedient.

And Moses did as the Lord commanded him: and he took Joshua, and set him before Eleazar the priest, and before all the congregation: and he laid his hands upon him, and gave him a charge as the Lord commanded by the hand of Moses.

Exogamy Is Discouraged

And Moses commanded the children of Israel according to the word of the Lord, saying, The tribe of the sons of Joseph hath said well.

This is the thing which the Lord doth command concerning the daughters of Zelophehad, saying, Let them marry to whom they think best; only to the family of the tribe of their father shall they marry. So shall not the inheritance of the children of Israel remove from tribe to tribe: for every one of the children of Israel shall keep himself to the inheritance of the tribe of his fathers.

From the Book of Deuteronomy

For a Sign upon Thine Hand

Hear, O Israel: The Lord our God is one Lord:

And thou shalt love the Lord thy God with all thine heart, and with all thy soul, and with all thy might.

And these words which I command thee this day, shall be in thine heart: and thou shalt teach them diligently unto thy children, and shalt talk of them when thou sittest in thine house, and when thou walkest by the way, and when thou liest down, and when thou risest up.

And thou shalt bind them for a sign upon thine hand, and they shall be as frontlets between thine eyes. And thou shalt write them upon the posts of thy house, and on thy gates.

The Law of Release

And the end of every seven years thou shalt make a release. And this is the manner of the release: Every creditor that lendeth aught unto his neighbour shall release it; he shall not exact it of his neighbour, or of his brother; because it is called the Lord's release.

Of a foreigner thou mayest exact it again: but that which is thine with thy brother thine hand shall release: save when there shall be no poor among you; for the Lord shall greatly bless thee in the land which the Lord thy God giveth thee for an inheritance to possess it: only if thou carefully hearken unto the voice of the Lord thy God, to observe to do all these commandments which I command thee this day.

For the Lord thy God blesseth thee, as he promised

thee: and thou shalt lend unto many nations, but thou shalt not borrow; and thou shalt reign over many nations, but they shall not reign over thee.

Trial and Punishment

If there be found among you, within any of thy gates which the Lord thy God giveth thee, man or woman that hath wrought wickedness in the sight of the Lord thy God, in transgressing his covenant, and hath gone and served other gods, and worshipped them, either the sun, or moon, or any of the host of heaven, which I have not commanded; and it be told thee, and thou hast heard of it, and inquired diligently, and behold, it be true, and the thing certain, that such abomination is wrought in Israel: then shalt thou bring forth that man or that woman, which have committed that wicked thing, unto thy gates, even that man or that woman, and shalt stone them with stones, till they die.

At the mouth of two witnesses, or three witnesses, shall he that is worthy of death be put to death; but at the mouth of one witness he shall not be put to death. The hands of the witnesses shall be first upon him to put him to death, and afterward the hands of all the people. So thou shalt put the evil away from among you.

The Coming of a Prophet Foretold

And the Lord said, I will raise them up a Prophet from among their brethren, and will put my words in his mouth; and he shall speak unto them all that I shall command him. And it shall come to pass, that whosoever will not hearken unto my words which he shall speak in my name, I will require it of him.

But the prophet, which shall presume to speak a word in my name, which I have not commanded him to speak, or that shall speak in the name of other gods, even that prophet shall die.

And if thou say in thine heart, How shall we know the word which the Lord hath not spoken? When a prophet speaketh in the name of the Lord, if the thing follow not, nor come to pass, that is the thing which the Lord hath not spoken, but the prophet hath spoken it presumptuously: thou shalt not be afraid of him.

The Law of False Witness

If a false witness rise up against any man to testify against him that which is wrong; then both the men between whom the controversy is shall stand before the Lord, before the priests and the judges, which shall be in those days; and the judges shall make diligent inquisition; and behold, if the witness be a false witness, and hath testified falsely against his brother; then shall ye do unto him, as he had thought to have done unto his brother: so shalt thou put the evil away from among you.

And those which remain shall hear, and fear, and shall henceforth commit no more any such evil among you. And thine eye shall not pity; but life shall go for life, eye for eye, tooth for tooth, hand for hand, foot for foot.

Of Sanctuary

Thou shalt not deliver unto his master the servant which is escaped from his master unto thee: he shall dwell with thee, even among you in that place which he shall choose in one of thy gates where it liketh him best: thou shalt not oppress him.

The Law of Divorce

When a man hath taken a wife, and married her, and it come to pass that she find no favour in his eyes, because he hath found some uncleanness in her: then let him write her a bill of divorcement, and give it in her hand, and send her out of his house. And when she is departed out of his house, she may go and be another man's wife.

And if the latter husband hate her, and write her a bill of divorcement, and giveth it in her hand, and sendeth her out of his house; or if the latter husband die, which took her to be his wife; her former husband which sent her away, may not take her again to be his wife, after that she is defiled; for that is abomination before the Lord: and thou shalt not cause the land to sin, which the Lord thy God giveth thee for an inheritance.

Of Master and Servant

Thou shalt not oppress an hired servant that is poor and needy, whether he be of thy brethren, or of thy strangers that are in thy land within thy gates: at his day thou shalt give him his hire, neither shall the sun go down upon it, for he is poor, and setteth his heart upon it: lest he cry against thee unto the Lord, and it be sin unto thee.

Of Individual Responsibility

The fathers shall not be put to death for the children, neither shall the children be put to death for the fathers: every man shall be put to death for his own sin.

The Duty of an Husband's Brother

If brethren dwell together, and one of them die and have no child, the wife of the dead shall not marry without unto a stranger: her husband's brother shall go in unto her, and take her to him to wife, and perform the duty of an husband's brother unto her.

And it shall be, that the first-born which she beareth, shall succeed in the name of his brother which is dead, that his name be not put out of Israel.

The Cursed of Israel

Cursed be the man that maketh any graven or molten image, an abomination unto the Lord, the work of the hands of the craftsman, and putteth it in a secret place. Cursed be he that setteth light by his father or his mother. Cursed be he that removeth his neighbour's land-mark. Cursed be he that maketh the blind to wander out of the way. Cursed be he that perverteth the judgment of the stranger, fatherless, and widow. Cursed be he that lieth with his father's wife; because he uncovereth his father's skirt. Cursed be he that lieth with any manner of beast. Cursed be he that lieth with his sister, the daughter of his father, or the daughter of his mother. Cursed be he that lieth with his mother-in-law. Cursed be he that smiteth his neighbour secretly. Cursed be he that taketh reward to slay an innocent person. Cursed be he that confirmeth not all the words of this law to do them.

The Blessed of Israel

And it shall come to pass, if thou shalt hearken diligently unto the voice of the Lord thy God, to observe and to do all his commandments which I command thee this day: that the Lord thy God will set thee on high above all nations of the earth: and all these blessings shall come on thee, and overtake thee, if thou shalt hearken unto the voice of the Lord thy God.

Blessed shalt thou be in the city, and blessed shalt thou be in the field.

Blessed shall be the fruit of thy body, and the fruit of thy ground, and the fruit of thy cattle, the increase of thy kine, and the flocks of thy sheep.

Blessed shall be thy basket and thy store.

Blessed shalt thou be when thou comest in, and blessed shalt thou be when thou goest out.

The Lord shall cause thine enemies that rise up against thee to be smitten before thy face: they shall come out against thee one way, and flee before thee seven ways.

The Lord shall command the blessing upon thee in thy store-houses, and in all that thou settest thine hand unto: and he shall bless thee in the land which the Lord thy God giveth thee.

The Lord shall establish thee an holy people unto himself, as he hath sworn unto thee, if thou shalt keep the commandments of the Lord thy God, and walk in his ways. The Lord shall open unto thee his good treasure, the heaven to give the rain unto thy land in his season, and to bless all the work of thine hand: and thou shalt lend unto many nations, and thou shalt not borrow.

And the Lord shall make thee the head, and not the tail; and thou shalt be above only, and thou shalt not be beneath; if that thou hearken unto the commandments of the Lord thy God, which I command thee this day, to observe and to do them.

The Death of Moses

And the Lord spake unto Moses that self-same day, saying, Get thee up into this mountain Abarim, unto mount Nebo, which is in the land of Moab, that is over against Jericho; and behold the land of Canaan which I give unto the children of Israel for a possession: and die in the mount wither thou goest up, and be gathered unto thy people; as Aaron thy brother died in mount Hor, and was gathered unto his people: because ye trespassed against me among the children of Israel at the waters of Meribah-Kadesh, in the wilderness of Zin; because ye sanctified me not in the midst of the children of Israel. Yet thou shalt see the land before thee; but thou shalt not go thither unto the land which I give the children of Israel.

And Moses went up from the plains of Moab, unto the mountain of Nebo, to the top of Pisgah, that is over against Jericho: and the Lord shewed him all the land of Gilead, unto Dan, and all Naphtali, and the land of Ephraim, and Manasseh, and all the land of Judah, unto the utmost sea, and the south, and the plain of the valley of Jericho, the city of palm-trees, unto Zoar.

And the Lord said unto him, This is the land which I sware unto Abraham, unto Isaac, and unto Jacob, saying, I will give it unto thy seed: I have caused thee to see it with thine eye, but thou shalt not go over thither.

So Moses the servant of the Lord died there in the land of Moab, according to the word of the Lord. And he buried him in a valley in the land of Moab, over against Beth-peor: but no man knoweth of his sepulchre unto this day.

And Moses was an hundred and twenty years old

when he died: his eye was not dim, nor his natural force abated.

And the children of Israel wept for Moses in the plains of Moab thirty days: so the days of weeping and mourning for Moses were ended.

And Joshua the son of Nun was full of the spirit of wisdom; for Moses had laid his hands upon him: and the children of Israel hearkened unto him, and did as the Lord commanded Moses.

And there arose not a prophet since in Israel like unto Moses, whom the Lord knew face to face, in all the signs and the wonders which the Lord sent him to do in the land of Egypt, to Pharaoh, and to all his servants, and to all his land; and in all that mighty hand, and in all the great terror which Moses shewed in the sight of all Israel.

From the Book of Joshua

Joshua Instructs His People

And it came to pass, a long time after that the Lord had given rest unto Israel from all their enemies round about, that Joshua waxed old and stricken in age. And Joshua called for all Israel, and for their elders, and for their heads, and for their judges, and for their officers, and said unto them, I am old and stricken in age: and ye have seen all that the Lord your God hath done unto all these nations because of you; for the Lord your God is he that hath fought for you.

Be ye therefore very courageous to keep and to do all that is written in the book of the law of Moses, that ye turn not aside therefrom to the right hand or to the left; that ye come not among these nations, these that remain among you; neither make mention of the name of their gods, nor cause to swear by them, neither serve them, nor bow yourselves unto them: but cleave unto the Lord your God, as ye have done unto this day.

And behold, this day I am going the way of all the earth; and ye know in all your hearts and in all your souls, that not one thing hath failed of all the good things which the Lord your God spake concerning you; all are come to pass unto you, and not one thing hath failed thereof.

The Death of Joshua

And Joshua gathered all the tribes of Israel to Shechem, and called for the elders of Israel, and for their heads, and for their judges, and for their officers; and they presented themselves before God.

And Joshua said unto all the people, Thus saith the Lord God of Israel, Your fathers dwelt on the other side of the flood in old time, even Terah, the father of Abraham, and the father of Nachor: and they served other gods. And I took your father Abraham from the other side of the flood, and led him throughout all the land of Canaan, and multiplied his seed, and gave him Isaac. I sent Moses also and Aaron, and I plagued Egypt, according to that which I did among them: and afterward I brought you out.

Now therefore fear the Lord, and serve him in sincerity and in truth; and put away the gods which your fathers served on the other side of the flood, and in Egypt; and serve ye the Lord. And if it seem evil unto you to serve the Lord, choose you this day whom ye will serve, whether the gods which your fathers served that were on the other side of the flood, or the gods of the Amorites in whose land ye dwell: but as for me and my house, we will serve the Lord.

And the people answered, and said, God forbid that we should forsake the Lord, to serve other gods.

And Joshua said unto the people, Ye are witnesses against yourselves that ye have chosen you the Lord, to serve him. And they said, We are witnesses.

Now therefore put away (said he) the strange gods which are among you, and incline your heart unto the Lord God of Israel.

And the people said unto Joshua, The Lord our God will we serve, and his voice will we obey.

And it came to pass after these things, that Joshua the son of Nun the servant of the Lord died, being an hundred and ten years old.

From the Book of Judges

The Anger of the Lord

And the children of Israel dwelt among the Canaanites, Hittites, and Amorites, and Perizzites, and Hivites, and Jebusites: and they took their daughters to be their wives, and gave their daughters to their sons, and served their gods. And the children of Israel did evil in the sight of the Lord, and forgat the Lord their God, and served Baalim, and the groves.

Therefore the anger of the Lord was hot against Israel, and he sold them into the hand of Chushan-rishathaim king of Mesopotamia: and the children of Israel served Chushan-rishathaim eight years.

From the First Book of the Kings

The Divided Kingdom

And Rehoboam went to Shechem: for all Israel were come to Shechem to make him king.

And it came to pass, when Jeroboam the son of Nebat, who was yet in Egypt, heard of it, (for he was fled from the presence of king Solomon, and Jeroboam dwelt in Egypt); that they sent and called him. And Jeroboam and all the congregation of Israel came, and spake unto Rehoboam, saying, Thy father made our yoke grievous: now therefore make thou the grievous service of thy father, and his heavy yoke which he put upon us, lighter, and we will serve thee. And he said unto them, Depart yet for three days, then come again to me. And the people departed.

And king Rehoboam consulted with the old men that stood before Solomon his father while he yet lived, and said, How do ye advise that I may answer this people? And they spake unto him, saying, If thou wilt be a servant unto this people this day, and wilt serve them, and answer them, and speak good words to them, then they will be thy servants for ever.

But he forsook the counsel of the old men, which they had given him, and consulted with the young men that were grown up with him, and which stood before him: and he said unto them, What counsel give ye that we may answer this people, who have spoken to me, saying, Make the yoke which thy father did put upon us lighter?

And the young men that were grown up with him spake unto him, saying, Thus shalt thou speak unto this people that spake unto thee, saying, Thy father made our yoke heavy, but make thou it lighter unto us; thus shalt thou say unto them, My little finger shall be thicker than my father's loins. And now whereas my father did lade you with a heavy yoke, I will add to your yoke: my father hath chastised you with whips, but I will chastise you with scorpions.

So Jeroboam and all the people came to Rehoboam the third day, as the king had appointed, saying, Come to me again the third day.

And the king answered the people roughly, and forsook the old men's counsel that they gave him; and spake to them after the counsel of the young men, saying, My father made your yoke heavy, and I will add to your yoke: my father also chastised you with whips, but I will chastise you with scorpions. Wherefore the king hearkened not unto the people: for the cause was from the Lord, that he might perform his saying, which the Lord spake by Ahijah and Shilonite unto Jeroboam the son of Nebat.

So when all Israel saw that the king hearkened not unto them, the people answered the king, saying, What portion have we in David? neither have we inheritance in the son of Jesse: to your tents, O Israel: now see to thine own house, David. So Israel departed unto their tents.

But as for the children of Israel which dwelt in the cities of Judah, Rehoboam reigned over them.

Then king Rehoboam sent Adoram, who was over the tribute; and all Israel stoned him with stones, that he died. Therefore king Rehoboam made speed to get him up to his chariot, to flee to Jerusalem.

So Israel rebelled against the house of David unto this day.

And it came to pass when all Israel heard that Jeroboam was come again, that they sent and called him unto the congregation, and made him king over all Israel: there was none that followed the house of David, but the tribe of Judah only.

And when Rehoboam was come to Jerusalem, he assembled all the house of Judah, with the tribe of Benjamin, an hundred and four score thousand chosen men, which were warriors, to fight against the house of Israel, to bring the kingdom again to Rehoboam the son of Solomon.

But the word of God came unto Shemaiah the man of God, saying, Speak unto Rehoboam the son of Solomon, king of Judah, and unto all the house of Judah and Benjamin, and to the remnant of the people, saying, Thus saith the Lord, Ye shall not go up, nor fight against your brethren the children of Israel: return every man to his house; for this thing is from me. They hearkened therefore to the word of the Lord, and returned to depart, according to the word of the Lord.

Then Jeroboam built Shechem in mount Ephraim, and dwelt therein; and went out from thence, and built Penuel.

And Jeroboam said in his heart, Now shall the kingdom return to the house of David. If this people go up to do sacrifice in the house of the Lord at Jerusalem, then shall the heart of this people turn again unto their lord, even unto Rehoboam king of Judah, and they shall kill me, and go again to Rehoboam king of Judah.

Whereupon the king took counsel, and made two calves of gold, and said unto them, It is too much for you to go up to Jerusalem: behold thy gods, O Israel, which brought thee up out of the land of Egypt. And he set the one in Beth-el, and the other put he in Dan.

And this thing became a sin: for the people went to worship before the one, even unto Dan.

And he made an house of high places, and made priests of the lowest of the people, which were not of the sons of Levi.

And Jeroboam ordained a feast in the eighth month, on the fifteenth day of the month, like unto the feast that is in Judah, and he offered upon the altar. So did he in Beth-el, sacrificing unto the calves that he had made: and he placed in Beth-el the priests of the high places which he had made. So he offered upon the altar which he had made in Beth-el the fifteenth day of the eighth month, even in the month which he had devised of his own heart; and ordained a feast unto the children of Israel: and he offered upon the altar, and burnt incense.

Elijah Proves God

And it came to pass after many days, that the word of the Lord came to Elijah in the third year, saying, Go, shew thyself unto Ahab; and I will send rain upon the earth. And Elijah went to shew himself unto Ahab. And there was a sore famine in Samaria.

And it came to pass when Ahab saw Elijah, that Ahab said unto him, Art thou he that troubleth Israel? And he answered, I have not troubled Israel; but thou, and thy father's house, in that ye have forsaken the commandments of the Lord, and thou hast followed Baalim. Now therefore send, and gather to me all Israel unto mount Carmel, and the prophets of Baal four hundred and fifty, and the prophets of the groves four hundred, which eat at Jezebel's table.

So Ahab sent unto all the children of Israel, and gathered the prophets together unto mount Carmel.

And Elijah came unto all the people, and said, How long halt ye between two opinions? if the Lord be God, follow him: but if Baal, then follow him. And the people answered him not a word.

Then said Elijah unto the people, I, even I only, remain a prophet of the Lord; but Baal's prophets are four hundred and fifty men. Let them therefore give us two bullocks; and let them choose one bullock for themselves, and cut it in pieces, and lay it on wood, and put no fire under: and I will dress the other bullock, and lay it on wood, and put no fire under. And call ye on the name of your gods, and I will call on the name of the Lord: and the God that answereth by fire, let him be God. And all the people answered and said, It is well spoken.

And Elijah said unto the prophets of Baal, Choose you one bullock for yourselves, and dress it first; for ye are many; and call on the name of your gods, but put no fire under.

And they took the bullock which was given them, and they dressed it, and called on the name of Baal from morning even until noon, saying, O Baal, hear us. But there was no voice, nor any that answered. And they leaped upon the altar which was made.

And it came to pass at noon, that Elijah mocked them, and said, Cry aloud: for he is a god: either he is talking, or he is pursuing, or he is in a journey, or peradventure he sleepeth, and must be awaked.

And Elijah said unto all the people, Come near unto me. And all the people came near unto him. And he repaired the altar of the Lord that was broken down. And Elijah took twelve stones, according to the number of the tribes of the sons of Jacob, unto whom the word of the Lord came, saying, Israel shall be thy name. And with the stones he built an altar in the name of the

Lord: and he made a trench about the altar, as great as would contain two measures of seed. And he put the wood in order, and cut the bullock in pieces, and laid him on the wood, and said, Fill four barrels with water, and pour it on the burnt-sacrifice, and on the wood. And he said, Do it the second time. And they did it the second time. And he said, Do it the third time. And they did it the third time. And the water ran round about the altar; and he filled the trench also with water.

And it came to pass at the time of the offering of the evening sacrifice, that Elijah the prophet came near and said, Lord God of Abraham, Isaac, and of Israel, let it be known this day that thou art God in Israel, and that I am thy servant, and that I have done all these things at thy word. Hear me, O Lord, hear me, that this people may know that thou art the Lord God, and that thou hast turned their heart back again.

Then the fire of the Lord fell, and consumed the burnt-sacrifice, and the wood, and the stones, and the dust, and licked up the water that was in the trench. And when all the people saw it, they fell on their faces: and they said, The Lord, he is the God; the Lord, he is the God.

And Elijah said unto them, Take the prophets of Baal; let not one of them escape. And they took them; and Elijah brought them down to the brook Kishon, and slew them there.

From the Book of Job

What Is the Almighty?

How should man be just with God? If he will contend with him, he cannot answer him one of a thousand.

He is wise in heart, and mighty in strength: who hath hardened himself against him, and hath prospered? which removeth the mountains, and they know not: which overturneth them in his anger; which shaketh the earth out of her place, and the pillars thereof tremble; which commandeth the sun, and it riseth not; and sealeth up the stars; which alone spreadeth out the heavens, and treadeth upon the waves of the sea; which maketh Arcturus, Orion, and Pleiades, and the chambers of the south; which doeth great things past finding out; yea, and wonders without number.

Lo, he goeth by me, and I see him not: he passeth on also, but I perceive him not. Behold, he taketh away, who can hinder him? who will say unto him, What doest thou?

If I speak of strength, lo, he is strong: and if of judgment, who shall set me a time to plead? If I justify myself, mine own mouth shall condemn me: If I say I am perfect, it shall also prove me perverse. Though I were perfect, yet would I not know my soul: I would despise my life.

This is one thing, therefore I said it, He destroyeth the perfect and the wicked.

I am as one mocked of his neighbour, who calleth upon God, and he answereth him: the just upright man is laughed to scorn. He that is ready to slip with his feet is as a lamp despised in the thought of him that is at ease. The tabernacles of robbers prosper, and they that provoke God are secure; into whose hand God bringeth abundantly.

But ask now the beasts, and they shall teach thee; and the fowls of the air, and they shall tell thee; or speak to the earth, and it shall teach thee; and the fishes of the sea shall declare unto thee.

Who knoweth not in all these that the hand of the Lord hath wrought this?

Lo, mine eye hath seen all this, mine ear hath heard and understood it.

Man that is born of a woman is of few days, and full of trouble. He cometh forth like a flower, and is cut down: he fleeth also as a shadow, and continueth not.

And dost thou open thine eyes upon such an one, and bringest me into judgment with thee? Who can bring a clean thing out of an unclean? not one.

Seeing his days are determined, the number of his months are with thee, thou hast appointed his bounds that he cannot pass; turn from him, that he may rest, till he shall accomplish, as an hireling, his day. For there is hope of a tree, if it be cut down, that it will sprout again, and that the tender branch thereof will not cease.

Though the root thereof wax old in the earth, and the stock thereof die in the ground; yet through the scent of water it will bud, and bring forth boughs like a plant. But man dieth, and wasteth away: yea, man giveth up the ghost, and where is he?

As the waters fail from the sea, and the flood decayeth and drieth up: so man lieth down, and riseth not: till the heavens be no more, they shall not awake nor be raised out of their sleep.

O that my words were now written! O that they were

printed in a book! that they were graven with an iron pen and lead in the rock for ever!

For I know that my Redeemer liveth, and that he shall stand at the latter day upon the earth, and though after my skin worms destroy this body, yet in my flesh shall I see God.

Even when I remember I am afraid, and trembling taketh hold on my flesh.

Wherefore do the wicked live, become old, yea, are mighty in power? Their seed is established in their sight with them, and their offspring before their eyes. Their houses are safe from fear, neither is the rod of God upon them. They spend their days in wealth, and in a moment go down to the grave. Therefore they say unto God, Depart from us; for we desire not the knowledge of thy ways.

What is the Almighty, that we should serve him? and what profit should we have, if we pray unto him?

Lo, their good is not in their hand: the counsel of the wicked is far from me. How oft is the candle of the wicked put out? and how oft cometh their destruction upon them? God distributeth sorrows in his anger.

They are as stubble before the wind, and as chaff that the storm carrieth away.

God layeth up his iniquity for his children: he rewardeth him, and he shall know it. His eyes shall see his destruction, and he shall drink of the wrath of the Almighty. For what pleasure hath he in his house after him, when the number of his months is cut off in the midst?

Shall any teach God knowledge? seeing he judgeth those that are high.

Oh that I knew where I might find him! that I might come even to his seat! Behold, I go forward, but he is not there; and backward, but I cannot perceive him: on the left hand, where he doth work, but I cannot behold him: he hideth himself on the right hand, that I cannot see him: but he knoweth the way that I take: when he hath tried me, I shall come forth as gold.

My foot hath held his steps, his way have I kept, and not declined. Neither have I gone back from the commandment of his lips; I have esteemed the words of his mouth more than my necessary food.

But he is in one mind, and who can turn him? and what his soul desireth, even that he doeth.

Surely there is a vein for the silver, and a place for gold where they fine it. Iron is taken out of the earth, and brass is molten out of the stone.

He setteth an end to darkness, and searcheth out all perfection: the stones of darkness, and the shadow of death. The flood breaketh out from the inhabitant; even the waters forgotten of the foot: they are dried up, they are gone away from men. As for the earth, out of it cometh bread: and under it is turned up as it were fire. The stones of it are the place of sapphires: and it hath dust of gold.

There is a path which no fowl knoweth, and which the vulture's eye hath not seen: the lion's whelps have not trodden it, nor the fierce lion passed by it.

He putteth forth his hand upon the rock; he overturneth the mountains by the roots. He cutteth out rivers among the rocks; and his eye seeth every precious thing. He bindeth the floods from overflowing; and the thing that is hid bringeth he forth to light.

But where shall wisdom be found? and where is the place of understanding? Man knoweth not the price thereof; neither is it found in the land of the living. The depth saith, It is not in me: and the sea saith, It is not with me. It cannot be gotten for gold, neither shall silver be weighed for the price thereof. It cannot be valued with the gold of Ophir, with the precious onyx, or the sapphire.

Whence then cometh wisdom? and where is the place of understanding? seeing it is hid from the eyes of all living, and kept close from the fowls of the air. Destruction and death say, We have heard the fame thereof with our ears.

God understandeth the way thereof, and he knoweth the place thereof. For he looketh to the ends of the earth, and seeth under the whole heaven; to make the weight for the winds; and he weigheth the waters by measure.

When he made a decree for the rain, and a way for the lightning of the thunder; then did he see it, and declare it; he prepared it, yea, and searched it out. And unto man he said, Behold, the fear of the Lord, that is wisdom; and to depart from evil is understanding.

Is not destruction to the wicked? and a strange punishment to the workers of iniquity? Doth not he see my ways, and count all my steps?

Oh that one would hear me! Behold, my desire is, that the Almighty would answer me, and that mine adversary had written a book. Surely I would take it upon my shoulder, and bind it as a crown to me. I would declare unto him the number of my steps; as a prince would I go near unto him. If my land cry against me, or that the furrows likewise thereof complain: if I have eaten the fruits thereof without money, or have caused the owners thereof to lose their life: let thistles grow instead of wheat, and cockle instead of barley. The words of Job are ended.

Then the Lord answered Job out of the whirlwind, and said, Who is this that darkeneth counsel by words without knowledge?

Gird up now thy loins like a man; for I will demand of thee, and answer thou me.

Where wast thou when I laid the foundations of the earth? declare, if thou hast understanding. Who hath laid the measures thereof, if thou knowest? or who hath stretched the line upon it? Whereupon are the foundations thereof fastened? or who laid the corner-stone thereof: when the morning stars sang together, and all the sons of God shouted for joy?

Or who shut up the sea with doors, when it brake forth, as if it had issued out of the womb? When I made the cloud the garment thereof, and thick darkness a swaddling band for it, and brake up for it my decreed place, and set bars and doors, and said, Hitherto shalt thou come, but no further: and here shall thy proud waves be stayed?

Hast thou commanded the morning since thy days; and caused the day-spring to know his place; that it might take hold of the ends of the earth, that the wicked might be shaken out of it?

It is turned as clay to the seal; and they stand as a garment. And from the wicked their light is withholden, and the high arm shall be broken.

Hast thou entered into the springs of the sea? or hast thou walked in the search of the depth? Have the gates of death been opened unto thee? or hast thou seen the doors of the shadow of death? Hast thou perceived the breadth of the earth? declare if thou knowest it all.

Where is the way where light dwelleth? and as for darkness, where is the place thereof, that thou shouldest take it to the bound thereof, and that thou shouldest know the paths to the house thereof? Knowest thou it, because thou wast then born? or because the number of thy days is great?

Hast thou entered into the treasures of the snow? or hast thou seen the treasures of the hail, which I have reserved against the time of trouble, against the day of battle and war?

By what way is the light parted, which scattereth the east wind upon the earth? Who hath divided a watercourse for the overflowing of waters, or a way for the lightning of thunder; to cause it to rain on the earth, where no man is; on the wilderness, wherein there is no man; to satisfy the desolate and waste ground; and to cause the bud of the tender herb to spring forth?

Hath the rain a father? or who hath begotten the drops of dew? Out of whose womb came the ice? and the hoary frost of heaven, who hath gendered it?

The waters are hid as with a stone, and the face of the deep is frozen.

Canst thou bind the sweet influences of Pleiades, or loose the bands of Orion? Canst thou bring forth Mazzaroth in his season? or canst thou guide Arcturus with his sons? Knowest thou the ordinances of heaven? canst thou set the dominion thereof in the earth? Canst thou lift up thy voice to the clouds, that abundance of waters may cover thee? Canst thou send lightnings, that they may go, and say unto thee, Here we are? Who hath put wisdom in the inward parts? or who hath given understanding to the heart? Who can number the clouds in wisdom? or who can stay the bottles of heaven, when the dust groweth into hardness, and the clods cleave fast together? Wilt thou hunt the prey for the lion? or fill the appetite of the young lions, when they couch in their dens, and abide in the covert to lie in wait? Who provideth for the raven his food? when his young ones cry unto God, they wander for lack of meat.

Knowest thou the time when the wild goats of the

rock bring forth? or canst thou mark when the hinds do calve? Canst thou number the months that they fulfil? or knowest thou the time when they bring forth?

They bow themselves, they bring forth their young ones, they cast out their sorrows. Their young ones are in good liking, they grow up with corn; they go forth, and return not unto them.

Who hath sent out the wild ass free? or who hath loosed the bands of the wild ass? whose house I have made the wilderness, and the barren land his dwellings.

He scorneth the multitude of the city, neither regardeth he the crying of the driver. The range of the mountains is his pasture, and he searcheth after every green thing.

Will the unicorn be willing to serve thee, or abide by thy crib? Canst thou bind the unicorn with his band in the furrow? or will he harrow the valleys after thee? Wilt thou trust him, because his strength is great? or wilt thou leave thy labour to him? Wilt thou believe him, that he will bring home thy seed, and gather it into thy barn?

Gavest thou the goodly wings unto the peacocks? or wings and feathers unto the ostrich? which leaveth her eggs in the earth, and warmeth them in the dust, and forgetteth that the foot may crush them, or that the wild beast may break them. She is hardened against her young ones, as though they were not hers: her labour is in vain without fear; because God hath deprived her of wisdom, neither hath he imparted to her understanding. What time she lifteth up herself on high, she scorneth the horse and his rider.

Hast thou given the horse strength? hast thou clothed his neck with thunder? Canst thou make him afraid as a grasshopper? the glory of his nostrils is terrible. He paweth in the valley, and rejoiceth in his strength: he goeth on to meet the armed men.

He mocketh at fear, and is not affrighted; neither turneth he back from the sword. The quiver rattleth against him, the glittering spear and the shield. He swalloweth the ground with fierceness and rage; neither believeth he that it is the sound of the trumpet. He saith among the trumpets, Ha! Ha! and he smelleth the battle afar off, the thunder of the captains, and the shouting.

Doth the hawk fly by thy wisdom, and stretch her wings toward the south? Doth the eagle mount up at thy command, and make her nest on high? She dwelleth and abideth on the rock, upon the crag of the rock, and the strong place. From thence she seeketh the prey, and her eyes behold afar off. Her young ones also suck up blood: and where the slain are, there is she.

Shall he that contendeth with the Almighty instruct him? he that reproveth God, let him answer it.

Then Job answered the Lord, and said, Behold, I am vile; what shall I answer thee? I will lay my hand upon my mouth. Once have I spoken; but I will not answer: yea, twice; but I will proceed no further.

Then answered the Lord unto Job out of the whirlwind, and said, Gird up thy loins now like a man: I will demand of thee, and declare thou unto me.

Wilt thou also disannul my judgment? wilt thou condemn me, that thou mayest be righteous? Hast thou an arm like God? or canst thou thunder with a voice like him?

Deck thyself now with majesty and excellency; and array thyself with glory and beauty. Cast abroad the rage of thy wrath: and behold every one that is proud, and abase him. Look on every one that is proud, and bring him low; and tread down the wicked in their place. Hide them in the dust together; and bind their faces in secret. Then will I also confess unto thee that thine own right hand can save thee.

Behold now Behemoth, which I made with thee; he eateth grass as an ox. Lo now, his strength is in his loins, and his force is in the navel of his belly. He moveth his tail like a cedar; the sinews of his stones are wrapped together. His bones are as strong pieces of brass; his bones are like bars of iron. He is the chief of the ways of God: he that made him can make his sword to approach unto him. Surely the mountains bring him forth food, where all the beasts of the field play. He lieth under the shady trees, in the covert of the reed, and fens. The shady trees cover him with their shadow; the willows of the brook compass him about. Behold, he drinketh up a river, and hasteth not: he trusteth that he can draw up Jordan into his mouth. He taketh it with his eyes: his nose pierceth through snares.

Canst thou draw out leviathan with an hook? or his tongue with a cord which thou lettest down? Canst thou put an hook into his nose? or bore his jaw through with a thorn? Will he make many supplications unto thee? will he speak soft words unto thee? Will he make a covenant with thee? wilt thou take him for a servant for ever? Wilt thou play with him as with a bird? or wilt thou bind him or thy maidens? Shall thy companions make a banquet of him? shall they part him among the merchants? Canst thou fill his skin with barbed irons? or his head with fish-spears?

Then Job answered the Lord, and said, I know that thou canst do everything, and that no thought can be withholden from thee.

Who is he that hideth counsel without knowledge? therefore have I uttered that I understood not; things too wonderful for me, which I knew not. Hear, I beseech thee, and I will speak: I will demand of thee, and declare thou unto me. I have heard of thee by the hearing of the ear: but now mine eye seeth thee: wherefore I abhor myself, and repent in dust and ashes.

From the Psalms

The Godly and the Ungodly
(PSALM I)

Blessed is the man that walketh not in the counsel of the ungodly, nor standeth in the way of sinners, nor sitteth in the seat of the scornful.

But his delight is in the law of the Lord; and in his law doth he meditate day and night. And he shall be like a tree planted by the rivers of water, that bringeth forth his fruit in his season; his leaf also shall not wither; and whatsoever he doeth shall prosper.

The ungodly are not so: but are like the chaff which the wind driveth away.

Therefore the ungodly shall not stand in the judgment, nor sinners in the congregation of the righteous.

For the Lord knoweth the way of the righteous: but the way of the ungodly shall perish.

Prophecy of a Son of God
(PSALM II)

Why do the heathen rage, and the people imagine a vain thing?

The kings of the earth set themselves, and the rulers take counsel together, against the Lord, and against his Annointed, saying,

Let us break their bands asunder, and cast away their cords from us.

He that sitteth in the heavens shall laugh: the Lord shall have them in derision.

Then shall he speak unto them in his wrath, and vex them in his sore displeasure.

Yet have I set my King upon my holy hill of Zion.

I will declare the decree: the Lord hath said unto me, thou art my Son; this day have I begotten thee.

Ask of me, and I shall give thee the heathen for thine inheritance, and the uttermost parts of the earth for thy possession.

Thou shalt break them with a rod of iron; thou shalt dash them in pieces like a potter's vessel.

Be wise now therefore, O ye kings: be instructed, ye judges of the earth.

Serve the Lord with fear, and rejoice with trembling.

Kiss the Son, lest he be angry, and ye perish from the way, when his wrath is kindled but a little. Blessed are all they that put their trust in him.

When I Consider Thy Heavens

(PSALM VIII)

O Lord our Lord, how excellent is thy name in all the earth! who hast set thy glory above the heavens.

Out of the mouth of babes and sucklings hast thou ordained strength because of thine enemies, that thou mightest still the enemy and the avenger.

When I consider thy heavens, the work of thy fingers; the moon and the stars, which thou hast ordained;

What is man, that thou art mindful of him? and the son of man, that thou visitest him?

For thou hast made him a little lower than the angels, and hast crowned him with glory and honour

Thou madest him to have dominion over the works
of thy hands; thou hast put all things under his feet:

All sheep and oxen, yea, and the beasts of the field;

The fowl of the air, and the fish of the sea, and whatsoever passeth through the paths of the seas.

O Lord our Lord, how excellent is thy name in all
the earth!

Hymn of Trust

(PSALM XI)

In the Lord put I my trust: how say ye to my soul,
Flee as a bird to your mountain?

For lo, the wicked bend their bow, they make ready
their arrow upon the string, that they may privily
shoot at the upright in heart.

If the foundations be destroyed, what can the righteous do?

The Lord is in his holy temple, the Lord's throne is
in heaven: his eyes behold, his eyelids try the children
of men.

The Lord trieth the righteous: but the wicked and
him that loveth violence his soul hateth.

Upon the wicked he shall rain snares, fire and brim-
stone, and an horrible tempest: this shall be the portion
of their cup.

For the righteous Lord loveth righteousness; his
countenance doth behold the upright.

Who Walks Uprightly

(PSALM XV)

Lord, who shall abide in thy tabernacle? who shall
dwell in thy holy hill?

He that walketh uprightly, and worketh righteousness, and speaketh the truth in his heart.

He that backbiteth not with his tongue, nor doeth evil to his neighbour, nor taketh up a reproach against his neighbour.

In whose eyes a vile person is contemned; but he honoureth them that fear the Lord. He that sweareth to his own hurt, and changeth not.

He that putteth not out his money to usury, nor taketh reward against the innocent. He that doeth these things shall never be moved.

The Glory of God

(PSALM XIX)

The heavens declare the glory of God; and the firmament sheweth his handiwork.

Day unto day uttereth speech, and night unto night sheweth knowledge.

There is no speech nor language, where their voice is not heard.

Their line is gone out through all the earth, and their words to the end of the world. In them hath he set a tabernacle for the sun,

Which is as a bridegroom coming out of his chamber, and rejoiceth as a strong man to run a race.

His going forth is from the end of the heaven, and his circuit unto the ends of it: and there is nothing hid from the heat thereof.

The law of the Lord is perfect, converting the soul: the testimony of the Lord is sure, making wise the simple.

The statutes of the Lord are right, rejoicing the heart: the commandment of the Lord is pure, enlightening the eyes.

The fear of the Lord is clean, enduring for ever: the judgments of the Lord are true and righteous altogether.

More to be desired are they than gold, yea, than much fine gold: sweeter also than honey and the honey-comb.

Moreover, by them is thy servant warned; and in keeping of them there is great reward.

Who can understand his errors? cleanse thou me from secret faults.

Keep back thy servant also from presumptuous sins; let them not have dominion over me: then shall I be upright, and I shall be innocent from the great transgression.

Let the words of my mouth, and the meditation of my heart, be acceptable in thy sight, O Lord, my strength, and my redeemer.

A Cry of Despair

(PSALM XXII)

My God, my God, why hast thou forsaken me? why art thou so far from helping me, and from the words of my roaring?

O my God, I cry in the daytime, but thou hearest not; and in the night season, and am not silent.

But thou art holy, O thou that inhabitest the praises of Israel.

Our fathers trusted in thee: they trusted, and thou didst deliver them.

They cried unto thee, and were delivered: they trusted in thee, and were not confounded.

But I am a worm, and no man; a reproach of men, and despised of the people.

All they that see me laugh me to scorn: they shoot out the lip, they shake the head, saying,

He trusted on the Lord that he would deliver him: let him deliver him, seeing he delighted in him.

But thou art he that took me out of the womb: thou didst make me hope when I was upon my mother's breasts.

I was cast upon thee from the womb: thou art my God from my mother's belly.

Be not far from me; for trouble is near; for there is none to help.

Many bulls have compassed me: strong bulls of Bashan have beset me round.

They gaped upon me with their mouths, as a ravening and a roaring lion.

I am poured out like water, and all my bones are out of joint; my heart is like wax: it is melted in the midst of my bowels.

My strength is dried up like a potsherd; and my tongue cleaveth to my jaws; and thou hast brought me into the dust of death.

For dogs have compassed me: the assembly of the wicked have inclosed me: they pierced my hands and my feet.

I may tell all my bones: they look and stare upon me.

They part my garments among them and cast lots upon my vesture.

But be not thou far from me, O Lord: O my strength, haste thee to help me.

Deliver my soul from the sword, my darling from the power of the dog.

Save me from the lion's mouth: for thou hast heard me from the horns of the unicorns.

I will declare thy name unto my brethren: in the midst of the congregation will I praise thee.

Ye that fear the Lord, praise him; all ye the seed of Jacob, glorify him; and fear him, all ye the seed of Israel.

For he hath not despised nor abhorred the affliction of the afflicted; neither hath he hid his face from him; but when he cried unto him, he heard.

My praise shall be of thee in the great congregation: I will pay my vows before them that fear him.

The meek shall eat and be satisfied: they shall praise the Lord that seek him: your heart shall live for ever.

All the ends of the world shall remember and turn unto the Lord: and all the kindreds of the nations shall worship before thee.

For the kingdom is the Lord's: and he is the governor among the nations.

All they that be fat upon earth shall eat and worship: all they that go down to the dust shall bow before him: and none can keep alive his own soul.

A seed shall serve him; it shall be accounted to the Lord for a generation.

They shall come, and shall declare his righteousness unto a people that shall be born, that he hath done this.

The Shepherd's Psalm

(PSALM XXIII)

The Lord is my shepherd; I shall not want.

He maketh me to lie down in green pastures: he leadeth me beside the still waters.

He restoreth my soul: he leadeth me in the paths of righteousness for his name's sake.

Yea, though I walk through the valley of the shadow of death, I will fear no evil: for thou art with me; thy rod and thy staff they comfort me.

Thou preparest a table before me in the presence of mine enemies: thou anointest my head with oil; my cup runneth over.

Surely goodness and mercy shall follow me all the days of my life; and I will dwell in the house of the Lord for ever.

The King of Glory

(PSALM XXIV)

The earth is the Lord's and the fulness thereof; the world, and they that dwell therein.

For he hath founded it upon the seas, and established it upon the floods.

Who shall ascend into the hill of the Lord? and who shall stand in his holy place?

He that hath clean hands, and a pure heart; who hath not lifted up his soul unto vanity, nor sworn deceitfully.

He shall receive the blessing from the Lord, and righteousness from the God of his salvation.

This is the generation of them that seek him, that seek thy face, O Jacob.

Lift up your heads, O ye gates; and be ye lifted up, ye everlasting doors; and the King of glory shall come in.

Who is this King of glory? the Lord strong and mighty, the Lord mighty in battle.

Lift up your heads, O ye gates; even lift them up, ye everlasting doors; and the King of glory shall come in.

Who is this King of glory? the Lord of hosts, he is the King of glory.

A Hymn of Faith

(PSALM XXVII)

The Lord is my light and my salvation; whom shall I fear? the Lord is the strength of my life; of whom shall I be afraid?

When the wicked, even mine enemies and my foes, came upon me to eat up my flesh, they stumbled and fell.

Though an host should encamp against me, my heart shall not fear: though war should rise against me, in this will I be confident.

One thing have I desired of the Lord, that will I seek after; that I may dwell in the house of the Lord all the days of my life, to behold the beauty of the Lord, and to inquire in his temple.

For in the time of trouble he shall hide me in his pavilion: in the secret of his tabernacle shall he hide me; he shall set me up upon a rock.

And now shall mine head be lifted up above mine enemies round about me: therefore will I offer in his tabernacle sacrifices of joy; I will sing, yea, I will sing praises unto the Lord.

Hear, O Lord, when I cry with my voice: have mercy also upon me, and answer me.

When thou saidst, Seek ye my face; my heart said unto thee, Thy face, Lord, will I seek.

Hide not thy face far from me; put not thy servant away in anger; thou hast been my help; leave me not, neither forsake me, O God of my salvation.

When my father and my mother forsake me, then the Lord will take me up.

Teach me thy way, O Lord, and lead me in a plain path, because of mine enemies.

Deliver me not over unto the will of mine enemies: for false witnesses are risen up against me, and such as breathe out cruelty.

I had fainted, unless I had believed to see the goodness of the Lord in the land of the living.

Wait on the Lord: be of good courage, and he shall strengthen thine heart: wait, I say, on the Lord.

The Gentleness of God

(PSALM CIII)

Bless the Lord, O my soul: and all that is within me, bless his holy name.

Bless the Lord, O my soul, and forget not all his benefits:

Who forgiveth all thine iniquities; who healeth all thy diseases;

Who redeemeth thy life from destruction; who crowneth thee with loving-kindness and tender mercies;

Who satisfieth thy mouth with good things; so that thy youth is renewed like the eagle's.

The Lord executeth righteousness and judgment for all that are oppressed.

He made known his ways unto Moses, his acts unto the children of Israel.

The Lord is merciful and gracious, slow to anger, and plenteous in mercy.

He will not always chide; neither will he keep his anger for ever.

He hath not dealt with us after our sins; nor rewarded us according to our iniquities.

For as the heaven is high above the earth, so great is his mercy toward them that fear him.

As far as the east is from the west, so far hath he removed our transgressions from us.

Like as a father pitieth his children, so the Lord pitieth them that fear him.

For he knoweth our frame; he remembereth that we are dust.

As for man, his days are as grass: as a flower of the field, so he flourisheth.

For the wind passeth over it, and it is gone; and the place thereof shall know it no more.

But the mercy of the Lord is from everlasting to everlasting upon them that fear him, and his righteousness unto children's children;

To such as keep his covenant, and to those that remember his commandments to do them.

The Bounty of God

(PSALM CIV)

Bless the Lord, O my soul. O Lord my God, thou art very great; thou art clothed with honour and majesty:

Who coverest thyself with light as with a garment: who stretchest out the heavens like a curtain:

Who layeth the beams of his chambers in the waters: who maketh the clouds his chariot: who walketh upon the wings of the wind:

Who maketh his angels spirits; his ministers a flaming fire:

Who laid the foundations of the earth, that it should not be removed for ever.

Thou coveredst it with the deep as with a garment: the waters stood above the mountains.

At thy rebuke they fled; at the voice of thy thunder they hasted away.

They go up by the mountains; they go down by the valleys unto the place which thou hast founded for them.

Thou hast set a bound that they may not pass over; that they turn not again to cover the earth.

He sendeth the springs into the valleys, which run among the hills.

They give drink to every beast of the field: the wild asses quench their thirst.

By them shall the fowls of the heaven have their habitation, which sing among the branches.

He watereth the hills from his chambers: the earth is satisfied with the fruit of thy works.

He causeth the grass to grow for the cattle, and herb for the service of man: that he may bring forth food out of the earth:

And wine that maketh glad the heart of man, and oil to make his face to shine, and bread which strengtheneth man's heart.

The trees of the Lord are full of sap; the cedars of Lebanon, which he hath planted;

Where the birds make their nests: as for the stork, the fir-trees are her house.

The high hills are a refuge for the wild goats; and the rocks for the conies.

He appointed the moon for seasons: the sun knoweth his going down.

Thou makest darkness, and it is night: wherein all the beasts of the forest do creep forth.

The young lions roar after their prey, and seek their meat from God.

The sun ariseth, they gather themselves together, and lay them down in their dens.

Man goeth forth unto his work and to his labour until the evening.

O Lord, how manifold are thy works! in wisdom hast thou made them all: the earth is full of thy riches.

So is this great and wide sea, wherein are things creeping innumerable, both small and great beasts.

There go the ships: there is that leviathan, whom thou hast made to play therein.

These wait all upon thee; that thou mayest give them their meat in due season.

That thou givest them, they gather: thou openest thine hand, they are filled with good.

Thou hidest thy face, they are troubled: thou takest away their breath, they die, and return to their dust.

Thou sendest forth thy spirit, they are created: and thou renewest the face of the earth.

The glory of the Lord shall endure for ever: the Lord shall rejoice in his works.

He looketh on the earth, and it trembleth: he toucheth the hills, and they smoke.

I will sing unto the Lord as long as I live: I will sing praise to my God while I have my being.

My meditation of him shall be sweet: I will be glad in the Lord.

Let the sinners be consumed out of the earth, and let the wicked be no more. Bless thou the Lord, O my soul. Praise ye the Lord.

Whence Help Cometh

(PSALM CXXI)

I will lift up mine eyes unto the hills, from whence cometh my help.

My help cometh from the Lord, which made heaven and earth.

He will not suffer thy foot to be moved: he that keepeth thee will not slumber.

Behold, he that keepeth Israel shall neither slumber nor sleep.

The Lord is thy keeper: the Lord is thy shade upon thy right hand.

The sun shall not smite thee by day, nor the moon by night.

The Lord shall preserve thee from all evil: he shall preserve thy soul.

The Lord shall preserve thy going out and thy coming in from this time forth, and even for evermore.

He Giveth His Beloved Sleep

(PSALM CXXVII)

Except the Lord build the house, they labour in vain that build it: except the Lord keep the city, the watchman waketh but in vain.

It is vain for you to rise up early, to sit up late, to eat the bread of sorrows: for so he giveth his beloved sleep.

Lo, children are an heritage of the Lord: and the fruit of the womb is his reward.

As arrows are in the hand of a mighty man; so are children of the youth.

Happy is the man that hath his quiver full of them: they shall not be ashamed, but they shall speak with the enemies in the gate.

The Goodness of Unity

(PSALM CXXXIII)

Behold, how good and how pleasant it is for brethren to dwell together in unity!

It is like the precious ointment upon the head, that ran down upon the beard, even Aaron's beard: that went down to the skirts of his garments;

As the dew of Hermon, and as the dew that descended upon the mountains of Zion: for there the Lord commanded the blessing, even life for evermore.

From the Book of Proverbs

Proverbs

The proverbs of Solomon the son of David, king of Israel:

The fear of the Lord is the beginning of knowledge: but fools despise wisdom and instruction.

Wisdom crieth without; she uttereth her voice in the streets; she crieth in the chief places of concourse, in the openings of the gates: in the city she uttereth her words, saying, How long, ye simple ones, will ye love simplicity? and the scorners delight in their scorning, and fools hate knowledge? Turn you at my reproof: behold, I will pour out my spirit unto you, I will make known my words unto you.

Let not mercy and truth forsake thee: bind them about thy neck; write them upon the table of thine heart.

Happy is the man that findeth wisdom, and the man that getteth understanding. For the merchandise of it is better than the merchandise of silver, and the gain thereof than fine gold. She is more precious than rubies: and all the things thou canst desire are not to be compared unto her. Length of days is in her right hand; and in her left hand riches and honour. Her ways are ways of pleasantness, and all her paths are peace. She is a tree of life to them that lay hold upon her: and happy is every one that retaineth her.

The Lord by wisdom hath founded the earth; by understanding hath he established the heavens. By his knowledge the depths are broken up, and the clouds drop down the dew.

Be not afraid of sudden fear, neither of the desolation of the wicked, when it cometh.

Wisdom is the principal thing; therefore get wisdom: and with all thy getting get understanding. Exalt her, and she shall promote thee: she shall bring thee to honour, when thou dost embrace her. She shall give to thine head an ornament of grace: a crown of glory shall she deliver to thee.

Go to the ant, thou sluggard; consider her ways, and be wise; which having no guide, overseer, or ruler, provideth her meat in the summer, and gathereth her food in the harvest. How long wilt thou sleep, O sluggard? when wilt thou arise out of thy sleep?

Yet a little sleep, a little slumber, a little folding of the hands to sleep: so shall thy poverty come as one that travelleth, and thy want as an armed man.

These six things doth the Lord hate; yea, seven are an abomination unto him: a proud look, a lying tongue, and hands that shed innocent blood, an heart that deviseth wicked imaginations, feet that be swift in running to mischief, a false witness that speaketh lies, and he that soweth discord among brethren.

I Wisdom dwell with prudence, and find out knowledge of witty inventions. By me kings reign, and princes decree justice. By me princes rule, and nobles, even all the judges of the earth. I love them that love me: and those that seek me early shall find me. I lead in the way of righteousness, in the midst of the paths of judgment.

The Lord possessed me in the beginning of his way, before his works of old. I was set up from everlasting, from the beginning, or ever the earth was. When there were no depths, I was brought forth; when there were no fountains abounding with water. Before the mountains were settled, before the hills was I brought forth:

while as yet he had not made the earth, nor the fields, nor the highest part of the dust of the world. When he prepared the heavens, I was there: when he set a compass upon the face of the depth: when he established the clouds above: when he strengthened the fountains of the deep: when he gave to the sea his decree, that the waters should not pass his commandment; when he appointed the foundations of the earth: then I was by him, as one brought up with him: and I was daily his delight, rejoicing always before him.

Hatred stirreth up strifes: but love covereth all sins.

Where no counsel is, the people fall: but in the multitude of counsellors there is safety.

He that tilleth his land shall be satisfied with bread: but he that followeth vain persons is void of understanding.

He that spareth his rod hateth his son: but he that loveth him chasteneth him betimes.

A soft answer turneth away wrath: but grievous words stir up anger.

Better is little with the fear of the Lord, than great treasure and trouble therewith.

Pride goeth before destruction, and an haughty spirit before a fall.

Whoso mocketh the poor reproacheth his Maker: and he that is glad at calamities shall not be unpunished.

A merry heart doeth good like a medicine: but a broken spirit drieth the bones.

Even a fool, when he holdeth his peace, is counted wise: and he that shutteth his lips is esteemed a man of understanding.

He that answereth a matter before he heareth it, it is folly and shame unto him.

A man that hath friends must shew himself friendly: and there is a friend that sticketh closer than a brother.

Wine is a mocker, strong drink is raging: and whosoever is deceived thereby is not wise.

A good name is rather to be chosen than great riches, and loving favour rather than silver and gold.

Train up a child in the way he should go: and when he is old, he will not depart from it.

Make no friendship with an angry man; and with a furious man thou shalt not go: lest thou learn his ways, and get a snare to thy soul.

Seest thou a man diligent in his business? he shall stand before kings; he shall not stand before mean men.

Rejoice not when thine enemy falleth, and let not thine heart be glad when he stumbleth: lest the Lord see it, and it displease him, and he turn away his wrath from him.

If thine enemy be hungry, give him bread to eat; and if he be thirsty, give him water to drink: for thou shalt heap coals of fire upon his head, and the Lord shall reward thee.

He that hath no rule over his own spirit is like a city that is broken down, and without walls.

The Unsatisfied and the Wonderful

The words of Agur the son of Jakeh, even the prophecy: the man spake unto Ithiel, even unto Ithiel and Ucal:

There are three things that are never satisfied, yea, four things say not, It is enough: the grave; and the barren womb; the earth that is not filled with water; and the fire that saith not, It is enough.

There be three things which are too wonderful for me, yea, four which I know not: the way of an eagle in the air; the way of a serpent upon a rock; the way

of a ship in the midst of the sea; and the way of a man
with a maid.

For three things the earth is disquieted, and for four
which it cannot bear: for a servant when he reigneth;
and a fool when he is filled with meat; for an odious
woman when she is married; and an handmaid that is
heir to her mistress.

There be four things which are little upon the earth,
but they are exceeding wise: the ants are a people not
strong, yet they prepare their meat in the summer; the
conies are but a feeble folk, yet make they their houses
in the rocks; the locusts have no king, yet go they forth
all of them by bands; the spider taketh hold with her
hands, and is in kings' palaces.

There be three things which go well, yea, four are
comely in going: a lion, which is strongest among
beasts, and turneth not away for any; a greyhound;
an he-goat also; and a king, against whom there is no
rising up.

If thou hast done foolishly in lifting up thyself, or if
thou hast thought evil, lay thine hand upon thy mouth.

Surely the churning of milk bringeth forth butter, and
the wringing of the nose bringeth forth blood: so the
forcing of wrath bringeth forth strife.

From the Book of Ecclesiastes

The Vanity of Man

The words of the Preacher, the son of David, king
in Jerusalem.

Vanity of vanities, saith the Preacher, vanity of vanities; all is vanity.

What profit hath a man of all his labour which he taketh under the sun?

One generation passeth away, and another generation cometh: but the earth abideth for ever.

The sun also ariseth, and the sun goeth down, and hasteth to his place where he arose. The wind goeth toward the south, and turneth about unto the north; it whirleth about continually, and the wind returneth again according to his circuits. All the rivers run into the sea; yet the sea is not full: unto the place from whence the rivers come, thither they return again.

All things are full of labour; a man cannot utter it: the eye is not satisfied with seeing, nor the ear filled with hearing.

The thing that hath been, it is that which shall be; and that which is done is that which shall be done: and there is no new thing under the sun. Is there anything whereof it may be said, See, this is new? it hath been already of old time, which was before us. There is no remembrance of former things; neither shall there be any remembrance of things that are to come with those that shall come after.

I have seen all the works that are done under the sun; and behold, all is vanity and vexation of Spirit.

I said in mine heart, Go to now, I will prove thee with mirth; therefore enjoy pleasure: and behold, this also is vanity. I said of laughter, It is mad: and of mirth, What doeth it?

I sought in mine heart to give myself unto wine, yet acquainting mine heart with wisdom; and to lay hold on folly, till I might see what was that good for the sons of men, which they should do under the heaven all the days of their life.

I made me great works; I builded me houses; I planted me vineyards; I made me gardens and orchards, and I planted trees in them of all kind of fruits; I made me pools of water, to water therewith the wood that bringeth forth trees; I got me servants and maidens, and had servants born in my house; also I had great possessions of great and small cattle above all that were in Jerusalem before me; I gathered me also silver and gold, and the peculiar treasure of kings, and of the provinces; I gat me men-singers and women-singers, and the delights of the sons of men, as musical instruments, and that of all sorts.

So I was great, and increased more than all that were before me in Jerusalem: also my wisdom remained with me. And whatsoever mine eyes desired I kept not from them, I withheld not my heart from any joy; for my heart rejoiceth in all my labour: and this was my portion of all my labour.

Then I looked on all the works that my hands had wrought, and on the labour that I had laboured to do: and behold, all was vanity and vexation of spirit, and there was no profit under the sun.

And I turned myself to behold wisdom, and madness, and folly: for what can the man do that cometh after the king? even that which hath been already done. Then I saw that wisdom excelleth folly, as far as light excelleth darkness. The wise man's eyes are in his head; but the fool walketh in darkness: and I myself perceived also that one event happeneth to them all.

Then said I in my heart, As it happeneth to the fool, so it happeneth even to me; and why was I then more wise? Then I said in my heart, that this also is vanity.

For there is no remembrance of the wise more than of the fool for ever; seeing that which now is in the days to come shall all be forgotten. And how dieth the wise man? as the fool. Therefore I hated life; because the work that is wrought under the sun is grievous unto me: for all is vanity, and vexation of spirit.

Yea, I hated all my labour which I had taken under the sun: because I should leave it unto the man that shall be after me. And who knoweth whether he shall be a wise man or a fool? yet shall he have rule over all my labour wherein I have laboured, and wherein I have shewed myself wise under the sun. This is also vanity. Therefore I went about to cause my heart to despair of all the labour which I took under the sun.

There is nothing better for a man than that he should eat and drink, and that he should make his soul enjoy good in his labour. This also I saw, that it was from the hand of God. For who can eat, or who else can hasten hereunto more than I?

For God giveth to a man that is good in his sight, wisdom, and knowledge, and joy: but to the sinner he giveth travail, to gather and to heap up, that he may give to him that is good before God. This also is vanity and vexation of spirit.

To everything there is a season, and a time to every purpose under the heaven: a time to be born, and a time to die; a time to plant, and a time to pluck up that which is planted; a time to kill, and a time to heal; a time to break down, and a time to build up; a time to weep, and a time to laugh; a time to mourn, and a time to dance; a time to cast away stones, and a time to gather stones together; a time to embrace, and a time to refrain from embracing; a time to get, and a time to lose; a time to keep, and a time to cast away; a time to rend, and a time to sew; a time to keep silence, and a time to speak; a time to love, and a time to hate; a time of war, and a time of peace.

So I returned, and considered all the oppressions

that are done under the sun: and behold the tears of such were oppressed, and they had no comforter; and on the side of their oppressors there was power; but they had no comforter.

Wherefore I praised the dead which are already dead more than the living which are yet alive. Yea, better is he than both they, which hath not yet been, who hath not seen the evil work that is done under the sun.

Two are better than one; because they have a good reward for their labour. For if they fall, the one will lift up his fellow: but woe to him that is alone when he falleth; for he hath not another to help him up. Again, if two lie together, then they have heat: but how can one be warm alone? And if one prevail against him, two shall withstand him; and a threefold cord is not quickly broken.

A good name is better than precious ointment; and the day of death than the day of one's birth. It is better to go to the house of mourning, than to go to the house of feasting: for that is the end of all men; and the living will lay it to his heart. Sorrow is better than laughter: for by the sadness of the countenance the heart is made better.

There is one event to the righteous and to the wicked; to the good, and to the clean, and to the unclean; to him that sacrificeth, and to him that sacrificeth not: as is the good, so is the sinner; and he that sweareth, as he that feareth an oath.

Go thy way, eat thy bread with joy, and drink thy wine with a merry heart. Live joyfully with the wife whom thou lovest all the days of the life of thy vanity, which He hath given thee under the sun, all the days of thy vanity: for that is thy portion in this life, and in thy labour which thou takest under the sun. Whatsoever thy hand findeth to do, do it with thy might; for there is no work, nor device, nor knowledge, nor wisdom, in the grave, whither thou goest.

Remember now thy Creator in the days of thy youth, while the evil days come not, nor the years draw nigh, when thou shalt say, I have no pleasure in them; while the sun, or the light, or the moon, or the stars, be not darkened, nor the clouds return after the rain: in the day when the keepers of the house shall tremble, and the strong men shall bow themselves, and the grinders cease because they are few, and those that look out of the windows be darkened, and the doors shall be shut in the streets, when the sound of the grinding is low, and he shall rise up at the voice of the bird, and all the daughters of music shall be brought low. Also when they shall be afraid of that which is high, and fears shall be in the way, and the almond-tree shall flourish, and the grasshopper shall be a burden, and desire shall fail: because man goeth to his long home, and the mourners go about the streets: or ever the silver cord be loosed, or the golden bowl be broken, or the pitcher be broken at the fountain, or the wheel broken at the cistern. Then shall the dust return to the earth as it was: and the spirit shall return unto God who gave it.

Vanity of vanities, saith the Preacher; all is vanity.

And further, by these, my son, be admonished: of making many books there is no end; and much study is a weariness of the flesh.

Let us hear the conclusion of the whole matter: Fear God, and keep his commandments: for this is the whole duty of man. For God shall bring every work into judgment, with every secret thing, whether it be good, or whether it be evil.

From the Pre-Exilic Prophets

From the Book of Amos

Can two walk together, except they be agreed?

Seek the Lord and ye shall live; lest he break out like a fire in the house of Joseph, and devour it, and there be none to quench it in Bethel.

Ye who turn judgment to wormwood, and leave off righteousness in the earth, seek him that maketh the seven stars and Orion, and turneth the shadow of death into the morning, and maketh the day dark with night; that called for the waters of the sea, and poureth them out upon the face of the earth; the Lord is his name, that strengtheneth the spoiled against the strong, so that the spoiled shall come against the fortress.

Forasmuch, therefore, as your treading is upon the poor, and ye take from him burdens of wheat, ye have built houses of hewn stone, but ye shall not dwell in them; ye have planted pleasant vineyards, but ye shall not drink of the wine.

Seek good, and not evil, that ye may live; and so the Lord, the God of hosts, shall be with you as ye have spoken. Hate the evil and love the good, and establish judgment in the gate; it may be that the Lord God of hosts will be gracious unto the remnant of Joseph.

I hate, I despise your feast days, and I will not smell in your solemn assemblies. Though ye offer me burnt-offerings and your meat-offerings, I will not accept them; neither will I regard the peace-offerings of your fat beasts. Take thou away from me the noise of your songs; for I will not hear the melody of thy viols. But let judgment run down as waters, and righteousness as a mighty stream.

Hear this, O ye that swallow up the needy, even to make the poor of the land to fail, saying, when will the new moon be gone that we may sell corn? And the Sabbath, that we may set forth wheat, making the ephaḥ small, and the sheckel great, and falsifying the balances by deceit? That we may buy the poor for silver, and the needy for a pair of shoes, yea, and sell the refuse of the wheat?

The Lord hath sworn by the excellency of Jacob, surely I will never forget any of their works. Shall not the land tremble for this, and every one mourn that dwelleth therein? And it shall come to pass in that day, saith the Lord God, that I will cause the sun to go down at noon, and I will darken the earth in the clear day; and I will turn your feasts into mourning, and all your songs into lamentation, and I will make it as the mourning of an only son, and the end thereof as a bitter day.

From the Book of Hosea

Hear the word of the Lord, ye children of Israel: for the Lord hath a controversy with the inhabitants of the land, because there is no truth, nor mercy, nor knowledge of God in the land.

By swearing, and lying, and killing, and stealing, and committing adultery, they break out, and blood toucheth blood. Therefore, shall the land mourn, and every one that dwelleth therein shall languish, with the beasts of the field, and with the fowls of heaven; yea, the fishes of the sea also shall be taken away. Yet let no man strive, nor reprove another; for thy people are as they that strive with the priest. Therefore, shalt thou fall in the day, and the prophet also shall fall with thee in the night, and I will destroy thy mother.

My people are destroyed for lack of knowledge: because thou hast rejected knowledge, I will also reject thee, that thou shalt be no priest to me: seeing thou hast forgotten the law of thy God, I will also forget thy children. As they were increased, so they sinned against me: therefore will I change their glory into shame. They eat up the sin of my people, and they set their heart on their iniquity.

Come, and let us return unto the Lord: for he hath torn, and he will heal us; he hath smitten, and he will bind us up. After two days will he revive us: in the third day he will raise us up, and we shall live in his sight. Then shall we know, if we follow on to know the Lord: his going forth is prepared as the morning; and he shall come unto us as the rain, as the latter and former rain unto the earth.

For I desired mercy, and not sacrifice, and the knowledge of God more than burnt-offerings.

For they have sown the wind, and they shall reap the whirlwind; it hath no stalks; the bud shall yield no meal; if so be it yield, the strangers shall swallow it up. Israel is swallowed up; now shall they be among the Gentiles as a vessel wherein is no pleasure.

From the Book of Micah

But in the last days it shall come to pass, that the mountain of the house of the Lord shall be established in the top of the mountains, and it shall be exalted above the hills; and people shall flow unto it. And many nations shall come, and say, Come, and let us go up to the mountain of the Lord, and to the house of the God of Jacob; and he will teach us of his ways, and we will walk in his paths: for the law shall go forth of Zion, and the word of the Lord from Jerusalem.

And he shall judge among many people, and rebuke strong nations afar off; and they shall beat their swords into plough-shares, and their spears into pruning-hooks: nation shall not lift up a sword against nation, neither shall they learn war any more. But they shall sit every man under his vine and under his fig-tree; and none shall make them afraid: for the mouth of the Lord of hosts hath spoken it. For all people will walk every one in the name of his god, and we will walk in the name of the Lord our God for ever and ever.

Now gather thyself in troops, O daughter of troops: he hath laid siege against us: they shall smite the judge of Israel with a rod upon the cheek. But thou, Bethlehem Ephratah, though thou be little among the thousands of Judah, yet out of thee shall he come forth unto me that is to be Ruler in Israel; whose goings forth have been from of old, from everlasting. Therefore will he give them up until the time that she which travaileth hath brought forth: then the remnant of his brethren shall return unto the children of Israel.

Wherewith shall I come before the Lord, and bow myself before the high God? Shall I come before him with burnt-offerings, with calves of a year old? Will the Lord be pleased with thousands of rams, or with ten thousands of rivers of oil? Shall I give my first-born for my transgression, the fruit of my body for the sin of my soul?

He hath showed thee, O man, what is good; and what doth the Lord require of thee, but to do justly, and to love mercy, and to walk humbly with thy God?

From the Book of the First Isaiah

The vision of Isaiah the son of Amoz, which he saw concerning Judah and Jerusalem in the days of Uzziah, Jotham, Ahaz, and Hezekiah, kings of Judah.

Hear the word of the Lord, ye rulers of Sodom: give ear unto the law of our God, ye people of Gomorrah.

To what purpose is the multitude of your sacrifices unto me? saith the Lord: I am full of the burnt-offerings of rams, and the fat of fed beasts; and I delight not in the blood of bullocks, or of lambs, or of he-goats. When ye come to appear before me, who hath required this at your hand, to tread my courts? Bring no more vain oblations: incense is an abomination unto me; the new-moons and sabbaths, the calling of assemblies, I cannot away with; it is iniquity, even the solemn meeting. Your new-moons and your appointed feasts my soul hateth: they are a trouble unto me; I am weary to bear them. And when ye spread forth your hands, I will hide mine eyes from you; yea, when ye make many prayers, I will not hear: your hands are full of blood.

Wash you, make you clean: put away the evil of your doings from before mine eyes; cease to do evil; learn to do well; seek judgment, relieve the oppressed, judge the fatherless, plead for the widow.

Come now, and let us reason together, saith the Lord: though your sins be as scarlet, they shall be as white as snow; though they be red like crimson, they shall be as wool.

If ye be willing and obedient, ye shall eat the good of the land: but if ye refuse and rebel, ye shall be devoured with the sword: for the mouth of the Lord hath spoken it.

The Lord spake also unto me again, saying,

The people that walked in darkness have seen a great light: they that dwell in the land of the shadow of death, upon them hath the light shined. Thou hast multiplied the nation, and not increased the joy: they joy before thee according to the joy in harvest, and as men rejoice when they divide the spoil. For thou hast broken the yoke of his burden, and the staff of his shoulder, the rod of his oppressor, as in the day of Midian. For every battle of the warrior is with confused noise, and garments rolled in blood; but this shall be with burning and fuel of fire.

For unto us a child is born, unto us a son is given: and the government shall be upon his shoulder: and his name shall be called Wonderful, Counsellor, The Mighty God, The Everlasting Father, The Prince of Peace. Of the increase of his government and peace there shall be no end, upon the throne of David, and upon his kingdom, to order it, and to establish it with judgment and with justice from henceforth even for ever. The zeal of the Lord of hosts will perform this.

And there shall come forth a rod out of the stem of Jesse, and a Branch shall grow out of his roots. And the Spirit of the Lord shall rest upon him, the spirit of wisdom and understanding, the spirit of counsel and might, the spirit of knowledge and of the fear of the Lord, and shall make him of quick understanding in the fear of the Lord: and he shall not judge after the sight of his eyes, neither reprove after the hearing of his ears, but with righteousness shall he judge the poor, and reprove with equity for the meek of the earth: and he shall smite the earth with the rod of his mouth, and with the breath of his lips shall he slay the wicked. And righteousness shall be the girdle of his loins, and faithfulness the girdle of his reins.

The wolf also shall dwell with the lamb, and the leopard shall lie down with the kid; and the calf and the young lion and the fatling together; and a little child shall lead them. And the cow and the bear shall feed; their young ones shall lie down together: and the lion shall eat straw like the ox. And the suckling child shall play on the hole of the asp, and the weaned child shall put his hand on the cockatrice's den. They shall not hurt nor destroy in all my holy mountain: for the earth shall be full of the knowledge of the Lord, as the waters cover the sea.

And in that day there shall be a root of Jesse, which shall stand for an ensign of the people; to it shall the Gentiles seek: and his rest shall be glorious.

From the Book of Jeremiah

Woe be unto the pastors that destroy and scatter the sheep of my pasture! saith the Lord. Ye have scattered my flock, and driven them away, and have not visited them: behold, I will visit upon you the evil of your doings, saith the Lord.

And I will gather the remnant of my flock out of all countries whither I have driven them, and will bring them again to their folds; and they shall be fruitful and increase. And I will set up shepherds over them, which shall feed them: and they shall fear no more, nor be dismayed, neither shall they be lacking, saith the Lord.

Behold, I am against the prophets, saith the Lord,

that use their tongues. Behold, I am against them that prophesy false dreams, saith the Lord, and do tell them, and cause my people to err by their lies, and by their lightness; yet I sent them not, nor commanded them; therefore they shall not profit this people at all, saith the Lord.

Therefore behold, I even I, will utterly forget you, and I will forsake you, and the city that I gave you and your fathers, and cast you out of my presence: and I will bring an everlasting reproach upon you, and a perpetual shame, which shall not be forgotten.

From the Book of the Second Isaiah

A Voice in the Wilderness

Comfort ye, comfort ye my people, saith your God. Speak ye comfortably to Jerusalem, and cry unto her, that her warfare is accomplished, that her iniquity is pardoned: for she hath received of the Lord's hand double for all her sins.

The voice of him that crieth in the wilderness, Prepare ye the way of the Lord, make straight in the desert a highway for our God. Every valley shall be exalted, and every mountain and hill shall be made low: and the crooked shall be made straight, and the rough places plain. And the glory of the Lord shall be revealed, and all flesh shall see it together: for the mouth of the Lord hath spoken it.

The voice said, Cry.

And he said, What shall I cry? All flesh is grass, and all the goodliness thereof is as the flower of the field. The grass withereth, the flower fadeth: because the spirit of the Lord bloweth upon it: surely the people is grass. The grass withereth, the flower fadeth: but the word of our God shall stand for ever.

O Zion, that bringest good tidings, get thee up into the high mountain. O Jerusalem, that bringest good tidings, lift up thy voice with strength; lift it up, be not afraid; say unto the cities of Judah, Behold your God! Behold the Lord God will come with strong hand, and his arm shall rule for him: behold, his reward is with him, and his work before him. He shall feed his flock like a shepherd: he shall gather the lambs with his arm, and carry them in his bosom, and shall gently lead those that are with young.

Who hath measured the waters in the hollow of his hand, and meted out heaven with the span, and comprehended the dust of the earth in a measure, and weighed the mountains in scales, and the hills in a balance? Who hath directed the Spirit of the Lord, or being his counsellor hath taught him? With whom took he counsel, and who instructed him, and taught him in the path of judgment, and taught him knowledge, and shewed to him the way of understanding?

Behold, the nations are as a drop of a bucket, and are counted as the small dust of the balance: behold, he taketh up the isles as a very little thing. And Lebanon is not sufficient to burn, nor the beasts thereof sufficient for a burnt-offering. All nations before him are as nothing; and they are counted to him less than nothing, and vanity.

To whom then will ye liken God? or what likeness will ye compare unto him?

The workman melteth a graven image, and the goldsmith spreadeth it over with gold, and casteth silver chains. He that is so impoverished that he hath no oblation chooseth a tree that will not rot; he seeketh unto him a cunning workman to prepare a graven image that shall not be moved.

Have ye not known? have ye not heard? hath it not been told you from the beginning? have ye not understood from the foundations of the earth?

It is he that sitteth upon the circle of the earth, and the inhabitants thereof are as grasshoppers; that stretcheth out the heavens as a curtain, and spreadeth them out as a tent to dwell in; that bringeth the princes to nothing; he maketh the judges of the earth as vanity.

Yea, they shall not be planted; yea, they shall not be sown; yea, their stock shall not take root in the earth: and he shall also blow upon them, and they shall wither, and the whirlwind shall take them away as stubble.

To whom then will ye liken me, or shall I be equal? saith the Holy One.

Lift up your eyes on high, and behold who hath created these things, that bringeth out their host by number: he calleth them all by names, by the greatness of his might, for that he is strong in power; not one faileth.

Why sayest thou, O Jacob, and speakest, O Israel, My way is hid from the Lord, and my judgment is passed over from my God?

Hast thou not known, hast thou not heard, that the everlasting God, the Lord, the Creator of the ends of the earth, fainteth not, neither is weary? there is no searching of his understanding. He giveth power to the faint; and to them that have no might he increaseth strength. Even the youths shall faint and be weary, and the young men shall utterly fall. But they that wait upon the Lord shall renew their strength; they shall mount up with wings as eagles; they shall run, and not be weary; and they shall walk, and not faint.

Fear thou not; for I am with thee: be not dismayed; for I am thy God: I will strengthen thee; yea, I will help thee; yea, I will uphold thee with the right hand of my righteousness.

The Omnipotence of God

Thus saith the Lord to his anointed, to Cyrus, whose right hand I have holden, to subdue nations before him; and I will loose the loins of kings, to open before him the two-leaved gates, and the gates shall not be shut. I will go before thee, and make the crooked places straight: I will break in pieces the gates of brass, and cut in sunder the bars of iron. And I will give thee the treasures of darkness, and hidden riches of secret places, that thou mayest know that I, the Lord, which call thee by thy name, am the God of Israel. For Jacob my servant's sake, and Israel mine elect, I have even called thee by thy name: I have surnamed thee, though thou hast not known me.

I am the Lord, and there is none else, there is no God besides me: I girded thee, though hast not known me, that they may know from the rising of the sun, and from the west, that there is none besides me. I am the Lord, and there is none else. I form the light, and create darkness; I make peace, and create evil; I the Lord do all these things. Drop down, ye heavens, from above, and let the skies pour down righteousness: let the earth open, and let them bring forth salvation, and let righteousness spring up together; I the Lord have created it.

Woe unto him that striveth with his Maker! Let the potsherd strive with the potsherds of the earth. Shall the clay say to him that fashioneth it, What makest thou? or thy work, He hath no hands?

Woe unto him that saith unto his father, What begettest thou? or to the woman, What hast thou brought forth?

Thus saith the Lord, the Holy One of Israel, and his Maker, Ask me of things to come concerning my sons, and concerning the work of my hands command ye me. I have made the earth, and created man upon it: I, even my hands, have stretched out the heavens, and all their host have I commanded. I have raised him up in righteousness, and I will direct all his ways: he shall build my city, and he shall let go my captives, not for price nor reward, saith the Lord of hosts.

A Promise of Joy and Peace

Ho, every one that thirsteth, come ye to the waters, and he that hath no money; come ye, buy, and eat; yea, come, buy wine and milk without money and without price.

Wherefore do ye spend money for that which is not bread? and your labour for that which satisfieth not? hearken diligently unto me, and eat ye that which is good, and let your soul delight itself in fatness.

Incline your ear, and come unto me; hear, and your soul shall live; and I will make an everlasting covenant with you, even the sure mercies of David. Behold, I have given him for a witness to the people, a leader and commander to the people. Behold, thou shalt call a nation that thou knowest not, and nations that knew not thee shall run unto thee, because of the Lord thy God, and for the Holy One of Israel; for he hath glorified thee.

Seek ye the Lord while he may be found, call ye upon him while he is near. Let the wicked forsake his way, and the unrighteous man his thoughts: and let him return unto the Lord, and he will have mercy upon him; and to our God, for he will abundantly pardon.

For my thoughts are not your thoughts, neither are your ways my ways, saith the Lord. For as the heavens are higher than the earth, so are my ways higher than your ways, and my thoughts than your thoughts.

For as the rain cometh down, and the snow from heaven, and returneth not thither, but watereth the earth, and maketh it bring forth and bud, that it may give seed to the sower, and bread to the eater, so shall my word be that goeth forth out of my mouth: it shall not return unto me void, but it shall accomplish that which I please, and it shall prosper in the thing whereto I sent it.

For ye shall go out with joy, and be led forth with peace: the mountains and the hills shall break forth before you into singing, and all the trees of the field shall clap their hands. Instead of the thorn shall come up the fir-tree, and instead of the brier shall come up the myrtle-tree: and it shall be to the Lord for a name, for an everlasting sign that shall not be cut off.

Arise, shine; for thy light is come, and the glory of the Lord is risen upon thee. For behold, the darkness shall cover the earth, and gross darkness the people: but the Lord shall arise upon thee, and his glory shall be seen upon thee. And the Gentiles shall come to thy light, and kings to the brightness of thy rising.

THE NEW TESTAMENT

The Life of Christ

The Miraculous Conception of Jesus

(FROM THE GOSPEL OF LUKE)

The angel Gabriel was sent from God unto a city of Galilee, named Nazareth, to a virgin espoused to a man whose name was Joseph, of the house of David; and the virgin's name was Mary.

And the angel came in unto her, and said, Hail, thou that art highly favoured, the Lord is with thee: blessed art thou among women.

And when she saw him, she was troubled at his saying, and cast in her mind what manner of salutation this should be.

And the angel said unto her, Fear not, Mary: for thou hast found favour with God. And, behold, thou shalt conceive in thy womb, and bring forth a son, and shalt call his name JESUS. He shall be great, and shall be called the Son of the Highest; and the Lord God shall give unto him the throne of his father David: and he shall reign over the house of Jacob for ever; and of his kingdom there shall be no end.

Then said Mary unto the angel, How shall this be, seeing I know not a man?

And the angel answered and said unto her, The Holy Ghost shall come upon thee, and the power of the Highest shall overshadow thee: therefore also that holy thing which shall be born of thee shall be called the Son of God.

And Mary said, Behold the handmaid of the Lord; be it unto me according to thy word. And the angel departed from her.

The Birth of Jesus

(FROM THE GOSPEL OF LUKE)

And it came to pass in those days, that there went out a decree from Caesar Augustus, that all the world should be taxed. (And this taxing was first made when Cyrenius was governor of Syria.) And all went to be taxed, every one into his own city.

And Joseph also went up from Galilee, out of the city of Nazareth, into Judea, unto the city of David, which is called Bethlehem, (because he was of the house and lineage of David,) to be taxed with Mary his espoused wife, being great with child.

And so it was, that, while they were there, the days were accomplished that she should be delivered. And she brought forth her firstborn son, and wrapped him in swaddling clothes, and laid him in a manger; because there was no room for them in the inn.

And there were in the same country shepherds abiding in the field, keeping watch over their flock by night. And, lo, the angel of the Lord came upon them, and the glory of the Lord shone round about them; and they were sore afraid.

And the angel said unto them, Fear not: for, behold, I bring you good tidings of great joy, which shall be to all people. For unto you is born this day in the city of David a Saviour, which is Christ the Lord. And this shall be a sign unto you; Ye shall find the babe wrapped in swaddling clothes, lying in a manger.

And suddenly there was with the angel a multitude

of the heavenly host praising God, and saying, Glory
to God in the highest, and on earth peace, good will
toward men.

And it came to pass, as the angels were gone away
from them into heaven, the shepherds said one to another, Let us now go even unto Bethlehem, and see
this thing which is come to pass, which the Lord hath
made known unto us.

And they came with haste, and found Mary and
Joseph, and the babe lying in a manger.

And when they had seen it, they made known
abroad the saying which was told them concerning this
child. And all they that heard it wondered at those
things which were told them by the shepherds.

But Mary kept all these things, and pondered them
in her heart.

And the shepherds returned, glorifying and praising
God for all the things that they had heard and seen, as
it was told unto them.

And when eight days were accomplished for the
circumcising of the child, his name was called JESUS,
which was so named of the angel before he was conceived in the womb.

The Genealogy of Jesus

(FROM THE GOSPEL OF MATTHEW)

The book of the generation of Jesus Christ, the son
of David, the son of Abraham.

Abraham begat Isaac; and Isaac begat Jacob; and
Jacob begat Judas and his brethren; and Judas begat
Phares and Zara of Thamar; and Phares begat Esrom;
and Esrom begat Aram; and Aram begat Aminadab;
and Aminadab begat Naasson; and Naasson begat Salmon; and Salmon begat Booz of Rachab; and Booz

begat Obed of Ruth; and Obed begat Jesse; and Jesse
begat David the king.

And David the king begat Solomon of her that had
been the wife of Urias; and Solomon begat Roboam;
and Roboam begat Abia; and Abia begat Asa; and Asa
begat Josaphat; and Josaphat begat Joram; and Joram
begat Ozias; and Ozias begat Joatham; and Joatham
begat Achaz; and Achaz begat Ezekias; and Ezekias
begat Manasses; and Manasses begat Amon; and Amon
begat Josias; and Josias begat Jechonias and his brethren, about the time they were carried away to Babylon.

And after they were brought to Babylon, Jechonias
begat Salathiel; and Salathiel begat Zorobabel; and
Zorobabel begat Abiud; and Abiud begat Eliakim; and
Eliakim begat Azor; and Azor begat Sadoc; and Sadoc
begat Achim; and Achim begat Eliud; and Eliud begat
Eleazar; and Eleazar begat Matthan; and Matthan
begat Jacob; and Jacob begat Joseph the husband of
Mary, of whom was born Jesus, who is called Christ.

So all the generations from Abraham to David are
fourteen generations; and from David until the carrying
away into Babylon are fourteen generations; and from
the carrying away into Babylon unto Christ are fourteen generations.

The Flight into Egypt

(FROM THE GOSPEL OF MATTHEW)

Now when Jesus was born in Bethlehem of Judea in
the days of Herod the king, behold, there came wise
men from the east to Jerusalem, saying, Where is he
that is born King of the Jews? for we have seen his star
in the east, and are come to worship him.

When Herod the king had heard these things, he
was troubled, and all Jerusalem with him.

And when he had gathered all the chief priests and scribes of the people together, he demanded of them where Christ should be born.

And they said unto him, In Bethlehem of Judea: for thus it is written by the prophet, And thou Bethlehem, in the land of Juda, art not the least among the princes of Juda: for out of thee shall come a Governor, that shall rule my people Israel.

Then Herod, when he had privily called the wise men, inquired of them diligently what time the star appeared. And he sent them to Bethlehem, and said, Go and search diligently for the young child; and when ye have found him, bring me word again, that I may come and worship him also.

When they had heard the king, they departed; and, lo, the star, which they saw in the east, went before them, till it came and stood over where the young child was. When they saw the star, they rejoiced with exceeding great joy.

And when they were come into the house, they saw the young child with Mary his mother, and fell down, and worshipped him: and when they had opened their treasures, they presented unto him gifts; gold, and frankincense, and myrrh. And being warned of God in a dream that they should not return to Herod, they departed into their own country another way.

And when they were departed, behold, the angel of the Lord appeareth to Joseph in a dream, saying, Arise, and take the young child and his mother, and flee into Egypt, and be thou there until I bring thee word: for Herod will seek the young child to destroy him.

When he arose, he took the young child and his mother by night, and departed into Egypt, and was there until the death of Herod: that it might be fulfilled which was spoken of the Lord by the prophet, saying, Out of Egypt have I called my son.

Then Herod, when he saw that he was mocked of the wise men, was exceeding wroth, and sent forth, and slew all the children that were in Bethlehem, and in all the coasts thereof, from two years old and under, according to the time which he had diligently inquired of the wise men. Then was fulfilled that which was spoken by Jeremy the prophet, saying, In Rama was there a voice heard, lamentation, and weeping, and great mourning, Rachel weeping for her children, and would not be comforted, because they are not.

But when Herod was dead, behold, an angel of the Lord appeareth in a dream to Joseph in Egypt, saying, Arise, and take the young child and his mother, and go into the land of Israel: for they are dead which sought the young child's life. And he arose, and took the young child and his mother, and came into the land of Israel.

But when he heard that Archelaus did reign in Judea in the room of his father Herod, he was afraid to go thither: notwithstanding, being warned of God in a dream, he turned aside into the parts of Galilee. And he came and dwelt in a city called Nazareth: that it might be fulfilled which was spoken by the prophets, He shall be called a Nazarene.

The Baptism of Jesus

(FROM THE GOSPEL OF JOHN)

In the beginning was the Word, and the Word was with God, and the Word was God. The same was in the beginning with God. All things were made by him; and without him was not anything made that was made. In him was life; and the life was the light of men. And the light shineth in darkness; and the darkness comprehended it not.

There was a man sent from God, whose name was John. The same came for a witness, to bear witness of the Light, that all men through him might believe. He was not that Light, but was sent to bear witness of that Light.

That was the true Light, which lighteth every man that cometh into the world. He was in the world, and the world was made by him, and the world knew him not. He came unto his own, and his own received him not. But as many as received him, to them gave he power to become the sons of God, even to them that believe on his name, which were born, not of blood, nor of the will of the flesh, nor of the will of man, but of God.

And the Word was made flesh, and dwelt among us, (and we beheld his glory, the glory as of the only begotten of the Father,) full of grace and truth.

John bare witness of him, and cried, saying, This was he of whom I spake, He that cometh after me is preferred before me; for he was before me. And of his fulness have all we received, and grace for grace. For the law was given by Moses, but grace and truth came by Jesus Christ.

No man hath seen God at any time; the only begotten Son, which is in the bosom of the Father, he hath declared him.

And this is the record of John, when the Jews sent priests and Levites from Jerusalem to ask him, Who art thou?

And he confessed, and denied not; but confessed, I am not the Christ.

And they asked him, What then? Art thou Elias? And

he saith, I am not. Art thou that Prophet? And he answered, No.

Then said they unto him, Who art thou? that we may give an answer to them that sent us. What sayest thou of thyself?

He said, I am the voice of one crying in the wilderness, Make straight the way of the Lord, as said the prophet Esaias.

And they which were sent were of the Pharisees.

And they asked him, and said unto him, Why baptizest thou then, if thou be not that Christ, nor Elias, neither that Prophet?

John answered them, saying, I baptize with water: but there standeth one among you, whom ye know not. He it is, who coming after me is preferred before me, whose shoe-latchet I am not worthy to unloose.

These things were done in Bethabara beyond Jordan, where John was baptizing.

The next day John seeth Jesus coming unto him, and saith, Behold the Lamb of God, which taketh away the son of the world! This is he of whom I said, After me cometh a man who is preferred before me; for he was before me. And I knew him not; but that he should be made manifest to Israel, therefore am I come baptizing with water.

And John bare record, saying, I saw the Spirit descending from heaven like a dove, and it abode upon him. And I knew him not; but he that sent me to baptize with water, the same said unto me, Upon whom thou shalt see the Spirit descending, and remaining on him, the same is he which baptizeth with the Holy Ghost. And I saw, and bare record that this is the Son of God.

Jesus Is Tempted by the Devil

(FROM THE GOSPEL OF LUKE)

And Jesus being full of the Holy Ghost returned from Jordan, and was led by the Spirit into the wilderness, being forty days tempted of the devil. And in those days he did eat nothing: and when they were ended, he afterward hungered.

And the devil said unto him, If thou be the Son of God, command this stone that it be made bread.

And Jesus answered him, saying, It is written, That man shall not live by bread alone, but by every word of God.

And the devil, taking him up into a high mountain, showed unto him all the kingdoms of the world in a moment of time. And the devil said unto him, All this power will I give thee, and the glory of them: for that is delivered unto me; and to whomsoever I will, I give it. If thou therefore wilt worship me, all shall be thine.

And Jesus answered and said unto him, Get thee behind me, Satan: for it is written, Thou shalt worship the Lord thy God, and him only shalt thou serve.

And he brought him to Jerusalem, and set him on a pinnacle of the temple, and said unto him, If thou be the Son of God, cast thyself down from hence, for it is written, He shall give his angels charge over thee, to keep thee, and in their hands they shall bear thee up, lest at any time thou dash thy foot against a stone.

And Jesus answering said unto him, It is said, Thou shalt not tempt the Lord thy God.

And when the devil had ended all the temptation, he departed from him for a season.

The Healer

(FROM THE GOSPEL OF LUKE)

And (he) came down to Capernaum, a city of Galilee, and taught them on the sabbath days, and they were astonished at his doctrine: for his word was with power.

And in the synagogue there was a man, which had a spirit of an unclean devil, and cried out with a loud voice, saying, Let us alone; what have we to do with thee, thou Jesus of Nazareth? art thou come to destroy us? I know thee who thou art; the Holy One of God.

And Jesus rebuked him, saying, Hold thy peace, and come out of him. And when the devil had thrown him in the midst, he came out of him, and hurt him not.

And they were all amazed, and spake among themselves, saying, What a word is this! for with authority and power he commandeth the unclean spirits, and they come out.

And the fame of him went out into every place of the country round about.

And he rose out of the synagogue, and entered into Simon's house. And Simon's wife's mother was taken with a great fever; and they besought him for her. And he stood over her, and rebuked the fever; and it left her: and immediately she arose and ministered unto them.

Now when the sun was setting, all they that had any sick with divers diseases brought them unto him; and he laid his hands on every one of them, and healed them. And devils also came out of many, crying out, and saying, Thou art Christ the Son of God. And he rebuking them suffered them not to speak: for they knew that he was Christ.

And when it was day, he departed and went into a desert place: and the people sought him, and came unto him, and stayed him, that he should not depart from them. And he said unto them, I must preach the kingdom of God to other cities also: for therefore am I sent.

And he preached in the synagogues of Galilee.

The First Disciples

(FROM THE GOSPEL OF LUKE)

And it came to pass, that, as the people pressed upon him to hear the word of God, he stood by the lake of Gennesaret, and saw two ships standing by the lake: but the fishermen were gone out of them, and were washing their nets. And he entered into one of the ships, which was Simon's, and prayed him that he would thrust out a little from the land. And he sat down, and taught the people out of the ship.

Now when he had left speaking, he said unto Simon, Launch out into the deep, and let down your nets for a draught.

And Simon answering said unto him, Master, we have toiled all the night, and have taken nothing: nevertheless at thy word I will let down the net.

And when they had this done, they enclosed a great multitude of fishes: and their net brake. And they beckoned unto their partners, which were in the other ship, that they should come and help them. And they came, and filled both the ships, so that they began to sink.

When Simon Peter saw it, he fell down at Jesus' knees, saying, Depart from me; for I am a sinful man, O Lord. For he was astonished, and all that were with him, at the draught of the fishes which they had taken. And so was also James, and John, the sons of Zebedee, which were partners with Simon.

And Jesus said unto Simon, Fear not; from henceforth thou shalt catch men.

And when they had brought their ships to land, they forsook all, and followed him.

And it came to pass, when he was in a certain city, behold a man full of leprosy; who seeing Jesus fell on his face, and besought him, saying, Lord, if thou wilt, thou canst make me clean. And he put forth his hand, and touched him, saying, I will: be thou clean. And immediately the leprosy departed from him. And he charged him to tell no man: but go, and show thyself to the priest, and offer for thy cleansing, according as Moses commanded, for a testimony unto them.

But so much the more went there a fame abroad of him: and great multitudes came together to hear, and to be healed by him of their infirmities.

And he withdrew himself into the wilderness, and prayed.

A Crippled Man Is Healed

(FROM THE GOSPEL OF LUKE)

And it came to pass on a certain day, as he was teaching, that there were Pharisees and doctors of the law sitting by, which were come out of every town of Galilee, and Judea, and Jerusalem: and the power of the Lord was present to heal them.

And, behold, men brought in a bed a man which was taken with a palsy: and they sought means to bring him in, and to lay him before him. And when they could not find by what way they might bring him in because of the multitude, they went upon the housetop, and let him down through the tiling with his couch into the midst before Jesus.

And when he saw their faith, he said unto him, Man, thy sins are forgiven thee.

And the scribes and the Pharisees began to reason, saying, Who is this which speaketh blasphemies? Who can forgive sins, but God alone?

But when Jesus perceived their thoughts, he answering said unto them, What reason ye in your hearts? Whether is easier, to say, Thy sins be forgiven thee; or to say, Rise up and walk? But that ye may know that the Son of man hath power upon earth to forgive sins, (he said unto the sick of the palsy,) I say unto thee, Arise, and take up thy couch, and go into thine house.

And immediately he rose up before them, and took up that whereon he lay, and departed to his own house, glorifying God.

And they were all amazed, and they glorified God, and were filled with fear, saying, We have seen strange things to-day.

And after these things he went forth, and saw a publican, named Levi, sitting at the receipt of custom: and he said unto him, Follow me. And he left all, rose up, and followed him.

And Levi made him a great feast in his own house: and there was a great company of publicans and of others that sat down with them. But their scribes and Pharisees murmured against his disciples, saying, Why do ye eat and drink with publicans and sinners?

And Jesus answering said unto them, They that are whole need not a physician; but they that are sick. I came not to call the righteous, but sinners to repentance.

To Keep Holy the Sabbath

(FROM THE GOSPEL OF LUKE)

And it came to pass on the second sabbath after the first, that he went through the corn fields; and his disciples plucked the ears of corn, and did eat, rubbing them in their hands. And certain of the Pharisees said unto them, Why do ye that which is not lawful to do on the sabbath day?

And Jesus answering them said, Have ye not read so much as this, what David did, when himself was ahungered, and they which were with him, how he went into the house of God, and did take and eat the showbread, and gave also to them that were with him; which it is not lawful to eat but for the priests alone? And he said unto them, That the Son of man is Lord also of the sabbath.

And it came to pass also on another sabbath, that he entered into the synagogue and taught: and there was a man whose right hand was withered. And the scribes and Pharisees watched him, whether he would heal on the sabbath day; that they might find an accusation against him. But he knew their thoughts, and said to the man which had the withered hand, Rise up, and stand forth in the midst. And he arose and stood forth.

Then said Jesus unto them, I will ask you one thing; Is it lawful on the sabbath day to do good, or to do evil? to save life, or to destroy it?

And looking round about upon them all, he said unto the man, Stretch forth thy hand. And he did so: and his hand was restored whole as the other.

And they were filled with madness; and communed one with another what they might do to Jesus.

And it came to pass in those days, that he went out

into a mountain to pray, and continued all night in prayer to God.

And when it was day, he called unto him his disciples: and of them he chose twelve, whom also he named apostles; Simon, (whom he also named Peter,) and Andrew his brother, James and John, Philip and Bartholomew, Matthew and Thomas, James the son of Alpheus, and Simon called Zelotes, and Judas the brother of James, and Judas Iscariot, which also was the traitor.

And he came down with them, and stood in the plain, and the company of his disciples, and a great multitude of people out of all Judea and Jerusalem, and from the seacoast of Tyre and Sidon, which came to hear him, and to be healed of their diseases, and they that were vexed with unclean spirits: and they were healed.

And the whole multitude sought to touch him: for there went virtue out of him, and healed them all.

And, behold, there was a woman which had a spirit of infirmity eighteen years, and was bowed together, and could in no wise lift up herself.

And when Jesus saw her, he called her to him, and said unto her, Woman, thou art loosed from thine infirmity. And he laid his hands on her: and immediately she was made straight, and glorified God.

And the ruler of the synagogue answered with indignation, because that Jesus had healed on the sabbath day, and said unto the people, There are six days in which men ought to work: in them therefore come and be healed, and not on the sabbath day.

The Lord then answered him, and said, Thou hypocrite, doth not each one of you on the sabbath loose his ox or his ass from the stall, and lead him away to watering? And ought not this woman, being a daughter of Abraham, whom Satan hath bound, lo, these eighteen years, be loosed from this bond on the sabbath day?

And when he had said these things, all his adversaries were ashamed: and all the people rejoiced for all the glorious things that were done by him.

What Manner of Man Is This?

(FROM THE GOSPEL OF LUKE)

And it came to pass afterward, that he went throughout every city and village, preaching and showing the glad tidings of the kingdom of God.

And the twelve were with him, and certain women, which had been healed of evil spirits and infirmities, Mary called Magdalene, out of whom went seven devils, and Joanna the wife of Chuza Herod's steward, and Susanna, and many others, which ministered unto him of their substance.

Then came to him his mother and his brethren, and could not come at him for the press. And it was told him by certain which said, Thy mother and thy brethren stand without, desiring to see thee. And he answered and said unto them, My mother and my brethren are these which hear the word of God, and do it.

Now it came to pass on a certain day, that he went into a ship with his disciples: and he said unto them, Let us go over unto the other side of the lake. And they launched forth.

But as they sailed, he fell asleep: and there came down a storm of wind on the lake; and they were filled with water, and were in jeopardy. And they came to him, and awoke him, saying, Master, Master, we perish. Then he arose, and rebuked the wind and the raging of the water: and they ceased, and there was a calm.

And he said unto them, Where is your faith? And they being afraid wondered, saying one to another, What manner of man is this! for he commandeth even the winds and water, and they obey him.

And they arrived at the country of the Gadarenes, which is over against Galilee.

And, behold, there came a man named Jairus, and he was a ruler of the synagogue; and he fell down at Jesus' feet, and besought him that he would come into his house, for he had one only daughter, about twelve years of age, and she lay a dying. But as he went the people thronged him.

And a woman having an issue of blood twelve years, which had spent all her living upon physicians, neither could be healed of any, came behind him, and touched the border of his garment: and immediately her issue of blood stanched.

And Jesus said, Who touched me? When all denied, Peter and they that were with him said, Master, the multitude throng thee and press thee, and sayest thou, Who touched me?

And Jesus said, Somebody hath touched me: for I perceive that virtue is gone out of me.

And when the woman saw that she was not hid, she came trembling, and falling down before him, she declared unto him before all the people for what cause she had touched him, and how she was healed immediately.

And he said unto her, Daughter, be of good comfort: thy faith hath made thee whole; go in peace.

While he yet spake, there cometh one from the ruler of the synagogue's house, saying to him, Thy daughter is dead; trouble not the Master.

But when Jesus heard it, he answered him, saying, Fear not: believe only, and she shall be made whole.

And when he came into the house, he suffered no man to go in, save Peter, and James, and John, and the father and the mother of the maiden. And all wept, and bewailed her: but he said, Weep not; she is not dead, but sleepeth.

And they laughed him to scorn, knowing that she was dead.

And he put them all out, and took her by the hand, and called, saying, Maid, arise.

And her spirit came again, and she arose straightway: and he commanded to give her meat. And her parents were astonished: but he charged them that they should tell no man what was done.

The Twelve Apostles Named

(FROM THE GOSPEL OF MATTHEW)

And when he had called unto him his twelve disciples, he gave them power against unclean spirits, to cast them out, and to heal all manner of sickness and all manner of disease.

Now the names of the twelve apostles are these; The first, Simon, who is called Peter, and Andrew his brother; James the son of Zebedee, and John his brother; Philip, and Bartholomew; Thomas, and Matthew the publican; James the son of Alpheus, and Lebbeus, whose surname was Thaddeus; Simon the Canaanite, and Judas Iscariot, who also betrayed him.

The Rock of the Christian Church

(FROM THE GOSPEL OF MATTHEW)

When Jesus came into the coasts of Caesarea Philippi, he asked his disciples, saying, Whom do men say that I, the Son of man, am?

And they said, Some say that thou art John the Baptist; some, Elias; and others, Jeremias, or one of the prophets.

He saith unto them, But whom say ye that I am?

And Simon Peter answered and said, Thou art the Christ, the Son of the living God.

And Jesus answered and said unto him, Blessed art thou, Simon Barjona: for flesh and blood hath not revealed it unto thee, but my Father which is in heaven. And I say also unto thee, That thou art Peter, and upon this rock I will build my church; and the gates of hell shall not prevail against it. And I will give unto thee the keys of the kingdom of heaven: and whatsoever thou shalt bind on earth shall be bound in heaven; and whatsoever thou shalt loose on earth shall be loosed in heaven.

Then charged he his disciples that they should tell no man that he was Jesus the Christ.

From that time forth began Jesus to show unto his disciples, how that he must go unto Jerusalem, and suffer many things of the elders and chief priests and scribes, and be killed, and be raised again the third day.

Then Peter took him, and began to rebuke him, saying, Be it far from thee, Lord: this shall not be unto thee.

But he turned, and said unto Peter, Get thee behind me, Satan: thou art an offence unto me: for thou savourest not the things that be of God, but those that be of men.

The Loaves and Fishes

(FROM THE GOSPEL OF MARK)

And the apostles gathered themselves together unto Jesus, and told him all things, both what they had done, and what they had taught. And he said unto them, Come ye yourselves apart into a desert place, and rest a while: for there were many coming and going, and they had no leisure so much as to eat. And they departed into a desert place by ship privately.

And the people saw them departing, and many knew him, and ran afoot thither out of all cities, and outwent them, and came together unto him. And Jesus, when he came out, saw much people, and was moved with compassion toward them, because they were as sheep not having a shepherd: and he began to teach them many things.

And when the day was now far spent, his disciples came unto him, and said, This is a desert place, and now the time is far passed. Send them away, that they may go into the country round about, and into the villages, and buy themselves bread: for they have nothing to eat.

He answered and said unto them, Give ye them to eat.

And they say unto him, Shall we go and buy two hundred pennyworth of bread, and give them to eat?

He saith unto them, How many loaves have ye? go and see.

And when they knew, they say, Five, and two fishes.

And he commanded them to make all sit down by companies upon the green grass. And they sat down in ranks, by hundreds, and by fifties. And when he had taken the five loaves and the two fishes, he looked up to heaven, and blessed, and brake the loaves, and

gave them to his disciples to set before them; and the
two fishes divided he among them all. And they did
all eat, and were filled. And they took up twelve baskets full of the fragments, and of the fishes. And they
that did eat of the loaves were about five thousand
men.

The Transfiguration

(FROM THE GOSPEL OF LUKE)

And he took Peter and John and James, and went up
into a mountain to pray. And as he prayed, the fashion
of his countenance was altered, and his raiment was
white and glistening. And, behold, there talked with
him two men, which were Moses and Elias, who appeared in glory, and spake of his decease which he
should accomplish at Jerusalem.

But Peter and they that were with him were heavy
with sleep: and when they were awake, they saw his
glory, and the two men that stood with him.

And it came to pass, as they departed from him,
Peter said unto Jesus, Master, it is good for us to be
here: and let us make three tabernacles; one for thee,
and one for Moses, and one for Elias: not knowing
what he said.

While he thus spake, there came a cloud, and over-
shadowed them: and they feared as they entered into
the cloud. And there came a voice out of the cloud,
saying, This is my beloved Son: hear him.

And when the voice was past, Jesus was found alone.
And they kept it close, and told no man in those days
any of those things which they had seen.

Suffer the Little Children

(FROM THE GOSPEL OF MARK)

And they brought young children to him, that he should touch them; and his disciples rebuked those that brought them.

But when Jesus saw it, he was much displeased, and said unto them, Suffer the little children to come unto me, and forbid them not; for of such is the kingdom of God. Verily I say unto you, Whosoever shall not receive the kingdom of God as a little child, he shall not enter therein.

And he took them up in his arms, put his hands upon them, and blessed them.

Announcement of Destiny

(FROM THE GOSPEL OF LUKE)

Then he took unto him the twelve, and said unto them, Behold, we go up to Jerusalem, and all things that are written by the prophets concerning the Son of man shall be accomplished. For he shall be delivered unto the Gentiles, and shall be mocked, and spitefully entreated, and spitted on. And they shall scourge him, and put him to death; and the third day he shall rise again.

The Woman Taken in Adultery

(FROM THE GOSPEL OF JOHN)

Jesus went unto the mount of Olives.

And early in the morning he came again into the temple, and all the people came unto him; and he sat down, and taught them.

And the scribes and Pharisees brought unto him a

woman taken in adultery; and when they had set her in the midst, they say unto him, Master, this woman was taken in adultery, in the very act. Now Moses in the law commanded us, that such should be stoned: but what sayest thou? This they said, tempting him, that they might have to accuse him.

But Jesus stooped down, and with his finger wrote on the ground, as though he heard them not. So when they continued asking him, he lifted up himself, and said unto them, He that is without sin among you, let him first cast a stone at her. And again he stooped down, and wrote on the ground.

And they which heard it, being convicted by their own conscience, went out one by one, beginning at the eldest, even unto the last; and Jesus was left alone, and the woman standing in the midst.

When Jesus had lifted up himself, and saw none but the woman, he said unto her, Woman, where are those thine accusers? hath no man condemned thee? She said, No man, Lord. And Jesus said unto her, Neither do I condemn thee: go, and sin no more.

Lazarus Arises from Death

(FROM THE GOSPEL OF JOHN)

Now a certain man was sick, named Lazarus, of Bethany, the town of Mary and her sister Martha. (It was that Mary which anointed the Lord with ointment, and wiped his feet with her hair, whose brother Lazarus was sick.) Therefore his sisters sent unto him, saying, Lord, behold, he whom thou lovest is sick.

When Jesus heard that, he said, This sickness is not unto death, but for the glory of God, that the Son of God might be glorified thereby.

Now Jesus loved Martha, and her sister, and Lazarus.

When he had heard therefore that he was sick, he abode two days still in the same place where he was. Then after that saith he to his disciples, Let us go into Judea again.

Then when Jesus came, he found that he had lain in the grave four days already.

Now Bethany was nigh unto Jerusalem, about fifteen furlongs off. And many of the Jews came to Martha and Mary, to comfort them concerning their brother. Then Martha, as soon as she heard that Jesus was coming, went and met him: but Mary sat still in the house.

Then said Martha unto Jesus, Lord, if thou hadst been here, my brother had not died. But I know, that even now, whatsoever thou wilt ask of God, God will give it thee.

Jesus saith unto her, Thy brother shall rise again.

Martha saith unto him, I know that he shall rise again in the resurrection at the last day.

Jesus said unto her, I am the resurrection, and the life: he that believeth in me, though he were dead, yet shall he live. And whosoever liveth and believeth in me shall never die. Believest thou this?

She saith unto him, Yea, Lord: I believe that thou art the Christ, the Son of God, which should come into the world.

And when she had so said, she went her way, and called Mary her sister secretly, saying, The Master is come, and calleth for thee.

Then when Mary was come where Jesus was, and saw him, she fell down at his feet, saying unto him, Lord, if thou hadst been here, my brother had not died.

When Jesus therefore saw her weeping, and the Jews also weeping which came with her, he groaned in the spirit, and was troubled, and said, Where have ye laid him? They said unto him, Lord, come and see.

Jesus wept.

Jesus therefore again groaning in himself cometh to the grave. It was a cave, and a stone lay upon it. Jesus said, Take ye away the stone. Martha, the sister of him that was dead, saith unto him, Lord, by this time he stinketh: for he hath been dead four days.

Jesus saith unto her, Said I not unto thee, that, if thou wouldest believe, thou shouldest see the glory of God?

Then they took away the stone from the place where the dead was laid. And Jesus lifted up his eyes, and said, Father, I thank thee that thou hast heard me. And I knew that thou hearest me always, but because of the people which stand by I said it, that they may believe that thou hast sent me. And when he thus had spoken, he cried with a loud voice, Lazarus, come forth.

And he that was dead came forth, bound hand and foot with graveclothes; and his face was bound about with a napkin. Jesus saith unto them, Loose him, and let him go.

Then many of the Jews which came to Mary, and had seen the things which Jesus did, believed on him. But some of them went their ways to the Pharisees, and told them what things Jesus had done.

Then gathered the chief priests and the Pharisees a council, and said, What do we? for this man doeth many miracles. If we let him thus alone, all men will believe on him; and the Romans shall come and take away both our place and nation.

And one of them, named Caiaphas, being the high priest that same year, said unto them, Ye know nothing at all, nor consider that it is expedient for us, that one man should die for the people, and that the whole nation perish not.

And this spake he not of himself: but being high priest that year, he prophesied that Jesus should die for that nation, and not for that nation only, but that also he should gather together in one the children of God that were scattered abroad.

Then from that day forth they took counsel together for to put him to death.

Entry into Jerusalem

(FROM THE GOSPEL OF LUKE)

And when he had thus spoken, he went before, ascending up to Jerusalem. And it came to pass, when he was come nigh to Bethphage and Bethany, at the mount called the mount of Olives, he sent two of his disciples, saying, Go ye into the village over against you; in the which at your entering ye shall find a colt tied, whereon yet never man sat: loose him, and bring him hither. And if any man ask you, Why do ye loose him? thus shall ye say unto him, Because the Lord hath need of him.

And they that were sent went their way, and found even as he had said unto them. And as they were loosing the colt, the owners thereof said unto them, Why loose ye the colt? And they said, The Lord hath need of him.

And they brought him to Jesus: and they cast their garments upon the colt, and they set Jesus thereon.

And as he went, they spread their clothes in the way. And when he was come nigh, even now at the descent of the mount of Olives, the whole multitude of the disciples began to rejoice and praise God with a loud voice for all the mighty works that they had seen, saying, Blessed be the King that cometh in the name of the Lord: peace in heaven, and glory in the highest.

And some of the Pharisees from among the multitude said unto him, Master, rebuke thy disciples.

And he answered and said unto them, I tell you that, if these should hold their peace, the stones would immediately cry out.

And he went into the temple, and began to cast out them that sold therein, and them that bought, saying unto them, It is written, My house is the house of prayer; but ye have made it a den of thieves.

And he taught daily in the temple. But the chief priests and the scribes and the chief of the people sought to destroy him, and could not find what they might do: for all the people were very attentive to hear him.

The Price of a Saviour

(FROM THE GOSPEL OF MATTHEW)

Then one of the twelve, called Judas Iscariot, went unto the chief priests, and said unto them, What will ye give me, and I will deliver him unto you? And they covenanted with him for thirty pieces of silver. And from that time he sought opportunity to betray him.

The Last Supper

(FROM THE GOSPEL OF JOHN)

And supper being ended, the devil having now put into the heart of Judas Iscariot, Simon's son, to betray him; Jesus knowing that the Father had given all things into his hands, and that he was come from God, and went to God; he riseth from supper, and laid aside his garments; and took a towel, and girded himself.

After that he poureth water into a basin, and began to wash the disciples' feet, and to wipe them with the towel wherewith he was girded.

Then cometh he to Simon Peter: and Peter saith unto him, Lord, dost thou wash my feet? Jesus answered and said unto him, What I do thou knowest not now; but thou shalt know hereafter.

Peter saith unto him, Thou shalt never wash my feet. Jesus answered him, If I wash thee not, thou hast no part with me. Simon Peter saith unto him, Lord, not my feet only, but also my hands and my head.

Jesus saith to him, He that is washed needeth not save to wash his feet, but is clean every whit: and ye are clean, but not all. For he knew who should betray him; therefore said he, Ye are not all clean.

So after he had washed their feet, and had taken his garments, and was set down again, he said unto them, Know ye what I have done to you? Ye call me Master and Lord: and ye say well; for so I am. If I then, your Lord and Master, have washed your feet; ye also ought to wash one another's feet. For I have given you an example, that ye should do as I have done to you. Verily, verily, I say unto you. The servant is not greater than his lord; neither he that is sent greater than he that sent him. If ye know these things, happy are ye if ye do them.

I speak not of you all: I know whom I have chosen: but that the Scripture may be fulfilled, He that eateth bread with me hath lifted up his heel against me.

Now I tell you before it come, that, when it is come to pass, ye may believe that I am he. Verily, verily, I say unto you, He that receiveth whomsoever I send receiveth me; and he that receiveth me receiveth him that sent me.

When Jesus had thus said, he was troubled in spirit, and testified, and said, Verily, verily, I say unto you, that one of you shall betray me.

Then the disciples looked one on another, doubting of whom he spake.

Now there was leaning on Jesus' bosom one of his disciples, whom Jesus loved. Simon Peter therefore beckoned to him, that he should ask who it should be of whom he spake.

He then lying on Jesus' breast saith unto him, Lord, who is it? Jesus answered, He it is, to whom I shall give a sop, when I have dipped it. And when he had dipped the sop, he gave it to Judas Iscariot, the son of Simon.

And after the sop Satan entered into him. Then said Jesus unto him, That thou doest, do quickly. Now no man at the table knew for what intent he spake this unto him. For some of them thought, because Judas had the bag, that Jesus had said unto him, Buy those things that we have need of against the feast; or, that he should give something to the poor. He then, having received the sop, went immediately out; and it was night.

Therefore, when he was gone out, Jesus said, Now is the Son of man glorified, and God is glorified in him. If God be glorified in him, God shall also glorify him in himself, and shall straightway glorify him.

Little children, yet a little while I am with you. Ye shall seek me; and as I said unto the Jews, Whither I go, ye cannot come; so now I say to you. A new commandment I give unto you, That ye love one another; as I have loved you, that ye also love one another. By this shall all men know that ye are my disciples, if ye have love one to another.

Simon Peter said unto him, Lord, whither goest thou? Jesus answered him, Whither I go, thou canst not follow me now; but thou shalt follow me afterward. Peter said unto him, Lord, why cannot I follow thee now? I will lay down my life for thy sake. Jesus answered him, Wilt thou lay down thy life for my sake? Verily, verily, I say unto thee, The cock shall not crow, till thou hast denied me thrice.

Gethsemane

(FROM THE GOSPEL OF LUKE)

And he came out, and went, as he was wont, to the mount of Olives; and his disciples also followed him. And when he was at the place, he said unto them, Pray that ye enter not into temptation.

And he was withdrawn from them about a stone's cast, and kneeled down, and prayed, saying, Father, if thou be willing, remove this cup from me: nevertheless, not my will, but thine, be done.

And there appeared an angel unto him from heaven, strengthening him.

And being in an agony he prayed more earnestly: and his sweat was as it were great drops of blood falling down to the ground.

And when he rose up from prayer, and was come to his disciples, he found them sleeping for sorrow, and said unto them. Why sleep ye? rise and pray, lest ye enter into temptation.

And while he yet spake, behold a multitude, and he that was called Judas, one of the twelve, went before them, and drew near unto Jesus to kiss him. But Jesus said unto him, Judas, betrayest thou the Son of man with a kiss?

When they which were about him saw what would

follow, they said unto him, Lord shall we smite with the sword? And one of them smote the servant of the high priest, and cut off his right ear. And Jesus answered and said, Suffer ye thus far. And he touched his ear, and healed him.

Then Jesus said unto the chief priests, and captains of the temple, and the elders, which were come to him, Be ye come out, as against a thief, with swords and staves? When I was daily with you in the temple, ye stretched forth no hands against me: but this is your hour, and the power of darkness.

Then took they him, and led him, and brought him into the high priest's house. And Peter followed afar off.

And when they had kindled a fire in the midst of the hall, and were set down together, Peter sat down among them. But a certain maid beheld him as he sat by the fire, and earnestly looked upon him, and said, This man was also with him. And he denied him, saying, Woman, I know him not.

And after a little while another saw him, and said, Thou are also of them. And Peter said, Man, I am not.

And about the space of one hour after another confidently affirmed, saying, Of a truth this fellow also was with him; for he is a Galilean. And Peter said, Man, I know not what thou sayest. And immediately while he yet spake, the cock crew.

And the Lord turned, and looked upon Peter. And Peter remembered the word of the Lord, how he had said unto him, Before the cock crow, thou shalt deny me thrice. And Peter went out and wept bitterly.

And the men that held Jesus mocked him, and smote him. And when they had blind-folded him, they struck him on the face, and asked him, saying, Prophesy, who is it that smote thee? And many other things blasphemously spake they against him.

And as soon as it was day, the elders of the people and the chief priests and the scribes came together, and led him into their council, saying, Art thou the Christ? tell us. And he said unto them, If I tell you, ye will not believe: and if I also ask you, ye will not answer me, nor let me go. Hereafter shall the Son of man sit on the right hand of the power of God.

Then said they all, Art thou then the Son of God? And he said unto them, Ye say that I am. And they said, What need we any further witness? for we ourselves have heard of his own mouth.

The Trial of Jesus

(FROM THE GOSPEL OF JOHN)

Pilate then went out unto them, and said, What accusation bring ye against this man?

They answered and said unto him, If he were not a malefactor, we would not have delivered him up unto thee.

Then said Pilate unto them, Take ye him, and judge him according to your law.

The Jews therefore said unto him, It is not lawful for us to put any man to death; that the saying of Jesus might be fulfilled, which he spake, signifying what death he should die.

Then Pilate entered into the judgment hall again, and called Jesus, and said unto him, Art thou the King of the Jews?

Jesus answered him, Sayest thou this thing of thyself, or did others tell it thee of me?

Pilate answered, Am I a Jew? Thine own nation and the chief priests have delivered thee unto me: what hast thou done?

Jesus answered, My kingdom is not of this world; if

my kingdom were of this world, then would my servants fight, that I should not be delivered to the Jews: but now is my kingdom not from hence.

Pilate therefore said unto him, Art thou a king then?

Jesus answered, Thou sayest that I am a king. To this end was I born, and for this cause came I into the world, that I should bear witness unto the truth. Every one that is of the truth heareth my voice.

Pilate saith unto him, What is truth? And when he had said this, he went out again unto the Jews, and saith unto them, I find in him no fault at all. But ye have a custom, that I should release unto you one at the passover: will ye therefore that I release unto you the King of the Jews?

Then cried they all again, saying, Not this man, but Barabbas. Now Barabbas was a robber.

Condemnation

(FROM THE GOSPEL OF JOHN)

Then Pilate therefore took Jesus, and scourged him. And the soldiers platted a crown of thorns, and put it on his head, and they put on him a purple robe, and said, Hail, King of the Jews! and they smote him with their hands.

Pilate therefore went forth again, and saith unto them, Behold, I bring him forth to you, that ye may know that I find no fault in him.

Then came Jesus forth, wearing the crown of thorns, and the purple robe. And Pilate saith unto them, Behold the man!

When the chief priests therefore and officers saw him, they cried out, saying, Crucify him, crucify him. Pilate saith unto them, Take ye him, and crucify him: for I find no fault in him. The Jews answered him, We have a law, and by our law he ought to die, because he made himself the Son of God.

When Pilate therefore heard that saying, he was the more afraid; and went again into the judgment hall, and saith unto Jesus, Whence art thou? But Jesus gave him no answer. Then saith Pilate unto him, Speakest thou not unto me? Knowest thou not that I have power to crucify thee, and have power to release thee? Jesus answered, Thou couldest have no power at all against me, except it were given thee from above: therefore he that delivered me unto thee hath the greater sin. And from thenceforth Pilate sought to release him: but the Jews cried out, saying, If thou let this man go, thou art not Caesar's friend: whosoever maketh himself a king speaketh against Caesar.

When Pilate therefore heard that saying, he brought Jesus forth, and sat down in the judgment seat in a place that is called the Pavement, but in the Hebrew, Gabba-tha. And it was the preparation of the passover, and about the sixth hour: and he saith unto the Jews, Behold your King!

But they cried out, Away with him, away with him, crucify him. Pilate saith unto them, Shall I crucify your King? The chief priests answered, We have no king but Caesar.

Then delivered he him therefore unto them to be crucified. And they took Jesus, and led him away.

The Crucifixion

I

(FROM THE GOSPEL OF JOHN)

And he bearing his cross went forth into a place called the place of a skull, which is called in the Hebrew Golgotha: where they crucified him, and two others with him, on either side one, and Jesus in the midst.

And Pilate wrote a title, and put it on the cross. And the writing was, JESUS OF NAZARETH THE KING OF THE JEWS. This title then read many of the Jews; for the place where Jesus was crucified was nigh to the city: and it was written in Hebrew, and Greek, and Latin. Then said the chief priests of the Jews to Pilate, Write not, The King of the Jews; but that he said, I am King of the Jews. Pilate answered, What I have written I have written.

II

(FROM THE GOSPEL OF LUKE)

Then said Jesus, Father, forgive them; for they know not what they do.

And they parted his raiment, and cast lots. And the people stood beholding. And the rulers also with them derided him, saying, He saved others; let him save himself, if he be Christ, the chosen of God. And the soldiers also mocked him, coming to him, and offering him vinegar, and saying, If thou be the King of the Jews, save thyself.

And one of the malefactors which were hanged railed on him, saying, If thou be Christ, save thyself and us.

But the other answering rebuked him, saying, Dost not thou fear God, seeing thou art in the same condemnation? And we indeed justly; for we receive the due reward of our deeds: but this man hath done nothing amiss. And he said unto Jesus, Lord, remember me when thou comest into thy kingdom.

And Jesus said unto him, Verily I say unto thee, To-day shalt thou be with me in paradise.

III

(FROM THE GOSPEL OF MATTHEW)

Now from the sixth hour there was darkness over all the land unto the ninth hour. And about the ninth hour Jesus cried with a loud voice, saying, Eli, Eli, lama sabachtha-ni? that is to say, My God, my God, why hast thou forsaken me?

Some of them that stood there, when they heard that, said, This man calleth for Elias. And straightway one of them ran, and took a sponge, and filled it with vinegar, and put it on a reed, and gave him to drink. The rest said, Let be, let us see whether Elias will come to save him.

Jesus, when he had cried again with a loud voice, yielded up the ghost. And, behold, the veil of the temple was rent in twain from the top to the bottom; and the earth did quake, and the rocks rent; and the graves were opened; and many bodies of the saints which slept arose, and came out of the graves after his resurrection, and went into the holy city, and appeared unto many.

Now when the centurion, and they that were with him, watching Jesus, saw the earthquake, and those things that were done, they feared greatly, saying, Truly this was the Son of God.

And many women were there beholding afar off, which followed Jesus from Galilee, ministering unto him: among which was Mary Magdalene, and Mary the mother of James and Joses, and the mother of Zebedee's children.

Burial

(FROM THE GOSPEL OF JOHN)

The Jews therefore, because it was the preparation, that the bodies should not remain upon the cross on the sabbath day (for that sabbath day was a high day,) besought Pilate that their legs might be broken, and that they might be taken away. Then came the soldiers, and brake the legs of the first, and of the other which was crucified with him.

But when they came to Jesus, and saw that he was dead already, they brake not his legs: but one of the soldiers with a spear pierced his side, and forthwith came there out blood and water. And he that saw it bare record, and his record is true; and he knoweth that he saith true, that ye might believe. For these things were done, that the Scripture should be fulfilled, A bone of him shall not be broken. And again another Scripture saith, They shall look on him whom they pierced.

And after this Joseph of Arimathea, being a disciple of Jesus, but secretly for fear of the Jews, besought Pilate that he might take away the body of Jesus: and Pilate gave him leave. He came therefore, and took the body of Jesus.

And there came also Nicodemus, which at the first came to Jesus by night, and brought a mixture of myrrh and aloes, about a hundred pound weight.

Then took they the body of Jesus, and wound it in linen clothes with the spices, as the manner of the Jews is to bury. Now in the place where he was crucified there was a garden; and in the garden a new sepulchre, wherein was never man yet laid. There laid they Jesus therefore because of the Jews' preparation day; for the sepulchre was nigh at hand.

The Tomb Is Sealed

(FROM THE GOSPEL OF MATTHEW)

Now the next day, that followed the day of the preparation, the chief priests and Pharisees came together unto Pilate, saying, Sir, we remember that that deceiver said, while he was yet alive, After three days I will rise again. Command therefore that the sepulchre be made sure until the third day, lest his disciples come by night, and steal him away, and say unto the people, He is risen from the dead: so the last error shall be worse than the first.

Pilate said unto them, Ye have a watch: go your way, make it as sure as ye can.

So they went, and made the sepulchre sure, sealing the stone, and setting a watch.

The Resurrection

(FROM THE GOSPEL OF JOHN)

The first day of the week cometh Mary Magdalene early, when it was yet dark, unto the sepulchre, and seeth the stone taken away from the sepulchre. Then she runneth, and cometh to Simon Peter, and to the other disciple, whom Jesus loved, and saith unto them, They have taken away the Lord out of the sepulchre, and we know not where they have laid him.

Peter therefore went forth, and that other disciple, and came to the sepulchre. So they ran both together: and the other disciple did outrun Peter, and came first to the sepulchre. And he stooping down, and looking in, saw the linen clothes lying; yet went he not in.

Then cometh Simon Peter following him, and went into the sepulchre, and seeth the linen clothes lie, and the napkin, that was about his head, not lying with the linen clothes, but wrapped together in a place by itself. Then went in also that other disciple, which came first to the sepulchre, and he saw, and believed. For as yet they knew not the Scripture, that he must rise again from the dead.

Then the disciples went away again unto their own home.

But Mary stood without at the sepulchre weeping: and as she wept, she stooped down, and looked into the sepulchre, and seeth two angels in white sitting, the one at the head, and the other at the feet, where the body of Jesus had lain.

And they say unto her, Woman, why weepest thou? She saith unto them, Because they have taken away my Lord, and I know not where they have laid him. And when she had thus said, she turned herself back, and saw Jesus standing, and knew not that it was Jesus.

Jesus saith unto her, Woman, why weepest thou? whom seekest thou? She, supposing him to be the gardener, saith unto him, Sir, if thou have borne him hence, tell me where thou hast laid him, and I will take him away. Jesus saith unto her, Mary. She turned herself, and saith unto him, Rabboni; which is to say, Master.

Jesus saith unto her, Touch me not; for I am not yet ascended to my Father: but go to my brethren, and say unto them, I ascend unto my Father, and your Father; and to my God, and your God.

Mary Magdalene came and told the disciples that she had seen the Lord, and that he had spoken these things unto her.

The Risen Christ

(FROM THE GOSPEL OF MATTHEW)

Then the eleven disciples went away into Galilee, into a mountain where Jesus had appointed them. And when they saw him, they worshipped him: but some doubted.

And Jesus came and spake unto them, saying, All power is given unto me in heaven and in earth. Go ye therefore, and teach all nations, baptizing them in the name of the Father, and of the Son, and of the Holy Ghost: teaching them to observe all things whatsoever I have commanded you: and, lo, I am with you always, even unto the end of the world. Amen.

Sermons and Sayings of Jesus

The Sermon on the Mount

(FROM THE GOSPEL OF MATTHEW)

And seeing the multitudes, he went up into a mountain: and when he was set, his disciples came unto him: and he opened his mouth, and taught them, saying:

Blessed are the poor in spirit: for theirs is the kingdom of heaven. Blessed are they that mourn: for they shall be comforted. Blessed are the meek: for they shall inherit the earth. Blessed are they which do hunger and thirst after righteousness: for they shall be filled. Blessed are the merciful: for they shall obtain mercy. Blessed are the pure in heart: for they shall see God. Blessed are the peacemakers: for they shall be called the children of God. Blessed are they which are persecuted for righteousness' sake: for theirs is the kingdom of heaven. Blessed are ye, when men shall revile you, and persecute you, and shall say all manner of evil against you falsely, for my sake. Rejoice, and be exceeding glad: for great is your reward in heaven: for so persecuted they the prophets which were before you.

Ye are the salt of the earth: but if the salt have lost his savour, wherewith shall it be salted? it is thenceforth good for nothing, but to be cast out, and to be trodden under foot of men.

Ye are the light of the world. A city that is set on a hill cannot be hid. Neither do men light a candle, and put it under a bushel, but on a candlestick; and it giveth light unto all that are in the house. Let your light so shine before men, that they may see your good works, and glorify your Father which is in heaven.

Think not that I am come to destroy the law, or the prophets: I am not come to destroy, but to fulfil. For verily I say unto you, Till heaven and earth pass, one jot or one tittle shall in no wise pass from the law, till all be fulfilled. Whosoever therefore shall break one of these least commandments, and shall teach men so, he shall be called the least in the kingdom of heaven: but whosoever shall do and teach them, the same shall be called great in the kingdom of heaven. For I say unto you, That except your righteousness shall exceed the righteousness of the scribes and Pharisees, ye shall in no case enter into the kingdom of heaven.

Ye have heard that it was said by them of old time, Thou shalt not kill; and whosoever shall kill shall be in danger of the judgment. But I say unto you, That whosoever is angry with his brother without a cause shall be in danger of the judgment: and whosoever shall say to his brother, Raca, shall be in danger of the council: but whosoever shall say, Thou fool, shall be in danger of hell fire. Therefore if thou bring thy gift to the altar, and there rememberest that thy brother hath aught against thee, leave there thy gift before the altar, and go thy way; first be reconciled to thy brother, and then come and offer thy gift.

Agree with thine adversary quickly, while thou art in the way with him; lest at any time the adversary deliver thee to the judge, and the judge deliver thee to the officer, and thou be cast into prison. Verily I say unto thee, Thou shalt by no means come out thence, till thou hast paid the uttermost farthing.

Ye have heard that it was said by them of old time, Thou shalt not commit adultery. But I say unto you, That whosoever looketh on a woman to lust after her hath committed adultery with her already in his heart.

And if thy right eye offend thee, pluck it out, and cast it from thee: for it is profitable for thee that one of thy members should perish, and not that thy whole body should be cast into hell. And if thy right hand offend thee, cut it off, and cast it from thee: for it is profitable for thee that one of thy members should perish, and not that thy whole body should be cast into hell.

It hath been said, Whosoever shall put away his wife, let him give her a writing of divorcement. But I say unto you, That whosoever shall put away his wife, saving for the cause of fornication, causeth her to commit adultery: and whosoever shall marry her that is divorced committeth adultery.

Again, ye have heard that it hath been said by them of old time, Thou shalt not forswear thyself, but shalt perform unto the Lord thine oaths. But I say unto you, Swear not at all; neither by heaven; for it is God's throne; nor by the earth; for it is his footstool; neither by Jerusalem; for it is the city of the great King. Neither shalt thou swear by thy head, because thou canst not make one hair white or black. But let your communication be, Yea, yea; Nay, nay: for whatsoever is more than these cometh of evil.

Ye have heard that it hath been said, An eye for an eye, and a tooth for a tooth. But I say unto you, That ye resist not evil: but whosoever shall smite thee on thy right cheek, turn to him the other also. And if any man will sue thee at the law, and take away thy coat, let him have thy cloak also. And whosoever shall compel thee to go a mile, go with him twain. Give to him that asketh thee, and from him that would borrow of thee turn not thou away.

Ye have heard that it hath been said, Thou shalt love thy neighbour, and hate thine enemy. But I say unto you, Love your enemies, bless them that curse you, do good to them that hate you, and pray for them which despitefully use you, and persecute you, that ye may be the children of your Father which is in heaven: for he maketh his sun to rise on the evil and on the good, and sendeth rain on the just and on the unjust.

For if ye love them which love you, what reward have ye? do not even the publicans the same? And if ye salute your brethren only, what do ye more than others? do not even the publicans so?

Be ye therefore perfect, even as your Father which is in heaven is perfect.

Take heed that ye do not your alms before men, to be seen of them: otherwise ye have no reward of your Father which is in heaven. Therefore when thou doest thine alms, do not sound a trumpet before thee, as the hypocrites do in the synagogues and in the streets, that they may have glory of men. Verily I say unto you, They have their reward. But when thou doest alms, let not thy left hand know what thy right hand doeth, that thine alms may be in secret: and thy Father which seeth in secret himself shall reward thee openly.

And when thou prayest, thou shalt not be as the hypocrites are: for they love to pray standing in the synagogues and in the corners of the streets, that they may be seen of men. Verily I say unto you, They have their reward. But thou, when thou prayest, enter into thy closet, and when thou hast shut thy door, pray to thy Father which is in secret; and thy Father which seeth in secret shall reward thee openly. But when ye pray, use not vain repetitions, as the heathen do: for they think that they shall be heard for their much speaking. Be not ye therefore like unto them, for your Father knoweth what things ye have need of, before ye ask him.

After this manner therefore pray ye:

Our Father which art in heaven, Hallowed be thy name. Thy kingdom come. Thy will be done in earth, as it is in heaven. Give us this day our daily bread. And forgive us our debts, as we forgive our debtors. And lead us not into temptation, but deliver us from evil: For thine is the kingdom, and the power, and the glory, for ever. Amen.

For if ye forgive men their trespasses, your heavenly Father will also forgive you. But if ye forgive not men their trespasses, neither will your Father forgive your trespasses.

Moreover when ye fast, be not, as the hypocrites, of a sad countenance: for they disfigure their faces, that they may appear unto men to fast. Verily I say unto you, They have their reward. But thou, when thou fastest, anoint thine head, and wash thy face, that thou appear not unto men to fast, but unto thy Father which is in secret: and thy Father which seeth in secret shall reward thee openly.

Lay not up for yourselves treasures upon earth, where moth and rust doth corrupt, and where thieves break through and steal. But lay up for yourselves treasures in heaven, where neither moth nor rust doth corrupt, and where thieves do not break through nor steal; for where your treasure is, there will your heart be also.

The light of the body is the eye: if therefore thine eye be single, thy whole body shall be full of light. But if thine eye be evil, thy whole body shall be full of darkness. If therefore the light that is in thee be darkness, how great is that darkness!

No man can serve two masters: for either he will hate the one, and love the other; or else he will hold to the one, and despise the other. Ye cannot serve God and mammon.

Therefore I say unto you, Take no thought for your life, what ye shall eat, or what ye shall drink; nor yet for your body, what ye shall put on. Is not the life more than meat, and the body than raiment? Behold the fowls of the air: for they sow not, neither do they reap, nor gather into barns; yet your heavenly Father feedeth them. Are ye not much better than they? Which of you by taking thought can add one cubit unto his stature? And why take ye thought for raiment? Consider the lilies of the field, how they grow; they toil not, neither do they spin, and yet I say unto you, That even Solomon in all his glory was not arrayed like one of these. Wherefore, if God so clothe the grass of the field, which to-day is, and to-morrow is cast into the oven, shall he not much more clothe you, O ye of little faith?

Therefore take no thought, saying, What shall we eat? or, What shall we drink? or, Wherewithal shall we be clothed? (For after all these things do the Gentiles seek:) for your heavenly Father knoweth that ye have need of all these things. But seek ye first the kingdom of God, and his righteousness; and all these things shall be added unto you. Take therefore no thought for the morrow: for the morrow shall take thought for the things of itself. Sufficient unto the day is the evil thereof.

Judge not, that ye be not judged. For with what judgment ye judge, ye shall be judged: and with what measure ye mete, it shall be measured to you again. And why beholdest thou the mote that is in thy brother's eye, but considerest not the beam that is in thine own eye? Or how wilt thou say to thy brother, Let me pull out the mote out of thine eye; and, behold, a beam is in thine own eye? Thou hypocrite, first cast out the beam out of thine own eye; and then shalt thou see clearly to cast out the mote out of thy brother's eye.

Give not that which is holy unto the dogs, neither cast ye your pearls before swine, lest they trample them under their feet, and turn again and rend you.

Ask, and it shall be given you; seek, and ye shall find; knock, and it shall be opened unto you. For every one that asketh receiveth; and he that seeketh findeth; and to him that knocketh it shall be opened. Or what man is there of you, whom if his son ask bread, will he give him a stone? Or if he ask a fish, will he give him a serpent? If ye then, being evil, know how to give good gifts unto your children, how much more shall your Father which is in heaven give good things to them that ask him?

Therefore all things whatsoever ye would that men should do to you, do ye even so to them: for this is the law and the prophets.

Enter ye in at the strait gate: for wide is the gate,

and broad is the way, that leadeth to destruction, and many there be which go in thereat, because strait is the gate, and narrow is the way, which leadeth unto life, and few there be that find it.

Beware of false prophets, which come to you in sheep's clothing, but inwardly they are ravening wolves. Ye shall know them by their fruits. Do men gather grapes of thorns, or figs of thistles? Even so every good tree bringeth forth good fruit; but a corrupt tree bringeth forth evil fruit. A good tree cannot bring forth evil fruit, neither can a corrupt tree bring forth good fruit. Every tree that bringeth not forth good fruit is hewn down, and cast into the fire. Wherefore by their fruits ye shall know them.

Not every one that saith unto me, Lord, Lord, shall enter into the kingdom of heaven; but he that doeth the will of my Father which is in heaven. Many will say to me in that day, Lord, Lord, have we not prophesied in thy name? and in thy name have cast out devils? and in thy name done many wonderful works? And then will I profess unto them, I never knew you: depart from me, ye that work iniquity.

Therefore whosoever heareth these sayings of mine, and doeth them, I will liken him unto a wise man, which built his house upon a rock; and the rain descended, and the floods came, and the winds blew, and beat upon that house; and it fell not: for it was founded upon a rock.

And every one that heareth these sayings of mine, and doeth them not, shall be likened unto a foolish man, which built his house upon the sand; and the rain descended, and the floods came, and the winds blew, and beat upon that house; and it fell: and great was the fall of it.

And it came to pass, when Jesus had ended these

sayings, the people were astonished at his doctrine, for
he taught them as one having authority, and not as the
scribes.

Invitation to Christ

(FROM THE GOSPEL OF MATTHEW)

Come unto me, all ye that labour and are heavy
laden, and I will give you rest. Take my yoke upon you,
and learn of me; for I am meek and lowly in heart: and
ye shall find rest unto your souls. For my yoke is easy,
and my burden is light.

A Rebuke to Doubters

(FROM THE GOSPEL OF MATTHEW)

Every kingdom divided against itself is brought to
desolation; and every city or house divided against
itself shall not stand. And if Satan cast out Satan, he is
divided against himself; how shall then his kingdom
stand? And if I by Beelzebub cast out devils, by whom
do your children cast them out? therefore they shall be
your judges. But if I cast out devils by the Spirit of
God, then the kingdom of God is come unto you.

Or else, how can one enter into a strong man's house,
and spoil his goods, except he first bind the strong
man? and then he will spoil his house.

He that is not with me is against me; and he that
gathered not with me scattereth abroad.

Wherefore I say unto you, All manner of sin and
blasphemy shall be forgiven unto men: but the blasphemy against the Holy Ghost shall not be forgiven
unto men. And whosoever speaketh a word against the
Son of man, it shall be forgiven him: but whosoever
speaketh against the Holy Ghost, it shall not be for-

given him, neither in this world, neither in the world
to come.

Either make the tree good, and his fruit good; or else
make the tree corrupt, and his fruit corrupt: for the tree
is known by his fruit.

O generation of vipers, how can ye, being evil, speak
good things? for out of the abundance of the heart the
mouth speaketh. A good man out of the good treasure
of the heart bringeth forth good things: and an evil
man out of the evil treasure bringeth forth evil things.
But I say unto you, That every idle word that men
shall speak, they shall give account thereof in the day
of judgment. For by thy words thou shalt be justified,
and by thy words thou shalt be condemned.

*Then certain of the scribes and of the Pharisees
answered, saying, Master, we would see a sign from
thee.*

But he answered and said unto them,

An evil and adulterous generation seeketh after a
sign; and there shall no sign be given to it, but the
sign of the prophet Jonas; for as Jonas was three days
and three nights in the whale's belly; so shall the Son
of man be three days and three nights in the heart of
the earth. The men of Nineveh shall rise in judgment
with this generation, and shall condemn it: because
they repented at the preaching of Jonas; and, behold,
a greater than Jonas is here.

Of Forms and Meanings

(FROM THE GOSPEL OF MATTHEW)

*Then came to Jesus scribes and Pharisees, which
were of Jerusalem, saying, Why do thy disciples transgress the tradition of the elders? for they wash not their
hands when they eat bread.*

But he answered and said unto them,

Why do ye also transgress the commandment of God by your tradition? For God commanded, saying, Honour thy father and mother: and, He that curseth father or mother, let him die the death. But ye say, Whosoever shall say to his father or his mother, It is a gift, by whatsoever thou mightest be profited by me, and honour not his father or his mother, he shall be free. Thus have ye made the commandment of God of none effect by your tradition.

Ye hypocrites, well did Esaias prophesy of you, saying, This people draweth nigh unto me with their mouth, and honoureth me with their lips; but their heart is far from me. But in vain they do worship me, teaching for doctrines the commandments of men.

And he called the multitude, and said unto them,

Hear, and understand: not that which goeth into the mouth defileth a man; but that which cometh out of the mouth, this defileth a man. Do not ye yet understand, that whatsoever entereth in at the mouth goeth into the belly, and is cast out into the draught? But those things which proceed out of the mouth come forth from the heart; and they defile the man. For out of the heart proceed evil thoughts, murders, adulteries, fornications, thefts, false witness, blasphemies. These are the things which defile a man: but to eat with unwashen hands defileth not a man.

The Price of Salvation

(FROM THE GOSPEL OF MATTHEW)

Then said Jesus unto his disciples,

If any man will come after me, let him deny himself, and take up his cross, and follow me. For whosoever will save his life shall lose it: and whosoever will lose his life for my sake shall find it.

For what is a man profited, if he shall gain the whole world, and lose his own soul? or what shall a man give in exchange for his soul?

For the Son of man shall come in the glory of his Father with his angels; and then he shall reward every man according to his works.

Verily I say unto you, There be some standing here, which shall not taste of death, till they see the Son of man coming in his kingdom.

Until Seventy Times Seven

(FROM THE GOSPEL OF MATTHEW)

If thy brother shall trespass against thee, go and tell him his fault between thee and him alone: if he shall hear thee, thou hast gained thy brother. But if he will not hear thee, then take with thee one or two more, that in the mouth of two or three witnesses every word may be established. And if he shall neglect to hear them, tell it unto the church: but if he neglect to hear the church, let him be unto thee as a heathen man and a publican.

Verily I say unto you, Whatsoever ye shall bind on earth shall be bound in heaven; and whatsoever ye shall loose on earth shall be loosed in heaven.

Again I say unto you, That if two of you shall agree on earth as touching any thing that they shall ask, it shall be done for them of my Father which is in heaven. For where two or three are gathered together in my name, there am I in the midst of them.

Then came Peter to him, and said, Lord, how oft shall my brother sin against me, and I forgive him? till seven times?

Jesus saith unto him,

I say not unto thee, Until seven times, but, Until seventy times seven.

Of Marriage

(FROM THE GOSPEL OF MATTHEW)

The Pharisees also came unto him, tempting him, and saying unto him, Is it lawful for a man to put away his wife for every cause?

And he answered and said unto them,

Have ye not read, that he which made them at the beginning made them male and female, and said, For this cause shall a man leave father and mother, and shall cleave to his wife: and they twain shall be one flesh? Wherefore they are no more twain, but one flesh. What therefore God hath joined together, let not man put asunder.

They say unto him, Why did Moses then command to give a writing of divorcement, and to put her away?

He saith unto them,

Moses because of the hardness of your hearts suffered you to put away your wives: but from the beginning it was not so. And I say unto you, Whosoever shall put away his wife, except it be for fornication, and shall marry another, committeth adultery: and whoso marrieth her which is put away doth commit adultery.

His disciples say unto him, If the case of the man be so with his wife, it is not good to marry.

But he said unto them,

All men cannot receive this saying, save they to whom it is given. For there are some eunuchs, which were so born from their mother's womb: and there are some eunuchs, which were made eunuchs of men: and there be eunuchs, which have made themselves eunuchs for the kingdom of heaven's sake. He that is able to receive it, let him receive it.

Of Riches

(FROM THE GOSPEL OF MATTHEW)

And, behold, one came and said unto him, Good Master, what good thing shall I do, that I may have eternal life?

And he said unto him,

Why callest thou me good? there is none good but one, that is, God: but if thou wilt enter into life, keep the commandments.

He saith unto him, Which? Jesus said,

Thou shalt do no murder, Thou shalt not commit adultery, Thou shalt not steal, Thou shalt not bear false witness, Honour thy father and thy mother: and, Thou shalt love thy neighbour as thyself.

The young man saith unto him, All these things have I kept from my youth up: what lack I yet? Jesus said unto him,

If thou wilt be perfect, go, and sell that thou hast, and give to the poor, and thou shalt have treasure in heaven: and come and follow me.

But when the young man heard that saying, he went away sorrowful: for he had great possessions.

Then said Jesus unto his disciples,

Verily I say unto you, That a rich man shall hardly enter into the kingdom of heaven. And again I say unto you, It is easier for a camel to go through the eye of a needle, than for a rich man to enter into the kingdom of God.

When his disciples heard it, they were exceedingly

amazed, saying, Who then can be saved? But Jesus beheld them, and said unto them,

With men this is impossible; but with God all things are possible.

The Great Commandments

(FROM THE GOSPEL OF MARK)

And one of the scribes came, and having heard them reasoning together, and perceiving that he had answered them well, asked him, Which is the first commandment of all? And Jesus answered him,

The first of all the commandments is, Hear, O Israel; The Lord our God is one Lord: and thou shalt love the Lord thy God with all thy heart, and with all thy soul, and with all thy mind, and with all thy strength: this is the first commandment. And the second is like, namely this, Thou shalt love thy neighbour as thyself. There is none other commandment greater than these.

Jesus Rebukes the Scribes and Pharisees

(FROM THE GOSPEL OF MATTHEW)

Then spake Jesus to the multitude, and to his disciples, saying,

The scribes and the Pharisees sit in Moses' seat. All therefore whatsoever they bid you observe, that observe and do; but do not ye after their works, for they say, and do not. For they bind heavy burdens and grievous to be borne, and lay them on men's shoulders; but they themselves will not move them with one of their fingers. But all their works they do for to be seen of men; they make broad their phylacteries, and enlarge the borders of their garments, and love the uppermost rooms at feasts, and the chief seats in the synagogues, and greetings in the markets, and to be called of men, Rabbi, Rabbi.

But be not ye called Rabbi: for one is your Master, even Christ; and all ye are brethren. And call no man your father upon the earth: for one is your Father, which is in heaven. Neither be ye called masters, for one is your Master, even Christ. But he that is greatest among you shall be your servant. And whosoever shall exalt himself shall be abased; and he that shall humble himself shall be exalted.

But woe unto you, scribes and Pharisees, hypocrites! for ye shut up the kingdom of heaven against men, for ye neither go in yourselves, neither suffer ye them that are entering to go in. Woe unto you, scribes and Pharisees, hypocrites! for ye devour widows' houses, and for a pretense make long prayer: therefore ye shall receive the greater damnation. Woe unto you, scribes and Pharisees, hypocrites! for ye compass sea and land to make one proselyte, and when he is made, ye make him twofold more the child of hell than yourselves.

Woe unto you, ye blind guides, which say, Whosoever shall swear by the temple, it is nothing; but whosoever shall swear by the gold of the temple, he is a debtor! Ye fools and blind: for whether is greater, the gold, or the temple that sanctifieth the gold? And, Whosoever shall swear by the altar, it is nothing; but whosoever sweareth by the gift that is upon it, he is guilty. Ye fools and blind: for whether is greater, the gift, or the altar that sanctifieth the gift? Whoso therefore shall swear by the altar, sweareth by it, and by all things thereon. And whoso shall swear by the temple, sweareth by it, and by him that dwelleth therein. And he that shall swear by heaven, sweareth by the throne of God, and by him that sitteth thereon.

Woe unto you, scribes and Pharisees, hypocrites! for

ye pay tithe of mint and anise and cummin, and have omitted the weightier matters of the law, judgment, mercy, and faith: these ought ye to have done, and not to leave the other undone. Ye blind guides, which strain at a gnat, and swallow a camel.

Woe unto you, scribes and Pharisees, hypocrites! for ye make clean the outside of the cup and of the platter, but within they are full of extortion and excess. Thou blind Pharisee, cleanse first that which is within the cup and platter, that the outside of them may be clean also.

O Jerusalem, Jerusalem, thou that killest the prophets, and stonest them which are sent unto thee, how often would I have gathered thy children together, even as a hen gathereth her chickens under her wings, and ye would not! Behold, your house is left unto you desolate. For I say unto you, Ye shall not see me henceforth, till ye shall say, Blessed is he that cometh in the name of the Lord.

Second Coming

(FROM THE GOSPEL OF MATTHEW)

And Jesus went out, and departed from the temple: and his disciples came to him. And Jesus said unto them.

Take heed that no man deceive you. For many shall come in my name, saying, I am Christ; and shall deceive many. And ye shall hear of wars and rumours of wars: see that ye be not troubled: for all these things must come to pass, but the end is not yet. For nation shall rise against nation, and kingdom against kingdom: and there shall be famines, and pestilences, and earthquakes, in divers places. All these are the beginning of sorrows.

Then shall they deliver you up to be afflicted, and

shall kill you, and ye shall be hated of all nations for my name's sake. And then shall many be offended, and shall betray one another, and shall hate one another. And many false prophets shall rise, and shall deceive many. And because iniquity shall abound, the love of many shall wax cold. But he that shall endure unto the end, the same shall be saved.

Then if any man shall say unto you, Lo, here is Christ, or there; believe it not. For there shall arise false Christs, and false prophets, and shall show great signs and wonders; insomuch that, if it were possible, they shall deceive the very elect. Behold, I have told you before. Wherefore if they shall say unto you, Behold, he is in the desert; go not forth: behold, he is in the secret chambers; believe it not. For as the lightning cometh out of the east, and shineth even unto the west; so shall also the coming of the Son of man be. For wheresoever the carcass is, there will the eagles be gathered together.

Immediately after the tribulation of those days shall the sun be darkened, and the moon shall not give her light, and the stars shall fall from heaven, and the powers of the heavens shall be shaken. And then shall appear the sign of the Son of man in heaven: and then shall all the tribes of the earth mourn, and they shall see the Son of man coming in the clouds of heaven with power and great glory. And he shall send his angels with a great sound of a trumpet, and they shall gather together his elect from the four winds, from one end of heaven to the other.

Watch therefore; for ye know not what hour your Lord doth come. But know this, that if the goodman of the house had known in what watch the thief would come, he would have watched, and would not have suffered his house to be broken up. Therefore be ye also ready, for in such an hour as ye think not the Son of man cometh.

When the Son of man shall come in his glory, and all the holy angels with him, then shall he sit upon the throne of his glory. And before him shall be gathered all nations: and he shall separate them one from another, as a shepherd divideth his sheep from the goats. And he shall set the sheep on his right hand, but the goats on the left.

Then shall the King say unto them on his right hand, Come, ye blessed of my Father, inherit the kingdom prepared for you from the foundation of the world. For I was ahungered, and ye gave me meat; I was thirsty, and ye gave me drink; I was a stranger, and ye took me in; naked, and ye clothed me; I was sick, and ye visited me; I was in prison, and ye came unto me.

Then shall the righteous answer him, saying, Lord, when saw we thee ahungered, and fed thee? or thirsty, and gave thee drink? When saw we thee a stranger, and took thee in? or naked, and clothed thee? Or when saw we thee sick, or in prison, and came unto thee?

And the King shall answer and say unto them, Verily I say unto you, Inasmuch as ye have done it unto one of the least of these my brethren, ye have done it unto me.

Then shall he say also unto them on the left hand, Depart from me, ye cursed, into everlasting fire, prepared for the devil and his angels. For I was ahungered, and ye gave me no meat; I was thirsty, and ye gave me no drink; I was a stranger, and ye took me not in; naked, and ye clothed me not; sick, and in prison, and ye visited me not.

Then shall they also answer him, saying, Lord, when

saw we thee ahungered, or athirst, or a stranger, or
naked, or sick, or in prison, and did not minister unto
thee?

Then shall he answer them, saying, Verily I say
unto you, Inasmuch as ye did it not to one of the least
of these, ye did it not to me.

And these shall go away into everlasting punishment:
but the righteous into life eternal.

The Birth of the Spirit

(FROM THE GOSPEL OF JOHN)

*There was a man of the Pharisees, named Nicodemus,
a ruler of the Jews. The same came to Jesus by night,
and said unto him, Rabbi, we know that thou art a
teacher come from God: for no man can do these
miracles that thou doest, except God be with him. Jesus
answered and said unto him,*

Verily, verily, I say unto thee, Except a man be born
again, he cannot see the kingdom of God.

*Nicodemus saith unto him, How can a man be born
when he is old? can he enter the second time into his
mother's womb, and be born? Jesus answered,*

Verily, verily, I say unto thee, Except a man be
born of water and of the Spirit, he cannot enter into the
kingdom of God. That which is born of the flesh is
flesh; and that which is born of the Spirit is spirit.
Marvel not that I said unto thee, Ye must be born
again.

The wind bloweth where it listeth, and thou hearest
the sound thereof, but canst not tell whence it cometh,
and whither it goeth: so is every one that is born of the
Spirit.

*Nicodemus answered and said unto him, How can
these things be? Jesus answered and said unto him,*

Art thou a master of Israel, and knowest not these things? Verily, verily, I say unto thee, We speak that we do know, and testify that we have seen; and ye receive not our witness. If I have told you earthly things, and ye believe not, how shall ye believe, if I tell you of heavenly things? And no man hath ascended up to heaven, but he that came down from heaven, even the Son of man which is in heaven.

And as Moses lifted up the serpent in the wilderness, even so must the Son of man be lifted up, that whosoever believeth in him should not perish, but have eternal life.

For God so loved the world, that he gave his only begotten Son, that whosoever believeth in him should not perish, but have everlasting life. For God sent not his Son into the world to condemn the world; but that the world through him might be saved.

He that believeth on him is not condemned: but he that believeth not is condemned already, because he hath not believed in the name of the only begotten Son of God. And this is the condemnation, that light is come into the world, and men loved darkness rather than light, because their deeds were evil. For every one that doeth evil hateth the light, neither cometh to the light, lest his deeds should be reproved. But he that doeth truth cometh to the light, that his deeds may be made manifest, that they are wrought in God.

The Bread of Life

(FROM THE GOSPEL OF JOHN)

I am that bread of life. Your fathers did eat manna in the wilderness, and are dead. This is the bread which cometh down from heaven, that a man may eat thereof, and not die. I am the living bread which came down from heaven. If any man eat of this bread, he shall live for ever: and the bread that I will give is my flesh, which I will give for the life of the world.

The True Vine

(FROM THE GOSPEL OF JOHN)

I am the true vine, and my Father is the husbandman. Every branch in me that beareth not fruit he taketh away: and every branch that beareth fruit, he purgeth it, that it may bring forth more fruit.

Now ye are clean through the word which I have spoken unto you.

Abide in me, and I in you. As the branch cannot bear fruit of itself, except it abide in the vine; no more can ye, except ye abide in me. I am the vine, ye are the branches. He that abideth in me, and I in him, the same bringeth forth much fruit; for without me ye can do nothing. If a man abide not in me, he is cast forth as a branch, and is withered; and men gather them, and cast them into the fire, and they are burned. If ye abide in me, and my words abide in you, ye shall ask what ye will, and it shall be done unto you.

This is my commandment, That ye love one another, as I have loved you. Greater love hath no man than this, that a man lay down his life for his friends.

Of the Sower, the Tares, and the Mustard Seed

(FROM THE GOSPEL OF MATTHEW)

And he spake many things unto them in parables, saying,

Behold, a sower went forth to sow; and when he sowed, some seeds fell by the wayside, and the fowls came and devoured them up: some fell upon stony places, where they had not much earth: and forthwith they sprang up, because they had no deepness of earth, and when the sun was up, they were scorched; and because they had no root, they withered away. And some fell among thorns; and the thorns sprang up, and choked them; but other fell into good ground, and brought forth fruit, some a hundredfold, some sixtyfold, some thirtyfold.

Who hath ears to hear, let him hear.

And the disciples came, and said unto him, Why speakest thou unto them in parables? He answered and said unto them,

Because it is given unto you to know the mysteries of the kingdom of heaven, but to them it is not given. For whosoever hath, to him shall be given, and he shall have more abundance: but whosoever hath not, from him shall be taken away even that he hath. Therefore speak I to them in parables: because they seeing see not; and hearing they hear not, neither do they understand.

Hear ye therefore the parable of the sower. When any one heareth the word of the kingdom, and understandeth it not, then cometh the wicked one, and catcheth away that which was sown in his heart. This is he which received seed by the wayside. But he that received the seed into stony places, the same is he that heareth the word, and anon with joy receiveth it; yet hath he not root in himself, but dureth for a while; for when tribulation or persecution ariseth because of the word, by and by he is offended. He also that received seed among the thorns is he that heareth the word; and the care of this world, and the deceitfulness of riches, choke the word, and he becometh unfruitful. But he that received seed into the good ground is he that heareth the word, and understandeth it; which also beareth fruit, and bringeth forth, some a hundredfold, some sixty, some thirty.

Another parable put he forth unto them, saying,

The kingdom of heaven is likened unto a man which sowed good seed in his field. But while men slept, his enemy came and sowed tares among the wheat, and went his way. But when the blade was sprung up, and brought forth fruit, then appeared the tares also.

So the servants of the householder came and said unto him, Sir, didst not thou sow good seed in thy field? from whence then hath it tares?

He said unto them, An enemy hath done this.

The servants said unto him, Wilt thou then that we go and gather them up?

But he said, Nay; lest while ye gather up the tares, ye root up also the wheat with them. Let both grow together until the harvest, and in the time of harvest I will say to the reapers, Gather ye together first the tares, and bind them in bundles to burn them: but gather the wheat into my barn.

Another parable put he forth unto them, saying,

The kingdom of heaven is like to a grain of mustard seed, which a man took, and sowed in his field, which indeed is the least of all seeds, but when it is grown, it is the greatest among herbs, and becometh a tree, so that the birds of the air come and lodge in the branches thereof.

Another parable spake he unto them:

The kingdom of heaven is like unto leaven, which a woman took, and hid in three measures of meal, till the whole was leavened.

All these things spake Jesus unto the multitude in parables; and without a parable spake he not unto them, that it might be fulfilled which was spoken by

*the prophet, saying, I will open my mouth in parables;
I will utter things which have been kept secret from
the foundation of the world.*

*Then Jesus sent the multitude away, and went into
the house: and his disciples came unto him, saying,
Declare unto us the parable of the tares of the field.
He answered and said unto them,*

He that soweth the good seed is the Son of man;
the field is the world; the good seed are the children
of the kingdom; but the tares are the children of the
wicked one; the enemy that sowed them is the devil;
the harvest is the end of the world; and the reapers
are the angels. As therefore the tares are gathered and
burned in the fire; so shall it be in the end of this
world. The Son of man shall send forth his angels, and
they shall gather out of his kingdom all things that
offend, and them which do iniquity; and shall cast
them into a furnace of fire: there shall be wailing and
gnashing of teeth. Then shall the righteous shine forth
as the sun in the kingdom of their Father. Who hath
ears to hear, let him hear.

Again, the kingdom of heaven is like unto treasure
hid in a field; the which when a man hath found, he
hideth, and for joy thereof goeth and selleth all that
he hath, and buyeth that field.

Again, the kingdom of heaven is like unto a merchant-
man, seeking goodly pearls, who, when he had found
one pearl of great price, went and sold all that he had,
and bought it.

Again, the kingdom of heaven is like unto a net, that
was cast into the sea, and gathered of every kind,
which, when it was full, they drew to shore, and sat
down, and gathered the good into vessels, but cast the
bad away.

So shall it be at the end of the world: the angels

shall come forth, and sever the wicked from among the just, and shall cast them into the furnace of fire: there shall be wailing and gnashing of teeth.

Of the Good Samaritan

(FROM THE GOSPEL OF LUKE)

And, behold, a certain lawyer stood up, and tempted him, saying, Master, what shall I do to inherit eternal life? He said unto him,

What is written in the law? how readest thou?

And he answering said, Thou shalt love the Lord thy God with all thy heart, and with all thy soul, and with all thy strength, and with all thy mind; and thy neighbour as thyself. And he said unto him,

Thou hast answered right: this do, and thou shalt live.

But he, willing to justify himself, said unto Jesus, And who is my neighbour? And Jesus answering said,

A certain man went down from Jerusalem to Jericho, and fell among thieves, which stripped him of his raiment, and wounded him, and departed, leaving him half dead. And by chance there came down a certain priest that way; and when he saw him, he passed by on the other side. And likewise a Levite, when he was at the place, came and looked on him, and passed by on the other side. But a certain Samaritan, as he journeyed, came where he was; and when he saw him, he had compassion on him, and went to him, and bound up his wounds, pouring in oil and wine, and set him on his own beast, and brought him to an inn, and took care of him. And on the morrow when he departed, he took out two pence, and gave them to the host, and said unto him, Take care of him: and whatsoever thou spendest more, when I come again, I will repay thee.

Which now of these three, thinkest thou, was neighbour unto him that fell among the thieves?

And he said, He that showed mercy on him. Then said Jesus unto him,

Go, and do thou likewise.

Of One That Layeth Up Treasure

(FROM THE GOSPEL OF LUKE)

And he spake a parable unto them, saying,

The ground of a certain rich man brought forth plentifully. And he thought within himself, saying, What shall I do, because I have no room where to bestow my fruits? And he said, This will I do: I will pull down my barns, and build greater; and there will I bestow all my fruits and my goods. And I will say to my soul, Soul, thou hast much goods laid up for many years; take thine ease, eat, drink, and be merry.

But God said unto him, Thou fool, this night thy soul shall be required of thee: then whose shall those things be, which thou hast provided?

So is he that layeth up treasure for himself, and is not rich toward God.

Fear not, little flock; for it is your Father's good pleasure to give you the kingdom. Sell that ye have, and give alms; provide yourselves bags which wax not old, a treasure in the heavens that faileth not, where no thief approacheth, neither moth corrupteth. For where your treasure is, there will your heart be also.

Of the Two Men Who Prayed

(FROM THE GOSPEL OF LUKE)

And he spake this parable unto certain which trusted in themselves that they were righteous, and despised others:

Two men went up into the temple to pray; the one a Pharisee, and the other a publican.

The Pharisee stood and prayed thus with himself, God, I thank thee, that I am not as other men are, extortioners, unjust, adulterers, or even as this publican. I fast twice in the week, I give tithes of all that I possess.

And the publican, standing afar off, would not lift up so much as his eyes unto heaven, but smote upon his breast, saying, God be merciful to me a sinner.

I tell you, this man went down to his house justified rather than the other: for every one that exalteth himself shall be abased; and he that humbleth himself shall be exalted.

From the Acts of the Apostles

The Founding of the Christian Church

And in those days Peter stood up in the midst of the disciples and they appointed two, Joseph called Barsabas, who was surnamed Justus, and Matthias. And they prayed, and said, Thou, Lord, which knowest the hearts of all men, shew whether of these two thou hast chosen, that he may take part of this ministry and apostleship, from which Judas by transgression fell, that he might go to his own place. And they gave forth their lots; and the lot fell upon Matthias; and he was numbered with the eleven apostles.

And when the day of Pentecost was fully come, they were all with one accord in one place. And suddenly there came a sound from heaven, as of a rushing mighty wind, and it filled all the house where they were sitting. And there appeared unto them cloven tongues like as of fire, and it sat upon each of them. And they were all filled with the Holy Ghost, and began to speak with other tongues, as the Spirit gave them utterance.

And there were dwelling at Jerusalem Jews, devout men, out of every nation under heaven. And they were all amazed, and marvelled, saying one to another, Behold, are not all these which speak, Galileans? And how hear we every man in our own tongue, wherein we were born? Parthians, and Medes, and Elamites, and the dwellers in Mesopotamia, and in Judea, and Cappadocia, in Pontus, and Asia, Phrygia, and Pamphylia, in Egypt, and in the parts of Libya about Cyrene, and strangers of Rome, Jews and proselytes, Cretes and Arabians, we do hear them speak in our tongues the wonderful works of God. Others mocking, said, These men are full of new wine.

But Peter, standing up with the eleven, lifted up his voice, and said unto them, Ye men of Judea, and all ye that dwell at Jerusalem, be this known unto you, and hearken to my words: for these are not drunken, as ye suppose, seeing it is but the third hour of the day. But this is that which was spoken by the prophet Joel, And it shall come to pass in the last days, saith God, I will pour out of my Spirit upon all flesh: and your sons and your daughters shall prophesy, and your young men shall see visions, and your old men shall dream dreams. And on my servants and on my handmaidens, I will pour out in those days of my Spirit; and they shall prophesy.

And I will shew wonders in heaven above, and signs in the earth beneath; blood, and fire, and vapour of smoke. The sun shall be turned into darkness, and the moon into blood, before that great and notable day of the Lord come. And it shall come to pass, that whosoever shall call on the name of the Lord, shall be saved.

Ye men of Israel, hear these words; Jesus of Nazareth, a man approved of God among you by miracles, and wonders, and signs, which God did by him in the midst of you, as ye yourselves also know, Him, being delivered by the determinate counsel and foreknowledge of God, ye have taken, and by wicked hands have crucified and slain.

Now when they heard this, they were pricked in their hearts, and said unto Peter and to the rest of the apostles, Men and brethren, what shall we do?

Then Peter said unto them, Repent, and be baptized every one of you in the name of Jesus Christ, for the remission of sins, and ye shall receive the gift of the Holy Ghost. And with many other words did he testify and exhort, saying, Save yourselves from this untoward generation.

Then they that gladly received his word, were baptized: and the same day there were added unto them about three thousand souls. And they, continuing daily with one accord in the temple, and breaking bread from house to house, did eat their meat with gladness and singleness of heart, praising God, and having favour with all the people. And the Lord added to the church daily such as should be saved.

Saul's Conversion

And Saul, breathing out threatenings and slaughter against the disciples of the Lord, went unto the high priest, and desired of him letters to Damascus to the synagogues, that if he found any of this way, whether they were men or women, he might bring them bound unto Jerusalem.

And as he journeyed, he came near Damascus: and suddenly there shined round about him a light from heaven. And he fell to the earth, and heard a voice saying unto him, Saul, Saul, why persecutest thou me?

And he said, Who art thou, Lord? And the Lord said, I am Jesus whom thou persecutest. It is hard for thee to kick against the pricks.

And he trembling, and astonished, said, Lord, what wilt thou have me to do? And the Lord said unto him, Arise, and go into the city, and it shall be told thee what thou must do.

And the men which journeyed with him stood speechless, hearing a voice, but seeing no man.

And Saul arose from the earth; and when his eyes were opened, he saw no man: but they led him by the hand, and brought him into Damascus. And he was three days without sight, and neither did eat nor drink.

And there was a certain disciple at Damascus, named Ananias; and to him said the Lord in a vision, Ananias. And he said, Behold, I am here, Lord.

And the Lord said unto him, Arise, and go into the street which is called Straight, and inquire in the house of Judas for one called Saul of Tarsus: for behold, he prayeth, and hath seen in a vision a man named Ananias, coming in, and putting his hand on him, that he might receive his sight.

And Ananias went his way, and entered into the house: and putting his hands on him, said, Brother Saul, the Lord (even Jesus that appeared unto thee in the way as thou camest) hath sent me, that thou mightest receive thy sight, and be filled with the Holy Ghost.

And immediately there fell from his eyes as it had been scales: and he received sight forthwith, and arose, and was baptized. And when he had received meat, he was strengthened. Then was Saul certain days with the disciples which were at Damascus. And straightway he preached Christ in the synagogues, that he is the Son of God.

Peter's Vision of the Gentiles

As they went on their journey, and drew nigh unto the city, Peter went up upon the house-top to pray, about the sixth hour. And he became very hungry, and would have eaten: but while they made ready, he fell into a trance, and saw heaven opened, and a certain vessel descending unto him, as it had been a great sheet knit at the four corners, and let down to the earth, wherein were all manner of four-footed beasts of the earth, and wild beasts, and creeping things, and fowls of the air.

And there came a voice to him, Rise, Peter; kill, and eat.

But Peter said, Not so, Lord; for I have never eaten anything that is common or unclean.

And the voice spake unto him again the second time, What God hath cleansed, that call not thou common.

This was done thrice: and the vessel was received up again into heaven.

Then Peter opened his mouth, and said, Of a truth I perceive that God is no respector of persons, but in every nation, he that feareth him and worketh right-eousness, is accepted with him. Can any man forbid water, that these should not be baptized, which have received the Holy Ghost as well as we?

And the apostles and brethren that were in Judea, heard that the Gentiles had also received the word of God.

And when Peter was come up to Jerusalem, they that were of the circumcision contended with him, saying,

Thou wentest in to men uncircumcised, and didst eat with them.

But Peter rehearsed the matter from the beginning, and expounded it by order unto them.

When they heard these things, they held their peace, and glorified God, saying, Then hath God also to the Gentiles granted repentance unto life.

Now they which were scattered abroad upon the persecution that arose about Stephen, travelled as far as Phenice, and Cyprus, and Antioch, preaching the word to none but unto the Jews only. And some of them were men of Cyprus and Cyrene, which when they were come to Antioch, spake unto the Grecians, preaching the Lord Jesus.

And the hand of the Lord was with them: and a great number believed, and turned unto the Lord.

Then tidings of these things came unto the ears of the church which was in Jerusalem: and they sent forth Barnabas, that he should go as far as Antioch.

Then departed Barnabas to Tarsus, for to seek Saul. And when he had found him, he brought him unto Antioch. And it came to pass, that a whole year they assembled themselves with the church, and taught much people. And the disciples were called Christians first in Antioch.

And in these days came prophets from Jerusalem unto Antioch.

Paul and Barnabas Turn to the Gentiles

And the next sabbath-day came almost the whole city together to hear the word of God. But when the Jews saw the multitudes, they were filled with envy, and spake against those things which were spoken by Paul, contradicting and blaspheming.

Then Paul and Barnabas waxed bold, and said, It was necessary that the word of God should first have been spoken to you: but seeing you put it from you, and judge yourselves unworthy of everlasting life, lo, we turn to the Gentiles. For so hath the Lord commanded us, saying, I have set thee to be a light of the Gentiles, that thou shouldest be for salvation unto the ends of the earth.

And when the Gentiles heard this, they were glad, and glorified the word of the Lord: and as many as were ordained to eternal life, believed.

And certain men which came down from Judea, taught the brethren, and said, Except ye be circumcised after the manner of Moses, ye cannot be saved.

When therefore Paul and Barnabas had no small dissension and disputation with them, they determined that Paul and Barnabas, and certain other of them, should go up to Jerusalem unto the apostles and elders about this question.

And when they were come to Jerusalem, they were received of the church, and of the apostles and elders, and they declared all things that God had done with them.

Then pleased it the apostles and elders, with the whole church, to send chosen men of their own company to Antioch, with Paul and Barnabas; namely, Judas surnamed Barsabas, and Silas, chief men among the brethren.

And they wrote letters by them after this manner; The apostles, and elders, and brethren, send greeting unto the brethren which are of the Gentiles in Antioch, and Syria, and Cilicia. Forasmuch as we have heard, that certain which went out from us, have troubled you with words, subverting your souls, saying, Ye must be circumcised, and keep the law; to whom we gave no such commandment: it seemed good unto us, being assembled with one accord, to send chosen men unto you, with our beloved Barnabas and Paul: men that have hazarded their lives for the name of our Lord Jesus Christ. We have sent therefore Judas and Silas, who shall also tell you the same things by mouth. For it seemed good to the Holy Ghost, and to us, to lay upon you no greater burden than these necessary things; that ye abstain from meats offered to idols, and from blood, and from things strangled, and from fornication: from which if ye keep yourselves, ye shall do well. Fare ye well.

From the Epistles

To the Jew and Also to the Gentile

(FROM THE EPISTLE OF PAUL TO THE ROMANS)

I am debtor both to the Greeks, and to the Barbarians; both to the wise, and to the unwise. So, as much as in me is, I am ready to preach the gospel to you that are at Rome also.

For therein is the righteousness of God revealed from faith to faith: as it is written, The just shall live by faith. For the wrath of God is revealed from heaven against all ungodliness, and unrighteousness of men, who hold the truth in unrighteousness.

Tribulation and anguish, upon every soul of man that doeth evil; of the Jew first, and also of the Gentile; but glory, honour, and peace, to every man that worketh good; to the Jew first, and also to the Gentile. For there is no respect of persons with God.

For as many as have sinned without law, shall also

perish without law: and as many as have sinned in the law, shall be judged by the law.

For he is not a Jew, which is one outwardly; neither is that circumcision, which is outward in the flesh. But he is a Jew which is one inwardly; and circumcision is that of the heart, in the spirit, and not in the letter; whose praise is not of men, but of God.

What advantage then hath the Jew? or what profit is there of circumcision? Much every way: chiefly, because that unto them were committed the oracles of God.

But now the righteousness of God without the law is manifested, being witnessed by the law and the prophets; even the righteousness of God, which is by faith of Jesus Christ unto all, and upon all them that believe; for there is no difference: for all have sinned, and come short of the glory of God; being justified freely by his grace, through the redemption that is in Christ Jesus: whom God hath set forth to be a propitiation, through faith in his blood, to declare his righteousness for the remission of sins that are past, through the forbearance of God; to declare, I say, at this time his righteousness: that he might be just, and the justifier of him which believeth in Jesus.

Where is boasting then? It is excluded. By what law? of works? Nay; but by the law of faith. Therefore we conclude, that a man is justified by faith without the deeds of the law.

Is he the God of the Jews only? is he not also of the Gentiles? Yes, of the Gentiles also: seeing it is one God which shall justify the circumcision by faith, and uncircumcision through faith.

Do we then make void the law through faith? God forbid: yea, we establish the law.

Therefore being justified by faith, we have peace with God, through our Lord Jesus Christ, by whom also we have access by faith into this grace wherein we stand, and rejoice in hope of the glory of God. And not only so, but we glory in tribulations also; knowing that tribulation worketh patience; and patience, experience; and experience, hope; and hope maketh not ashamed: because the love of God is shed abroad in our hearts by the Holy Ghost which is given unto us.

Ye are not in the flesh, but in the Spirit, if so be that the Spirit of God dwell in you. Now, if any man have not the Spirit of Christ, he is none of his. And if Christ be in you, the body is dead because of sin; but the Spirit is life because of righteousness. But if the Spirit of him that raised up Jesus from the dead dwell in you, he that raised up Christ from the dead shall also quicken your mortal bodies by his Spirit that dwelleth in you.

Therefore, brethren, we are debtors not to the flesh, to live after the flesh. For if ye live after the flesh, ye shall die: but if ye through the Spirit do mortify the deeds of the body, ye shall live. For as many as are led by the Spirit of God, they are the sons of God.

What shall we then say to these things? If God be for us, who can be against us? He that spared not his own Son, but delivered him up for us all, how shall he not with him also freely give us all things?

Who shall lay anything to the charge of God's elect? It is God that justifieth: who is he that condemneth? It is Christ that died, yea rather, that is risen again, who is even at the right hand of God, who also maketh intercession for us. Who shall separate us from the love of Christ? shall tribulation, or distress, or persecution, or famine, or nakedness, or peril, or sword? As it is written, For thy sake we are killed all the day long;

we are accounted as sheep for the slaughter. Nay, in all these things we are more than conquerers, through him that loved us.

For I am persuaded, that neither death, nor life, nor angels, nor principalities, nor powers, nor things present, nor things to come, nor height, nor depth, nor any other creature, shall be able to separate us from the love of God which is in Christ Jesus our Lord.

Let love be without dissimulation. Abhor that which is evil; cleave to that which is good. Be kindly affectioned one to another with brotherly love; in honour preferring one another; not slothful in business; fervent in spirit; serving the Lord; rejoicing in hope; patient in tribulation; continuing instant in prayer; distributing to the necessity of saints; given to hospitality.

Bless them which persecute you; bless, and curse not. Rejoice with them that do rejoice, and weep with them that weep.

Be of the same mind one toward another. Mind not high things, but condescend to men of low estate. Be not wise in your own conceits.

Recompense to no man evil for evil. Provide things honest in the sight of all men.

If it be possible, as much as lieth in you, live peaceably with all men.

Dearly beloved, avenge not yourselves, but rather give place unto wrath: for it is written, Vengeance is mine; I will repay, saith the Lord. Therefore, if thine enemy hunger, feed him; if he thirst, give him drink; for in so doing thou shalt heap coals of fire on his head.

Be not overcome of evil, but overcome evil with good.

Let us therefore follow after the things which make for peace, and things wherewith one may edify another.

Paul Instructs the Christian Church

(FROM THE FIRST EPISTLE OF PAUL TO
THE CORINTHIANS)

Where is the wise? where is the scribe? where is the disputer of this world? hath not God made foolish the wisdom of this world? For after that in the wisdom of God the world by wisdom knew not God, it pleased God by the foolishness of preaching to save them that believe.

For the Jews require a sign, and the Greeks seek after wisdom: but we preach Christ crucified, unto the Jews a stumbling-block, and unto the Greeks foolishness; but unto them which are called, both Jews and Greeks, Christ the power of God, and the wisdom of God. Because the foolishness of God is wiser than men; and the weakness of God is stronger than men.

It is good for a man not to touch a woman. Nevertheless, to avoid fornication, let every man have his own wife, and let every woman have her own husband. Let the husband render unto the wife due benevolence: and likewise also the wife unto the husband. The wife hath not power of her own body, but the husband: and likewise also the husband hath not power of his own body, but the wife.

For I would that all men were even as I myself. But every man hath his proper gift of God, one after this manner, and another after that. I say therefore to the unmarried and widows, It is good for them if they abide even as I. But if they cannot contain, let them marry: for it is better to marry than to burn.

Art thou bound unto a wife? seek not to be loosed. Art thou loosed from a wife? seek not a wife. But and if thou marry, thou hast not sinned: and if a virgin marry, she hath not sinned.

But I would have you know, that the head of every man is Christ; and the head of the woman is the man; and the head of Christ is God. Every man praying or prophesying, having his head covered, dishonoureth his head. But every woman that prayeth or prophesieth with her head uncovered, dishonoureth her head: for that is even all one as if she were shaven.

For a man indeed ought not to cover his head, forasmuch as he is the image and glory of God: but the woman is the glory of the man. For the man is not of the woman, but the woman of the man. Neither was the man created for the woman, but the woman for the man.

Let your women keep silence in the churches; for it is not permitted unto them to speak: but they are commanded to be under obedience, as also saith the law. And if they will learn anything, let them ask their husbands at home; for it is a shame for women to speak in the church.

When ye come together therefore into one place, this is not to eat the Lord's supper. For in eating every one taketh before other his own supper: and one is hungry, and another is drunken. What! have ye not houses to eat and to drink in? or despise ye the church of God, and shame them that have not? What shall I say to you? shall I praise you in this? I praise you not.

For I have received of the Lord, that which also I delivered unto you, That the Lord Jesus, the same night in which he was betrayed, took bread: and when he had given thanks, he brake it, and said, Take, eat: this is my body, which is broken for you: this do in remembrance of me. After the same manner also he took the cup, when he had supped, saying, This cup is the new testament in my blood: this do ye, as oft as ye drink it, in remembrance of me. For as often as ye eat this bread, and drink this cup, ye do shew the Lord's death till he come.

Wherefore, whosoever shall eat this bread, and drink this cup of the Lord, unworthily, shall be guilty of the body and blood of the Lord. But let a man examine himself, and so let him eat of that bread, and drink of that cup. For he that eateth and drinketh unworthily, eateth and drinketh damnation to himself, not discerning the Lord's body.

Though I speak with the tongues of men and of angels, and have not charity, I am become as sounding brass, or a tinkling cymbal. And though I have the gift of prophecy, and understand all mysteries, and all knowledge; and though I have all faith, so that I could remove mountains, and have not charity, I am nothing. And though I bestow all my goods to feed the poor, and though I give my body to be burned, and have not charity, it profiteth me nothing.

Charity suffereth long, and is kind; charity envieth not; charity vaunteth not itself, is not puffed up, doth not behave itself unseemly, seeketh not her own, is not easily provoked, thinketh no evil, rejoiceth not in iniquity, but rejoiceth in the truth; beareth all things, believeth all things, hopeth all things, endureth all things.

Charity never faileth: but whether there be prophecies, they shall fail; whether there be tongues, they shall cease; whether there be knowledge, it shall vanish away.

For we know in part, and we prophesy in part. But when that which is perfect is come, then that which is in part shall be done away.

When I was a child, I spake as a child, I understood as a child, I thought as a child: but when I became a man, I put away childish things. For now we see through a glass, darkly; but then face to face: now I know in part; but then shall I know even as also I am known.

And now abideth faith, hope, charity, these three; but the greatest of these is charity.

Now if Christ be preached that he rose from the dead, how say some among you that there is no resurrection of the dead? But if there be no resurrection of the dead, then is Christ not risen: and if Christ be not risen, then is our preaching vain, and your faith is also vain. Yea, and we are found false witnesses of God; because we have testified of God that he raised up Christ: whom he raised not up, if so be that the dead rise not.

For if the dead rise not, then is not Christ raised: and if Christ be not raised, your faith is vain; ye are yet in your sins. Then they also which are fallen asleep in Christ are perished. If in this life only, we have hope in Christ, we are of all men most miserable.

But now is Christ risen from the dead, and become the first-fruits of them that slept. For since by man came death, by man came also the resurrection of the dead. For as in Adam all die, even so in Christ shall all be made alive.

O death, where is thy sting? O grave, where is thy victory? The sting of death is sin; and the strength of sin is the law. But thanks be to God, which giveth us the victory, through our Lord Jesus Christ.

Walk in the Spirit

(FROM PAUL'S EPISTLE TO THE GALATIANS)

Walk in the Spirit, and ye shall not fulfil the lust of the flesh. For the flesh lusteth against the Spirit, and the Spirit against the flesh: and these are contrary the one to the other; so that ye cannot do the things that ye would. But if ye be led by the Spirit, ye are not under the law.

Now the works of the flesh are manifest, which are these, adultery, fornication, uncleanness, lasciviousness, idolatry, witchcraft, hatred, variance, emulations, wrath, strife, seditions, heresies, envyings, murders, drunkenness, revellings, and such like: of the which I tell you before, as I have also told you in time past, that they which do such things shall not inherit the kingdom of God.

But the fruit of the Spirit is love, joy, peace, longsuffering, gentleness, goodness, faith, meekness, temperance: against such there is no law. And they that are Christ's have crucified the flesh, with the affections and lusts.

One Lord

(FROM PAUL'S EPISTLE TO THE EPHESIANS)

There is one body, and one Spirit, even as ye are called in one hope of your calling; one Lord, one faith, one baptism, one God and Father of all, who is above all, and through all, and in you all. But unto every one of us is given grace according to the measure of the gift of Christ.

Wherefore putting away lying, speak every man truth with his neighbour: for we are members one of another. Be ye angry, and sin not. Let not the sun go down upon your wrath. Neither give place to the devil. Let him that stole, steal no more: but rather let him labour, working with his hands the thing which is good, that he may have to give to him that needeth.

Let all bitterness, and wrath, and anger, and clamour, and evil-speaking, be put away from you, with all malice. And be ye kind one to another, tender-hearted, forgiving one another, even as God for Christ's sake hath forgiven you.

Be ye therefore followers of God as dear children, and walk in love, as Christ also hath loved us, and hath given himself for us an offering and a sacrifice to God for a sweet-smelling savour.

Hold Fast That Which Is Good

(FROM PAUL'S EPISTLE TO THE THESSALONIANS)

But ye, brethren, are not in darkness, that that day should overtake you as a thief. Ye are all the children of light, and the children of the day: we are not of the night, nor of darkness. Therefore let us not sleep, as do others; but let us watch and be sober. For they that sleep, sleep in the night; and they that be drunken, are drunken in the night. But let us, who are of the day, be sober, putting on the breast-plate of faith and love; and for an helmet, the hope of salvation.

For God hath not appointed us to wrath, but to obtain salvation by our Lord Jesus Christ, who died for us, that, whether we wake or sleep, we should live together with him. Wherefore comfort yourselves together, and edify one another, even as also ye do.

And we beseech you, brethren, to know them which labour among you, and are over you in the Lord, and admonish you, and to esteem them very highly in love for their work's sake. And be at peace among yourselves.

Now we exhort you, brethren, warn them that are unruly, comfort the feeble-minded, support the weak, be patient toward all men. See that none render evil for evil unto any man; but ever follow that which is good, both among yourselves, and to all men.

Rejoice evermore. Pray without ceasing. In every thing give thanks: for this is the will of God in Christ Jesus concerning you. Quench not the Spirit. Despise not prophesyings. Prove all things; hold fast that which is good. Abstain from all appearance of evil.

And the very God of peace sanctify you wholly; and I pray God your whole spirit, and soul, and body, be preserved blameless unto the coming of our Lord Jesus Christ.

The grace of our Lord Jesus Christ be with you. Amen.

The Power of Faith

(FROM THE EPISTLE TO THE HEBREWS)

Now faith is the substance of things hoped for, the evidence of things not seen: for by it the elders obtained a good report.

Through faith we understand that the worlds were framed by the word of God, so that things which are seen were not made of things which do appear.

By faith Abel offered unto God a more excellent sacrifice than Cain, by which he obtained witness that he was righteous, God testifying of his gifts: and by it he being dead yet speaketh.

By faith Enoch was translated, that he should not see death; and was not found, because God had translated him: for before his translation he had this testimony, that he pleased God. But without faith it is impossible to please him: for he that cometh to God must believe that he is, and that he is a rewarder of them that diligently seek him.

By faith Noah, being warned of God of things not seen as yet, moved with fear, prepared an ark to the saving of his house; by the which he condemned the world, and became heir of the righteousness which is by faith.

By faith Abraham, when he was called to go out into a place which he should after receive for an inheritance, obeyed; and he went out, not knowing whither he went. By faith he sojourned in the land of promise, as in a strange country, dwelling in tabernacles with Isaac and Jacob, the heirs with him of the same promise: for he looked for a city which hath foundations, whose builder and maker is God.

Through faith also Sara herself received strength to conceive seed, and was delivered of a child when she was past age, because she judged him faithful who had promised. Therefore sprang there even of one, and him as good as dead, so many as the stars of the sky in multitude, and as the sand which is by the seashore innumerable.

By faith Abraham, when he was tried, offered up Isaac: and he that had received the promises offered up his only-begotten son, of whom it was said, That in Isaac shall thy seed be called: accounting that God was able to raise him up, even from the dead; from whence also he received him in a figure.

By faith Isaac blessed Jacob and Esau concerning things to come.

By faith Jacob, when he was a dying, blessed both the sons of Joseph; and worshipped, leaning upon the top of his staff.

By faith Joseph, when he died, made mention of the departing of the children of Israel; and gave commandment concerning his bones.

By faith Moses, when he was born, was hid three months of his parents, because they saw he was a proper child; and they were not afraid of the king's commandment. By faith Moses, when he was come to years, refused to be called the son of Pharaoh's daughter, choosing rather to suffer affliction with the people of God, than to enjoy the pleasures of sin for a season; esteeming the reproach of Christ greater riches than the treasures in Egypt: for he had respect unto the recompense of the reward.

By faith the harlot Rahab perished not with them of the king: for he endured, as seeing him who is invisible. Through faith he kept the passover, and the sprinkling of blood, lest he that destroyed the firstborn should touch them. By faith they passed through the Red sea as by dry land: which the Egyptians assaying to do were drowned.

By faith the walls of Jericho fell down, after they were compassed about seven days.

By faith the harlot Rahab perished not with them that believed not, when she had received the spies with peace.

Wherefore lift up the hands which hang down, and the feeble knees; and make straight paths for your feet, lest that which is lame be turned out of the way; but let it rather be healed. Follow peace with all men, and holiness, without which no man shall see the Lord: looking diligently, lest any man fail of the grace of God; lest any root of bitterness springing up, trouble you, and thereby many be defiled.

Let brotherly love continue. Be not forgetful to entertain strangers: for thereby some have entertained angels unawares. Remember them that are in bonds, as bound with them; and them which suffer adversity, as being yourselves also in the body.

The Insufficiency of Faith Alone

(FROM THE GENERAL EPISTLE OF JAMES)

Pure religion and undefiled before God and the Father is this, To visit the fatherless and widows in their affliction, and to keep himself unspotted from the world.

Hearken, my beloved brethren, Hath not God chosen the poor of this world rich in faith, and heirs of the kingdom which he hath promised to them that love him? But ye have despised the poor. Do not rich men oppress you, and draw you before the judgment-seats? Do not they blaspheme that worthy name by the which ye are called? If you fulfil the royal law according to the scripture, Thou shalt love thy neighbour as thyself, ye do well: but if ye have respect to persons, ye commit sin, and are convinced of the law as transgressors. For whosoever shall keep the whole law, and yet offend in one point, he is guilty of all.

What doth it profit, my brethren, though a man say he hath faith, and have not works? can faith save him? If a brother or sister be naked, and destitute of daily food, and one of you say unto them, Depart in peace, be ye warmed and filled; notwithstanding ye give them not those things which are needful to the body; what doth it profit? Even so faith, if it hath not works, is dead, being alone.

Yea, a man may say, Thou hast faith, and I have works: shew me thy faith without thy works, and I will shew thee my faith by my works. Thou believest that there is one God; thou doest well: the devils also believe, and tremble. But wilt thou know, O vain man, that faith without works is dead?

From whence come wars and fightings among you? come they not hence, even of your lusts that war in your members? Ye lust and have not: ye kill, and desire to have, and cannot obtain: ye fight and war, yet ye have not, because ye ask not. Ye ask, and receive not, because ye ask amiss, that ye may consume it upon your lusts.

Submit yourselves therefore to God. Resist the devil, and he will flee from you. Draw nigh to God, and he will draw nigh to you. Cleanse your hands, ye sinners, and purify your hearts, ye double-minded.

Is any among you afflicted? let him pray. Is any merry? let him sing psalms. Is any sick among you? let him call for the elders of the church; and let them pray over him, anointing him with oil in the name of the Lord: and the prayer of faith shall save the sick, and the Lord shall raise him up; and if he have committed sins, they shall be forgiven him.

Confess your faults one to another, and pray one for another, that ye may be healed. The effectual fervent prayer of a righteous man availeth much.

Love Not the World

(FROM THE FIRST GENERAL EPISTLE OF JOHN)

Love not the world, neither the things that are in the world. If any man love the world, the love of the Father is not in him. For all that is in the world, the lust of the flesh, and the lust of the eyes, and the pride of life, is not of the Father, but is of the world. And the world passeth away, and the lust thereof: but he that doeth the will of God abideth for ever.

Behold what manner of love the Father hath bestowed upon us, that we should be called the sons of God! therefore the world knoweth us not, because it knew him not. Beloved, now are we the sons of God, and it doth not yet appear what we shall be: but we know that, when he shall appear, we shall be like him; for we shall see him as he is. And every man that hath this hope in him purifieth himself, even as he is pure.

But whoso hath this world's good, and seeth his brother have need, and shutteth up his bowels of compassion from him, how dwelleth the love of God in him? My little children, let us not love in word neither in tongue, but in deed and in truth.

Beloved, let us love one another: for love is of God; and every one that loveth is born of God, and knoweth God. He that loveth not, knoweth not God; for God is love. In this was manifested the love of God towards us, because that God sent his only begotten Son into the world, that we might live through him. Herein is love, not that we loved God, but that he loved us, and sent his Son to be the propitiation for our sins. Beloved, if God so loved us, we ought also to love one another. No man hath seen God at any time. If we love one another, God dwelleth in us, and his love is perfected in us.

THE MOSLEM

"There Is No God but Allah"

D eath is ever threatening and often slow and painful in the Arabian desert. It waits quietly in the
singing red sands which stretch barren for many miles
between oases. It flies on the wings of the whirling
sand-storms. It glints in the sunlight from the curved
sword blades of hostile tribesmen. The weak are oblit-
erated by the sun and the sands and the dryness. And
in the hour of the parched lip and arid tongue, on
whom is there to call for comfort and aid?

In the wide unpeopled stretches of wasteland, private
ownership is an abstraction. An object belongs to him
who has it and can hold it, or to him who can take it.
Who or what power is there to deny this? If a man
withholds his hand from murder and pillage of a
weaker traveller, or even shares his handful of dates
and his precious skin of fetid water with the less fortu-
nate one, it is the result of no religious compulsion.
Rather, it arises from a sense of family pride or perhaps
from the realization that the giver of bounty to-day may
be the pleader for his life to-morrow. Or so it was in
the sixth century A.D.

Yet for all that, desert wastes, so sparing in material
fertility, have always been fertile in the spawning of
religion, as India, Persia, and Palestine bear witness.
And the desert land of Arabia is no exception.

During the first half millennium of our era, when
Christianity was establishing itself firmly in Europe
and Zoroastrianism, having been stopped in its onward
march by the Greek victory at Salamis, was deterior-

ating in Persia, when in China Confucius and Lao Tze had become venerated saints of the distant past and Buddhism had spread far eastward from the land of its origin, the vast majority of the Semitic Arabian people still expressed their dim religious consciousness in primitive, unorganized polytheism. In the theology of the Arabs, there was a god for every sept—a deity who symbolized the state of union which existed between every living man and his ancestors. Above all these minor gods there was one higher god, *Allah*, whose sons and daughters the tribal deities were. Feasts and ceremonies paid tribute to the tribal gods but Allah was ignored in these propitiations. Holy oaths were sworn and documents sealed in his name but beyond this recognition of his existence he seems to have had little pertinence to the life of the average Arab.

In the conception and name of Allah, the Arabians were but carrying on a primitive vision of God and a word which existed before the beginning of their recorded history—one which fathered the conception of Jehovah as well as that of Allah. Just as a common ancestry of the Indians, the Persians, the Greeks, the Romans, and others, may be traced, through language and common theologies, to the Indo-European race, so has language research established knowledge of a common Semitic race which, before recorded history, scattered into southern or Arabic, northern or Aramaic, and middle or Hebrew, branches.

Among the deities common to all of these peoples was *El*, which meant "strong." In early Hebrew it occurs to mean "strong," "hero," and "God." In Babylonian inscriptions, the same designation occurs as *Ilu*, meaning "God." In Arabic *ilah*, standing alone, means any god; combined with an article, *Al-Ilah*, it becomes, through shortening, *Allah*, the far and distant God, whose sons and daughters were worshipped by the Arabian tribes.[1]

But there were influences modifying the ancient religion during these centuries in Arabia. To the east, across the Persian Gulf, lay Iran, the home of Zoroastrianism. To the north were Transjordan, Syria, Lebanon, and Iraq, watered by the Euphrates River, over which Abraham had led his people. In the great cities of Arabia, centers of trade and intellectual ferment, were many Jews and Christians living in close association with the Arabs. By the middle of the sixth century A.D., the influence of Greece and Persia had spread throughout the length and breadth of the Arabian peninsula. There was not a single independent Arabian state of any size or importance.

Yet the religions of these mixed peoples from abroad, as professed and practised in Arabia, had sunk to a low level. Arabian Christianity had become a shapeless mass of dogma. Arabian Judaism had become almost idolatry in which Ezra, the scribe who was believed to have written the *Torah*, was worshipped as a god. And among the Arabians even the old polytheistic religion had fallen so low that the tribal gods were neglected and often openly mocked.

Into this land of mixed and demeaning religious life was born Mohammed in Mecca, about A.D. 570. His father, Abdallah, died before his birth, and his mother when he was a child. After their deaths he was cared for first by his grandfather, and later by his maternal uncle, Abu Talib. He was kindly treated, but as part of a large and poor family, suffered the privations which were the lot of his cousins. He had no formal education and as a youth he learned to know the hardships of desert life through herding sheep.

[1] F. Max Muller, *The Science of Religion* (New York, 1872).

When he was twenty-five he entered the service of a rich widow, Khadijah, and became for her a camel driver and a conductor of caravans between Damascus and Jerusalem. Later he married Khadijah, though she was fifteen years his senior, and seems to have found in her a rare measure of support and comfort and inspiration during the years of bitter emotional conflicts and persecution which began during the period of his awakening religious consciousness and ended only when he was past fifty.

After his marriage he came into contact through his wife's cousin, Waraka, with a small group of thoughtful persons who called themselves *Hanifs*, or "penitents." These, strongly under the influences of the Jews, early Christians and Essenes of Arabia, and familiar with the Greek, Syrian and Abyssinian churches, believed in asceticism, meditation, and consecration of life in preparation for the Day of Judgment. They denied the existence of the many tribal gods and proclaimed that salvation could be achieved by man only through *islam*, or submission to the will of the one God, Allah. Man must return, they said, to the original Semitic religion of Abraham, the real fountainhead of both Judaism and Christianity.

Profoundly impressed, Mohammed frequently withdrew for long periods of meditation, fasting, and prayer to a cave on a lonely slope of the bare and desolate Mount Hira. Weakened by loss of food and the emotional storm which surged within him, he sometimes had physical seizures in which he saw visions and occasionally lost consciousness.

During one of these seizures, in the month of Ramadan, the Angel Gabriel appeared to him holding a scroll, saying that on it was written a passage from the heavenly book. And although Mohammed was unable to read or write, the angel commanded him to read what was written thereon. Later this passage became *Sura XCVI* of the *Koran*. Its words were: "Read! in the name of thy Lord who created, created man from clots of blood. Read! for thy Lord is the most beneficent, who hath taught the use of the pen, hath taught man that which he knew not. Nay, verily, man is most extravagant in wickedness because he seeth himself possessed of wealth. Verily unto the Lord is the return of all."

Rushing home in a frenzy of excitement Mohammed told Khadijah of his experience which greatly troubled him. Had his vision been authentic? And if so, what did it mean? Khadijah urged him to believe the evidence of his senses, and accept it as a command from Allah to prophesy and become the voice through which God could speak to mankind. Yet in spite of his faithful wife's assurance, Mohammed continued to doubt and sometimes even contemplated suicide in the agony of his soul. But after two or three years of this conflict, the Angel Gabriel appeared to him a second time with a second revelation, and after this there were no doubts in Mohammed's mind. He confidently went forward on his mission as revelation after revelation came to him.

He began by gaining followers within his own household, then among his friends, and soon a small community was formed, professing Hanif beliefs and following Hanif practices under the leadership of Mohammed. Thus he did not found an original religion nor attempt, as did Zoroaster, Gautama, and Jesus, to reform an old. Rather he set himself the task of spreading the doctrines of the Hanifs which he, and they, said constituted the one true creed, the ancient religion of Abraham.

One of the members of the group gave Mohammed a house to use as a meeting place, and here he preached and gained a few converts. But his influence at first was not great or widely spread. He had nothing to say which was new to his auditors. He at first delivered impersonal "revelations" in which he proclaimed a virile monotheism, dominated by the one God who required self-surrender and unconditional obedience, prayers, almsgiving, and temperance. But these were principles which the Hanifs had long held. All which Mohammed brought to old beliefs was his individual enthusiasm and the emotional intensity of his religious passion. And there were many who looked upon him with deep disfavour and criticized him openly because he drew so many of his supporters from the poor, the slave class, and the young.

Embittered by open criticism and lack of public support, his preaching became more personal and was filled with imprecations. His "revelations" now began to threaten infidels and those who did not believe in him as the prophet of God with the vengeance of Allah. The importance of moral behaviour was submerged by the importance of believing in Mohammed and the Allah whom he proclaimed. Going further, he attacked the worship of the old tribal gods and incurred the anger of powerful Meccans.

A group of these went to Mohammed's uncle, Abu Talib, and asked him either to persuade the prophet to desist from his insulting heresies or to withdraw his protection so that they could use their own methods of persuasion. At first Abu refused but when they returned, accompanying their request with threats, he called his nephew to him and asked him to stop preaching before he involved them both in ruin.

But Mohammed, weeping, replied, "Though they

gave me the sun in my right hand, and the moon in my left, to turn me from my undertaking, yet would I not pause until I saw the victory of the Lord's cause, or till I died for it." Stirred by this reply, Abu, though he was not one of his nephew's followers, said, "Go in peace, son of my brother, and say what thou wilt, for, by God, I will on no condition abandon thee."

Continuing his preaching in Mecca, Mohammed suffered almost daily insults. Because of his uncle's protection he was not subjected to actual violence, though some of his followers were cruelly treated and a number of them fled to Abyssinia where, among the Abyssinian Christians, they found a friendly welcome and sympathy.

In an attempt to heal the breach with his fellow Meccans, Mohammed now modified his preaching somewhat. On one occasion he even renounced his emphasis upon monotheism and delivered a "revelation" in which appeared a doctrine giving slight recognition to some of the tribal gods and goddesses of the Arabs. Surprised and delighted, those of his audience who were not Hanifs smiled and nodded in approval, and when at the end of the discourse the Prophet called upon all his listeners to bow down to Allah, the outsiders courteously and graciously bowed with the rest. Obviously in this one session Mohammed had gone far towards overcoming Meccan enmity. But that night in a vision he saw the Angel Gabriel who charged him with having spoken words which came not from God but from the Devil. In remorse Mohammed recalled his words, revising them so that the tribal gods were discredited, and his persecution began afresh and with greater fury than ever.

Shortly after this, about A.D. 620, both his faithful wife Khadijah and his uncle Abu died. Shorn of protection now and divested of the support and encouragement with which his wife had upheld him during all the years of his ministry, the Prophet decided that his case in Mecca was hopeless. Going northward to Taif, he asked the head of the town to furnish him with protection while he preached. But his request was refused and a mob drove him violently out of the city.

However, Medinah farther to the north was more receptive. A group there, Mohammed learned, were seeking a new religion and hoping for the coming of an Arabian Messiah. About a year after the Prophet fled the mob at Taif he met with twelve citizens of Medinah who made a sixfold pledge: to have no God but Allah, to withhold their hands from all which was not their own, to abstain from fornication, not to kill new-born infants, to shun slander, and to obey Mohammed so long as his demands upon them were not unreasonable. These returned to Medinah, began to solicit support for him, and, when it seemed sufficient to insure success, in the year A.D. 622 the Meccan faithful made a secret exodus to Medinah and were followed by the Prophet himself. Thus occurred the Hegira and thus was established the year (*Anno Hegira*) which marks the beginning of the Mohammedan era in the Moslem calendar, as the birth of Jesus marks the beginning of the Christian era.

In Medinah Mohammed and the Moslems ("those who submit") were quickly successful. Mohammed became not only a religious leader but a ruler for his followers. "Arabs could be swung on an idea as on a cord," wrote T. E. Lawrence, and the idea which Mohammed brought to them was nothing less than world domination for the religion of Allah, to be brought about through the unity and fanatic steadfastness of his worshippers. But the Prophet himself lived only ten years after the Hegira.

During this time he took eleven wives, though he had proclaimed a limit of four for each of his followers. His own violation of this rule he justified by special "revelations" which permitted the Prophet to take more wives than the people were allowed.

During his reign in Medinah—for it became more a reign than a ministry—he also changed, from Jerusalem to Mecca, the direction towards which worshippers faced when they prayed.

Mohammed's indoctrination was thorough in respect to the duty of spreading the religion of Islam throughout the world. Converts were to be made peacefully if possible, but by means of the sword if necessary.

After his death a succession of Caliphs, or successors to the Prophet, carried on the work of lawgiving and bloody proselytizing with amazing speed. During the life of the first of them the conquests of Islam extended over Palestine, Egypt, and Persia. Within less than a century the religion had been forcibly extended throughout North Africa and Southwest Spain, eastward to the borders of India and into Turkestan, and even into France.

In 732, exactly a century after the death of the Prophet, a powerful Saracen army, carrying the green banner and wielding the curved sword of Islam, stood at Tours within striking distance of Paris. Once again, as at Salamis in 480 B.C., the future religion of Europe was to be decided through ordeal by battle. The defeated leaders of Southern Gaul seemed hopelessly outnumbered.

But suddenly out of the north, at the head of a stouthearted army of Franks, came Charles Martel (whose grandson, born twelve years later, was to be called Charlemagne) to put the invader to rout, and European Christians were saved from the ruthless extermination which must have preceded the establishment of Islam on the Continent.

Moslem conquests did not cease with this defeat. Later Mohammedanism penetrated India (where it became a strong rival of Hinduism), China, and the islands of the Pacific. The number of its followers has constantly increased until to-day about 240,000,000 persons, comprising about a sixth of the world's total population, are Moslems.

The basic sacred book of Islam is the *Koran*. This is believed to be the divine law of God as uttered by Allah himself in revelations to Mohammed, and passed on by the Prophet through word of mouth. Mohammed's actual inspirations for the words of the sacred book seem to have been the traditions and folklore of the Arabs, Zoroastrian beliefs (for example, the devil, the angels, Judgment Day, and the resurrection), the Old Testament and teachings of the Jews with whom he came into contact, and the New Testament and teachings of the early Christians.

The book consists of 114 chapters, or *suras*, which make its volume less than that of the New Testament, and about a fourth that of the Old. Every *sura* save one begins with the words, "In the name of Allah, the compassionate, the merciful." The authority of the *Koran* is believed by good Moslems to be absolute. It is without any question the most influential, and the most widely read book in all Arabic literature, and probably the most faithfully read scripture in the world. It is the chief text-book of the modern Mohammedan university of Al-Azhar at Cairo.

Its theology and ethical code are simply stated.

Allah is the one God, who is the primary principle in the universe. He is "all-seeing, all-hearing, all-speaking, all-knowing, all-willing, all-powerful." Those whom Allah loves are those who do good, those who believe in and follow the principles of Mohammed, those who are not braggarts, and those who fight in his cause. He punishes the wicked in a fiery hell in which "they shall broil," and rewards the faithful in a very material paradise, by wedding them to "large-eyed maidens" and giving them all manner of sensual delights.

Robert Ernest Hume, in *The World's Living Religions*, list six beliefs and five duties of the good Moslem. The beliefs are: in the one God, Allah; in angels who intercede with Allah for the forgiveness of the faithful; in the *Koran* as the last of the sacred books, which include also the Jewish *Torah* and Psalms, and the words of Jesus; belief in the prophets of Allah, of whom twenty-eight are named in the *Koran,* including Adam, Enoch, Methuselah, Noah, Abraham, Lot, Ishmael, Isaac, Jacob, Moses, David, Solomon, Zechariah, John the Baptist, Jesus, Alexander the Great, and Mohammed, the last and greatest; in the final judgment, with the vividly described rewards and punishments that follow it; and in the divine decrees of Allah. The five duties are: to repeat every day in Arabic, "There is no God but Allah, and Mohammed is his prophet"; to pray at least three times a day, at daybreak, at noon, and at night, with the face turned towards Mecca; to give alms; to fast during the month of Ramadan; and to make at least one pilgrimage to Mecca during a lifetime.

While Mohammed lived, the law of the Moslems was administered by him, using as his authority the words of the *Koran*. When there were none which precisely fit the case in hand, he received special "revelations" to guide him. After his death the *Koran* (which was first recorded from memory during the years immediately following his death) continued to be the basic law. When its words were not specifically applicable the memories of "the companions of the Prophet" (those who had known him) were depended upon to tell what the Prophet said in similar circumstances. After their death the memories of those who had known "the companions" were drawn upon.

During the ninth century Al-Bakhair made a collection of about seven thousand "traditions" in the *Sahih* which were used as guidance. Throughout succeeding centuries many other collections of "traditions" have been made. Selections from one such collection, *The Forty-Two Traditions of An-Nawawi*, are reprinted in this volume.

Islam has suffered the same division into sects which has afflicted most of the religions of the world, in spite of Mohammed's frequent warnings against such divisions. To-day Mohammedan sects are almost as numerous as those of Christianity. One of these, the *Sufis*, has produced much that is fine in its mystic poetry. Selections from one of the Sufi books, the *Masnavi*, are included in this collection. The book is the work of Jalal-uddin Rumi, most famous of the Sufi poets, who was born at Balkh in 1207 and died in 1273.

Another offshoot from Islam is worth especial mention here because of its widely spread influence in both America and Europe. In 1844 Mirza Ali Mohammed, a merchant of Shiraz in Persia, announced himself as a new prophet. He called himself the *Bab*, or the gate, through which one could find God. Later he proclaimed that he was a personal incarnation of God. In a revolt from his leadership he was assassinated in 1850, but one of his followers, Bahaullah, called himself "He whom God manifests." He drew many followers to him quickly, who called themselves *Bahais*. Though the original Babism has declined, Bahaism has increased constantly and has many adherents both in America and abroad.

It is difficult for the Western reader to find a plane upon which he can evaluate the importance of Mohammed and his doctrine in the religious and cultural history of the world. In the scriptures of all of the other great religions of the world the Jew or Christian, no matter how well read he is in the sacred and secular literature of his own religious culture, can find much which enlarges his own perception of those three religious forces which dominate mankind—the search for a better understanding of the source of his being, the attempt to understand and evaluate himself, and the need for better relationships with his fellow-men. In the scriptures of Mohammedanism he is likely to find some conceptions which seem degrading, many which seem to him meaningless, and, at their best, some few things that seem to be mere reiterations of principles with which he is already familiar through his own scriptures.

But to judge the contribution of Islam on this basis is perhaps to make a false approach to it. It must be remembered that Judaism, Hinduism, Buddhism, Confucianism, Taoism, Zoroastrianism, and even Christianity, the youngest of this group, were old and well-established religions when Arabia was still in the grip of a primitive form of polytheism that made almost no pretense at a social code. Furthermore, the leaders of these older religions had behind them a comparatively high degree of religious culture and tradition, whereas Mohammed was an illiterate whose vision was so far beyond that of his average compatriots that he was incomparably above them in religious thought. That he brought a conception of monotheism and a code of social conduct to one of the world's most backward countries and furnished a religion which could be comprehended and accepted by other backward peoples, thus enabling them to take a single step forward out of the darkness, will, perhaps, make it apparent that the Prophet of Allah was one of the great among the world's religious leaders.

MOHAMMEDAN SCRIPTURES

From the Koran

In the Name of God, the Compassionate, the Merciful

Clots of Blood

Read! in the name of thy Lord who created;—
Created man from Clots of Blood:—
Read! For thy Lord is the most beneficent,
Who hath taught the use of the pen;—
Hath taught man that which he knew not.

Nay, verily, man is most extravagant in wickedness
Because he seeth himself possessed of wealth.
Verily unto the Lord is the return of all.
What thinkest thou of him who forbiddeth
A servant of God when he prayeth?
What thinkest thou? that he hath followed the true
    guidance or enjoined piety?
What thinkest thou, if he hath treated the truth as a
    lie and turned his back?
Doth he not know that God seeth?

Nay, verily, if he desist not, we will assuredly seize him
    by the forelock,
The lying sinful forelock!
Then let him summon his associates;

We too will summon the guards of hell:
Nay! obey him not; but adore, and draw nigh to God.

The Enwrapped

O thou Enwrapped in thy mantle!
Arise and warn!
And thy Lord—magnify him!
And thy raiment—purify it!
And the abomination—flee it!
And bestow not favours that thou mayest receive again
    with increase;
And for thy Lord wait thou patiently.
For when there shall be a trump on the trumpet,
That then shall be a distressful day,
A day, to the unbelievers, devoid of ease.

Nay, by the moon!
And by the night when it retreateth!
And by the morn when it brighteneth!
Verily, hell is one of the most grievous woes,
Fraught with warning to man,
To him among you who desireth to press forward, or
    to remain behind.
For its own works lieth every soul in pledge. But they
    of God's right hand
In their gardens make inquiry of the wicked;—
"What hath cast you into hell-fire?"
They will say, "We were not of those who prayed,
And we were not of those who fed the poor,
And we plunged into vain disputes with vain disputers,
And we rejected as a lie the day of reckoning,
Till the certainty came upon us"—
Therefore intercession of interceders shall not avail
    them.

What then hath come to them that they turn aside
    from the warning
As if they were affrighted asses fleeing from a lion?
But every one of them would fain have open pages
    given to him out of heaven!
Nay, but they fear not the life to come.
Nay, verily this Koran is a warning, and whoso will,
    beareth it in mind;
But not unless God please, will they bear it in mind.
    Meet is he to be feared, and meet is forgiveness
    in him.

The Most High

Praise the name of thy Lord The Most High,
Who hath created and balanced all things,
And who hath fixed their destinies and guided them;
Who bringeth forth the pastures,
Then reduceth them to dusky stubble.
We will teach thee to recite the Koran, nor aught shalt
    thou forget,
Save what God pleaseth; he verily knoweth alike the
    manifest and what is hidden;
And we will make easy for thee the easiest way.

Warn therefore; verily the warning is profitable:
He that feareth God will receive the warning,—
And the greatest wretch only will turn aside from it,
Who shall be burned at the terrible fire;
Then shall he not die therein, and shall not live.
Happy he who is purified by Islam,
And remembereth the name of his Lord and prayeth.
But ye prefer this present life,
Though the life to come is better and more enduring.
This truly is in the books of old,
The books of Abraham and Moses.

Those Who Stint

Woe to those who stint the measure:
Who when they take by measure from others, exact
    the full;
But when they mete to them or weigh to them, minish—
Have they no thought that they shall be raised again
For a great day,
A day when mankind shall stand before the Lord of the
    worlds?

The Mountain

By the Mountain,
And by the Book written
On an outspread scroll,
And by the frequented fane,
And by heaven's lofty roof,
And by the swollen sea,
Verily, a chastisement from thy Lord is most imminent,
And none shall put it back.
With reeling on that day the heaven shall reel,
And with moving shall the mountains move,
And woe, on that day, to those who called the apostles
    liars,
Who plunged for pastime into vain disputes—
On that day shall they be thrust with thrusting to the
    fire of hell:—
"This is the fire which ye treated as a lie!
Is it magic, then? or, do ye not see it?
Burn ye therein: and bear it patiently or impatiently it
    will be the same to you: ye only receive the reward
    of your doings."

But 'mid gardens and delights shall they dwell who have feared God,

Rejoicing in what their Lord hath given them; and that from the pain of hell-fire hath their Lord preserved them.

"Eat and drink with healthy enjoyment, in recompense for your deeds."

On couches ranged in rows shall they recline; and to the damsels with large dark eyes will we wed them.

And to those who have believed, whose offspring have followed them in the faith, will we again unite their offspring; nor of the meed of their works will we in the least defraud them. Pledged to God is every man for his actions.

And fruits in abundance will we bestow on them, and such flesh as they shall desire;

Therein shall they present to one another the cup which shall engender no light discourse, no motive to sin:

And youths shall go round unto them beautiful as imbedded pearls:

And they shall accost one another and ask mutual questions.

"A time indeed there was," will they say, "when we were full of care as to the future lot of our families;

But kind hath God been to us, and from the pestilential torment of the scorching wind hath he preserved us;

Verily, heretofore we called upon him—and he of a truth, he is the Beneficent, the Merciful."

Warn thou, then. For thou by the favour of thy Lord art neither soothsayer nor possessed.

The Poets

Verily from the Lord of the worlds hath this Book
    come down;
The faithful spirit hath come down with it
Upon thy heart, that thou mightest become a warner—
In the clear Arabic tongue:
And truly it is foretold in the scriptures of them of
    yore.
Shall it not be a sign to them that the learned among
    the children of Israel recognized it?
If we had sent it down unto any foreigner,
And he had recited it to them, they had not believed.
In such sort have we influenced the heart of the wicked
    ones,
That they will not believe it till they see the grievous
    chastisement.

Call not thou then on any other god with God, lest
    thou be of those consigned to torment:
But warn thy relatives of nearer kin,
And kindly lower thy wing over the faithful who follow
    thee,
And if they disobey thee, then say: "I verily am clear
    of your doings";—
And put thy trust in the Mighty, the Merciful,
Who seeth thee when thou standest in prayer,
And thy demeanour among those who worship;
Verily he is the hearer, the knower.

Shall I tell you on whom the satans descend?
They descend on every lying, wicked person:
They impart what they have heard; but most of them
    are liars.

It is the poets whom the erring follow:
Seest thou not how they rove distraught in every valley?
And that they say that which they do not?
Save those who believe and do good works, and oft
    remember God;
And who defend themselves when unjustly treated.
    But they who treat them unjustly shall find out
    what a lot awaiteth them hereafter.

God Has No Son

The Book sent down from God, the Mighty, the Wise!
Verily we have sent down the Book to thee with the
    truth: serve thou God then, showing forth to him
    a pure religion—
Is not a pure worship due to God?
But they who have taken others beside him as lords,
    saying, "We serve them only that they may bring
    us near unto God,"—of a truth, God will judge
    between them and the faithful, concerning that
    wherein they have differed.
Verily God guideth not him who is a liar, and un-
    believer.
Had God desired to have had a son, He had surely
    chosen what he pleased out of his own creation.
    But praise be to him! He is God, the One, the
    Almighty.

The Spider

Yes, and God is well acquainted with those who have
    believed, and he is well acquainted with the
    hypocrites.
Also the unbelievers say to the faithful, "Follow ye our

way, and we will surely bear your sins." But not aught of their sins will they bear—verily they are indeed liars!

But their own burdens, and burdens together with their own burdens shall they surely bear: and inquisition shall surely be made of them on the day of resurrection as to their false devices.

The likeness for those who take to themselves guardians beside God is the likeness of the Spider who buildeth her a house: but verily, frailest of all houses surely is the house of the spider. Did they but know this!

Recite the portions of the Book which have been revealed to thee and discharge the duty of prayer: verily prayer restraineth from the filthy and the blameworthy. And assuredly the gravest duty is the remembrance of God; and God knoweth what ye do.

Dispute ye not, unless in kindliest sort, with the people of the Book; save with such of them as have dealt wrongfully with you: and say ye, "We believe in what hath been sent down to us and hath been sent down to you. Our God and your God is one, and to him are we self-surrendered" (Muslims).

And thus have we sent down the Book of the Koran to thee: and they to whom we have given the Book of the law believe in it: and of these Arabians there are those who believe in it: and none, save the infidels, reject our signs.

Say: God is a sufficient witness between me and you: He knoweth all that is in the heavens and the earth, and they who believe in vain things and disbelieve in God—these shall suffer loss.

O my servants who have believed! Vast truly is my
earth: me, therefore! yea worship me.

Every soul shall taste of death: afterwards to us shall
ye return.

But those who have believed and wrought righteousness will we assuredly lodge in gardens with lofty
apartments, beneath which the rivers flow, to
abide therein for ever. Goodly the reward of those
who labour,

Who patiently endure, and put their trust in their Lord!

And this present life is no other than a pastime and a
disport: but truly the future mansion is life indeed!
Would that they knew this!

Then when they embark on shipboard, they call upon
God, professing to him the purity of their faith;
but when he bringeth them safe to land, behold
they join partners with him;

Believing not in our revelation, and yet take their fill
of good things: but in the end they shall know
their folly.

Do they not see that we have established a safe precinct
while all around them men despoil? Will they then
believe in vain idols, and not own the goodness
of God?

Relation to Jews and Christians

The unbelievers among the people of the Book, and
among the idolaters, do not wish that any good
should be sent down to you from your Lord: but
God will show his special mercy to whom he will,
for God is of great bounty.

Whatever verse we cancel, or cause thee to forget, we

bring a better or its like. Knowest thou not that
God hath power over all things?

Knowest thou not that the dominion of the heavens
and of the earth is God's? and that ye have neither
patron nor helper, save God?

Would ye ask of your apostle as of old it was asked of
Moses? But he who hath exchanged faith for unbelief, hath already erred from the even way.

Many of those who have scripture would like to bring
you back to unbelief after ye have believed, out
of selfish envy, even after the truth hath been
clearly shown to them. Forgive them then, and
shun them till God shall come with his decree.
Truly God hath power over all things.

And observe prayer and pay the legal impost: and
whatever good thing ye have sent on before for
your soul's sake, ye shall find it with God. Verily
God seeth what ye do.

And they say, "By no means shall any but Jews or
Christians enter paradise:" This is their belief.
Say: Give your proofs if ye speak the truth—

But, they who set their face with resignation Godward,
and do what is right,—their reward is therefore
with their Lord, and no fear shall come on them,
neither shall they be grieved.

Moreover, the Jews say, "The Christians lean on
nought:" "On nought lean the Jews," say the
Christians: Yet both are readers of the Book. So
with like words say they who have no knowledge.
But on the resurrection day, God shall judge between them as to that in which they have differed.

The East and the West is God's: therefore, whichever
way ye turn, there is the face of God: Truly God
is immense, knowing (omnipresent, omniscient).

And they say, "God hath begotten a son." Glory be to him! Nay rather—his, whatever is in the heavens and the earth! All obeyeth him,—

Sole maker of the heavens and of the earth! And when he decreeth a thing, he only saith to it, "Be," and it is.

And they who have no knowledge say, "Why doth not God speak to us, or thou come to us with a sign?" So spake those who were before them the like of their words: their hearts are alike: Clear now have we made the signs (verses) for those who have firm faith:

Verily, with the truth have we sent thee, a bearer of good tidings and a warner: and concerning the inmates of hell thou shalt not be questioned.

But until thou follow their religion, neither the Jews nor the Christians will ever be satisfied with thee, Say: Verily, guidance of God,—that is the guidance! And if after "the Knowledge" which hath reached thee, thou follow their desires, thou shalt find from God neither helper nor protector.

They to whom we have given the Book, and who read it as it ought to be read,—these believe therein: but whoso believeth not therein, these are they who shall be the losers.

O children of Israel! remember my favour wherewith I have favoured you, and that above all creatures have I been bounteous to you:

And dread the day when not in aught shall soul satisfy for soul, nor shall any ransom be taken from it, nor shall any intercession avail, and they shall not be helped.

When his Lord made trial of Abraham by commands which he fulfilled, he said, "I am about to make

thee an Imam to mankind:" he said, "Of my offspring also:" "My covenant," said God, "em-
braceth not the evil-doers."

And remember when we appointed the holy house as
man's resort and safe retreat, and said, "Take ye
the station of Abraham for a place of prayer." And
we commanded Abraham and Ismael, "Purify my
house for those who shall go in procession round
it, and those who shall abide there for devotion,
and those who shall bow down and prostrate
themselves."

And when Abraham said, "Lord! make this land secure,
and supply its people with fruits, such of them as
believe in God and in the last days:" he said, "And
whoso believeth not, little therefore will I bestow
on him; then will I drive him to the torment of the
fire! and ill the passage!"

And when Abraham, with Ismael, raised the foundations of the house, they said, "O our Lord! accept
it from us; thou of a truth art the hearer, the
knower.

O our Lord! and make us thy Muslims (resigned to
thee), and our posterity a Muslim people; and
teach us our holy rites, and be turned towards us:
verily thou art He who turneth, the Merciful.

O our Lord! and raise up among them an apostle from
themselves who may rehearse thy signs unto them,
and teach them 'the Book,' and wisdom, and
purify them: of a truth thou art the Mighty, the
Wise."

And who but he that hath debased his soul to folly will
mislike the faith of Abraham, when we have
chosen him in this world, and truly in the world
to come he shall be assuredly of the just?

When his Lord said to him, "Resign thyself to me" (become a Muslim), he said, "I resign myself to the Lord of the worlds."

And this to his children did Abraham enjoin, and Jacob also, saying, "O my children! truly God hath chosen a religion for you; so die not without having become Muslims."

Were ye present when Jacob was at the point of death? when he said to his sons, "Whom will ye worship when I am gone?" They said, "We will worship thy God and the God of thy fathers Abraham and Ismael and Isaac, one God, and to him are we surrendered (Muslims)."

That people have now passed away; to them the meed of their deeds, and to you the meed of your deeds: but of their doings ye shall not be questioned.

They say, moreover, "Become Jews or Christians, that ye may have the true guidance." Say: Nay! the religion of Abraham, the sound in faith, and not one of those who join gods with God is our religion!

Say ye: "We believe in God, and that which hath been sent down to us, and that which hath been sent down to Abraham and Ismael and Isaac and Jacob and the tribes; and that which hath been given to Moses and to Jesus, and that which was given to the prophets from their Lord. No difference do we make between any of them: and to God are we resigned (Muslims)."

If therefore they believe the like of what ye believe, then have they true guidance; but if they turn back, then verily they are in a state of separation from you; and God will suffice to protect thee against them: and he is the hearer, the knower.

Moral and Ritual Prescriptions

There is no piety in turning your faces towards the east or the west, but he is pious who believeth in God and the last day and the angels and the scriptures and the prophets; who for the love of God disburseth his wealth to his kindred, and to the orphans, and the needy, and the wayfarer, and those who ask, and for ransoming; who observeth prayer, and payeth the legal alms, and who is one of those who are faithful to their engagements when they have engaged in them, and patient under ills and hardships and in time of trouble: these are they who are just, and these are they who fear God.

O believers! retaliation for bloodshedding is prescribed to you: the free man for the free, and the slave for the slave, and the woman for the woman: but he to whom his brother shall make any remission is to be dealt with equitably; and a payment should be made to him with liberality.

This is a relaxation from your Lord and a mercy. For him therefore who after this shall transgress, a sore punishment!

But in this law of retaliation is your security for life, O men of understanding! Haply ye will fear God.

It is prescribed to you when any one of you is at the point of death, that if he leave goods, he bequeath equitably to his parents and kindred; this is binding on those who fear God:—

Whoso then after he hath heard what a bequest is shall change it, the guilt of this shall be on those only who alter it; verily, God heareth, knoweth:

But he who feareth from the testator any mistake or

wrong, and shall make a settlement between the parties—that then shall be no guilt in him; verily, God is forgiving, merciful.

O believers! a fast is prescribed to you, as it was prescribed to those before you, that ye may fear God,
For certain days. But he among you who shall be sick, or on a journey, shall fast that same number of other days: and for those who are able to keep it and yet break it, there shall be as an expiation the maintenance of a poor man. And he who of his own accord performeth a good work, shall derive good from it: and that ye fast is good for you—if ye but knew it.
As to the month Ramadan in which the Koran was sent down to be man's guidance, and an explanation of that guidance, and an illumination, as soon as any one of you observeth the moon, let him set about the fast; but he who is sick, or upon a journey, shall fast a like number of other days. God wisheth you ease and wisheth not your discomfort, and that you fulfil the number of days, and that you glorify God for his guidance: and haply you will be thankful.
And when my servants ask thee concerning me, then verily will I be nigh unto them—will answer the cry of him that crieth, when he crieth unto me: but let them hearken unto me, and believe in me. Haply they will proceed aright.
You are allowed on the night of the fast to approach your wives: they are your garment and ye are their garment. God knoweth that ye have mutually defrauded yourselves therein; so he turneth unto you and remitteth unto you. Now, therefore, go in unto them with full desire for that which God hath

ordained for you; and eat and drink until ye can discern a white thread from a black thread by the daybreak: afterwards fast strictly till night, and go not in unto them, but pass the time in the Mosques. These are the bounds set up by God: therefore come not near to transgress them. Thus God maketh his signs clear to men: haply they will fear him.

Consume not your wealth among yourselves in vain things; nor offer it to judges as a bribe that ye may consume a part of men's wealth unjustly, while ye know the sin which ye commit.

They will ask thee of the new moons. Say: They are periods fixed for man's service and for the pilgrimage. But there is no piety in entering your houses at the back, but piety consists in the fear of God. Enter your houses then by their doors; and fear God: haply ye shall be prosperous.

The Holy War

And fight for the cause of God against those who fight against you: but commit not the injustice of attacking them first: verily God loveth not the unjust:

And kill them wherever ye shall find them, and eject them from whatever place they have ejected you; for seduction from the truth is worse than slaughter: yet attack them not at the sacred Mosque, until they attack you therein; but if they attack you, then slay them—Such the recompense of the infidels!—

But if they desist, then verily God is gracious, merciful—

And do battle against them until there be no more
seduction from the truth and the only worship be
that of God: but if they desist, then let there be
no hostility, save against wrong-doers.

War is prescribed to you; but to this ye have a repug-
nance:
Yet haply ye are averse from a thing, though it be good
for you, and haply ye love a thing though it be
bad for you: And God knoweth; but ye, ye know
not.
They will ask thee concerning war in the sacred month.
Say: The act of fighting therein is a grave crime:
but the act of turning others aside from the path
of God, and unbelief in him, and to prevent access
to the sacred Mosque, and to drive out his people,
is worse in the sight of God; and civil strife is
worse than bloodshed. But they will not cease to
war against you until they turn you from your
religion, if they be able; but whoever of you shall
turn from his religion and die an infidel, their
works shall be fruitless in this world and in the
next: and they shall be consigned to the fire; therein
to abide for aye.
But they who believe, and who fly their country, and
fight in the cause of God, may hope for God's
mercy: and God is gracious, merciful.

Other Prophets

Some of the apostles we have endowed more highly
than others: to some God hath spoken, and he
hath raised others of them to the loftiest grade;
and to Jesus the son of Mary we gave manifest
proofs of his mission, and we strengthened him

with the Holy Spirit. And if God had pleased, they who came after them would not have wrangled, after the clear proofs had reached them. But into disputes they fell: some of them believed, and some were unbelievers; yet if God had pleased, they would not have thus wrangled: but God doth what he will.

The Table

(CONCERNING INFIDELS)

O believers! take not the Jews or Christians as friends. They are but friends to one another; and if any one of you taketh them for his friends, then surely he is one of them! Verily God will not guide the evil-doers.

"Moreover, the hand of God," say the Jews, "is tied up." Their own hands shall be tied up—and for that which they have said shall they be cursed. Nay! outstretched are both his hands! At his own pleasure doth he bestow gifts, and that which hath been sent down to thee from thy Lord will surely increase the rebellion and unbelief of many of them; and we have put enmity and hatred between them that shall last till the day of the resurrection. Oft as they kindle a beacon fire for war shall God quench it! and they strive after violence on the earth: but God loveth not the abettors of violence.

Verily, they who believe, and the Jews, and the Sabeites, and the Christians—whoever of them believeth in God and in the last day, and doth what is right, on them shall come no fear, neither shall they be put to grief.

Of old we accepted the covenant of the children of Israel, and sent apostles to them. Oft as an apostle

came to them with that for which they had no
desire, some they treated as liars, and some they
slew;

And they reckoned that no harm would come of it:—
so they became blind and deaf! Then was God
turned unto them: then many of them again became blind and deaf! but God beheld what they
did.

Surely now are they infidels who say, "God is the
Messiah son of Mary"; for the Messiah said, "O
children of Israel! worship God, my Lord and your
Lord." Verily, those who join other gods with
God, God doth exclude from paradise, and their
abode the fire; and for the wicked no helpers!

They surely are infidels who say, "God is a third of
three": for there is no god but one God: and if
they refrain not from what they say, a grievous
chastisement shall assuredly befall such of them as
believe not.

Will they not, therefore, turn unto God, and ask pardon
of him? since God is forgiving, merciful!

The Messiah, son of Mary, is but an apostle; other
apostles have flourished before him; and his
mother was a just person: they both ate food.
Behold! how we make clear to them the signs!
then behold how they turn aside!

From the Masnavi

A Certain Person in the Time of 'Umar— May God Be Pleased with Him!—Imagines He Sees the New Moon

In the time of 'Umar the month of fast came round, and a number of men ran to the top of a hill with him to take an omen from the new moon of the month of fast. Said one of them: "There, 'Umar, is the new moon."

When 'Umar could not see the moon in the sky, he said: "This moon has arisen out of your imagination; for in the celestial spheres I am keener-sighted than you. Why then do I not see the pure crescent?" He continued: "Moisten your hand, and rub your eyebrows, and then look up towards the crescent."

When he had moistened his eyebrows, he could not see the moon. He said: "O King, it is not the moon; it has disappeared."

He answered: "Yea, the hair of your eyebrows had become as a bow, which shot an arrow of surmise at you."

A single hair deflected from his eyebrow led him into error, so that he boastingly claimed to have seen the moon. Since a deflected hair may veil the sky from you, how will it be when all your members have become deflected?

O you who would walk straight, make straight your members by means of the straight; turn not your face from the threshold of the righteous. The balance may make the balance true; the balance too may make the balance false.

Whoever adjusts his weights to those of the untrue, falls into deficiency and falseness, and his intellect becomes confused.

A Governor Orders a Man to Dig Up from the Road a Bramble-Bush Which He Has Planted

A certain unfeeling person of pleasant speech planted a bramble-bush in the middle of the road. The passers-by reproached him, and repeatedly told him to dig it up; but he did not do so.

And every moment that bramble-bush was getting larger, and the feet of the people were covered with blood from the wounds it inflicted. The clothes of the people were torn by its thorns; and the feet of the poor were miserably wounded.

When the governor enjoined him seriously to dig it up, he answered, "Yes, I will dig it up some day."

For a good time he promised to do it to-morrow and to-morrow; and in the meantime his bramble-bush grew firm and robust.

The governor said to him one day, "O promise-breaker, come forward in my business; do not creep back." He rejoined, "O uncle, the days are between us." The governor said, "Hasten; defer not the payment of my debt.

"You who say, 'To-morrow,' learn you this, that in every day which time brings, that evil tree grows younger, and this digger of it up gets more old and helpless. The bramble-bush is gaining strength and on the rise; whilst the proposed digger of it up is getting old and on the decline. The bramble-bush every day and every moment more green and fresh; the digger of it up every day more emaciated and withered. It is becoming younger, and you are becoming older; be quick therefore, and do not waste your time."

The Being of Man Is Like a Forest

The being of man is like a forest;—be full of caution of this being if you are of that breath. In our being there are thousands of wolves and hogs. In our being there is the righteous, the unrighteous; the fair and the foul.

That trait which is predominant decides the temperament: when gold exceeds copper in quantity, the substance is gold. The quality which is predominant in your being,—you will have to rise in the very form of that same quality.

At one moment wolfishness comes into man; at another moment, the moon-like beauty of the face of Joseph. Feelings of peace and of enmity go by a hidden road from bosom to bosom.

Nay, indeed, wisdom, knowledge, and skill pass from man even into the ox and the ass. The untrained horse, rough and unformed, becomes of good easy paces and docile; the bear dances, and the goat also salutes. From men the desire of doing something enters into the dog: he becomes a shepherd, or a hunter, or a guard.

Every moment a new species appears in the bosom; sometimes a demon, sometimes an angel, and sometimes wild beasts.

From that wonderful forest with which every lion is acquainted there is a hidden road to that snare, the bosoms of men.

Steal the pearl of the soul from hearts, O you who are less than a dog!—from the hearts, I would say, of the Sufi saints. Since you steal, steal at least that exquisite pearl; since you bear burdens, bear at least a noble one.

"Paradise Is Surrounded by Things Unpleasant to Us; the Fires Are Surrounded by Our Carnal Desires"

Green branches are the source of the food of the fire which shall burn you; but he who is burnt by the fire shall be in proximity to Kausar.

Whoever is suffering an affliction in prison,—that is the requital of a morsel or a carnal desire. Whoever has a share of felicity in a palace,—that is the reward of some combat and affliction. Whomsoever you see unequalled in the possession of gold and silver,—know that he has been patient in earning.

You have abandoned Jesus and cherished the ass; hence you are necessarily, as an ass, outside of the curtain. The fortune of Jesus is knowledge and deep spiritual knowledge; these are not the fortune of the ass, O asinine one.

You hear the cry of the ass, and you have compassion; then you know not that the ass is enjoining upon you the properties of the ass. Have compassion upon Jesus, and not upon the ass: do not make the carnal soul lord over your intellect.

If you have become sick in heart through Jesus, still health too comes from him; leave him not.

O sweet-breathed Messiah, how are you as to affliction? for there has never been in the world a treasure without a serpent. How are you, Jesus, at the sight of the Jews? How are you, Joseph, at the hands of the crafty and envious? For this raw people, night and day, you are a furtherer of life even as the night and day.

John the Baptist—on Him Be Peace!—in His Mother's Womb Inclines in Worship Before Jesus—on Him Be Peace!

The mother of John before giving birth to him said in private to Mary, "I have found for certain that you will give birth to a King, who will be a Lord of constancy, a wise Apostle. When I have happened to be opposite to you, my unborn child at once has inclined in worship. This embryo inclined in worship before that embryo, so that pain affected my body through its inclination."

Mary said, "I also have perceived within myself an inclination on the part of the infant in my womb."

Fools say, "Cancel this story, because it is an untruth and an error; since Mary at the time of her delivery was far both from strangers and from relatives;—until that woman of persuasive eloquence was delivered without the town, she really did not enter it. When she had given birth to him she then took him up in her arms and carried him to her kindred. Where did the mother of John see her to speak these words to her as to the supposed occurrence?"

Let the caviller know this, that to the man of mind that which is absent as to space is present. The mother of John when far from the eyes of Mary might be present to her spiritual vision. With closed eyes she might see a friend when she has made a lattice of the body.

And if she saw her neither without nor in her own mind, pay attention, simpleton, to the spirit of the story.

O my brother, the story is like a measure; the spirit in it is like the grain. The man of intellect takes the grain, the spirit; he does not pay attention to the measure though it be taken away.

The Contention as to Grapes of Four Persons, Each of Whom Knows Grapes by a Different Name

A man gave a diram to four persons. One of them, a Persian, said, "I will spend this on 'angur.'"

Another of them was an Arab; he said. "No, you rogue; I want 'inab,' not 'angur.'"

A third was a Turk; he said, "I do not want 'inab,' dear friend, I want 'uzum.'"

The fourth was a Greek; he said, "Stop this altercation; I wish for 'istafil.'"

Those persons began to fight against one another, because they were ignorant of the secret of the names. Through sheer ignorance they struck one another with their fists; they were full of ignorance and devoid of knowledge.

If one who knew the inner truth, an estimable man versed in many tongues, had been there, he would have reconciled them. He would have said, "With this one diram I will gratify the desire of all of you. If in all sincerity you entrust your hearts to me, this diram of yours will do so much for you. Your one diram will become as four, which is what is wanted; four enemies will become as one by concord."

Although your words appear uniform and in harmony, they are the source, in their effect, of contention and anger.

From the Forty-Two Traditions of An-Nawawi

Actions are to be judged only in accordance with intentions; and every one gets only what he intended; hence he whose emigration is for the sake of Allah and his apostle, his emigration is for the sake of Allah and his apostle; and he who emigrates for a worldly thing, to get it; so his emigration is that for which he emigrated.

Islam is built on five points:—the witness of there being no deity except Allah, and of Mohammed being the apostle of Allah; the performing of prayer; the giving of alms; the pilgrimage to the house; and the fast of Ramadan.

The one who introduces (as from himself) into our affair that which has nothing to do with it is a reprobate.

Religion is good advice. We said, "Whose?" He, the prophet, said, "Allah's and His Book's and His apostle's, and the Imams of the Muslims, and the generality of them."

I have been commanded to wage war upon people until they witness that there is no deity except Allah, and that Mohammed is the apostle of Allah; and that they perform the prayer and give alms. Then if they do that, so far as I am concerned, their lives and property will be protected, unless in conflict with the rights of Islam; and their account is with Allah Ta'ala.

Let go the things in which you are in doubt for the things in which there is no doubt.

Leaving alone things which do not concern him is one of the good things in a man's Islam.

No one of you is a believer until he loves for his brother what he loves for himself.

The blood of a Muslim man is not lawful but for one of three reasons:—an adulterous married person; an avenger of blood; and the one who leaves his religion, that is, splits the community.

He that believes in Allah and the last day, let him speak good or hold his peace; and he who believes in Allah and the last day, let him honour his neighbour; and he who believes in Allah and the last day, let him honour his guest.

A man said to the prophet, "Give me a command." He said, "Do not get angry." The man repeated the question several times, and he said, "Do not get angry."

Allah has prescribed *Ihsan* for everything; hence, if you kill, do it well; and if you slaughter, do it well; and let each one of you sharpen his knife and let his victim die at once.

Fear Allah, wherever thou art; and follow up bad actions with good, so as to wipe them out; and behave in a decent way to people.

Among the things which people comprehended from the material of the first prophecy was, If you are not ashamed, then do whatever you wish.

Almsgiving is incumbent upon every "bone" of people each day that the sun rises; it is almsgiving if you make adjustment between a couple; and if you help a man in the matter of his riding-animal and mount him upon her or lift his baggage for him upon her. A good word is almsgiving; and in every step you walk towards prayer there is an act of almsgiving; and it is almsgiving when you ward danger off the road.

Righteousness is goodness of character; and sinfulness is what is woven in the soul, and you hate that people should ascertain the matter.

I went to the apostle of Allah, and he said: "You have come to ask about righteousness." I said, "Yes." He said, "Ask your heart to decide; righteousness is what the soul and the heart feel tranquil about; and sinfulness is what is fixed in the soul, and roams about in the breast, even if people give their decision in your favour over and over again."

I, Mu'adh, said, "O apostle of Allah, inform me of a work which will bring me into the garden and keep me far from the fire." He said, "You have indeed made inquiry about something great; but indeed it is easy for one for whom Allah facilitates things; you should worship Allah without joining aught with him; you should perform prayer, give alms, and fast in Ramadan; and make pilgrimage to the house." Then he said, "Shall I not indicate to you the doors to good. Fasting is a protection, and almsgiving quenches sin as water quenches fire, and the prayer of a man at the dead of night."

Then he said, "Shall I not tell you about the 'pith' of the matter, and its base and the apex of its prominence?" I said, "Of course, O apostle of Allah." He said, "The 'pith' is Islam; and its base is prayer, and apex of its prominence is holy war." Then he said, "Shall I tell you how to get all this?" I said, "Of course, O apostle of Allah." So he took hold of his tongue, and said, "Control this." I said, "O prophet of Allah, we are indeed to blame for what we speak with it." So he said, "Your mother is bereft of you; will people be toppled into the fire on their faces except for the harvest of their tongues?"

Do not be envious of each other; and do not outbid each other; and do not hate each other; do not oppose each other; and do not undersell each other; and be, O slaves of Allah, as brothers. A Muslim is a brother to a Muslim, not oppressing him and not forsaking him; not lying to him and not despising him. Here is true piety (and he, Mohammed, would point to his breast three times)—it's quite bad enough for a man to despise his brother Muslim. A Muslim's life, property and honour are inviolate to a Muslim.

He who dispels from a believer one of the griefs of the world, Allah will dispel for him a grief on the day of resurrection; he who cheers up a person in difficulties, Allah will cheer him in this world and the next; he who shields a Muslim, Allah will shield him in this world and the next. Allah is there to help his slave, so long as he is out to help his brother, and he who walks a path seeking therein knowledge, Allah will make easy for him a path to paradise through it. And when a company meets together in one of the houses of Allah to pore over the book of Allah and to study it together amongst themselves, the Shechinah comes down to them and mercy overshadows them; and the angels surround them; and Allah remembers them among them that are his; and the one whose work makes him procrastinate will not be hastened along by the nobility of his ancestry.

Be in the world as if you were a stranger or a traveller: when evening time comes, expect not the morning; and when morning time comes expect not the evening; and prepare as long as you are in good health for sickness, and so long as you are alive for death.

Allah Ta'ala said: So long as you call upon me and hope in me, I forgive you all that originates from you; and I will not heed, O son of man, should your sins reach the horizon of the heavens, and then you asked my pardon and I would pardon you. O son of man, were you to come to me with almost an earthful of sins, and then you met me without joining anything with me in the godhead, then would I come to you with an earthful of forgiveness.

THE CONFUCIANIST

Master Kung

Out of the chaos which pervaded the primordial universe came *Yang*, the bright, the warm, the effusive, the heavenly, and *Yin*, the dark, the secretive, the silent, the deep, the earthly. Counterparts and conflicting opposites, they complemented each other in the formation of a creative force whose product was heaven and earth with its fruits, whose symbol is a circle divided into two embryonic shapes, one black, one white, and whose significance is life and the ordering of life, universal power, and the mysterious duality which lies in the souls of men.

Thus was creation and the mystery of life explained in the minds of the ancient sages of China who were articulate and made records of their beliefs perhaps fifteen hundred or two thousand years before Gautama began his ministry in India, Zarathushtra composed his *gathas* of praise to Ahura Mazda in Persia, and the writers of the *Upanishads* and the later Hebrew prophets began proclaiming the doctrine of a universal and all-powerful God.

There is no record to tell when or from where the earliest ancestors of the Chinese came to the land of vast spaces, of rugged mountains and fertile valleys which is now inhabited by one-fifth of the human race and boasts the world's oldest continuous culture. Some scholars have attempted to show that they were related to the Sumerians of Babylonia, or the Elamites, but others believe it more likely that they developed from Mongolian stock which may have had its origin in their own land. Plainly these people of the Turanian race are not of the Indo-European stock which produced the worshippers of *Dyaush pitar*, Indra, and Varuna, whose descendants became Hindus, Indian Buddhists, Jainas, Persian Zoroastrians, and the later Christians of Italy, Greece, Spain, and Western Europe. Nor are they related to the Semitic worshippers of Jehovah and Allah.

Whatever the source and origin of the people, the rise of religious consciousness and civilization among them was early and rapid. Chinese historians list dynasties which go back in an unbroken line to 2850 B.C. and mention traditions and heroes long prior to this date. Western scholars, however, find unconvincing all accounts of happenings earlier than 2258 B.C. when the Hia dynasty came to power. If even this later date is accepted as the beginning of Chinese history, it is seen that the Chinese were at least a partly civilized people before the birth of Abraham, when the Jews were unorganized, wandering tribes, without clearly fixed religious beliefs. Their civilization also probably antedates the time when the ancient Indo-European rishis were composing the *Rig-Veda*, oldest of all the Indian scriptures.

By the sixth century B.C. Chinese social and economic life was highly developed. There is ample evidence from that period of well-built houses, umbrellas, carefully made clothing, chairs, tables, leather shoes, pottery dishes, and sun dials for measuring time.

A theological system and a code of ethics had long since been stabilized as a state religion. It included reverence of good spirits on the one hand and fear of their evil counterparts on the other. From the Yang came the host of good spirits called *shen*; from the Yin, a host of evil spirits called *kwei*. Man's soul was thought to contain a mixture of these two spirits. The shen constituted his spirituality, the immaterial, ethereal, heaven-like quality from which arose his intellect and all of his virtues. From his kwei came his passions and vices, creatures of the dark earth. At his birth the two forces were blended within him; at his death they departed from his body, the shen to return to the parent Yang in heaven, the kwei to the Yin in earth.

But it was not only within himself that man encountered the shen and the kwei. They were everywhere and in everything. Against the kwei one had constantly to be on guard. They inhabited every bush and tree, they lay in wait at every turn of the road and every shadowed angle between the buildings of the cities, ready to pounce on an unwary passer-by and do him bodily or spiritual harm. One could protect himself from them by beating on drums or gongs or kettles, or carrying lighted torches at night.

But in heaven there were always the shen, gods and departed ancestors, who were more powerful than the kwei and would protect the virtuous and those who remembered them in sacrifices. And above them all, both spirits and living men, there was the universal principle of goodness, sometimes referred to by the impersonal *Tien* or Heaven, sometimes by the more personal if somewhat vaguely defined *Shang-ti* or God, the supreme ruler.

Worship of Shang-ti was the privilege only of the Emperor, who was himself thought to be the son of Heaven. The people must confine their supplications to the shen and the spirits of their ancestors. But the Emperor also offered sacrifices to these, and to the kwei as well. Sheep and pigs were burned on an elaborate altar in the southern suburb of the capital when the offering was to Heaven, and were buried in the earth at another altar in the northern suburb when the sacrifice was to earth. The spirits of heat and cold, of sun, wind, rain, the stars, the forests, the streams, mountains and valleys—all were propitiated in sacrifice.

Such was, in brief, the state religion of China which prevailed from a time unknown to history (but certainly far back into the bronze age) until the fall of the last Manchu dynasty when the Chinese Republic was formed in 1912.

In 551 B.C., in the province of Shantung, Confucius was born, the youngest of eleven children. His name in Chinese was K'ungfutze or "Master Kung." That by which he is known to the Western World is the latinized form. When he was three years old his father died and Confucius' early life was spent in hard work. But though fatherless and apparently in modest financial circumstances, the boy obviously received a good education and came early to love the ancient Chinese books which were the heritage of every literate Chinese. "At fifteen," he is reported to have said, "I had my mind bent on learning."

He was married at the early age of nineteen and had one son, but his marriage was not a happy one and he later divorced his wife.

Shortly after his marriage he was given a minor government post as keeper of the stores of grain, but soon left this position and opened a private school which became so popular that he is said to have had three thousand pupils. Even then he showed evidences of the emphasis which would appear in his wider teachings that were to come later, for while giving instruction in history, poetry, literature, the proprieties, music, natural science, and government, he avoided all references to the supernatural and deprecated feats of physical strength and lack of order.

Through his success as a school teacher he was

appointed chief magistrate of his town and advanced
steadily in governmental positions until he was chief
justice of his state. Here his preoccupation with affairs
of government, and his deep-seated conviction that the
function of government was not the accumulation of
revenue and the increase of power but rather the welfare of the people—those principles which he stressed
so often in his later preaching—were clearly evident.
During his period in office he succeeded in helping to
bring about a high degree of obedience to government,
order, peace, and even partial disarmament.

But political intrigues brought about his resignation
at the age of fifty-five, and when he failed in his effort
to obtain a government post in a neighbouring state, he
entered the most significant period of his life. Wandering from state to state with a group of pupils, he spread
the principles which have given him world-wide immortality. His followers were in many ways the parallels
of the disciples of Jesus and the *Bhikkus* of Gautama,
though Confucius was not accorded during his lifetime any aspect of divinity, nor did he ask for such
characterization. Rather, his companions thought of
themselves as pupils of the master. In his wanderings
he inculcated in them and in all who would listen
principles of government, of agriculture, of propriety,
and of benevolent public morality which have with-
stood the tests of nearly twenty-five hundred years.

During this period he also performed one of his
greatest services to the world in rescuing the ancient
Chinese classics from threatened oblivion, collecting
and editing them. These, as Confucius has left them to
us, are the *Shu King* or *Canon of History*, the *Shi King*
or *Canon of Poetry*, the *I King* or *Canon of Changes*—
a mystical system of divination, the *Li Ki* or *Book of
Rites*, the *Chun Chiu* or *Spring and Autumn Annals*—

a local history which Confucius himself wrote, and the *Hsiao King* or *Book of Filial Piety*. They now constitute the six canonical classics of Confucianism.

At the age of seventy-two the great man died, leaving behind him the canonical books and a devoted group of pupils who collected and edited a book in memory of their master which preserved, in a disconnected way, much information about him and a large number of the things which he had said to them. This book we know as *The Analects of Confucius*. It and the *Ta Hsio* or *Great Learning*, the *Chung Yung* or *Doctrine of the Steadfast Mean*, and *Meng-tze* or *Mencius* (which records the teachings of the great disciple of Confucius who was born a century after the master's death) make up "the four books" which have been added to the classics to form the whole Confucianist canon. There have been later philosophers who have added to the list—such men as Moh Ti, Wang Chung, and Chu Hsi—but the six "Classics" and the four "Books" are by far the most important in Confucianist religious literature.

Like many a philosopher and prophet Confucius has been given greater honour in his own country since his death than he was given in life. Nearly two hundred years before the birth of Christ the Emperor of China offered a sacrifice at the tomb of the great teacher. About the beginning of the Christian era he was given the official title, "*Duke Ni*, all complete and illustrious." Half a century later an imperial edict ordered regular sacrifices to be made to his spirit. In A.D. 492 he was canonized. Other elevations in the conception of him followed until in 1906 he was raised by imperial decree to the rank of "Co-Assessor with the deities of Heaven and Earth." When the last Manchu dynasty fell and many imperial decrees were cancelled by the Repub-

'lican government, the worship of Confucius was continued by governmental edict.

Confucius did not originate a religion nor did he attempt to reform one in the sense in which Christ and the Buddha tried to reform theirs. Rather he organized the one which had existed in the land of his birth from time immemorial, giving form to its books, dignity to its formalities, and emphasis to its moral precepts. His way of life was one of formalism, of the proprieties, of a lack of extremes in all things. He is reported to have observed all the ancient conventions scrupulously and to have urged them on others.

Yet in spite of his formalism and deep respect for the proprieties, there was in Confucius a firm conviction of the instinctive righteousness of humanity and a never failing love of and respect for the informal, direct goodness of nature and the virtue to be found in communion with it, even when not materially productive. When four of his students were asked by Confucius to express their wishes, the lute-playing Tsang Hsi said that since it was spring he would like to go swimming with a dozen young companions and return home singing, and Confucius gave his approval although the other three students had expressed desires to be busy in highly social activities. In this philosophic tendency Master Kung had much in common with his somewhat older contemporary Lao Tze. (See the Introduction to the Taoist scriptures.)

Confucius' social philosophy is typified by the Golden Rule and the form in which he stated it: "What you do not want done to yourself, do not do to others." Here is not only the principle of reciprocity, but also the fine Eastern doctrine of "letting alone." Wisdom, benevolence, and fortitude Confucius called the universal virtues.

The chief interest of Confucianism is human behaviour rather than theology. Confucius himself, when asked about God, said "I prefer not speaking." Yet even he, in the midst of disappointment, when complaining of the lack of appreciation which his contemporaries gave him, took comfort in saying, "But Heaven knows me!" He also said "without recognizing the ordinances of Heaven, it is impossible to be a superior man," and "the superior man stands in awe of the ordinances of Heaven." He is reported to have used only once the term *Shang-Ti*, which means God, preferring the more general and impersonal word *Tien*, which means Heaven or the intangible order of goodness which rules the universe. This was not through any lack of belief in a supreme universal power, nor yet from any lack of reverence, as many passages in his teachings show. Rather he seemed to feel that there was a certain lack of propriety in speaking of these things. "Does Heaven speak?" he asked. "The four seasons pursue their course, and all things are continually being produced. But does Heaven say anything?" Also he seemed to feel, as Gautama did, that questions about God and personal immortality were "questions which tended not to edification." When Chi Lu asked about death, he answered, "While you do not know life, how can you know about death?"

Throughout his life the effort of Confucius seems to have been to turn men's minds away from contemplation of the eternal imponderables and to fix them upon the ever-present, the practical, and the more easily understandable problems of human behaviour. His attitudes towards heaven and earth are well summarized in his words, "To give one's self to the duties due to men, and, while respecting spiritual beings, to keep aloof from them, may be called wisdom." The religion of China which now bears his name has carried on this emphasis, though not to the extent which Master Kung intended it should, for the spirit of Confucius himself is now worshipped by Confucianists.

Intermixed with instruction in social and political righteousness there is much which concerns itself with love as a motivation for human goodness. When Fan Ch'ih asked about benevolence, Confucius answered, "It is to love all men." When his pupil asked about knowledge, he said, "It is to know all men." And though he once complained that none but Heaven knew him, he also said, "I will not be afflicted at men's not knowing me; I will be afflicted that I do not know men."

Yet a stern sense of reality in human relations also pervades his teachings. "Have no friends not equal to yourself," he said. When asked for his opinion as to the Taoist (and later Christian) principle that injury should be recompensed with kindness, he answered, "With what then will you recompense kindness? Recompense injury with justice, and recompense kindness with kindness."

Because of the emphasis on moral conduct and the small amount of theology in Confucianism, many have said that it is not a religion at all but only a code of ethical behaviour.

Yet is there any more exalted religious motivation than that which led one man to spend his life seeking to elevate the lives of all others through conformity with "the ordinances of heaven"? Like Abou ben Adhem, Confucius was one who loved his fellow-man. Could the Angel of the Lord choose a lower place for Master Kung on the list of immortal spiritual leaders than for any of the rest?

CONFUCIANIST SCRIPTURES

From the Li Ki

The Nature of the Universe and Man

Man is the product of the attributes of heaven and earth, by the interaction of the dual forces of nature, the union of the animal and intelligent souls, and the finest subtile matter of the five elements.

Heaven exercises the control of the strong and light force, and hangs out the sun and stars. Earth exercises the control of the dark and weaker force, and gives vent to it in the hills and streams. The five elements are distributed through the four seasons, and it is by their harmonious action that the moon is produced, which therefore keeps waxing for fifteen days and waning for fifteen.

The five elements in their movements alternately displace and exhaust one another. Each one of them, in the revolving course of the twelve months of the four seasons, comes to be in its turn the fundamental one for the time.

The five notes of harmony, with their six upper musical accords, and the twelve pitch tubes, come each, in their revolutions among themselves, to be the first note of the scale.

The five flavours, with the six condiments, and the twelve articles of diet, come each one, in their revolutions in the course of a year, to give its character to the food.

The five colours, with the six elegant figures, which they form on the two robes, come each one, in their revolutions among themselves, to give the character of the dress that is worn.

Therefore man is the heart and mind of heaven and earth, and the visible embodiment of the five elements. He lives in the enjoyment of all flavours, the discriminating of all notes of harmony, and the enrobing of all colours.

Thus it was that when the sages would make rules for men, they felt it necessary to find the origin of all things in heaven and earth; to make the two forces of nature the commencement of all; to use the four seasons as the handle of their arrangements; to adopt the sun and stars as the recorders of time, the moon as the measurer of work to be done, the spirits breathing in nature as associates, the five elements as giving substance to things, rules of propriety and righteousness as their instruments, the feelings of men as the field to be cultivated, and the four intelligent creatures as domestic animals to be reared.

The origin of all things being found in heaven and earth, they could be taken in hand, one after the other.

The Feelings of Men

What are the feelings of men? They are joy, anger, sadness, fear, love, disliking, and liking. These seven feelings belong to men without their learning them. What are "the things which men consider right"? Kindness on the part of the father, and filial duty on that of the son; gentleness on the part of the elder brother, and obedience on that of the younger; righteousness on the part of the husband, and submission on that of the wife; kindness on the part of elders, and deference on that of juniors; with benevolence on the part of the ruler, and loyalty on that of the minister:—these ten are the things which men consider to be right.

Truthfulness in speech and the cultivation of harmony constitute what are called "the things advantageous to men." Quarrels, plundering, and murders are "the things disastrous to men."

Hence when a ruler would regulate the seven feelings of men, cultivate the ten virtues that are right, promote truthfulness of speech, and the maintenance of harmony, show his value for kindly consideration and complaisant courtesy, and put away quarrelling and plundering: if he neglect the rules of propriety, how shall he succeed?

The things which men greatly desire are comprehended in meat and drink and sexual pleasure; those which they greatly dislike are comprehended in death, exile, poverty, and suffering. Thus liking and disliking are the great elements in men's minds. But men keep them hidden in their minds, where they cannot be fathomed or measured. The good and the bad of them being in their minds, and no outward manifestation of them being visible, if it be wished to determine these qualities in one uniform way, how can it be done without the rules of propriety?

The Functions of the Ruler

Heaven produces the seasons. Earth produces all the sources of wealth. Man is begotten by his father, and instructed by his teacher. The ruler correctly uses these four agencies, and therefore he stands in the place where there is no error.

Hence the ruler is he to whose brightness men look; he does not seek to brighten men. It is he whom men

support; he does not seek to support men. It is he whom
men serve; he does not seek to serve men. Therefore
the people imitate the ruler and we have their self-
government; they nourish the ruler, and they find
their security in doing so; they serve the ruler, and find
their distinction in doing so.

Therefore the ruler, making use of the wisdom of
others, will put away the cunning to which that wisdom might lead him; using their courage, he will put
away passion; and using their benevolence, he will put
away covetousness.

Therefore when it is said that the ruler, being a sage,
can look on all under the sky as one family, and on all
in the middle states as one man, this does not mean
that he will do so on premeditation and purpose. He
must know men's feelings, lay open to them what they
consider right, show clearly to them what is advantageous, and comprehend what are their calamities.
Being so furnished, he is then able to effect the thing.

From the Shih King

The Song of How-tsieh

The first birth of our people
Was from Keang Yuen.
How did she give birth to our people?
She had presented a pure offering and sacrifice,
That her childlessness might be taken away.
She then trod on a toe-print made by God, and was
       moved,
In the large place where she rested.
She became pregnant; she dwelt retired;

She gave birth to, and nourished a son,
Who was How-tsieh.

When she had fulfilled her months,
Her first-born son came forth like a lamb,
There was no bursting, nor rending,
No injury, no hurt;—
Showing how wonderful he would be.
Did not God give her the comfort?
Had he not accepted her pure offering and sacrifice,
So that thus easily she brought forth her son?

He was placed in a narrow lane,
But the sheep and oxen protected him with loving care.
He was placed in a wide forest,
Where he was met with by the woodcutters.
He was placed on the cold ice,
And a bird screened and supported him with its wings.

Charged with a large state, he commanded success.
He followed his rules of conduct without error;
Wherever he inspected the people, they responded to
    his instructions.
Then came Hsiang-thu all ardent,
And all within the four seas, beyond the middle regions,
    acknowledged his restraints.

Plea to an Ancestor

Alas for me, who am a little child,
On whom has devolved the unsettled state!
Solitary am I and full of distress.
Oh! my great father,
All thy life long, thou wast filial.

Thou didst think of my great grandfather,
Seeing him, as it were, ascending and descending in
the court;
I, the little child,
Day and night will be as reverent.

Oh! ye great kings,
As your successor, I will strive not to forget you.

How Vast Is God!

How vast is God,
The ruler of men below!
How arrayed in terrors is God,
With many things irregular in his ordinations.
Heaven gave birth to the multitudes of the people,
But the nature it confers is not to be depended on.
All are good at first,
But few prove themselves to be so at the last.

In Praise of Ancestors

Small is the cooing dove,
But it flies aloft up to heaven.
My heart is wounded with sorrow,
And I think of our forefathers.
When the dawn is breaking, and I cannot sleep,
The thoughts in my breast are of our parents.

Men who are grave and wise,
Though they drink, are mild and masters of themselves;
But those who are benighted and ignorant
Are devoted to drink, and more so daily.
Be careful, each of you, of your deportment;—
What heaven confers, when once lost, is not regained.

We must be mild, and humble,
As if we were perched on trees.
We must be anxious and careful,
As if we were on the brink of a valley.
We must be apprehensive and cautious,
As if we were treading upon thin ice.

On Letting Alone

Do not push forward a wagon;—
You will only raise the dust about yourself.
Do not think of all your anxieties;—
You will only make yourself ill.

Admonition

Do not try to cultivate fields too large;—
The weeds will only grow luxuriantly.
Do not think of winning people far away;—
Your toiling heart will be grieved.

From the Analects of Confucius

The Master said, "Is it not pleasant to learn with a
constant perseverance and application? Is it not delightful to have friends coming from distant quarters? Is he
not a man of complete virtue who feels no discomposure
though men may take no note of him?

"Fine words and an insinuating appearance are
seldom associated with true virtue."

The philosopher Tsang said, "I daily examine myself
on three points:—whether, in transacting business for

others, I may have been not faithful;—whether, in intercourse with friends, I may have been not sincere;—whether I may have not mastered and practised the instructions of my teacher."

The Master said, "To rule a country of a thousand chariots, there must be reverent attention to business, and sincerity; economy in expenditure, and love for men; and the employment of the people at the proper seasons."

Tsze-hsia said, "If a man withdraws his mind from the love of beauty, and applies it as sincerely to the love of the virtuous; if, in serving his parents, he can exert his utmost strength; if, in serving his prince, he can devote his life; if, in his intercourse with his friends, his words are sincere:—although men say that he has not learned, I will certainly say that he has."

The philosopher Yu said, "When agreements are made according to what is right, what is spoken can be made good. When respect is shown according to what is proper, one keeps far from shame and disgrace. When the parties upon whom a man leans are proper persons to be intimate with, he can make them his guides and masters."

The Master said, "He who aims to be a man of complete virtue in his food does not seek to gratify his appetite, nor in his dwelling-place does he seek the appliances of ease; he is earnest in what he is doing, and careful in his speech; he frequents the company of men of principle that he may be rectified:—such a person may be said indeed to love to learn.

"I will not be afflicted at men's not knowing me; I will be afflicted that I do not know men."

The Master said, "He who exercises government by means of his virtue may be compared to the north polar star which keeps its place and all the stars turn towards it.

"If the people be led by laws, and uniformity sought to be given them by punishments, they will try to avoid the punishment, but have no sense of shame. If they be led by virtue, and uniformity sought to be given them by the rules of propriety, they will have the sense of shame, and moreover will become good.

"At fifteen, I had my mind bent on learning. At thirty, I stood firm. At forty, I had no doubts. At fifty, I knew the decrees of heaven. At sixty, my ear was an obedient organ for the reception of truth. At seventy, I could follow what my heart desired, without transgressing what was right.

"I have talked with Hui for a whole day, and he has not made any objection to anything I said;—as if he were stupid. He has retired, and I have examined his conduct when away from me, and found him able to illustrate my teachings. Hui!—He is not stupid.

"See what a man does. Mark his motives. Examine in what things he rests. How can a man conceal his character?

"If a man keeps cherishing his old knowledge, so as continually to be acquiring new, he may be a teacher of others."

Tsze-kung asked what constituted the superior man. The Master said, "He acts before he speaks, and afterwards speaks according to his actions. The superior man is universally minded and no partisan. The inferior man is a partisan and not universal."

The Master said, "Yu, shall I teach you what knowledge is? When you know a thing, to hold that you know it; and when you do not know a thing, to allow that you do not know it;—this is knowledge."

The duke Ai asked, saying, "What should be done

in order to secure the submission of the people?" Confucius replied, "Advance the upright and set aside the crooked, then the people will submit. Advance the crooked and set aside the upright, then the people will not submit."

The Master said, "The superior man, in the world, does not set his mind either for anything, or against anything; what is right he will follow. The superior man thinks of virtue; the small man thinks of comfort. The superior man thinks of the sanctions of law; the small man thinks of favours which he may receive.

"He who acts with a constant view to his own advantage will be much murmured against.

"A man should say, I am not concerned that I have no place, I am concerned how I may fit myself for one. I am not concerned that I am not known, I seek to be worthy to be known."

The Master said of Tsze-ch'an that he had four of the characteristics of a superior man:—in his conduct of himself, he was humble; in serving his superiors, he was respectful; in nourishing the people, he was kind; in ordering the people, he was just.

The Master said, "Respectfulness, without the rules of propriety, becomes laborious bustle; carefulness, without the rules of propriety, becomes timidity; boldness, without the rules of propriety, becomes insubordination; straightforwardness, without the rules of propriety, becomes rudeness. When those who are in high stations perform well all their duties to their relations, the people are aroused to virtue. When old friends are not neglected by them, the people are preserved from inferiority."

The Master said, "The linen cap is that prescribed by the rules of ceremony, but now a silk one is worn. It is economical, and I follow the common practice. The rules of ceremony prescribe the bowing below the hall, but now the practice is to bow only after ascending it. That is arrogant. I continue to bow below the hall, though I oppose the common practice."

There were four things from which the Master was entirely free. He had no foregone conclusions, no arbitrary pre-determinations, no obstinacy, and no egoism.

The Master said, "I have not seen one who loves virtue as he loves beauty.

"A youth is to be regarded with respect. How do we know that his future will not be equal to our present? If he reach the age of forty or fifty, and has not made himself heard of, then indeed he will not be worth being regarded with respect.

"Hold faithfulness and sincerity as first principles. Have no friends not equal to yourself. When you have faults, do not fear to abandon them."

Confucius, in his village, looked simple and sincere, and as if he were not able to speak.

When he was in the prince's ancestorial temple, or in the court, he spoke minutely on every point, but cautiously.

When he was waiting at court, in speaking with the great officers of the lower grade, he spoke freely, but in a straightforward manner; in speaking with those of the higher grade, he did so blandly, but precisely.

When the ruler was present, his manner displayed respectful uneasiness; it was grave, but self-possessed.

He ascended the reception hall, holding up his robe with both his hands, and his body bent; holding in his breath also, as if he dared not breathe.

When he came out from the audience, as soon as he had descended one step, he began to relax his countenance, and had a satisfied look. When he had got to the bottom of the steps, he advanced rapidly to his place, with his arms like wings, and on occupying it, his manner still showed respectful uneasiness.

The stable being burned down, when he was at court, on his return he said, "Has any man been hurt?" He did not ask about the horses.

Chi Lu asked about serving the spirits of the dead. The Master said, "While you are not able to serve men, how can you serve their spirits?" Chi Lu added, "I venture to ask about death." He was answered, "While you do not know life, how can you know about death?"

Tsze-kung asked which of the two, Shih or Shang, was the superior. The Master said, "Shih goes beyond the due mean, and Shang does not come up to it." "Then," said Tsze-kung, "the superiority is with Shih, I suppose." The Master said, "To go beyond is as wrong as to fall short."

Tsze-lu, Tsang Hsi, Yen Yu, and Kung-hsi Hwa were sitting by the Master. He said to them, "Though I am a day or so older than you, do not think of that. From day to day you are saying, 'We are not known.' If some ruler were to know you, what would you like to do?"

Tsze-lu hastily and lightly replied, "Suppose the case of a state of ten thousand chariots; let it be straitened between other large states; let it be suffering from invading armies; and to this let there be added a famine in corn and in all vegetables:—if I were entrusted with the government of it, in three years' time I could make the people to be bold, and to recognize the rules of righteous conduct." The Master smiled at him.

Turning to Yen Yu, he said, "Ch'iu, what are your wishes?" Ch'iu replied, "Suppose a state of sixty or seventy li square, or one of fifty or sixty, and let me have the government of it;—in three years' time, I could make plenty to abound among the people. As to teaching them the principles of propriety, and music, I must wait for the rise of a superior man to do that."

"What are your wishes, Ch'ih," said the Master next to Kung-hsi Hwa. Ch'ih replied, "I do not say that my ability extends to these things, but I should wish to learn them. At the services of the ancestral temple, and at the audiences of the princes with the sovereign, I should like, dressed in the dark square-made robe and the black linen cap, to act as a small assistant."

Last of all, the Master asked Tsang Hsi, "Tien, what are your wishes?" Tien, pausing as he was playing on his lute, while it was yet twanging, laid the instrument aside, and rose. "My wishes," he said, "are different from the cherished purposes of these three gentlemen." "What harm is there in that?" said the Master; "do you also, as well as they, speak out your wishes." Tien then said, "In this, the last month of spring, with the dress of the season all complete, along with five or six young men who have assumed the cap, and six or seven boys, I would wash in the I, enjoy the breeze among the rain altars, and return home singing." The master heaved a sigh and said, "I give my approval to Tien."

Yen Yuan asked about perfect virtue. The Master said, "To subdue one's self and return to propriety, is perfect virtue. If a man can for one day subdue himself and return to propriety, all under heaven will ascribe perfect virtue to him."

Chung-kung asked about perfect virtue. The Master

said, "It is, when you go abroad, to behave to every one as if you were receiving a great guest; to employ the people as if you were assisting at a great sacrifice; not to do to others as you would not wish done to yourself; to have no murmuring against you in the country, and none in the family."

Tsze-chang asked what constituted intelligence. The Master said, "He with whom neither slander that gradually soaks into the mind, nor statements that startle like a wound in the flesh, are successful, may be called intelligent indeed."

Tsze-kung asked about government. The Master said, "The requisites of government are that there be sufficiency of food, sufficiency of military equipment, and the confidence of the people in their ruler."

Tsze-kung said, "If it cannot be helped, and one of these must be dispensed with, which of the three should be foregone first?" "The military equipment," said the Master.

Tsze-kung again asked, "If it cannot be helped, and one of the remaining two must be dispensed with, which of them should be foregone?" The Master answered, "Part with the food. From of old, death has been the lot of all men; but if the people have no faith in their rulers, there is no standing for the state."

Chi K'ang asked Confucius about government, saying, "What do you say to killing the unprincipled for the good of the principled?" Confucius replied, "Sir, in carrying on your government, why should you use killing at all? Let your evinced desires be for what is good, and the people will be good. The relation between superiors and inferiors is like that between the wind and the grass. The grass must bend, when the wind blows across it."

Fan Ch'ih asked about benevolence. The Master

said, "It is to love all men." He asked about knowledge. The Master said, "It is to know all men."

Tsze-lu said, "The ruler of Wei has been waiting for you, in order with you to administer the government. What will you consider the first thing to be done?"

The Master replied, "What is necessary is to rectify names. If names be not correct, language is not in accordance with the truth of things. If language be not in accordance with the truth of things, affairs cannot be carried on to success.

"When affairs cannot be carried on to success, proprieties and music will not flourish. When proprieties and music do not flourish, punishments will not be properly awarded. When punishments are not properly awarded, the people do not know how to move hand or foot.

"Therefore a superior man considers it necessary that the names he uses may be spoken appropriately, and also that what he speaks may be carried out appropriately. What the superior man requires is just that in his words there may be nothing incorrect."

When the Master went to Wei, Zan Yu acted as driver of his carriage. The Master observed, "How numerous are the people!" Yu said, "Since they are thus numerous, what more shall be done for them?" "Enrich them," was the reply. "And when they have been enriched, what more shall be done?" The Master said, "Teach them."

Tsze-kung asked, saying, "What do you say of a man who is loved by all the people of his neighbourhood?" The Master replied, "We may not for that accord our approval of him." "And what do you say of him who is hated by all the people of his neighbourhood?" The Master said, "We may not for that conclude that he is bad. It is better than either of these cases that the good in the neighbourhood love him, and the bad hate him."

The Master said, "The superior man is easy to serve and difficult to please. If you try to please him in any way which is not accordant with right, he will not be pleased. But in his employment of men, he uses them according to their capacity. The inferior man is difficult to serve, and easy to please. If you try to please him, though it be in a way which is not accordant with right, he may be pleased. But in his employment of men, he wishes them to be equal to everything."

Someone said, "What do you say concerning the principle that injury should be recompensed with kindness?" The Master said, "With what then will you recompense kindness? Recompense injury with justice and recompense kindness with kindness."

The Master said, "Alas! there is no one that knows me." Tsze-kung said, "What do you mean by thus saying—that no one knows you?" The Master replied, "I do not murmur against heaven. I do not grumble against men. My studies lie low, and my penetration rises high. But there is heaven;—that knows me!"

The Master said, "The determined scholar and the man of virtue will not seek to live at the expense of injuring their virtue. They will even sacrifice their lives to preserve their virtue complete."

The Master said, "If a man take no thought about what is distant, he will find sorrow near at hand.

"He who requires much from himself and little from others, will keep himself from being the object of resentment.

"The superior man is distressed by his want of ability. He is not distressed by men's not knowing him.

"The superior man is dignified, but does not wrangle. He is sociable, but not a partisan."

Tsze-kung asked, saying, "Is there one word which may serve as a rule of practice for all one's life?" The Master said, "Is not Reciprocity such a word? What you do not want done to yourself, do not do to others."

The Master said, "The object of the superior man is truth. Food is not his object. The superior man is anxious lest he should not get truth; he is not anxious lest poverty should come upon him.

"In teaching there should be no distinction of classes."

Tsze-chang asked Confucius about perfect virtue. Confucius said, "To be able to practise five things everywhere under heaven constitutes perfect virtue." He begged to ask what they were, and was told, "Gravity, generosity of soul, sincerity, earnestness, and kindness. If you are grave you will not be treated with disrespect. If you are generous, you will win all. If you are sincere, people will repose trust in you. If you are earnest, you will accomplish much. If you are kind, this will enable you to employ the services of others."

The Master said, "I would prefer not speaking." Tsze-kung said, "If you, Master, do not speak, what shall we, your disciples, have to record?" The Master said, "Does heaven speak? The four seasons pursue their courses, and all things are continually being produced, but does heaven say anything?"

Tsze-kung said, "Has the superior man his hatreds also?" The Master said, "He has his hatreds. He hates those who proclaim the evil of others. He hates the man who, being in a low station, slanders his superiors, he hates those who have valour merely, and are unobservant of propriety. He hates those who are forward and

determined, and, at the same time, of contracted understanding."

The Master then inquired, "Ts'ze, have you also your
hatreds?" Tsze-kung replied, "I hate those who pry
out matters, and ascribe the knowledge to their wisdom.
I hate those who are only not modest, and think that
they are valorous. I hate those who make known
secrets, and think that they are straightforward."

From the Great Learning

The Root of Everything

The ancients who wished to illustrate illustrous virtue throughout the kingdom first ordered well their
own states. Wishing to order well their states, they
first regulated their families. Wishing to regulate their
families they first cultivated their persons. Wishing to
cultivate their persons, they first rectified their hearts.
Wishing to rectify their hearts, they first sought to be
sincere in their thoughts. Wishing to be sincere in their
thoughts, they first extended to the utmost their knowledge. Such extension of knowledge lay in the investiga-
tion of things.

Things being investigated, knowledge became complete. Their knowledge being complete, their thoughts
were sincere. Their thoughts being sincere, their hearts
were then rectified. Their hearts being rectified, their
persons were cultivated. Their persons being cultivated,
their families were regulated. Their families being
regulated, their states were rightly governed. Their
states being rightly governed, the whole kingdom was
made tranquil and happy.

From the Son of Heaven down to the mass of the people, all must consider the cultivation of the person the root of everything besides.

From the Doctrine of the Steadfast Mean (Chung Yung)

The Middle Way

My master, the philosopher Ch'ang says: "Being without inclination to either side is called *Chung*; admitting of no change, is called *Yung*. By *Chung* is denoted the correct course to be pursued by all under heaven; by *Yung* is denoted the fixed principle regulating all under heaven. This work contains the law of the mind, which was handed down from one to another in the Confucian school till Tsze-sze committed it to writing and delivered it to Mencius."

What heaven has conferred is called the nature; and accordance with this nature is called the Path of Duty; the regulation of this path is called instruction. The path may not be left for an instant. If it could be left it would not be the path.

There is nothing more visible than what is secret, and nothing more manifest than what is minute. Therefore the superior man is watchful over himself, when he is alone.

While there are no stirrings of pleasure, anger, sorrow, or joy, the mind may be said to be in the state of equilibrium. When those feelings have been stirred, and they act in their due degree, there ensues what may be called the state of harmony. This equilibrium is the great root from which grow all the human actings in the world, and this harmony is the universal path which they all should pursue. Let the states of equilibrium and harmony exist in perfection, and a happy order will prevail throughout heaven and earth, and all things will be nourished and flourish.

The Master said, "Perfect is the virtue which is according to the Mean! Rare have they long been among the people, who could practise it!

"I know how it is that the path of the Mean is not walked in:—The knowing go beyond it, and the stupid do not come up to it. I know how it is that the path of the Mean is not understood:—The men of talents and virtue go beyond it, and the worthless do not come up to it.

"The superior man cultivates a friendly harmony, without being weak. How firm is he in his energy! He stands erect in the middle, without inclining to either side. How firm is he in his energy! When good principles prevail in the government of his country, he does not change from what he was in retirement.— How firm is he in his energy! When bad principles prevail in the country, he maintains his course to death without changing.—How firm is he in his energy!"

The Master said, "The path is not far from man. When men try to pursue a course which is far from the common indications of consciousness, this course cannot be considered the path. When one cultivates to the utmost the principles of his nature, and exercises them on the principle of reciprocity, he is not far from the path. What you do not like when done to yourself, do not do to others.

"In the way of the superior man there are four things, to not one of which have I as yet attained.—To serve my father, as I would require my son to serve me: to this I have not attained; to serve my prince, as I would require my minister to serve me: to this I have not attained; to serve my elder brother, as I would require my younger brother to serve me: to this I have not attained; to set the example in behaving to a friend, as I would require him to behave to me: to this I have not attained."

The superior man does what is proper to the station in which he is; he does not desire to go beyond this.

In a position of wealth and honour, he does what is proper to a position of wealth and honour. In a poor and low position, he does what is proper to a poor and low position. Situated among barbarous tribes, he does what is proper to a situation among barbarous tribes. In a position of sorrow and difficulty, he does what is proper to a position of sorrow and difficulty. The superior man can find himself in no situation in which he is not himself.

In a high situation, he does not treat with contempt his inferiors. In a low situation, he does not court the favour of his superiors. He rectifies himself, and seeks for nothing from others, so that he has no dissatisfactions. He does not murmur against heaven, nor grumble against men.

Thus it is that the superior man is quiet and calm, waiting for the appointments of heaven, while the inferior man walks in dangerous paths, looking for lucky occurrences.

The duke Ai asked about government.

The Master said, "Let there be the men and the government will flourish; but without the men, their government decays and ceases. With the right men the growth of government is rapid, just as vegetation is rapid in the earth; and moreover their government might be called an easily-growing rush. Therefore the administration of government lies in getting proper men.

"Benevolence is the characteristic element of humanity, and the great exercise of it is in loving relatives. Righteousness is the accordance of actions with what is right, and the great exercise of it is in honouring the worthy. The decreasing measures of the love due to relatives, and the steps in the honour due to the worthy, are produced by the principle of propriety."

The Master said, "To be fond of learning is to be near to knowledge. To practise with vigour is to be near to magnanimity. To possess the feeling of shame is to be near to energy. He who knows these three things, knows how to cultivate his own character. Knowing how to cultivate his own character, he knows how to govern other men. Knowing how to govern other men, he knows how to govern the kingdom with all its states and families.

"In all things success depends on previous preparation, and without such previous preparation there is sure to be failure. If what is to be spoken be previously determined, there will be no stumbling. If affairs be previously determined, there will be no difficulty with them. If one's actions have been previously determined, there will be no sorrow in connexion with them. If principles of conduct have been previously determined, the practice of them will be inexhaustible.

"Sincerity is the way of heaven. The attainment of sincerity is the way of men. He who possesses sincerity is he who, without an effort, hits what is right, and apprehends without the exercise of thought;—he is the sage who naturally and easily embodies the right way. He who attains to sincerity is he who chooses what is good, and firmly holds it fast. To this attainment there

are requisite the extensive study of what is good, accurate inquiry about it, careful reflection on it, the
clear discrimination of it, and the earnest practice of it."

The heaven now before us is only this bright shining
spot; but when viewed in its inexhaustible extent, the
sun, moon, stars, and constellations of the zodiac are
suspended in it, and all things are overspread by it.
The earth before us is but a handful of soil; but when
regarded in its breadth and thickness, it sustains mountains like the Hwa and the Yo, without feeling their
weight, and contains the rivers and seas, without their
leaking away. The mountain now before us appears
only a stone; but when contemplated in all the vastness
of its size, we see how the grass and trees are produced on it, and birds and beasts dwell on it, and
precious things which men treasure up are found on it.
The water now before us appears but a ladleful; yet
extending our view to its unfathomable depths, the
largest tortoises, iguanas, iguanodons, dragons, fishes,
and turtles are produced in them, articles of value and
sources of wealth abound in them.

All things are nourished together without their injuring one another. The courses of the seasons, and of
the sun and moon, are pursued without any collision
among them. The smaller energies are like river currents; the greater energies are seen in mighty transformations. It is this which makes heaven and earth so
great.

From the Works of Mencius

The Function of Government

King Hwuy of Leang said, "Small as my virtue is, in the government of my kingdom I do indeed exert my mind to the utmost. On examining the government of the neighbouring kingdoms, I do not find that there is any prince who employs his mind as I do. And yet the people of the neighbouring kingdoms do not decrease, nor do my people increase. How is this?"

Mencius replied, "If the seasons of husbandry be not interfered with, the grain will be more than can be eaten. If close nets are not allowed to enter the pools and ponds, the fishes and turtles will be more than can be consumed. If the axes and bills enter the hills and forests only at the proper time, the wood will be more than can be used. When the grain and fish and turtles are more than can be eaten, and there is more wood than can be used, this enables the people to nourish their living and bury their dead, without any feeling against any. This condition, in which the people nourish their living and bury their dead without any feeling against any, is the first step of royal government.

"Let mulberry trees be planted about the homesteads and persons of fifty years may be clothed with silk. In keeping fowls, pigs, dogs, and swine, let not their times of breeding be neglected, and persons of seventy years may eat flesh. Let there not be taken away the time that is proper for the cultivation of the farm and the family of several mouths that is supported by it shall not suffer from hunger. Let careful attention he paid to education in schools, inculcating in it especially the filial and fraternal duties, and grey-haired men will not be seen upon the roads, carrying burdens on their backs or on their heads. It never has been that the ruler of a state where such results were seen,—persons of seventy wearing silk and eating flesh, and the black-haired people suffering neither from hunger nor cold, —did not attain to the imperial dignity.

"Your dogs and swine eat the food of men, and you do not know to make any restrictive arrangements. There are people dying from famine on the roads, and you do not know to issue the stores of your granaries for them. When people die, you say, 'It is not owing to me; it is owing to the year.' In what does this differ from stabbing a man and killing him, and then saying, 'It was not I; it was the weapon'? Let your Majesty cease to lay the blame on the year, and instantly from all the empire the people will come to you.

"In your kitchen there is fat meat; in your stables there are fat horses. But your people have the look of hunger, and on the wilds there are those who have died of famine. This is leading on beasts to devour men. Beasts devour one another, and men hate them for doing so. When a prince, being the parent of his people, administers his government so as to be chargeable with leading on beasts to devour men, where is that parental relation to the people?

"You collect your equipments of war, endanger your soldiers and officers, and excite the resentment of the other princes;—do these things cause you pleasure in your mind?"

The king replied, "No. How should I derive pleasure from these things? My object in them is to seek for what I greatly desire."

Mencius said, "May I hear from you what it is that you greatly desire?" The king laughed and did not speak. Mencius resumed, "Are you led to desire it, because you have not enough of rich and sweet food for your mouth? Or because you have not enough of light and warm clothing for your body? Or because you have not enough of beautifully coloured objects to delight your eyes? Of because you have not voices and tones enough to please your ears? Or because you have not enough of attendants and favourites to stand before you and receive your orders? Your Majesty's various officers are sufficient to supply you with those things. How can your Majesty be led to entertain such a desire on account of them?" "No," said the king; "my desire is not on account of them." Mencius added, "Then, what your Majesty greatly desires may be known. You wish to enlarge your territories, to have Ts'in and Ts'oo wait at your court, to ule the Middle Kingdom, and to attract to you the barbarous tribes that surround it. But to do what you do to seek for what you desire, is like climbing a tree to seek for fish."

The king said, "Is it so bad as that?" "It is even worse," was the reply. "If you climb a tree to seek for fish, although you do not get the fish, you will not suffer any subsequent calamity. But if you do what you do to seek for what you desire, doing it moreover with all your heart, you will assuredly afterwards meet with calamities.

"Now, if your Majesty will institute a government whose action shall all be benevolent, this will cause all the officers in the empire to wish to stand in your Majesty's court, and the farmers all to wish to plough in your Majesty's fields, and the merchants, both travelling and stationary, all to wish to store their goods in your Majesty's market-places, and travelling strangers all to wish to make their tours on your Majesty's roads, and all throughout the empire who feel aggrieved by their rulers to wish to come and complain to your

Majesty. And when they are so bent, who will be able to keep them back?"

Mencius said, "He who, using force, makes a pretence to benevolence, is the leader of the princes. A leader of the princes requires a large kingdom. He who, using virtue, practises benevolence—is the sovereign of the empire. To become the sovereign of the empire, a prince need not wait for a large kingdom. T'ang did it with only seventy le, and king Wan with only a hundred.

"When one by force subdues men, they do not submit to him in heart. They submit because their strength is not adequate to resist. When one subdues men by virtue, in their hearts' core they are pleased, and sincerely submit."

Division of Labour

Ch'in Seang, having an interview with Mencius, related: "The prince of T'ang is indeed a worthy prince. He has not yet heard, however, the real doctrines of antiquity. Now, wise and able princes should cultivate the ground equally and along with their people, and eat the fruit of their labour. They should prepare their own meals, morning and evening, while at the same time they carry on their government. But now, the prince of T'ang has his granaries, treasuries, and arsenals, which is an oppressing of the people to nourish himself.—How can he be deemed a real worthy prince?"

Mencius said, "I suppose that Heu Hing sows grain and eats the produce. Is it not so?" "It is so," was the answer. "I suppose also he weaves cloth, and wears his own manufacture. Is it not so?" "No. Heu wears clothes of haircloth." "Does he wear a cap?" "He wears a cap." "What kind of cap?" "A plain cap." "Is it woven by himself?" "No. He gets it in exchange for grain." "Why does Heu not weave it himself?" "That would injure his husbandry." "Does Heu cook his food in boilers and earthen-ware pans, and does he plough with an iron share?" "Yes." "Does he make those articles himself?" "No. He gets them in exchange for grain."

Mencius then said, "The getting those various articles in exchange for grain is not oppressive to the potter and the founder, and the potter and the founder in their turn, in exchanging their various articles for grain, are not oppressive to the husbandman. How should such a thing be supposed? And moreover, why does not Heu act the potter and founder, supplying himself with the articles which he uses solely from his own establishment? Why does he go confusedly dealing and exchanging with the handicraftsmen? Why does he not spare himself so much trouble?" Ch'in Seang replied, "The business of the handicraftsman can by no means be carried on along with the business of husbandry."

Mencius resumed, "Then, is it the government of the empire which alone can be carried on along with the practice of husbandry? Great men have their proper business, and little men have their proper business. Moreover, in the case of any single individual, whatever articles he can require are ready to his hand, being produced by the various handicraftsmen:—if he must first make them for his own use, this way of doing would keep the whole empire running about upon the roads. Hence, there is the saying, 'Some labour with their minds, and some labour with their strength. Those who labour with their minds govern others; those who labour with their strength are governed by others. Those who are governed by others support them; those who govern others are supported by them.' This is a principle universally recognized.

"It is the nature of things to be of unequal quality. Some are twice, some five times, some ten times, some a hundred times, some a thousand times, some ten thousand times as valuable as others. If you reduce them all to the same standard, that must throw the empire into confusion."

The Flood

In the time of Yaou, the waters, flowing out of their channels, inundated the Middle Kingdom. Snakes and dragons occupied it, and the people had no place where they could settle themselves. In the low grounds they made nests for themselves, and in the high grounds they made caves. It is said in the Book of History, "The waters in their wild course warned me." Those "waters in their wild course" were the waters of the great inundation.

Shun employed Yu to reduce the waters to order. Yu dug open their obstructed channels, and conducted them to the sea. He drove away the snakes and dragons, and forced them into the grassy marshes. On this, the waters pursued their course through the country, even the waters of the Keang, the Hwae, the Ho, and the Han, and the dangers and obstructions which they had occasioned were removed. The birds and beasts which had injured the people also disappeared, and after this men found the plains available for them, and occupied them.

The Root of the State

Mencius said, "People have this common saying,— 'The empire, the state, the family.' The root of the empire is in the state. The root of the state is in the family. The root of the family is in the person of its head.

"There was a boy singing,

" 'When the water of the Ts'ang-lang is clear,
It does to wash the strings of my cap;
When the water of the Ts'ang-lang is muddy,
It does to wash my feet.'

"Confucius said, 'Hear what he sings, my children. When clear, then he will wash his cap-strings, and when muddy, he will wash his feet with it. This different application is brought by the water on itself.'

"A man must first despise himself, and then others will despise him. A family must first destroy itself, and then others will destroy it. A kingdom must first smite itself, and then others will smite it."

Mencius said, "With those who do violence to themselves, it is impossible to speak. With those who throw themselves away, it is impossible to do anything. To disown in his conversation propriety and righteousness, is what we mean by doing violence to one's self. To say—'I am not able to dwell in benevolence or pursue the path of righteousness,' is what we mean by throwing one's self away.

"Benevolence is the tranquil habitation of man, and righteousness is his straight path.

"Alas for them, who leave the tranquil dwelling empty, and do not reside in it, and who abandon the right path and do not pursue it!"

The Man with the Heart of a Child

Acts of propriety which are not really proper, and acts of righteousness which are not really righteous, the great man does not do.

Those who keep the Mean, train up those who do

not, and those who have abilities, train up those who have not, and hence men rejoice in having fathers and elder brothers who are possessed of virtue and talent. If they who keep the Mean spurn those who do not, and they who have abilities spurn those who have not, then the space between them—those so gifted and the ungifted—will not admit an inch.

Men must be decided on what they will not do, and then they are able to act with vigour in what they ought to do.

The great man does not think beforehand of his words that they may be sincere, nor of his actions that they may be resolute;—he simply speaks and does what is right.

The great man is he who does not lose his child's-heart.

That whereby man differs from the lower animals is but small. The mass of people cast it away, while superior men preserve it.

Of Friendships and Gifts

Wan Chang asked Mencius saying, "I venture to ask the principles of friendship." Mencius replied, "Friendship should be maintained without any presumption on the ground of one's superior age, or station, or the circumstances of his relatives. Friendship with a man is friendship with his virtue, and does not admit of assumptions of superiority.

"Respect shown by inferiors to superiors is called giving to the noble the observance due to rank. Respect shown by superiors to inferiors is called giving honour to talents and virtue. The rightness in each case is the same."

Man's Nature Is Good

The tendency of man's nature to good is like the tendency of water to flow downwards. There are none but have this tendency to good, just as all water flows downwards.

Now by striking water and causing it to leap up, you may make it go over your forehead, and, by damming and leading it, you may force it up a hill;— but are such movements according to the nature of water? It is the force applied which causes them. When men are made to do what is not good, their nature is dealt with in this way.

In good years the children of the people are most of them good, while in bad years the most of them abandon themselves to evil. It is not owing to their natural powers conferred by heaven that they are thus different. The abandonment is owing to the circumstances through which they allow their minds to be ensnared and drowned in evil.

All things which are the same in kind are like to one another;—why should we doubt in regard to man, as if he were a solitary exception to this? The sage and we are the same in kind.

The trees of the New mountain were once beautiful. Being situated, however, in the borders of a large state, they were hewn down with axes and bills;—and could they retain their beauty? Still through the activity of the vegetative life day and night, and the nourishing influence of the rain and dew, they were not without buds and sprouts springing forward, but then came the cattle and goats and browsed upon them. To these things is owing the bare and stript appearance of the mountain, which when people see, they think it was never finely wooded. But is this the nature of the mountain?

And so also of what properly belongs to man;—shall it be said that the mind of any man was without benevolence and righteousness? The way in which a man loses his proper goodness of mind is like the way in which the trees are denuded by axes and bills. Hewn down day after day, can it—the mind—retain its beauty? But there is a development of its life day and night, and in the calm air of the morning, just between night and day, the mind feels in a degree those desires and aversions which are proper to humanity, but the feeling is not strong, and it is fettered and destroyed by what takes place during the day. This fettering taking place again and again, the restorative influence of the night is not sufficient to preserve the proper goodness of the mind; and when this proves insufficient for that purpose, the nature becomes not much different from that of the irrational animals, which when people see, they think that it never had those powers which I assert. But does this condition represent the feelings proper to humanity?

Now chess-playing is but a small art, but without his whole mind being given, and his will bent to it, a man cannot succeed at it. Chess Ts'ew is the best chess-player in all the kingdom. Suppose that he is teaching two men to play.—The one gives to the subject his whole mind and bends to it all his will, doing nothing but listening to Chess Ts'ew. The other, although he seems to be listening to him, has his whole mind running on a swan which he thinks is approaching, and wishes to bend his bow, adjust the string to the arrow, and shoot it. Although he is learning along with the other, he does not come up to him. Why?—because his intelligence is not equal? Not so.

I like fish and I also like bear's paws. If I cannot have the two together, I will let the fish go, and take the bear's paws. So, I like life, and I also like righteousness. If I cannot keep the two together, I will let life go and choose righteousness.

There are cases when men by a certain course might preserve life, and they do not employ it; when by certain things they might avoid danger, and they will not do them.

Therefore, men have that which they like more than life, and that which they dislike more than death. They are not men of distinguished talents and virtue only who have this mental nature. All men have it; what belongs to such men is simply that they do not lose it.

The disciple Kung-too said, "All are equally men, but some are great men, and some are little men;—how is this?" Mencius replied, "Those who follow that part of themselves which is great are great men; those who follow that part which is little are little men. To the mind belongs the office of thinking. By thinking, it gets the right view of things; by neglecting to think, it fails to do this. Let a man first stand fast in the supremacy of the nobler part of his constitution, and the inferior part will not be able to take it from him. It is simply this which makes the great man."

Convention and Emergency

A man of Jin asked the disciple Uh-loo, saying, "Is an observance of the rules of propriety in regard to eating, or the eating, the more important?" The answer was, "The observance of the rules of propriety is the more important."

"Is the gratifying the appetite of sex, or the doing so only according to the rules of propriety, the more important?" The answer again was, "The observance of the rules of propriety in the matter is the more important."

The man pursued, "If the result of eating only according to the rules of propriety will be death by starvation, while by disregarding those rules we may get food, must they still be observed in such a case? If according to the rule that he shall go in person to meet his wife a man cannot get married, while by disregarding that rule he may get married, must he still observe the rule in such a case?"

Uh-loo was unable to reply to these questions, and the next day he went to Tsow, and told them to Mencius. Mencius said, "Go and answer him thus, 'If, by twisting your elder brother's arm, and snatching from him what he is eating, you can get food for yourself, while, if you do not do so, you will not get anything to eat, will you so twist his arm? If by getting over your neighbour's wall, and dragging away his virgin daughter, you can get a wife, while if you do not do so, you will not be able to get a wife, will you so drag her away?'"

All Things Are Complete in Us

He who has exhausted all his mental constitution knows his nature. Knowing his nature, he knows heaven. To preserve one's mental constitution, and nourish one's nature, is the way to serve heaven.

There is an appointment for everything. A man should receive submissively what may be correctly ascribed thereto. Therefore, he who has the true idea of what is heaven's appointment will not stand beneath a precipitous wall. Death sustained in the discharge of one's duties may correctly be ascribed to the appointment of heaven. Death under handcuffs and fetters cannot correctly be so ascribed.

All things are complete in us.

If one acts with a vigorous effort at the law of reciprocity, when he seeks for the realization of perfect virtue, nothing can be closer than his approximation to it.

Let a man not do what his own sense of righteousness tells him not to do, and let him not desire what his sense of righteousness tells him not to desire;—to act thus is all he has to do.

Men who are possessed of intelligent virtue and prudence in affairs will generally be found to have been in sickness and troubles. They are the friendless minister and concubine's son, who keep their hearts under a sense of peril, and use deep precautions against calamity. On this account they become distinguished for their intelligence.

To stand in the centre of the empire, and tranquillize the people within the four seas;—the superior man delights in this, but the highest enjoyment of his nature is not here.

What belong by his nature to the superior man are benevolence, righteousness, propriety, and knowledge. These are rooted in his heart; their growth and manifestation are a mild harmony appearing in the countenance, a rich fullness in the back, and the character imparted to the four limbs. Those limbs understand to arrange themselves, without being told.

There are men who say—"I am skilful at marshalling troops, I am skilful at conducting a battle!"—They are great criminals. If the sovereign of a state love benevolence, he will have no enemy in the empire.

If men of virtue and ability be not confided in, a state will become empty and void. Without the rules of propriety and distinctions of right, the high and the low will be thrown into confusion. Without the great principles of government and their various business, there will not be wealth sufficient for the expenditure.

Words which are simple, while their meaning is far-reaching, are good words. Principles which, as held, are compendious, while their application is extensive, are good principles. The principle which the superior man holds is that of personal cultivation, but the empire is thereby tranquillized. The disease of men is this:— that they neglect their own fields, and go to weed the fields of others, and that what they require from others is great, while what they lay upon themselves is light.

From the Book of Filial Piety (The Hsiao King)

The Three Powers

On hearing what Confucius said about filial duty, Tseng Tze remarked: "How great is the use of filial duty!" Here Confucius continued: "Filial duty is the constant doctrine of heaven, the natural righteousness of earth, and the practical duty of man. Every member of the community ought to observe it with the greatest care. We do what is dictated by heaven and what is good for the general public in order to organize the community. On this account our education is wide-spread, though it is not compulsory, and our government is sound, though it is not rigorous."

The Question of Remonstrance

Tseng Tze said: "I have heard all that you said about parental love, filial love, reverence to elders, how to treat parents every day, and how to please them by making oneself known for good conduct; and now I will venture to ask you whether it is filial that a son should obey every command of his father, whether right or wrong?"

"What do you say?—what do you say?" replied Confucius. "Once upon a time there was a certain emperor who would have lost his empire through his wickedness but that he had seven good ministers who often checked his illegal actions by strong protests; there was also a feudal baron who would have lost his feudal estate through wantonness, but for the fact that he had five good men who often made strong remonstrances to him; and there was also a statesman who would have brought frightful calamity upon his family, but for the fact that he had three good servants who often strongly advised him not to do what he ought not.

"If a man has a good friend to resist him in doing bad actions, he will have his reputation preserved; so if a father has a son to resist his wrong commands, he will be saved from committing serious faults.

"When the command is wrong, a son should resist his father, and a minister should resist his august master.

"The maxim is, 'Resist when wrongly commanded.' Hence how can he be called filial who obeys his father when he is commanded to do wrong?"

THE TAOIST

The Way

Great movements seldom find their expressions in single and isolated exponents or in complete agreement between those who give them voice. In India the fertile period of Gautama Buddha was also the time of Mahavira, the Jina; in Israel Hillel, the rabbi of Judaism, and Jesus of Nazareth, the rejected Jew who became a prototype for the Christian, were contemporaries; in China the time of religious awakening which produced Confucius, the great realist and moral philosopher who "preferred not speaking" about things unseen, was also marked by the teachings of Lao Tze, the mystic, who spoke chiefly of the unseen and intangible.

There is little that is trustworthy in the personal history of the latter, founder of the religion known as Taoism. Lao Tze was not his real name, but an appellation which may be translated either "Old Boy" or "Old Philosopher." The *Shan Hsien Chwan* (*Account of Spirits and Immortals*), written by Ko Hung in the fourth century A.D., says that he was miraculously conceived and that his mother carried him in her womb for seventy-two years, so that when he was born his hair was already white with age. Thus he explains the name "Old Boy." On the other hand the *Kia Yu* (*Narratives of the Confucian School*), compiled in the third century A.D. from documents said to have been preserved by descendants of Confucius, and a short biography of Lao Tze written by Sze-ma Ch'ien about A.D. 100 used "Old Philosopher" or "Venerable Philosopher" and intimated that the term, implying respect, was first used by Confucius.

The real name of the "Venerable Philosopher" was Li Uhr. He was a native of the state of Ch'u in Honan Province, and librarian, recorder, and historiographer at the court of Chau. The date of his birth is uncertain, but it was apparently 604 B.C. If this is accurate he was fifty-three years old when Confucius was born.

Whatever the exact date, he was certainly a contemporary of Confucius and an old man when Master Kung began his teaching, for both Taoist and Confucianist texts refer to meetings of the two sages. Indeed one of the most entertaining philosophic feuds in history is reflected by frequent references in late Taoist literature to Confucius and his followers and their confusion in the face of Taoist principles which they seem ever incapable of understanding. (See "Confucius at the Cataract," p. 566.) Yet there is always respectful affection behind the sly digs which Taoism confers on Confucianism, and above all urbanity. And the Confucianist references invariably show an awe and admiration for the Venerable Philosopher which never varies.

One meeting between the two is reported when Confucius was thirty-four years old. When he spoke to Lao Tze about his desire to increase respect for the ancient sages of China, the latter said to the young man, "The men about whom you talk are dead, and their bones are dust. Put away your proud airs and many desires."

When Confucius asked about Tao, saying that he had read many books but could not find it, Lao Tze replied, "If the Tao could be offered to men, who would not wish to offer it to his prince? If it could be presented to men, who would not wish to present it to his parents? If it could be announced to men, who would not wish to announce it to his brethren? If it could be transmitted to men, who would not wish to transmit it to his children? Why do you not obtain it? This is the reason: Because you do not give it an asylum in your heart."

When Confucius returned to his disciples in some confusion, one of them asked him for a report on the visit. At a loss for words, Kung replied: "I know how the birds fly, how the fishes swim, how animals run. But there is the Dragon. I cannot tell how it mounts on the wind through the clouds and flies through heaven. Today I have seen the Dragon." (For another account of what is apparently this same visit, see "Confucius and Lao Tze," p. 561.)

How Lao Tze, at a very advanced age, made his exit from public life in China, is told by Sze-ma Ch'ien. According to this account the old man, seeing corruption and decay at court, decided to leave his state. Coming to the city gates he was met by the gate warden, Yin Hsi, who, grieving over the philosopher's departure, begged him to leave his wisdom behind him. Thus importuned, Lao Tze stopped long enough to write an abstruse document of about five thousand characters and departed, not to be heard from again. The book which he left behind him, the *Tao-Te King*, has become the basic scripture of Taoism.

What does the title mean? The word *Te* is clearly and simply "Virtue." Translation of the word *Tao*, the basic term of the religion which Lao Tze founded, has been the subject of discussion among Western scholars for many years. It is perhaps most frequently rendered (when translated at all) as "the Way" or "the Path." It has also been translated as "reason," "nature," "God," and as "the word," in the sense of *Logos*. Chinese translations of the Gospel of John render the first verse, "In the beginning was the *Tao*, and the *Tao* was with God, and the *Tao* was God." Thus one might say that *Tao-Te King* means "Canon of Reason-Path-Word-Nature-God and Virtue."

But the apparent fact is that there is no one English word or phrase which will exactly translate the word *Tao* in all its uses, since it seems to have a number of closely interrelated and always obscure meanings. Probably it is better not to attempt a translation. Each reader must make his own interpretation according to his own perception whenever he meets the word in a Taoist text, evaluating it by the context in which it occurs. He will find plenty of occasions for exercising his perception in the *Tao-Te King*.

By this strangely mystical work, which often expresses its meanings in paradoxes, we are told that "the Tao which can be expressed is not the eternal Tao." Yet there are many attempts to express it. It is "infinite profundity." It "seems to be the origin of all things." It "looks like the predecessor of nature." It is "the mystic mother." It "seems ever to endure. In use it can never be exhausted." It is a stabilizing force, for "where Tao is equilibrium is. When Tao is lost, out come all the differences in things." It is "invisible and intangible, yet there are forms . . . substance . . . essence in it." It is "inherent and natural, motionless and fathomless. It stands alone and never changes, pervades everywhere." It "existed before heaven and earth." It is "supreme." Heaven follows its laws, but it "follows the laws of its intrinsic nature" (in other words its Tao). "By it all things came into being and it does not reject them." Yet "it does not claim mastery over them." (In other words, there seems to be a certain measure of free will.) It "is ever inactive, yet there is nothing that it does not do." It is "the nameless simplicity." "In progress it seems regressive, in straightness, rugged." It is "the eternal." The great way of Tao "is very plain and easy." "Tao is the source of all things, the treasure of good men, and the sustainer of bad men." (This is reminiscent of Isaiah's statement, attributing both good and evil to Jehovah.) "As Tao is to the world, so are streams and valleys to rivers and seas." It "does not contend, yet it surely wins the victory." It "does not speak, yet it surely responds." It "does not call, yet all things come of their own accord." It "shows no partiality."

Obviously in these characterizations the writer is thinking of the primary universal principle, of harmony with that universal principle, and of the way or path to that harmony. This principle, this harmony, this ability to achieve harmony, is, in Taoist doctrine, innate in all men. That innateness, that nature, that ability to find the way, that living "word" (as St. John used the term) is man's Tao. But just as the *Upanishads* found it impossible to express all of the attributes of Brahma by a single name (therefore the Upanishadic explanation that the names of the gods are but designations of the powers of Brahma), so is it impossible to translate Tao in all its uses by one English word.

In one passage of the *Tao-Te King* these phrases are used, "the Tao of heaven," "the Tao of man," "the Tao of the sage," and "Tao," in such a way that if translation were attempted several terms would have to be used.

The passage, as rendered by Ch'u Ta-Kao (whose translation is used in this volume) is as follows: "The Tao of heaven is to lessen the redundant and fill up the insufficient. The Tao of man, on the contrary, is to take from the insufficient and give to the redundant. Who can take from the redundant and give to the insuffi-

cient? Only he who has Tao. . . . The Tao of the sage
acts, but never contends."

In evaluating this passage it must be remembered
that the Chinese word Tien (Heaven) does not mean
the paradise to which righteous men's souls obtain after
death in Christian theology, but the divine order which
rules the universe—perhaps Tao itself, in one of its
meanings. With this in mind I venture a statement of
what this passage means to me, changing the word
"Heaven" to what I think is meant in this context, and
italicizing the words which designate what seem to
me to be the meanings of Tao here.

"The *nature* of the universal divine order is to lessen
the redundant and fill up the insufficient. The *nature* of
man, on the contrary, is to take from the insufficient
and give to the redundant. Who can take from the redundant and give to the insufficient? Only he who *is in
harmony with the divine order*. . . . The *divine force
which is within* the sage (*due to the harmony which
he has achieved with the primary universal principle*)
acts but never contends."

This is not an attempt to revise Mr. Ch'u's translation, which I am far from capable of doing, but only
to demonstrate the one way in which true and useful
meaning may be found in the conception of Tao
through reading Taoist texts. Perhaps the passage will
mean other things to other readers. For the Tao of the
word Tao is profound and obscure, and its meaning
dependent upon the Tao of the perceiver!

In the conception of Tao, then, we have Lao Tze's
approach to an expression of the universal creative and
ruling force which Jews and Christians have personalized as Jehovah, Parsis as Ahura Mazda, and Mohammedans as Allah. Hindus have called it the Atman and
Brahman. Gautama said that questions about it "tended

not to edification." Mahavira by implication denied its existence. Confucius "preferred not speaking."

What of duties of men in the world which Tao pervades? What of the way of life of the good Taoist, as the founder of the religion conceived it? Again we find the answers in the *Tao-Te King*.

The man of Tao "keeps what is within himself" (in other words, lets his communication be yea, yea, and nay, nay) "for he who talks more is sooner exhausted." He "is not self-interested." (In other words, as St. Paul put it, he does not count life dear unto himself.) Like water he "stays in places others despise." His heart is "deep." He "keeps on good terms with men." He "abides by good order." In business he "takes things easy." He "keeps the soul concentrated from straying." He "makes provision for the stomach and not for the eye." (In other words, he does not bother with the formal ceremonials which Confucius honoured.) He "loves the world as he does his own person" (in other words, his neighbour as himself). "He is subtle, penetrating, and profound." He is simple, "like an infant." He is cautious, modest, yielding. He "keeps to the state of perfect peace." He is humble, and thus "he remains entire." He does not "display himself," nor "praise himself." He "knows honour, yet keeps to humility." He "avoids excess, extravagance, and indulgence." He does not "force the world with arms," for "they are implements of ill omen. They are not implements for the man of Tao." He "aims only at carrying out relief, and does not venture to force his power upon others." He "knows where to stop." He "knows himself." He "conquers himself." He "knows others." He does not "deviate from his proper place." (Very Confucianist, this.) He is "free from desire." (Very Buddhist, this.) He "makes the self of the people his self." (Very Christian, this.) He acts to the good or to the bad "with goodness," and to the faithful or the faithless "with faith." He "follows the eternal." He makes no distinction between "male and female, yet he has sexual development." He "is in the perfect harmony." He "loves quietude." He "makes no fuss." "In ruling men and serving heaven" he "uses only moderation." He "regards the small as great" and "the few as many." He has "three treasures, love, moderation, and not venturing to go ahead of the world." He "returns love for great hatred" (even as the Buddha, less than a century after Lao Tze, and Christ, six hundred years later, admonished the world to do).

These, then, are the generalities of the Taoist life, as Lao Tze laid them down twenty-five hundred years ago, and there are few admonitions in his teachings which are more specific than these. Just as many of the principles are essentially those which Christ later enunciated, so is the enunciation of them always in generalities, as were most of Christ's admonitions. To Lao Tze as to Christ, righteousness was a matter of the spirit. Reiteration of specific laws was unnecessary to one who "had Tao" (or, as Christ would have put it, who knew God) and ineffective to one who did not.

If we may state it as a premise that a religious attitude consists of three related parts—a spiritual approach to the divine principle of the universe (Tao, Brahma, God), ethical human conduct, and an attitude towards one's self—then we may say that Lao Tze and Confucius, contemporaries in China, were the perfect complements to each other, each making an approach to a complete religion from opposite directions. To Confucius human conduct must be made righteous, and then man's relation to God and the universe would take care of itself. To Lao Tze man must establish himself in harmony with the universal principle (or Tao, through his own Tao) and righteous human conduct would follow through its own intrinsic nature.

Two centuries later than Lao Tze, Chuang Tze greatly furthered the spread of Taoism through teaching it in terms and idioms which were much more understandable than those of the *Tao-Te King*. Writing in parables or fables, he gave the world some of the most delightful and at the same time profound stories in any literature.

As is so often the tragic case of organized religions, Taoism has deteriorated sadly since the days of its founding. To-day it is demeaned by polytheism, witchcraft, demonolatry, and a degenerate papacy far removed from the purity of Lao Tze's conception. Its followers are estimated as numbering about 43,000,000.

Yet the *Tao-Te King* and the works of Chuang Tze remain and no amount of deterioration in the Taoist church can dim their brightness, any more than the failures justly chargeable to the Jewish congregation and the Christian Church can detract from the meaning of the great Hebrew prophets and Jesus, or Indian idolatry and polytheism can diminish the glory of the *Rig-Veda*, the *Upanishads*, and the *Bhagavad Gita*.

TAOIST SCRIPTURES

From the Tao-Te King

The Mother of All Things

The Tao that can be expressed is not the eternal Tao;
The name that can be defined is not the unchanging
name.
Non-existence is called the antecedent of heaven and
earth;
Existence is the mother of all things.
From eternal non-existence, therefore, we serenely observe the mysterious beginning of the universe;
From eternal existence we clearly see the apparent distinctions.
These two are the same in source and become different
when manifested.
This sameness is called profundity. Infinite profundity
is the gate whence comes the beginning of all parts
of the universe.

Government by Non-Action

Not exalting the worthy keeps the people from emula-
tion. Not valuing rare things keeps them from theft.
Not showing what is desirable keeps their hearts from
confusion. Therefore the sage rules

By emptying their hearts,
Filling their stomachs,
Weakening their ambitions
And strengthening their bones.

He always keeps them from knowing what is evil and

desiring what is good; thus he gives the crafty ones no chance to act. He governs by non-action; consequently there is nothing un-governed.

The Highest Goodness

The highest goodness is like water. Water is beneficent to all things but does not contend. It stays in places which others despise. Therefore it is near Tao.

In dwelling, think it a good place to live;
In feeling, make the heart deep;
In friendship, keep on good terms with men;
In words, have confidence;
In ruling, abide by good order;
In business, take things easy;
In motion, make use of the opportunity.
Since there is no contention, there is no blame.

Letting Alone

Holding and keeping a thing to the very full—it is better to leave it alone;
Handling and sharpening a blade—it cannot be long sustained;
When gold and jade fill the hall, no one can protect them;
Wealth and honour with pride bring with them destruction:
To have accomplished merit and acquired fame, then retire—
This is the Tao of heaven.

Favour and Disgrace

"Favour and disgrace are like fear; fortune and disaster are like our body."

What does it mean by "Favour and disgrace are like
fear"? Favour is in a higher place, and disgrace in a
lower place. When you win them you are like being
in fear, and when you lose them you are also like being
in fear. So favour and disgrace are like fear.

What does it mean by "Fortune and disaster are
like our body"? We have fortune and disaster because
we have a body. When we have no body, how can
fortune or disaster befall us?

Therefore he who regards the world as he does the
fortune of his own body can govern the world. He who
loves the world as he does his own body can be entrusted with the world.

The Perfect Man of Tao

In old times the perfect man of Tao was subtle, penetrating and so profound that he can hardly be understood. Because he cannot be understood, I shall endeavour to picture him:

He is cautious, like one who crosses a stream in
winter;
He is hesitating, like one who fears his neighbours;
He is modest, like one who is a guest;
He is yielding. like ice that is going to melt;
He is simple, like wood that is not yet wrought;
He is vacant, like valleys that are hollow;
He is dim, like water that is turbid.

For who is able to purify the dark till it becomes
    slowly light?
Who is able to calm the turbid till it slowly clears?
Who is able to quicken the stagnant till it slowly makes
    progress?
He who follows these principles does not desire
    fullness.
Because he is not full, therefore when he becomes
    decayed he can renew.

Do Away with Learning

Do away with learning, and grief will not be known.
Do away with sageness and eject wisdom, and the
    people will be more benefited a hundred times.
Do away with benevolence and eject righteousness, and
    the people will return to filial duty and parental
    love.
Do away with artifice and eject gains, and there will be
    no robbers and thieves.
These four, if we consider them as culture, are not
    sufficient.
Therefore let there be what the people can resort to:
Appear in plainness and hold to simplicity;
Restrain selfishness and curtail desires.

What Difference Between Yea and Nay?

Between yea and nay, how much difference is there?
Between good and evil, how much difference is there?
What are feared by others we must fear;
Vastly are they unlimited!
The people in general are so happy as if enjoying a
    great feast,
Or, as going up a tower in spring.

I alone am tranquil, and have made no signs,
Like a baby who is yet unable to smile;
Forlorn as if I had no home to go to.
Others all have more than enough,
And I alone seem to be in want.
Possibly mine is the mind of a fool,
Which is so ignorant!
The vulgar are bright,
And I alone seem to be dull.
The vulgar are discriminative, and I alone seem to be
        blunt.

I am negligent as if being obscure;
Drifting, as if being attached to nothing.
The people in general all have something to do,
And I alone seem to be impractical and awkward.
I alone am different from others.
But I value seeking sustenance from the Mother.

Be Humble

"Be humble, and you will remain entire."
Be bent, and you will remain straight.
Be vacant, and you will remain full.
Be worn, and you will remain new.
He who has little will receive.
He who has much will be embarrassed.
Therefore the sage keeps to One and becomes the
        standard for the world.
He does not display himself; therefore he shines.
He does not approve himself; therefore he is noted.
He does not praise himself; therefore he has merit.
He does not glory in himself; therefore he excels.
And because he does not compete; therefore no one in
        the world can compete with him.

The Eternal Tao

There is a thing inherent and natural,
Which existed before heaven and earth.
Motionless and fathomless,
it stands alone and never changes;
It pervades everywhere and never becomes exhausted.
It may be regarded as the Mother of the Universe.
I do not know its name.
If I am forced to give it a name,
I call it Tao, and I name it as supreme.
Supreme means going on;
Going on means going far;
Going far means returning.
Therefore Tao is supreme; heaven is supreme; earth
    is supreme; and man is also supreme. There are in
    the universe four things supreme, and man is one
    of them.
Man follows the laws of earth;
Earth follows the laws of heaven;
Heaven follows the laws of Tao;
Tao follows the laws of its intrinsic nature.

He Who Assists with Tao

He who assists a ruler of men with Tao does not
force the world with arms. He aims only at carrying out
relief, and does not venture to force his power upon
others.

So far as arms are concerned, they are implements of
ill-omen. They are not implements for the man of Tao.
For the actions of arms will be well requited: where
armies have been quartered brambles and thorns grow.
Great wars are for certain followed by years of scarcity.
The man of Tao when dwelling at home makes the left

as the place of honour, and when using arms makes the right as the place of honour. He uses them only when he cannot avoid it. In his conquests he takes no delight. If he took delight in them, it would mean that he enjoys the slaughter of men. He who takes delight in the slaughter of men cannot have his will done in the world.

He Who Knows Others

He who knows others is wise;
He who knows himself is enlightened.
He who conquers others is strong;
He who conquers himself is mighty.
He who knows contentment is rich.
He who keeps on his course with energy has will.
He who does not deviate from his proper place will
    long endure.
He who may die but not perish has longevity.

The Nameless Simplicity

Tao is ever inactive, and yet there is nothing that it
    does not do.
If princes and kings could keep to it, all things would
    of themselves become developed.
When they are developed, desire would stir in them;
I would restrain them by the nameless Simplicity,
In order to make them free from desire.
Free from desire, they would be at rest;
And the world would of itself become rectified.

Without Going Out of the Door

Without going out of the door
One can know the whole world;
Without peeping out of the window
One can see the Tao of heaven.
The further one travels
The less one knows.

The Sage Has No Self

The sage has no self to call his own;
He makes the self of the people his self.
To the good I act with goodness;
To the bad I also act with goodness:
Thus goodness is attained.
To the faithful I act with faith;
To the faithless I also act with faith:
Thus faith is attained.
The sage lives in the world in concord, and rules over
    the world in simplicity.
Yet what all the people turn their ears and eyes to,
The sage looks after as a mother does her children.

The Great Way

Let me have sound knowledge and walk on the great
    way (Tao);
Only I am in fear of deviating.
The great way is very plain and easy,
But the people prefer by-paths.
While the royal palaces are very well kept,
The fields are left weedy
And the granaries empty.
To wear embroidered clothes,

To carry sharp swords,
To be satiated in drink and food,
To be possessed of redundant riches—
This is called encouragement to robbery.
Is it not deviating from Tao?

Blunt All That Is Sharp

Blunt all that is sharp;
Cut all that is divisible;
Blur all that is brilliant;
Mix with all that is humble as dust;
This is called absolute equality.
Therefore it cannot be made intimate;
Nor can it be alienated.
It cannot be benefited;
Nor can it be harmed.
It cannot be exalted;
Nor can it be debased.
Therefore it is the most valuable thing in the world.

Three Treasures

I have three treasures, which I hold and keep safe:
The first is called love;
The second is called moderation;
The third is called not venturing to go ahead of the
    world.
Being loving, one can be brave;
Being moderate, one can be ample;
Not venturing to go ahead of the world, one can be
    the chief of all officials.
Instead of love, one has only bravery;
Instead of moderation, one has only amplitude;
Instead of keeping behind, one goes ahead:

These lead to nothing but death.
For he who fights with love will win the battle;
He who defends with love will be secure.
Heaven will save him, and protect him with love.

The Best Soldier

The best soldier is not soldierly;
The best fighter is not ferocious;
The best conqueror does not take part in war;
The best employer of men keeps himself below them.
This is called the virtue of not contending;
This is called the ability of using men;
This is called the supremacy of consorting with heaven.

The Strength of Weakness

The weakest things in the world can overmatch the
strongest things in the world.
Nothing in the world can be compared to water for its
weak and yielding nature; yet in attacking the
hard and the strong nothing proves better than it.
For there is no other alternative to it.
The weak can overcome the strong and the yielding
can overcome the hard.

Return Love for Hatred

Return love for great hatred.
Otherwise, when a great hatred is reconciled, some of
it will surely remain.
How can this end in goodness?
Therefore the sage holds to the left half of an agreement but does not exact what the other holder
ought to do

The virtuous resort to agreement;
The virtueless resort to exaction.
"The Tao of heaven shows no partiality;
It abides always with good men."

From the Works of Chuang Tze

All Things Are One

Tze Ch'i of Nan-kuo sat leaning on a table. Looking up to heaven, he sighed and became silent, as though soul and body had parted.

Yen Ch'eng Tze Yu, who was standing by him, exclaimed, "What are you thinking about that your body should thus become like dry wood, your mind like dead ashes?"

"My friend," replied Tze Ch'i, "great knowledge embraces the whole: small knowledge a part only. Great speech is universal: small speech is particular.

"For whether when the mind is locked in sleep or whether when in waking hours the body is released, we are subject to daily mental perturbations,—indecision, want of penetration, concealment, fretting fear, and trembling terror. Now like a javelin the mind flies forth, the arbiter of right and wrong. Now like a solemn covenanter it remains firm, the guardian of rights secured. Then, as under autumn and winter's blight, comes gradual decay, a passing away, like the flow of water, never to return. Finally, the block when all is choked up like an old drain,—the failing mind which shall not see light again.

"Joy and anger, sorrow and happiness, caution and remorse, come upon us by turns, with ever-changing mood. They come like music from hollowness, like mushrooms from damp. Daily and nightly they alternate within us, but we cannot tell whence they spring. Can we then hope in a moment to lay our finger upon their very cause?

"But for these emotions I should not be. But for me, they would have no scope. So far we can go; but we do not know what it is that brings them into play. 'Twould seem to be a soul; but the clue to its existence is wanting. That such a power operates, is credible enough, though we cannot see its form. It has functions without form.

"Take the human body with all its manifold divisions. Which part of it does a man love best? Does he not cherish all equally, or has he a preference? Do not all equally serve him? And do these servitors then govern themselves, or are they subdivided into rulers and subjects?

"Viewed from the standpoint of Tao, a beam and a pillar are identical. So are ugliness and beauty, greatness, wickedness, perverseness, and strangeness. Separation is the same as construction: construction is the same as destruction. Nothing is subject either to construction or to destruction, for these conditions are brought together into one.

"Only the truly intelligent understand this principle of the identity of all things. They do not view things as apprehended by themselves, subjectively; but transfer themselves into the position of the things viewed. And viewing them thus they are able to comprehend them, nay, to master them;—and he who can master them is near. So it is that to place oneself in subjective relation with externals, without consciousness of their objectivity,—this is Tao. But to wear out one's intellect in an obstinate adherence to the individuality of things, not recognizing the fact that all things are one,—this is called *Three in the Morning*."

"What is *Three in the Morning*?" asked Tze Yu.

"A keeper of monkeys," replied Tze Ch'i, "said with regard to their rations of chestnuts that each monkey was to have three in the morning and four at night. But at this the monkeys were very angry, so the keeper said they might have four in the morning and three at night, with which arrangement they were all well pleased.

"If there was a beginning, then there was a time before that beginning. And a time before the time which was before the time of that beginning.

"If there is existence, there must have been non-existence. And if there was a time when nothing existed, then there must have been a time before that—when even nothing did not exist. Suddenly, when nothing came into existence, could one really say whether it belonged to the category of existence or of non-existence? Even the very words I have just now uttered,— I cannot say whether they have really been uttered or not.

"There is nothing under the canopy of heaven greater than the tip of an autumn spikelet. A vast mountain is a small thing. Neither is there any age greater than that of a child cut off in infancy. P'eng Tsu himself died young. The universe and I came into being together; and I, and everything therein, are one."

No Absolute

If a man sleeps in a damp place, he gets lumbago and dies. But how about an eel? And living up in a tree is precarious and trying to the nerves;—but how about monkeys? Of the man, the eel, and the monkey, whose habitat is the right one, absolutely? Human beings feed on flesh, deer on grass, centipedes on snakes, owls and crows on mice. Of these four, whose is the right taste, absolutely? Monkey mates with monkey, the buck with the doe; eels consort with fishes, while men admire Mao Ch'iang and Li Chi, at the sight of whom fishes plunge deep down in the water, birds soar high in the air, and deer hurry away. Yet who shall say which is the correct standard of beauty? In my opinion, the standard of human virtue, and of positive and negative, is so obscured that it is impossible to actually know it as such.

The Dream and the Dreamer

Chu Ch'iao addressed Chang Wu Tze as follows:—"I heard Confucius say, 'The true sage pays no heed to mundane affairs. He neither seeks gain nor avoids injury. He asks nothing at the hands of man. He adheres, without questioning, to Tao. Without speaking, he can speak; and he can speak and yet say nothing. And so he roams beyond the limits of this dusty world. These,' added Confucius, 'are wild words.' Now to me they are the skilful embodiment of Tao. What, sir, is your opinion?"

"Points upon which the Yellow Emperor doubted," replied Chang Wu Tze, "how should Confucius know? Those who dream of the banquet, wake to lamentation and sorrow. Those who dream of lamentation and sorrow wake to join the hunt. While they dream, they do not know that they dream. Some will even interpret the very dream they are dreaming; and only when they awake do they know it was a dream. By and by comes the Great Awakening, and then we find out that this life is really a great dream. Fools think they are awake now, and flatter themselves they know if they are really princes or peasants. Confucius and you are both dreams; and I who say you are dreams,—I am but a dream myself. This is a paradox. To-morrow a sage may arise to explain it; but that to-morrow will not be until ten thousand generations have gone by.

"Granting that you and I argue. If you beat me, and not I you, are you necessarily right and I wrong? Or if I beat you and not you me, am I necessarily right and you wrong? Or are we both partly right and partly wrong? Or are we both wholly right and wholly wrong? You and I cannot know this, and consequently the world will be in ignorance of the truth.

"Whom shall I employ as arbiter between us? If I employ someone who takes your view, he will side with you. How can such a one arbitrate between us? If I employ someone who takes my view, he will side with me. How can such a one arbitrate between us? And if I employ someone who either differs from, or agrees with, both of us, he will be equally unable to decide between us. Since then you, and I, and man, cannot decide, must we not depend upon another? Such dependence is as though it were not dependence. We are embraced in the obliterating unity of God. There is perfect adaptation to whatever may eventuate; and so we complete our allotted span.

"Take no heed of time, nor of right and wrong. But passing into the realm of the Infinite, take your final rest therein."

Once upon a time, I, Chuang Tze, dreamt I was a butterfly, fluttering hither and thither, to all intents and purposes a butterfly. I was conscious only of following my fancies as a butterfly, and was unconscious of my individuality as a man. Suddenly, I awoke, and there I lay, myself again. Now I do not know whether I was

then a man dreaming I was a butterfly, or whether I
am now a butterfly dreaming I am a man.

The Nature of God

He who knows what God is, and who knows what
man is, has attained. Knowing what God is, he knows
that he himself proceeded therefrom. Knowing what
man is, he rests in the knowledge of the known, waiting
for the knowledge of the unknown. Working out one's
allotted span, and not perishing in mid career,—this
is the fullness of knowledge.

God is a principle which exists by virtue of its own
intrinsicality, and operates spontaneously, without self-
manifestation.

Herein, however, there is a flaw. Knowledge is
dependent upon fulfilment. And as this fulfilment is
uncertain, how can it be known that my divine is not
really human, my human really divine?

The Degradation of Horses and Men

Horses have hoofs to carry them over frost and snow;
hair, to protect them from wind and cold. They eat
grass and drink water, and fling up their heels over the
champaign. Such is the real nature of horses. Palatial
dwellings are of no use to them.

One day Poh Loh appeared, saying, "I understand
the management of horses."

So he branded them, and clipped them, and pared
their hoofs, and put halters on them, tying them up by
the head and shackling them by the feet, and disposing
them in stables, with the result that two or three in
every ten died. Then he kept them hungry and thirsty,
trotting them and galloping them, and grooming, and

trimming, with the misery of the tasselled bridle before and the fear of the knotted whip behind, until more than half of them were dead. Nevertheless, every age extols Poh Loh for his skill in managing horses.

Now I regard government of the empire from quite a different point of view.

The people have certain natural instincts;—to weave and clothe themselves, to till and feed themselves. These are common to all humanity, and all are agreed thereon. Such instincts are called "Heaven-sent."

And so in the days when natural instincts prevailed, men moved quietly and gazed steadily. At that time, there were no roads over mountains, nor boats, nor bridges over water. All things were produced, each for its own proper sphere. Birds and beasts multiplied; trees and shrubs grew up. The former might be led by the hand; you could climb up and peep into the raven's nest. For then man dwelt with birds and beasts, and all creation was one. There were no distinctions of good and bad men. Being all equally without knowledge, their virtue could not go astray. Being all equally without evil desires, they were in a state of natural integrity, the perfection of human existence.

But when sages appeared, tripping people over charity and fettering with duty to one's neighbour, doubt found its way into the world. And then with their gushing over music and fussing over ceremony, the empire became divided against itself.

Horses live on dry land, eat grass and drink water. When pleased, they rub their necks together. When angry, they turn round and kick up their heels at each other. Thus far only do their natural dispositions carry them. But bridled and bitted, with a plate of metal on their foreheads, they learn to cast vicious looks, to turn the head to bite, to resist, to get the bit out of the mouth or the bridle into it. And thus their natures become depraved,—the fault of Poh Loh.

In the days of Ho Hsu the people did nothing in particular when at rest, and went nowhere in particular when they moved. Having food, they rejoiced; having full bellies, they strolled about. Such were the capacities of the people. But when the sages came to worry them with ceremonies and music in order to rectify the form of government, and dangled charity and duty to one's neighbour before them in order to satisfy their hearts,— then the people began to develop a taste for knowledge and to struggle one with the other in their desire for gain. This was the error of the sages.

On Letting Alone

There has been such a thing as letting mankind alone; there has never been such a thing as governing mankind.

Letting alone springs from fear lest men's natural dispositions be perverted and their virtue laid aside. But if their natural dispositions be not perverted nor their virtue laid aside, what room is there left for government?

Because men are made to rejoice and to sorrow and to displace their centre of gravity, they lose their steadiness, and are unsuccessful in thought and action. And thus it is that the idea of surpassing others first came into the world.

Ts'ui Chu asked Lao Tze, saying, "If the empire is not to be governed, how are men's hearts to be kept in order?"

"Be careful," replied Lao Tze, "not to interfere with

the natural goodness of the heart of man. Man's heart may be forced down or stirred up. In each case the issue is fatal.

"By gentleness, the hardest heart may be softened. But try to cut and polish it,—'twill glow like fire or freeze like ice. In the twinkling of an eye it will pass beyond the limits of the Four Seas. In repose, profoundly still; in motion, far away in the sky. No bolt can bar, no bond can bind,—such is the human heart."

The Tao of God

The Tao of God operates ceaselessly; and all things are produced. The Tao of the sovereign operates ceaselessly; and the empire rallies around him. The Tao of the sage operates ceaselessly; and all within the limit of surrounding ocean acknowledge his sway. He who apprehends God, who is in relation with the sage, and who recognizes the radiating virtue of the sovereign,— his actions will be to him unconscious, the actions of repose.

The repose of the sage is not what the world calls repose. His repose is the result of his mental attitude. All creation could not disturb his equilibrium: hence his repose.

When water is still, it is like a mirror, reflecting the beard and the eyebrows. It gives the accuracy of the water-level, and the philosopher makes it his model. And if water thus derives lucidity from stillness, how much more the faculties of the mind? The mind of the sage being in repose becomes the mirror of the universe, the speculum of all creation.

Repose, tranquillity, stillness, inaction,—these were the levels of the universe, the ultimate perfection of Tao. Therefore wise rulers and sages rest therein.

Repose, tranquillity, stillness, inaction,—these were the source of all things. Keep to this when coming forward to pacify a troubled world, and your merit shall be great and your name illustrious, and the empire united into one. In your repose you will be wise; in your movements, powerful. By inaction you will gain honour; and by confining yourself to the pure and simple, you will hinder the whole world from struggling with you for show.

The Circling Sky

The sky turns round; the earth stands still; sun and moon pursue one another. Who causes this? Who directs this? Who has leisure enough to see that such movements continue?

Some think there is a mechanical arrangement which makes these bodies move as they do. Others think that they revolve without being able to stop.

The clouds cause rain; rain causes clouds. Whose kindly bounty is this? Who has leisure enough to see that such result is achieved?

Wind comes from the north. It blows now east, now west; and now it whirls aloft. Who puffs it forth? Who has leisure enough to be flapping it this way or that? I should like to know the cause of all this.

Confucius and Lao Tze

Confucius visited Lao Tze, and spoke of charity and duty to one's neighbour.

Lao Tze said, "The chaff from winnowing will blind a man's eyes so that he cannot tell the points of the compass. Mosquitoes will keep a man awake all night with their biting. And just in the same way this talk of charity and duty to one's neighbour drives me nearly crazy. Sir! strive to keep the world to its own original simplicity. And as the wind bloweth where it listeth, so let virtue establish itself. Wherefore such undue energy, as though searching for a fugitive with a big drum?

"The snow-goose is white without a daily bath. The raven is black without daily colouring itself. The original simplicity of black and of white is beyond the reach of argument. The vista of fame and reputation is not worthy of enlargement. When the pond dries up and the fishes are left upon dry ground, to moisten them with the breath or to damp them with a little spittle is not to be compared with leaving them in the first instance in their native rivers and lakes."

On returning from this visit to Lao Tze, Confucius did not speak for three days. A disciple asked him, saying, "Master, when you saw Lao Tze, in what direction did you admonish him?"

"I saw a dragon," replied Confucius, "—a dragon which by convergence showed a body, by radiation became colour, and riding upon the clouds of heaven, nourished the two principles of creation. My mouth was agape: I could not shut it. How then do you think I was going to admonish Lao Tze?"

Conceit

Conceit and assurance, which lead men to quit society, and be different from their fellows, to indulge in tall talk and abuse of others,—these are nothing more than personal over-estimation, the affectation of recluses and those who have done with the world and have closed their hearts to mundane influences.

Preaching of charity and duty to one's neighbour,

of loyalty and truth, of respect, of economy, and of humility,—this is but moral culture, affected by would-be pacificators and teachers of mankind, and by scholars at home or abroad.

Preaching of meritorious services, of fame, of ceremonial between sovereign and minister, of due relationship between upper and lower classes,—this is mere government, affected by courtiers or patriots who strive to extend the boundaries of their own state and to swallow up the territory of others.

But in self-esteem without conceit, in moral culture without charity and duty to one's neighbour, in government without rank and fame, in retirement without solitude, in health without hygiene,—there we have oblivion absolute coupled with possession of all things; an infinite calm which becomes an object to be attained by all.

Such is the Tao of the universe, such is the virtue of the sage. Wherefore it has been said, "In tranquillity, in stillness, in the unconditioned, in inaction, we find the levels of the universe, the very constitution of Tao."

The Choice of Chuang Tze

Chuang Tze was fishing in the P'u when the prince of Ch'u sent two high officials to ask him to take charge of the administration of the Ch'u State.

Chuang Tze went on fishing, and without turning his head said, "I have heard that in Ch'u there is a sacred tortoise which has been dead now some three thousand years. And that the prince keeps this tortoise carefully enclosed in a chest on the altar of his ancestral people. Now would this tortoise rather be dead and have its remains venerated, or be alive and wagging its tail in the mud?"

"It would rather be alive," replied the two officials, "and wagging its tail in the mud."

"Begone!" cried Chuang Tze. "I too will wag my tail in the mud."

The Death of Chuang Tze's Wife

When Chuang Tze's wife died, Hui Tze went to condole. He found the widower sitting on the ground, singing, with his legs spread out at a right angle, and beating time on a bowl.

"To live with your wife," exclaimed Hui Tze, "and see your eldest son grow up to be a man, and then not to shed a tear over her corpse,—this would be bad enough. But to drum on a bowl, and sing; surely this is going too far."

"Not at all," replied Chuang Tze. "When she died, I could not help being affected by her death. Soon, however, I remembered that she had already existed in a previous state before birth, without form, or even substance; that while in that unconditioned condition, substance was added to spirit; that this substance then assumed form; and that the next stage was birth. And now, by virtue of a further change, she is dead, passing from one phase to another like the sequence of spring, summer, autumn, and winter. And while she is thus lying asleep in eternity, for me to go about weeping and wailing would be to proclaim myself ignorant of these natural laws. Therefore I refrain."

The Wisdom of the Skull

Chuang Tze one day saw an empty skull, bleached but still preserving its shape. Striking it with his riding whip, he said, "Wert thou once some ambitious citizen

whose inordinate yearnings brought him to this pass?—
some statesman who plunged his country into ruin and
perished in the fray?—some wretch who left behind
him a legacy of shame?—some beggar who died in the
pangs of hunger and cold? Or didst thou reach this
state by the natural course of old age?"

When he had finished speaking, he took the skull,
and placing it under his head as a pillow, went to sleep.
In the night, he dreamt that the skull appeared to him
and said, "You speak well, sir; but all you say has refer-
ence to the life of mortals, and to mortal troubles. In
death there are none of these. Would you like to hear
about death?"

Chuang Tze having replied in the affirmative, the
skull began:—"In death, there is no sovereign above,
and no subject below. The working of the four seasons
are unknown. Our existences are bounded only by
eternity. The happiness of a king among men cannot
exceed that which we enjoy."

Chuang Tze, however, was not convinced, and said,
"Were I to prevail upon God to allow your body to be
born again, and your bones and flesh to be renewed,
so that you could return to your parents, to your wife,
and to the friends of your youth,—would you be willing?"

At this, the skull opened its eyes wide and knitted
its brows and said, "How should I cast aside happiness
greater than that of a king, and mingle once again in
the toils and troubles of mortality?"

The Secret of Life

"A drunken man who falls out of a cart, though he
may suffer, does not die. His bones are the same as
other people's; but he meets his accident in a different

way. His spirit is in a condition of security. He is not conscious of riding in the cart; neither is he conscious of falling out of it. Ideas of life, death, fear, etc., cannot penetrate his breast; and so he does not suffer from contact with objective existences. And if such security is to be got from wine, how much more is it to be got from God. It is in God that the sage seeks his refuge and so he is free from harm."

Confucius at the Cataract

Confucius was looking at the cataract at Lu-liang. It fell from a height of thirty jen, and its foam reached forty li away. No scaly, finny creature could enter therein. Yet Confucius saw an old man go in, and thinking that he was suffering from some trouble and desirous of ending his life, bade a disciple run along the side to try to save him. The old man emerged about a hundred paces off, and with flowing hair went carolling along the bank. Confucius followed him and said, "I had thought, sir, you were a spirit, but now I see you are a man. Kindly tell me, is there any way to deal thus with water?"

"No," replied the old man; "I have no way. There was my original condition to begin with; then habit growing into nature; and lastly acquiescence in destiny. Plunging in with the whirl, I come out with the swirl. I accommodate myself to the water, not the water to me. And so I am able to deal with it after this fashion."

"What do you mean," inquired Confucius, "by your original condition to begin with, habit growing into nature, and acquiescence in destiny?"

"I was born," replied the old man, "upon dry land, and accommodated myself to dry land. That was my original condition. Growing up on the water, I accommodated myself to the water. That was what I meant by nature. And doing as I did without being conscious of any effort so to do, that was what I meant by destiny."

The Impossibility of Possessing

Shun asked Ch'eng, saying, "Can one get Tao so as to have it for one's own?"

"Your very body," replied Ch'eng, "is not your own. How should Tao be?"

"If my body," said Shun, "is not my own, pray whose is it?"

"It is the delegated image of God," replied Ch'eng. "Your life is not your own. It is the delegated harmony of God. Your individuality is not your own. It is the delegated adaptability of God. Your posterity is not your own. It is the delegated exuviae of God. You move, you know not how. You are at rest, but know not why. You taste, but know not the cause. These are the operation of God's laws. How then should you get Tao so as to have it for your own?"

All Things After Their Kinds

Confucius said to Lao Tze, "Today you are at leisure. Pray tell me about perfect Tao."

"Purge your heart by fasting and discipline," answered Lao Tze. "Wash your soul as white as snow. Discard your knowledge. Tao is abstruse and difficult of discussion. I will try, however, to speak to you of its outline.

"Heaven cannot but be high. Earth cannot but be broad. The sun and moon cannot but revolve. All creation cannot but flourish. To do so is their Tao.

"But it is not from extensive study that this may be known, nor by dialectic skill that this may be made clear. The true sage will have none of these. It is in addition without gain, in diminution without loss, that the true sage finds salvation.

"Unfathomable as the sea, wondrously ending only to begin again, informing all creation without being exhausted, the Tao of the perfect man is spontaneous in its operation. That all creation can be informed by it without exhaustion, is its Tao.

"In the Middle Kingdom there are men who recognize neither positive nor negative. They abide between heaven and earth. They act their part as mortals, and then return to the Cause.

"The reality of the formless, the unreality of that which has form,—this is known to all. Those who are on the road to attainment care not for these things, but the people at large discuss them. Attainment implies non-discussion; discussion implies non-attainment. Manifested, Tao has no objective value; hence silence is better than argument. It cannot be translated into speech; better then say nothing at all. This is called the great attainment."

Where Tao Is

Tung Kuo Tze asked Chuang Tze, saying, "What you call Tao,—where is it?"

"There is nowhere," replied Chuang Tze, "where it is not."

"Tell me one place at any rate where it is," said Tung Kuo Tze.

"It is in the ant," replied Chuang Tze.

"Why go so low down?" asked Tung Kuo Tze.

"It is in a tare," said Chuang Tze.

"Still lower," objected Tung Kuo Tze.

"It is in a potsherd," said Chuang Tze.

"Worse still!" cried Tung Kuo Tze.

"It is in ordure," said Chuang Tze. And Tung Kuo Tze made no reply.

The Wise Tender of Horses

When the Yellow Emperor went to see Tao upon the Chu-tz'u Mountain, Fang Ming was his charioteer, Ch'ang Yu sat on his right, Chang Jo and Hsi P'eng were his outriders, and K'un Hun and Hua Chi brought up the rear. On reaching the wilds of Hsiang-ch'eng, these seven sages lost their way and there was no one of whom to ask the road. By and by, they fell in with a boy who was grazing horses, and asked him, saying, "Do you know the Chu-tz'u Mountain?"

"I do," replied the boy.

"And can you tell us," continued the Sages, "where Tao abides?"

"I can," replied the boy.

"This is a strange lad," cried the Yellow Emperor. "Not only does he know where the Chu-tz'u Mountain is, but also where Tao abides! Come tell me, pray, how would you govern the empire?"

"I should govern the empire," said the boy, "just the same as I look after my horses. What else should I do?

"When I was a little boy and used to live within the points of the compass, my eyes got dim of sight. An old man advised me to mount the chariot of the sun and visit the wilds of Hsiang-ch'eng. My sight is now much better, and I continue to dwell without the points of the compass. I should govern the empire in just the same way. What else should I do?"

"Of course," said the Yellow Emperor, "government is not your trade. Still I should be glad to hear what you would do."

The boy declined to answer, but on being again urged, cried out, "What difference is there between governing the empire and looking after horses? See that no harm comes to the horses, that is all!"

Thereupon the Emperor prostrated himself before the boy; and addressing him as Divine Teacher, took his leave.

Chuang Tze on Death

When Chuang Tze was about to die, his disciples expressed a wish to give him a splendid funeral. But Chuang Tze said, "With heaven and earth for my coffin and shell; with the sun, moon, and stars as my burial regalia; and with all creation to escort me to the grave, —are not my funeral paraphernalia ready to hand?"

"We fear," argued the disciples, "lest the carrion kite should eat the body of our Master"; to which Chuang Tze replied, "Above ground I shall be food for kites; below I shall be food for mole-crickets and ants. Why rob one to feed the other?"

The Way to Tao

Nan Yung took some provisions, and after a seven days' journey arrived at the abode of Lao Tze.

"Have you come from Keng Sang Ch'u?" said the latter.

"I have," replied Nan Yung.

"But why," said Lao Tze, "bring all these people with you?"

Nan Yung looked back in alarm, and Lao Tze continued, "Do you not understand what I say?"

Nan Yung bent his head abashed, and then looking up, said with a sigh, "I have now forgotten how to answer, in consequence of missing what I came to ask."

"What do you mean?" said Lao Tze.

"If I do not know," replied Nan Yung, "men call me a fool. If I do know, I injure myself. If I am not charitable, I injure others. If I am, I injure myself. If I do not my duty to my neighbour, I injure others. If I do it, I injure myself. My trouble lies in not seeing how to escape from these three dilemmas. On the strength of my connexion with Keng Sang, I would venture to ask advice."

"When I saw you," said Lao Tze, "I knew in the twinkling of an eye what was the matter with you. And now what you say confirms my view. You are confused, as a child that has lost its parents. You would fathom the sea with a pole. You are astray. You are struggling to get back to your natural self, but cannot find the way. Alas! alas!"

"If a rustic is sick," said Nan Yung, "and another rustic goes to see him; and if the sick man can say what is the matter with him,—then he is not seriously ill. Yet my search after Tao is like swallowing drugs which only increase the malady. I beg therefore merely to ask the art of preserving life."

"The art of preserving life," replied Lao Tze, "consists in being able to keep all in one, to lose nothing, to estimate good and evil without divination, to know when to stop, and how much is enough, to leave others alone and attend to oneself, to be without cares and without knowledge,—to be in fact as a child. A child will cry all day and not become hoarse, because of the perfection of its constitutional harmony. It will keep its fist tightly closed all day and not open it, because of the concentration of its virtue. It will gaze all day without taking off its eyes, because its sight is not attracted by externals. In motion, it knows not whither it is bound; at rest, it is not conscious of doing anything; but unconsciously adapts itself to the exigencies of its environment. This is the art of preserving life."

"Is this then the virtue of the perfect man?" cried Nan Yung.

"Not so," said Lao Tze. "I am, as it were, but breaking the ice.

"The perfect man shares the food of this earth, but the happiness of God. He does not incur trouble either from men or things. He does not join in censuring, in plotting, in toadying. Free from care he comes, and unconscious he goes;—this is the art of preserving life."

"This then is perfection?" inquired Nan Yung.

"Not yet," said Lao Tze. "I specially asked if you could be as a child. A child acts without knowing what it does; moves without knowing whither.

"Those whose hearts are in a state of repose give forth a divine radiance, by the light of which they see themselves as they are. And only by cultivating such repose can man attain to the constant.

"Those who are constant are sought after by men and assisted by God. Those who are sought after by men are the people of God; those who are assisted by God are his chosen children.

"To study this is to study what cannot be learnt. To practise this is to practise what cannot be accomplished. To discuss this is to discuss what can never be proved. Let knowledge stop at the unknowable. That is perfection. And for those who do not follow this, God will destroy them!

"With such defences for the body, ever prepared for the unexpected, deferential to the rights of others,—if then calamities overtake you, these are from God, not from man. Let them not disturb what you have already achieved. Let them not penetrate into the soul's abode. For there resides the will. And if the will knows not what to will, it will not be able to will.

"Whatsoever is not said in all sincerity, is wrongly said. And not to be able to rid oneself of this vice is only to sink deeper towards perdition.

"Those who do evil in the open light of day,—men will punish them. Those who do evil in secret,—God will punish them. Who fears both man and God, he is fit to walk alone. Those who are devoted to the internal, in practice acquire no reputation. Those who are devoted to the external, strive for pre-eminence among their fellows. Practice without reputation throws a halo around the meanest. But he who strives for pre-eminence among his fellows, he is as a huckster whose weariness all perceive though he himself puts on an air of gaiety.

"He who is naturally in sympathy with man, to him all men come. But he who forcedly adapts, has no room even for himself, still less for others. And he who has no room for others, has no ties. It is all over with him.

"Birth is not a beginning; death is not an end. There is existence without limitation; there is continuity without a starting-point. Existence without limitation is space. Continuity without a starting-point is time. There is birth, there is death, there is issuing forth, there is entering in. That through which one passes in and out without seeing its form, that is the Portal of God.

"The Portal of God is non-existence. All things sprang from non-existence. Existence could not make existence existence. It must have proceeded from non-existence, and non-existence and nothing are one. Herein is the abiding-place of the sage.

"Discard the stimuli of purpose. Free the mind from disturbances. Get rid of entanglements to virtue. Pierce the obstructions to Tao.

"Honours, wealth, distinction, power, fame, gain,— these six stimulate purpose.

"Mien, carriage, beauty, arguments, influence, opinions,—these six disturb the mind.

"Hate, ambition, joy, anger, sorrow, pleasure,—these six are entanglements to virtue.

"Rejecting, adopting, receiving, giving, knowledge, ability,—these six are obstructions to Tao.

"If these twenty-four be not allowed to run riot, then the mind will be duly ordered. And being duly ordered, it will be in repose. And being in repose, it will be clear of perception. And being clear of perception, it will be unconditioned. And being unconditioned, it will be in that state of inaction by which there is nothing which cannot be accomplished."

GLOSSARY

AND

INDEX

Glossary

The following abbreviations are used after words taken from scriptural selections to indicate the scriptures in which they occur: (H) Hindu; (B) Buddhist; (Z) Zoroastrian; (JC) Judeo-Christian; (M) Mohammedan; (C) Confucianist; (T) Taoist.

Acarya. (B) A spiritual guide or teacher.

Achyuta. (H) "Unfallen." A designation of Vishnu or Krishna.

Aditi. (H) "Free, unbounded." Infinity. The boundless heaven. Deva-Matri, mother of the gods.

Adityas. (H) A group of gods, sons of Aditi, of whom Varuna was chief. Therefore he was *the* Aditya.

Agamas. (H) Not contradicting the sense of scripture. Orthodox, canonical. A group of Hindu religious treatises.

Agni. (H) One of the early Indo-European gods. In Hinduism one of the three great deities of the Veda. The fire god. (*Ignis*, from which our "to ignite.")

Agnihotra. (H) A priest of Agni, or Ayni as priest.

ahamkara. (H) Self-consciousness. The function of the soul which produces the false conception of the ego.

Aharman. (Z) Same as Angra Mainyu.

Ahriman. (Z) Same as Angra Mainyu.

Ahura. (Z) Zoroastrian equivalent of Asura in its meaning of a god.

Ahura Mazda. (Z) "Wise Lord," or "Lord of Wisdom." The supreme God of Zoroastrianism. Also apparently one of a number of gods of the pre-Zoroastrian Persian religion.

Ahuras. (H) A group of gods of the earth and darkness in Hinduism, the word having achieved, through passage of time, the opposite meaning of its origin, Asuras, who were gods of the sky. (Cf. our "azure.")

Airyana. (Z) Same as Sanskrit. *Aryan.* The Indo-European race.

Alaka. (B) Capital of Kuvera and home of Gandharvas on Mt. Meru.

'Ali. (M) Mohammed's son-in-law, one of the successors of the Prophet.

Allah. (M) Shortened form of *Al-Illah*, "the god." The high god of the early Arabian pantheon (a development in conception from the early Semitic *El*, "the Strong One," common to Hebrew, Aramaic, and Arabic peoples). Later the one God of Mohammedanism.

Amerodad. (Z) Immortality. Proper name of one of the Amesha Spentas.

Amesha Spentas. (Z) A group of seven saints, or superior genii, or archangels, who

577

may be compared to the Hindu Adityas, and the archangels of later Judaism.

Analects of Confucius. (C) *Lun Yu.* The collected sayings of Confucius. One of the four "books" of Confucianism which, with the six "classics," make up the canon.

Ananda. (HB) In (H) "joy." An appelation of Siva and a suffix to the names of many Hindu teachers. In (B) the name of Gautama's personal attendant and beloved disciple.

Angra Mainyu. (Z) The embodiment of evil in Zoroastrian belief. King of all evil and unclean spirits. Later called Ahriman or Aharman. Parallel with Satan of Christianity.

apahadha. (Z) A serious illness.

Apaosh. (Z) The evil spirit of drought.

Apsaras. (H) "Moving in the water." Nymphs of Indra's heaven. Wives or mistresses of the Gandharvas.

Arahant. (B) One who has followed the eightfold path to enlightenment.

Arahat. (B) Same as Arahant.

Arjuna. (H) "White." Name of the third Pandu prince, son of Indra. The episode in the *Bhagavad Gita* is but one of many in the long story of this warrior's life.

Aryans. Originally "faithfully devoted comrades." The name by which the Indo-European invaders of India and Persia called themselves to distinguish them from the original inhabitants of those countries.

asana. (H) The third stage of Yoga practice, including physical postures as a background for meditation.

Asha. (Z) The righteous order pervading all pure things.

Ashaist. (Z) A pure and righteous worshipper of Ahura Mazda.

asramas (or ashramas). (H) Stages in the religious development of a Brahmana.

Asura. (H) "Spiritual." "Divine." In early Vedic literature the supreme spirit. Applied to Indra, Agni, Varuna, and others. In later Hinduism it acquired the exactly opposite meaning and signified a demon, a spirit of earth and darkness, an enemy of the gods. (*See also* Ahura.)

Asvins (or Ashvins). (H) "Horsemen." Two Vedic deities, twin sons of the sun and sky. The carriers of light to the morning sky.

Asvaghosha (or Acvaghosha). (B) One of the most celebrated of Buddhist philosophers who lived about six hundred years after the death of Gautama, which is to say, early in the second century of the Christian era.

Atharva-Veda. (H) The latest of the four *Vedas*, so named because its rites were practised by atharvans, or priests. (*See* Introduction to the Hindu scriptures in this volume.)

atta. (B) Pali equivalent of Sanskrit *Atman*. In Buddhism, however, the term refers simply to the human personality, while the "Atman" or "Brahman" principle of the *Upanishads* is denied in many Buddhist scriptures.

Atma Bodha. (H) (*Atma* or *Atman* means "universal soul" or spirit. *Bodha* means "enlightenment.") "Knowledge of Spirit." Title of

Sankaracharya's discourse on gaining spiritual perception. Many of the conceptions of this work are included in the modern doctrine of Christian Science.

Atman. (H) The universal soul. The intangible supreme principle, especially as manifested within the human soul. Brahman. "The God within us." Often inadequately translated "Self." The higher self. The divine spark in man. Very like the conception of Tao in Taoism.

Aum (or Om). (H) The sacred word. Symbol of the Lord of created beings. The mystic word which precedes all prayers. Symbolic of the three major *Vedas*, and of Vishnu, Siva, and Brahma. The word is believed to exercise mystic power when meditated upon.

Aurora. Goddess of the dawn in Roman mythology. Parallel with *Ushas* in Indo-European and early Vedic religions and *Eos* or *Heos* in Greek.

Avatara. (HB) "A descent." Incarnation of a deity, especially of Vishnu. In Buddhism used to designate the coming of a Bodhisattva.

bab. (Arabic) "Gate" or "Temple."

baresma. (Z) A bunch of branches held by a Zoroastrian priest during religious ceremonies.

Bhagavad Gita. (H) "The Lord's Song." Title of the great devotional classic of Hinduism written about A.D. 1.

Bharata. (H) A king from whom descended the warriors called Bharatas.

bhikku. (B) Pali equivalent of Sanskrit *Bhikshu*. Originally a beggar; later general appelation for the followers of Gautama Buddha who had left the worldly life. The usual, inadequate translation is "monks."

Bhishma. (H) "The Terrible." Son of King Santanu by the River Goddess Ganga (the Ganges). His son was also named Bhishma or Santanava.

bodhi. (B) Enlightenment.

Bodhi Tree or Bo-tree. (B) The tree under which Gautama attained enlightenment at Buddha-Gaya.

Bodhisattva. (B) One whose being or essence is bodhi, or enlightenment, arising from a direct perception of truth. A being which, through its incarnations in many forms and in many realms of existence, prepares itself to become a Buddha, or teacher of the enlightened doctrine on earth. In Hinayana Buddhism, one who is to be a Buddha. In Mahayana Buddhism, one who, although having attained enlightenment, renounces Nirvana in order to be of service to humanity.

Book of Filial Piety. (C) The *Hsiao King*. One of the six canonical classics of Confucianism, edited by Confucius.

Book of Rites. (C) The *Li Ki*. One of the six canonical classics of Confucianism, edited by Confucius.

Brahma. (H) Personification of the essential principle of Brahman as the creator God, the Lord and Father of all. In the *Upanishads* the conception of Brahma approached monotheism.

Brahman. (H) The supreme

essence, the central principle or soul of the universe, the all pervading force, incorporeal, immaterial, invisible, uncreated, unborn, infinite. To achieve union and identification with it is the purpose of Hindu meditation. Similar in conception to Tao. The conception was denied by Buddhism.

Buddhaghosha (or Buddhaghosha). (B) "Voice of the Buddha." Name of several Buddhist writers.

Buddha. (HB) A title, derived from the root *budh*, to "know" (from which also *bodhi*, "knowledge" or "enlightenment"). "The enlightened one." In (B) the title given to Gautama and others. In (H) the Buddha is sometimes considered as the ninth incarnation of Vishnu.

Canon of Changes. (C) The *I King.* A system of divination. One of the six canonical classics of Confucianism. Edited by Confucius.

Canon of History. (C) The *Shu King.* One of the six canonical classics of Confucianism. Edited by Confucius.

Canon of Poetry. (C) The *Shi King.* One of the six canonical classics of Confucianism. Edited by Confucius.

Ch'i. (T) The great breath, the life, the soul, of the living universe.

Chinvad Bridge. (Z) The bridge between heaven and hell.

Chou (Chow) dynasty. (C) A celebrated Chinese dynasty which lasted from 1122 B. C. to 255 B. C.

Chuang Tze (or Chuang Tzu). (T) A celebrated Chinese

sage who lived about 400 B. C. Sometimes spoken of as the "St. Paul of Taoism" because of his popularization of the religion.

Chun Chiu. (C) *Spring and Autumn Annals.* A book of local history. One of the six canonical classics of Confucianism, and the only book written by Confucius.

Confucius. (CT) Latin form of Kungfutze, i.e., "Master Kung." The great ethical teacher who founded Confucianism and who lived 551-479 B.C.

Daevas. (Z) Malevolent spirits. Demons of darkness. But originally the same as the Devas of Hinduism.

Dakhma. (Z) A container for bones. A "tower of silence" where corpses are left for birds to devour.

Devas. (HB) "Shining Ones." Gods in Hinduism. Parallel etymologically with Daevas of Zoroastrianism, in which they are demons. In (B) spirits both good and bad, but all in need of salvation through the enlightened doctrine of the Buddha.

dhamma. (B) Pali equivalent of Sanskrit *dharma*. In (B) the word may mean, according to its context, any of the following: system, doctrine, religion, virtue, moral quality, righteousness, justice, duty, law, standard, norm, ideal, truth, form, condition, cause, phenomenon, thing, cosmic order.

Dhammapada. (B) "Verses on Dhamma." One of the canonical books of Buddhism.

dharma. (H) Sanskrit equivalent of Pali *dhamma*. (1) Justice. (2) A name of Yama as the judge of the dead. (3) Moral or religious duty.

Dharmakaya. (B) The embodied law. The Buddha as personification of truth.

dhyana. (HB) Mystic state of serene contemplation attained by meditation.

Doctrine of the Mean. (C) Chung Yung. One of the four "books" of Confucianism which, with the six classics, make up the canon.

Drug (or Druj). (Z) From the verb meaning "to lie." One of a group of female demons.

Drujist. (Z) One who worships the Drug or Druj.

Duzaka. (Z) Hell.

Dyani Buddha. (B) Spiritual counterpart of each of five Buddhas of whom Gautama was believed to be the fourth and Maitreya will be the fifth.

Dyaus. (H) The sky. Heaven. Of itself or, with pitar, a deity of the Indo-Europeans before their separation, and also of Vedic Hinduism. Etymologically related to Greek Zeus and Latin Jupiter. "Sky Father."

Eightfold Path. (B) The Buddhist formula for obtaining enlightenment.

El. Early Semitic designation meaning "strong," "hero," "a god." (See Allah.)

Frashoastra. (Z) Proper name. Brother of Yamaspa.

Fravashi. (Z) The soul of one who is dead.

Gatha. (ZBH) A song or one verse of a song. Same as Sanskrit gita. In Zoroastrian scriptures there are five Avestan songs called Gathas. They are the oldest in the Zoroastrian scrip-

tures and are believed to have been written by Zarathushtra.

Gayomard. (Z) The first man in Zoroastrian legend.

Great Learning. (C) The Ta Hsio. One of the four "books" of Confucianism which, with the six classics, make up the canon.

Govinda. (H) "Keeper of the cows." One of the appelations of Krishna.

Guru. (H) A spiritual teacher or tutor, whose complete spiritual authority a student must accept.

Haoma. (Z) The personified sacred plan of Persian mythology from which juice was extracted for sacred rites. Its worship is believed to have been common to Indians and Iranians before the Indo-European migrations and separation of the two groups. An Angel in Zoroastrianism, and, under the name "Soma," a god in Hinduism.

Hari. (HB) An appelation of divinity freely translated as "Lord." Usually used to designate Vishnu, but also applied to other gods.

Hinayana Buddhism. "The Little Vehicle" of Siam, Ceylon, and Burma, which does not deify Gautama.

Hsiao King. (C) The Book of Filial Piety. One of the six canonical classics of Confucianism. Edited by Confucius.

Ilah. Arabic word related to El and Ilu. Alone it means "a god." With article al, it means "the God," or Allah.

Ilu. Derivation of early Semitic word El. In Babylonian inscriptions, "God."

Indo-Europeans. The early

Aryan race which, in its migrations and separations, became Indian, Persian, Greek, Roman, Spanish, etc.

Indra. (H) One of the early Indo-European gods. In Hinduism the god who protected and led his people in battle. Also found in other early religions.

Islam. "Submission" (to Allah). Mohammedanism and the body of the Mohammedan doctrine and church.

Judaism. The religion of the Jews. Generally applied to their religion from the time of Moses to the present.

Judeo-Christian. Pertaining to the theology and ethics of the Old and New Testaments of the Western Holy Bible.

Janardana. (H) "The adored of mankind." An appelation of Krishna.

jhana. (B) Pali equivalent for Sanskrit *dhyana*.

kalpa. (H) A day and night of Brahma. 4,320,000,000 years.

karma. (HB) Sanskrit equivalent of Pali *kamma*. The law of the continuing affect of one's deeds, which determines one's state of being during earthly existences and in intervals between rebirths.

Kesava. (H) "Having much or fine hair." An appelation of Krishna and Vishnu.

Krishna. (H) "Black." "The Blessed Lord" of the *Bhagavad Gita*. Considered by some as an incarnation of Vishnu.

Kshatriya. (H) The second, or warrior and regal caste.

kwei. Evil spirits in ancient Chinese religion, related to the Yin.

Lao Tze. (CT) A Chinese philosopher who, according to tradition, lived about 600 B.C., and to whom is somewhat doubtfully attributed authorship of the *Tao-Te King*, basic scripture of Taoism.

li. (CT) (1) A measure of distance, equal to about a third of an English mile. (2) Absolute right. (3) Etiquette, propriety.

Li Ki. (C) *Book of Rites.* One of the six canonical classics of Confucianism, edited by Confucius.

Logos. (Greek) "The Word" in the sense of the universal divine principle or law. Used in the Gospel of John. Similar in conception to Tao and Brahman.

Lumbini Grove. (B) The grove in Lumbini Park near Kapilavastu where Gautama was born.

Lun Yu. (C) The *Analects of Confucius.* One of the four "books" of Confucianism which, with the six classics, make up the canon.

Mahayana Buddhism. "The Great Vehicle" doctrine which deifies Gautama.

Maitreya. (B) The Buddha who, Buddhists believe, will appear on earth five thousand years after the death of Gautama (or about A. D. 4500).

Mantram. (H) A hymn of the *Vedas*. A formula which, by the power of its sound, is believed to create certain beneficent effects in the human soul.

Manu. (H) The name given to each of the fourteen progenitors of the human race. To the first is attributed the *Ordinances of Manu.* The seventh is the one mentioned in the story of the flood.

Mara. (B) The killer. Death. Personification o f t h e death-power and of evil principle. The tempter. (Note etymological relation to Latin *mors* and English "nightmare.")

Maruts. (H) The storm gods, allies of Indra.

Mashya and Mashyoi. (Z) The first human pair of Zoroastrianism from whose union the race sprang. Same as Matro and Matroyao.

Matro and Matroyao. (Z) Same as Mashya and Mashyoi.

Maya. (H) Illusion, deception, the demoniac power. Personification of evil in a female of divine appearance whose purpose it is to delude humanity. Also the name of Gaya, a sacred city, and of a Daitya, who was a carpenter of the gods.

Mazda. (Z) "The Great Wisdom." Related to Sanskrit *Maha* (great). Part of the name of the one God, Ahura Mazda.

Mazdayasnian. (Z) A worshipper of Ahura Mazda.

Mencius. (C) Meng-tze. The great expositor of Confucianism who lived about three centuries after the Master. Also the title of the book which contains his teachings, one of the four books of Confucianism which, with the six classics, make up the canon.

Mengtze. (C) *See* Mencius.

Mithra. (Z) *See* Mitra.

Mitra. (H) A god of the Indo-Europeans b e f o r e their separation. In Hinduism a son of Aditi, a manifestation of the sun, ruler of the day. In Persia, Mithra, the sun god.

Moksha. (H) The state in which rebirths are un-necessary. Hindu equivalent of Buddhist Nirvana.

Moslem (or Muslim). "One who submits." A Mohammedan.

mow (or mou). (C) Chinese measure of land. About one-sixth of an acre.

nazu. (Z) Corpse.

Nirvana. (B) The supreme goal of Buddhism. Release from the limitations of existence. Release from the necessity of rebirths. That state in which all attributes relating to the phenomenal existence cease.

nivid. (H) Formula.

niyama. (H) The second stage of Yoga practice.

Om. (H) *See* Aum.

Pairidaeza. (Z) Paradise.

Pairikas. (Z) Name of a class of evil female beings who mislead men, seducing them with their great physical beauty. In later Persian mythology they became beautiful fairies.

Pali. The language in which the Buddhist sacred books were first written.

Pars. Persia.

Parsi. From Pars, or Persia. A Zoroastrian.

Partha. (H) Son of Prithi or Kunti. An appellation of Arjuna.

Peshotanu. (Z) A sinful person. A body afflicted with sin.

Prajapati. (H) "Lord of Creatures." Applied to several creative gods.

Privithi. (H) The earth goddess in Indo-European and early Vedic religion. Parallel with Greek *Gaia Meter*.

Purusha. (H) "Person." The original eternal one. The supreme goal. A designation of Brahma.

Pushan. (H) A Vedic deity. Keeper of flocks and herds and bringer of prosperity.

Ranjanya. (H) Same as Kshatriya.

Rajas. (H) The quality of rage. "Fierceness in battle."

Ramadan (or Ramadhan). (M) The holy month of Islam when all Muslims must fast and in which pilgrimages to Mecca are undertaken.

Ric. (H) The *Rig-Veda.*

Rig-Veda. (H) The first and most important of the four *Vedas,* earliest verse collection of the Hindus. Some of it probably antedates the migration into India and the separation of the Indo-European peoples.

Rishi. (HB) An inspired poet or sage. Seven are deified and represented in the sky by the seven stars of the Great Bear.

Sadvastaran, assembly of. (Z) The gathering for final judgment which takes place after the resurrection.

Sama. (H) The *Sama-Veda.*

Sama-Veda. (H) One of the four *Vedas* of Hinduism. (*See* Introduction to the Hindu scriptures in this volume.)

Sambodhi. (B) The supreme enlightenment through which a human soul may attain to Nirvana.

Saoshyant. (Z) Same as Soshyans.

satwa. (H) The quality of goodness and wisdom.

Savitar. (H) "Generator." "Stimulator." (1) A Vedic appelation for the sun. (2) An Aditya.

Self. (H) *See* Atman.

Shang-ti. Chinese designation for the heavenly power. Almost synonymous with,

but generally regarded as more personal than Tien. Usually translated a s "God," while Tien is usually translated as "heaven."

shen. Benevolent spirits in ancient Chinese religion, related to the Yang.

Shi King. (C) The *Canon of Poetry.* One of the six canonical classics of Confucianism, edited by Confucius.

Shu King (C) The *Canon of History.* One of the six canonical classics of Confucianism, edited by Confucius.

Shun. (C) *See* Yao.

Soma. (H) The fermented, and therefore intoxicating, juice of a sacred plant used in sacrificial rites. Personified, the god who animated the soma juice. Parallel with Zoroastrian Haoma.

Soshyans. (Z) "To be useful." The future saviour. The Messiah to come.

Spendarmad. (Z) One of the Amesha Spentas who is in conflict with Angra Mainyu and increases the power of Ahura Mazda.

Spenta Armati. (Z) Equivalent of Spendarmad.

Spitama. (Z) The name of Zarathushtra's clan.

Spring and Autumn Annals. (C) The *Chun Chiu.* A book of local history. One of the six canonical classics of Confucianism. The only book written by Confucius.

sraosha-karana. (Z) "A spur for horses." Any instrument for stimulating obedience. A whip.

Srotapatti. (B) "Entering the stream" which carries one into the ocean of salvation and Nirvana.

Sudra. (H) The lowest, or servant and serf, caste in Hinduism.

Surya. (H) The sun god of the Indo-European and Vedic religions. Parallel with Greek *Helios*.

sutra. (HB) Sanskrit equivalent of Pali *sutta*. A thread on which jewels are strung. A verse.

Ta Hsio. (C) The *Great Learning*. One of the four "books" of Confucianism which, with the six classics, make up the canon.

tamas. (H) The quality of stupidity.

Tao. (T) The universal divine principle of Taoism. For further discussion of its meaning *see* the Introduction to Taoist scriptures in this volume.

Tathagata. (B) A title of Gautama Buddha. Used by his followers and by him in speaking of himself. Its derivation is doubtful, but it is thought to mean "Thus come, thus gone," that is, "following the path of former Buddhas," or "coming from no place and going to no place."

"That One Thing." (H) The unnamed, ununderstood, primordial creative force.

Tien. Ancient Chinese. The spirit of heaven, whose ordinances rule the universe. Often used to mean "the Great One" or "God," yet less personal in meaning than Shang-ti. Related to *Tengri* (son of heaven) in Mongolian, and *Tang-li* in Hunnish.

Ushas. The dawn goddess of the Indo-Europeans. (*Eos* or *Heos* in Greek. *Aurora* in Latin.)

Vaisya. (H) The third caste of Hinduism, consisting of artisans, tradesmen, and farmers.

vara. (Z) A garden.

Varuna. (H) A god of the Indo-Europeans and one of the oldest Vedic gods. A god of the sky, ruler of the night and of the waters.

Veda. (H) "Knowledge." The holy books of Hinduism, regarded as primal revelation. Specifically applied to the early books which include the word in the title (*Rig-Veda*, *Sama-Veda*, *Yajur-Veda*, and *Atharva-Veda*) but also used to include other books of the early Hindu canon.

Visvedevas. (H) Deities of inferior rank.

Vohumano. (Z) "Spirit of Goodness." Name of one of the Amesha Spentas.

Yajus. (H) The *Yajur-Veda*.

Yajur-Veda. (H) One of the four early sacred books of the Hindus. (*See* Introduction to the Hindu scriptures in this volume.)

Yang. In ancient Chinese religion the eternal and powerful force of brightness, warmth, effusiveness, heavenliness. The spiritual counterpart and opposite of Yin.

Yao. (C) A Chinese monarch of antiquity held up by the Chinese as a model of piety and virtue. He ruled, according to tradition, from 2356-2280 B. C., when he abdicated in favour of Shun on account of Shun's reputation for filial piety and brotherly affection.

Yaweh. (JC) The early tribal god of Abraham. Later Jehovah, the one God of Judaism and Christianity.

Yazatas. (Z) "Venerable." Given name of several higher beings. There are heavenly, invisible Yazatas, of whom the head is Ahura

Mazda, and earthly ones, of whom the head is Zarathushtra. The Amesha Spentas are Yazatas. There are exactly 100,000 Yazatas in all.

Yellow Emperor. (C) Hwang-Ti, a legendary ruler of China who is said to have lived nearly three thousand years before the birth of Christ and to have invented the wheeled carriage, a medium of exchange, music, astronomical instruments, and other devices which marked the dawn of civilization.

Yima (or Yim). (Z) The first man of Zoroastrianism. Gayomard.

Yin. In ancient Chinese religion the force of darkness, secretiveness, earthliness. Counterpart and opposite of Yang.

Yoga. (HB) "Yoke." That which unites. A school of Hindu philosophy especially marked by regulated physical postures in connexion with meditation.

Yogin. (HB) One who practises Yoga.

yoyana. (B) A measure of distance equal to nine English miles.

Zen Buddhism (or Zen). A Chinese and Japanese modification of Buddhism which has more in common with Taoism than with Indian Buddhism. It urges dependence (without seeking or avoiding) upon one's inner nature. It places no importance on religious ritual or written scriptures, considering these mere representations of truth rather than truth itself.

Index

The following abbreviations are used after selections to indicate the scriptures from which they are taken: (H) Hindu; (B) Buddhist; (Z) Zoroastrian; (J-C) Judeo-Christian; (M) Mohammedan; (C) Confucianist; (T) Taoist.

587